Anticolonialism in British Politics

The Left and the End of Empire, 1918–1964

STEPHEN HOWE

CLARENDON PRESS · OXFORD
1993

Oxford University Press, Walton Street, Oxford OX2 6DP
Oxford New York Toronto
Delhi Bombay Calcutta Madras Karachi
Kuala Lumpur Singapore Hong Kong Tokyo
Nairobi Dar es Salaam Cape Town
Melbourne Auckland Madrid
and associated companies in
Berlin Ibadan

Oxford is a trade mark of Oxford University Press

Published in the United States
by Oxford University Press Inc., New York

British Library Cataloguing in Publication Data
Data available

Library of Congress Cataloging in Publication Data
Howe, Stephen, 1958–
Anticolonialism in British politics: the left and the end of
Empire, 1918–1964 / Stephen Howe.
p. cm. — (Oxford historical monographs)
Based on the author's thesis (D. Phil.)—Oxford, 1985.
Includes bibliographical references (p.) and index.
1. Great Britain—Colonies—Public opinion—History—20th century.
2. Decolonization—Public opinion—History—20th century. 3. Great
Britain—Politics and government—20th century. 4. Imperialism—
Public opinion—History—20th century. 5. Public opinion—Great
Britain. I. Title. II. Series.
DA18.H714 1993 325'.341'0904—dc20 93–10369
ISBN 0–19–820423–X

1 3 5 7 9 10 8 6 4 2

Typeset by Best-set Typesetter Ltd., Hong Kong
Printed in Great Britain
on acid-free paper by
Biddles Ltd., Guildford & King's Lynn

For My Parents

Preface

THIS study of anticolonialism in Britain during the years of decolonisation has two main aims. The first is to survey the attitudes and
activities on colonial issues of those groups in British politics who
defined themselves, or were defined, as distinctively anti-imperialist
and sympathetic to the aims of colonial nationalism. This discussion
encompasses both the left-wing of the Labour Party and groups
outside it; in the Communist Party, other independent left-wing
groups and single-issue campaigns. It centres on the operations of
pressure groups on the left concerned with colonial issues: the most
important of these being, from its foundation in 1954, the Movement
for Colonial Freedom. The primary focus is not, therefore, on the
evolution of official colonial policy, nor on the leaderships and formal
structures of the two main political parties—both subjects on which
there is now a fairly large literature—although it is hoped that at least
an oblique new light is shed on these through study of their radical
critics.

On the other hand, attention is not restricted to any particular
colonial territory or group of territories, although there is naturally
more extensive discussion of those colonial issues which aroused
especial controversy in Britain, such as the armed conflicts in Malaya,
Kenya, and Cyprus, the contest over the Central African Federation,
and the crises in British Guiana. The British colonial Empire is the
main object of attention, but, where the arguments about decolonisation
on the British left spilled over from this into issues of race and
immigration or of Third World development, I have followed them at
least part of the way. Similarly, while the independent states of the
Commonwealth rarely impinge directly on my subject one of them in
particular, the Union of South Africa, cast so long a shadow and was
embroiled in so many of the other issues that total silence on British
socialists' attitudes to it would be absurd.[1] By contrast, although
contacts and mutual influences between British Labour and the

---

[1] It may also be noted that British political discourse usually categorised South
African affairs as colonial subjects until at least the 1950s; as it also frequently did the
issues of immigration and race relations within Britain.

Australian and New Zealand Labour Parties were close, there seems to have been very little interaction between these and British radical attitudes to the subject Empire.

Other related themes too are regretfully but necessarily ignored, or dealt with in very cursory fashion below. Religious influences on left-wing hostility to Empire are discussed at various points, but the full story of the Churches' role in both imperialist and anti-imperialist politics falls outside the ambit of this study.[2] The relationship between anticolonialism and regional or national aspirations within the United Kingdom is not discussed, though the major role played by Scottish and Welsh activists in anticolonial campaigns is noted. Both the international policies of Welsh and Scottish Nationalists, and the political geography of British attitudes to Empire are subjects of great interest which have been almost wholly neglected by scholars. The same is true of the more fraught subject of Northern Ireland; though in this case the polemical literature on mainland British attitudes to the problem is vast. British socialist views on Northern Ireland are not surveyed here, for both formal and substantive reasons. The formal reason is that neither Ireland nor, after partition, Ulster was ever juridically a British colony. The more important reason is that to trace and evaluate the ways in which imperialism, colonialism, and anticolonialism may or may not be concepts appropriate to Northern Ireland would be too complex and too bitterly contested a theme to be manageable within the present context.[3]

My second aim is to evaluate the changing ways in which, arising out of the experience of Empire and decolonisation, more general ideas about imperialism, nationalism, and underdevelopment were expressed among British radicals during these years. The scope and presuppositions of this discussion are explained in my first chapter. This and the second chapter, which deals with British radical attitudes to Empire before 1936, may appear to devote excessive attention to historiographical and other matters which form only a background to

---

[2] On this theme, see Gerald Studdert-Kennedy, *British Christians, Indian Nationalists, and the Raj* (Delhi: Oxford University Press, 1991).

[3] Geoffrey Bell, *Troublesome Business* (Pluto, 1982), is a fairly comprehensive, if sometimes superficial and partisan, survey of Labour Party attitudes to Ireland. John Whyte, *Interpreting Northern Ireland* (Oxford: Oxford University Press, 1990), is a magisterial survey of literature on the conflict, including that which sees it in terms of imperialism, while Frank Wright, *Northern Ireland: A Comparative Analysis* (Dublin: Gill & Macmillan, 1988), offers suggestive parallels with other divided societies both colonial and non-colonial.

the main themes of the work. The reason for this is that to separate the narrative of political events from the analysis of ideologies in this field would be artificial and impoverishing; but to demonstrate their interrelation it is necessary to situate the thought and action of the groups which are my main concern in a series of wider perspectives.

British anticolonialism was in a sense an offshoot of a massive global upsurge of sentiment, which has dominated much of the history of this century. It was an unusual, even paradoxical offshoot, for it grew in the country which was long the most important imperial metropole. Arguably, anticolonialism was the most ubiquitous international ideology from the 1950s to the 1980s, uniting the whole Communist world, almost all articulate opinion in the developing countries, and most left-wing thought in the Western world.

The British radicals whom I discuss were involved both in the events of decolonisation and in the interpretation of those events. They were so involved against a background of many decades' writing and activity on these issues within Britain, and within a pre-eminently transnational context. Without detailed reference to that background and context neither their thought nor their activity can be understood. They have been subject to radically opposed judgements: fickle sentimentalists or determined toilers, major architects of decolonisation or irrelevancies to it. The evaluation of their role is necessarily dependent on one's interpretation of decolonisation as a whole: a field of study which is itself in its infancy. The studies of imperialism, colonial nationalism, underdevelopment, and the history of social thought impose the opposite problem; they have long been complex battlegrounds of sharply contending views. Thus a prior arena of debate cannot be taken as given: the establishment of points of departure and bearings must involve a process of critique.

British reactions to more recent events—to the Falklands or Gulf wars, to British race relations, or the end of South African apartheid—cannot fully be understood except in relation to the experience of decolonisation and the legacy of Empire. In that sense, I hope that what follows may be seen to have some contemporary relevance.

S. H.

Acknowledgements

I SHOULD like to thank the following for their help in providing information, granting interviews, or access to documents, and in giving advice on earlier drafts and papers:

Anthony Barnett, the late Kay Beauchamp, the Rt. Hon. Tony Benn, MP, the late Professor M. Omer Beshir, Michael Brock, A. X. Cambridge, Dr Michael Cowen, Idris Cox, the late Bob Edwards, the late Tony Gilbert, Dr David Goldsworthy, Sarah Gracie, Professor Partha Sarathi Gupta, Barbara Haq, Dr Brian Harrison, Richard Hart, Lord Hatch of Lusby, Liz Hodgkin, Robert Hughes MP, Joan Hymans, Deborah Johnson, Mary Klopper, Professor J. M. Lee, Joseph Murumbi, Stan Newens, MEP, Professor Ken Post, Patricia Pugh, Ernie Roberts, Raphael Samuel, the late John Stonehouse, Richard Symonds, Ann Thurston, and Daphna Vardi.

Thanks also to the librarians and archivists of Rhodes House, Queen Elizabeth House, the Bodleian Library, Christ Church, Corpus Christi, Nuffield, and Ruskin Colleges, Oxford; the Labour Party, Marx Memorial Library, and Institute of Commonwealth Studies, London; and Churchill College, Cambridge.

Four of the people to whom I am most indebted have died since the early stages of my research. I honour the memories of Lord Brockway, C. L. R. James, Dr Julius Lewin, and Dr Philip Williams.

This book derives in part from my 1985 Oxford D.Phil. thesis, and owes a great deal to the encouragement and criticism of my examiners, Professors Victor Kiernan and Ronald Robinson; and especially to my supervisor, Professor David Fieldhouse.

Responsibility for error remains, of course, mine alone.

Contents

List of Tables

List of Abbreviations

Organisations

AAM	Anti-Apartheid Movement
AATUF	All-African Trade Union Federation
AEU	Amalgamated Engineering Union
AFPFL	Anti-Fascist People's Freedom League
AUBTW	Amalgamated Union of Building Trade Workers
AUEN	Amalgameted Union of Engineering Workers
BCAI	British Centre Against Imperialism
BCCF	British Centre for Colonial Freedom
BSP	British Socialist Party
CLC	Caribbean Labour Congress
CLP	Constituency Labour Party
Cmd.	Command Paper
CO	Colonial Office
COPAI	Congress of Peoples Against Imperialism
CP	Communist Party
CPGB	Communist Party of Great Britain
CPI	Communist Party of India
CPP	Convention People's Party (Gold Coast/Ghana)
CSC	Commonwealth Subcommittee of the Labour Party National Executive
CWU	Chemical Workers' Union
ETU	Electrical Trades Union
FBU	Fire Brigades Union
FCB	Fabian Colonial Bureau
FLN	Front de la Libération Nationale (Algeria)
IASB	International African Service Bureau
ICFTU	International Confederation of Free Trade Unions
ICU	Industrial and Commercial Workers' Union
ILP	Independent Labour Party

KAU	Kenya African Union
LAI	League Against Imperialism
LCP	League of Coloured Peoples
LPACIQ	Labour Party Advisory Committee on Imperial Questions
LPCD	Labour Party Commonwealth Department
LPCSC	Labour Party Commonwealth Subcommittee
LRD	Labour Research Department
MCF	Movement for Colonial Freedom
MCP	Malayan Communist Party
MDU	Malaya Democratic Union
MLP	Malta Labour Party
MNA	Mouvement Nationaliste Algérien
NAC	National Administrative Committee of the ILP
NCCL	National Council for Civil Liberties
NCLC	National Council of Labour Colleges
NCNC	National Council of Nigeria and the Cameroons (renamed in 1961 the National Council of Nigerian Cirizens)
NEC	National Executive Committee of the Labour Party
NUM	National Union of Mineworkers
NUR	National Union of Railwaymen
PAP	People's Action Party (Singapore)
PLP	Parliamentary Labour Party
PNP	People's National Party (Jamaica)
PPP	People's Progressive Party (British Guiana)
PPU	Peace Pledge Union
RCP	Revolutionary Communist Party
RSL	Revolutionary Socialist League
SACTU	South African Congress of Trade Unions
SLP	Socialist Labour Party
TGWU	Transport and General Workers' Union
TUC	Trades Union Congress
UDC	Union of Democratic Control
USDAW	Union of Shop, Distributive and Allied Workers
USSE	United Socialist States of Europe

VFS	Victory for Socialism
WASU	West African Students' Union
WFTU	World Federation of Trade Unions
WIL	Workers' International League
WWLI	Workers' Welfare League of India
ZAPU	Zimbabwe African Peoples' Union

Journals

CIB	*Colonial Information Bulletin* (Communist Party)
DW	*Daily Worker* (Communist Party)
EcHR	*Economic History Review*
HWJ	*History Workshop Journal*
ITE	*Inside the Empire* (Communist Party)
JAH	*Journal of African History*
JCCP	*Journal of Commonwealth & Comparative Politics*
JCH	*Journal of Contemporary History*
JCPS	*Journal of Commonwealth Political Studies*
JICH	*Journal of Imperial and Commonwealth History*
LM	*Labour Monthly* (Communist dominated)
LPACR	*Labour Party Annual Conference Report*
NL	*New Leader* (ILP)
NLR	*New Left Review*
NS&N	*New Statesman (and Nation)*
PA	*Parliamentary Affairs*
PN	*Peace News*
PQ	*Political Quarterly*
SL	*Socialist Leader* (ILP)
SSLHB	*Bulletin of the Society for the Study of Labour History*
WIN	*West Indies Newsletter*
WNV (WN)	*World News and Views* (later *World News*; Communist Party)

1

The Left and Imperialism

'Anti-fascism', wrote George Lichtheim, 'is not a distinctive political creed, any more than is anti-Stalinism. However estimable such sentiments may be, they are too vague and diffuse to lend themselves to analytical treatment.'[1] Such, one might well think, is also the case for anticolonialism; an equally vague and diffuse current of political language, ideas, and action. Can it none the less be sufficiently clearly defined as to make it susceptible to analytical treatment? I shall argue that this can be done when, and only when, it is set in a number of broader contexts.

The most important of these is the debate, among both participants and subsequent commentators, on the meaning, causes, and consequences of colonialism and decolonisation themselves. This first chapter analyses relevant aspects of these debates and seeks to relate them to the perceptions and the actions of anticolonialists in Britain. First, though, I propose a rough working definition of anticolonialism; whilst noting that this will be substantially elaborated and qualified, and its constituent elements shown to have changed greatly over time, in the chapters that follow.

The political views defined here as anticolonialist comprised four main features.[2]

First, a claim that national independence or self-determination, political, economic, and cultural, is the right of all peoples subject to, or threatened by, external domination. This claim necessarily implies rejection of arguments suggesting that certain peoples are not ready for independence, and of justifications of colonialism in terms of the doctrine of trusteeship. It has ordinarily been held to imply that the colonised are justified, if other methods fail, in employing violent means to gain their independence.

[1] George Lichtheim, *Marxism in Modern France* (New York: Columbia University Press, 1966), 44.
[2] The definition which follows derives in part from that proposed by Thomas Hodgkin in an unpublished lecture, 'The Anti-Colonial Tradition in British Politics' (notes in Hodgkin papers).

Second, anticolonialism involves a claim that struggles for national independence are in some strong sense interdependent, that their successes or failures have important implications for similar struggles elsewhere, and hence that international joint action by groups pursuing anticolonial ends is a necessity. This claim distinguishes anticolonialism from a pure nationalism.

Third, there is an assertion of the basic equality of European and non-European peoples and cultures. This assertion necessarily implies a rejection of justifications for colonialism in terms of the civilising mission, and implies also a claim that anticolonialism is integrally related to the eradication of racism.

Fourth, there is a commitment to oppose the colonialism of one's own nation, both as a moral duty consequent on the first claim, and as a result of the characteristic belief that ending colonialism is a precondition for progress towards a freer, more democratic society in the former colonialist country.

A fifth claim has been widely but far from universally held among the groups discussed in this book. This is the belief, popularised in the writings of Lenin and his disciples, that colonialism is an integral feature or necessary consequence of modern capitalism. Therefore, it is argued, the struggle for the ending of colonialism implies also anti-capitalism and the building of a socialist society, in both colonised and colonising countries. I shall not be treating this claim as a necessary component of anticolonialist beliefs: many socialists and liberals, accepting the first four assertions, explicitly rejected this fifth. It will none the less be seen to have been a very influential view; even though the political purpose implicit in all such theories—the presumption or creation of a global united front between anti-capitalist movements in the advanced countries and anti-imperialist ones in the developing world—has come over succeeding decades to appear ever more threadbare a piece of wishful thinking.

I. DECOLONISATION: THE POVERTY OF HISTORIOGRAPHY

By comparison with the debate over the causes and character of European colonial expansion, which has been among the most vigorous in Western historiography, and with the more recent but no less contentious exchanges on the nature of post-colonial states and economies, historical work on the end of empire still displays notable inadequacies. Despite the proliferation of studies of decolonisation in particular regions and territories, increasingly sophisticated work on colonial nationalism, and a number of attempts at general overviews of British disengagement, it could still be said that 'there is no serious interpretive account of it as an overall process' or even that 'the history of decolonization remains to be written'.[3] This is so not in any sense that there has been lack of attention to the subject, but in pervasive deficiencies of conceptualisation and theorisation. These have manifested themselves in three ways.

First, whilst the acquisition of colonial empires has generally been understood as constituting, or at least reflecting, structural changes— shifts in the *longue durée*—in the world system, most of the literature on decolonisation has seen the process purely in the short view of particular events; or in Braudelian terms at best as conjunctural. Historians have not agreed on the nature of relationships between the conjunctures of colonial conquest and structural change in either the colonising or the colonised countries; but few have doubted that such a relationship existed or that it requires explanation. Indeed as one historian of colonialism says:

The reason why imperialism as a set of facts has been so much debated is that the facts, particularly for the period after about 1870, are so surprising that they have given rise to a number of complex explanations, each of which constitutes a theory of imperialism.[4]

The facts of decolonisation, especially for the period after about 1950, are no less 'surprising', but they have given rise to far fewer 'complex explanations', and to very few candidates for a theory of decolonisation. It is generally accepted that colonialism was an integral part of a wider transformation: the integration of Africa, Asia, and Latin America into a world economy.[5] It cannot be reduced

---

[3] Tony Smith, 'A Comparative Study of French and British Decolonisation', *Comparative Studies in Society & History*, 20/1 (1978), 70; Henri Brunschwig, Preface to Winfried Baumgart, *Imperialism: The Idea and Reality of British and French Colonial Expansion, 1880–1914* (Oxford: Oxford University Press, 1982), p. vi.

[4] D. K. Fieldhouse (ed.), *The Theory of Capitalist Imperialism* (Longmans, 1967), p. xiii.

[5] This is common ground across all sides of debate over world systems theory and its analogues: see Fernand Braudel, *Civilisation and Capitalism, iii. The Perspective of the World* (Collins, 1984); Immanuel Wallerstein, *The Modern World System*, 3 vols. (New York: Academic Press, 1974, 1980, 1989); Eric Wolf, *Europe and the People Without History* (Berkeley, Calif.: University of California Press, 1982); Peter Worsley, *The*

to a mere episode in the histories either of Europe or (despite the politically understandable protestations of some Third World historians[6]) of the colonised world. Yet there has been a general inclination to treat the *end* of colonial empires in just such episodic fashion.

It is perhaps less than self-evident that this absence of theorisation has been a bad thing. The study of nineteenth-century imperialism has in some ways fared the worse for being so long a battleground of competing grand theories. Much theoretical work on imperialism has been abstract, formalistic, and ultimately self-referring, some of its formulations 'a sort of conceptual sculpture that should be discussed by art critics rather than social scientists';[7] some of its terminology 'a Tower of Babel in which not even Marxists knew any longer how to find their way'.[8]

Equally, there is something to be said for the claim that decolonisation remains too recent and our knowledge of the record too patchy to allow adequate theorisation. Access to fresh empirical information, further studies of particular cases and facets, and a lengthening perspective of time will and must call into question existing theories and assumptions about it. Yet the accumulation of facts will not in itself generate explanation, nor are historical data themselves constituted independently of presuppositions and conceptual frameworks which grant them significance. The second major problem for our understanding of decolonisation is not lack of empirical material so much as the fragmentation of perceptions of that material. It needs integration. To adapt a phrase of Anil Seal, it requires identification of the forces which drove the politics of decolonisation upwards and outwards from the oddities of the locality, or downwards from the

---

Three Worlds (Weidenfeld & Nicolson, 1984). On structure, conjuncture, and event see also Fernand Braudel, *Écrits sur l'histoire* (Paris: Flammarion, 1969), esp. ch. 3.

[6] For instance J. F. Ade Ajayi: 'The Continuity of African Institutions under Colonialism', in T. O. Ranger (ed.), *Emerging Themes in African History* (Heinemann, 1968). For the extreme opposed view of an equally distinguished Africanist, arguing that the colonial impact irrevocably destroyed indigenous tradition, see Jan Vansina, *Paths in the Rainforests: Towards a History of Political Tradition in Equatorial Africa* (James Currey, 1990), ch. 8.

[7] Anthony Brewer, *Marxist Theories of Imperialism: A Critical Survey* (Routledge & Kegan Paul, 1980), 265.

[8] Giovanni Arrighi, *The Geometry of Imperialism: The Limits of Hobson's Paradigm* (New Left Books, 1978), 17. A more recent critique of theoretical overload in this field is essayed by Bruce Berman, *Control and Crisis in Colonial Kenya: The Dialectic of Domination* (James Currey, 1990), ch. 1.

hollow generalities of the Commonwealth.[9] This necessitates generalisation and explicit theorisation, the attempt to place the events of decolonisation in the big pictures of long-term structural change in both former metropoles and former colonies.

A further contrast between the literature on colonial expansion and that on contraction may serve to illuminate the third major weakness of the latter. The questions asked by historians of the era of expansion have centred on both causes and effects. For the era of decolonisation, however, questions about consequences have held the field almost to themselves, and causation has barely begun to be debated. Most of the time, in this area, the perceptions of the actors in the process itself have effectively been reproduced in the subsequent scholarship.

Discussion of decolonisation has thus been dominated by three paradigms: by a description of a transfer of power focused on the metropolitan capitals and on planning by officials; an identification of decolonisation with a colonial revolution; and an analysis seeing the process as one of substitution of indirect or neo-colonial modes of domination for direct colonial rule. The three are, of course, implicitly deeply opposed to one another. The first two attribute very different types of significance to the events with which they both deal, whilst the third offers a strong, if often unspecific challenge to the idea that these events had any great significance at all. Yet there has been little open debate between the three positions. The often narrow empiricism of the first, the revolutionary romanticism so frequently characteristic of the second, and the lack of attention to the specificity of the political apparently inherent in the third, have combined to obscure the need to measure these positions against one another and by some common standard of historical evidence.

II. COLONIAL REVOLUTION, TRANSFER OF POWER, OR TRANSITION TO NEO-COLONIALISM?

The clearest and simplest explanation of decolonisation was that given by the early advocates of radical nationalism themselves.

[9] 'Imperialism and Nationalism in India', in John Gallagher, Gordon Johnson, and Anil Seal (eds.), *Locality, Province and Nation* (Cambridge: Cambridge University Press, 1978), 4.

Taking as their cue Burke's belief that 'those who have been once intoxicated with power even though for one year, can never willingly abandon it',[10] they saw nationalist initiatives—a colonial revolution, in fact—as having pressurised colonial governments into granting an independence which but for the threat or actuality of mass revolt would never have come. Perhaps the most powerful early elaboration of this view was that of the Trinidadian Marxist C. L. R. James. He spoke of the 'myth' which he saw as governing all British thinking about the colonies. This myth could be summarised as a belief in the backwardness of the colonial and especially the African peoples, in the desire of the colonising power to draw its subjects out of that backwardness, and in a policy of granting responsible self-government and eventually independence by gradual stages corresponding to the colonial peoples' degree of preparation for it. James, and with him now two generations of nationalists, contended that on the contrary independence came only and always when the subject peoples made the cost of imperial rule unacceptably high. Withdrawals from power have been the consequence of defeat, not of benevolent policy. To claim otherwise was an 'impudent fraud' imposed upon the British people by their government.[11]

Yet the view which James castigated as myth and fraud remained predominant in Britain: in official pronouncements, in the popular, and even in much of the scholarly, literature on decolonisation. The perception of the granting of self-rule to British colonies as a peaceful and voluntary process, the successful outcome of a coherent plan for disengagement, has attained the status of a major theme for national self-congratulation in the post-war years. The leaders of the Labour Party have been among the loudest of these self-lauding voices. Clement Attlee reflected in 1960 that:

There have been many great Empires in the history of the world that have risen, flourished for a time, and then fallen . . . There is only one Empire where, *without external pressure or weariness at the burden of governing*, the ruling people has voluntarily surrendered its hegemony over subject peoples and has given them their freedom . . . This unique example is the British Empire.[12]

[10] As quoted by the then radical Ndabaningi Sithole, *African Nationalism* (2nd edn., Oxford: Oxford University Press, 1968), 115.

[11] C. L. R. James, *Nkrumah and the Ghana Revolution* (Allison & Busby, 1977; orig. pub. 1962), 35.

[12] Clement Attlee, *Empire into Commonwealth* (Oxford: Oxford University Press, 1961), 1. My emphasis.

Some, like John Strachey, sought to assert the special role played in this by the domestic political traditions with which they associated themselves. Britain, suggested Strachey, was unlikely to become destructively fixated upon her imperial legacy because of the flexibility of her parliamentary institutions, the strength of the anticolonial tradition in her Liberal and Labour movements, and the fact that few in Britain had ever felt that their own interests were closely bound up with imperialism.[13] Others, like Patrick Gordon Walker, identified the key to the peaceable expiry of Empire as being the transformative power of the Commonwealth ideal; inscribed into its foundations by the coexistence of Crown Colonies and colonies of settlement within it.[14]

The same sort of stance lies more or less deeply imbedded in much British scholarship on decolonisation. Whiggish, teleological, Anglocentric, and fixated on Whitehall, it is also imbued with the mystique of a stillborn dream of Commonwealth. The approach reached a kind of apotheosis in 1980 with Morgan's *Official History of Colonial Development*: five ill-organised volumes which never venture forth from the dusty files of Colonial Office plans and constitutional schemes to ask what effect, if any, these had on the ground. Morgan thus feels able to conclude with some satisfaction that 'except in Palestine and Aden, the transfer of power had been made smoothly with sentiments of mutual regard' and that economic and social development had 'made a fair start...made headway...a solid contribution'.[15] The air is very much that of a headmaster's report on a dull but well-meaning pupil. As a summary of the colonial record it is fatuous.

The inadequacy of this interpretation of British decolonisation hardly needs to be argued today, such is the evidence that much British planning was abortive, incoherent, or merely an *ex post facto* rationalisation for decisions taken in haste, under pressure, and for quite different reasons from those publicly presented. And whilst the end of Empire may have been a less bloody and traumatic affair for Britain than for France or Portugal, the record of armed conflict in

[13] John Strachey, *The End of Empire* (Gollancz, 1959), 205–9.
[14] Patrick Gordon Walker, *The Commonwealth* (Secker & Warburg, 1962), esp. 17, 20.
[15] D. J. Morgan, *The Official History of Colonial Development*, 5 vols. (Macmillan, 1980), v. 343–4.

Ireland, Palestine, Malaya, Kenya, Cyprus, and Aden hardly indicates a smoothly consensual process.

On the other hand, it is undeniable that, especially after the mid-1950s, British governments were ready, eventually eager, to hand over authority in most cases to suitable successors. This, coupled with the evident shallowness of most successor élites' political bases—cruelly exposed in endemic post-colonial instability—heavily qualify the often vainglorious claims of freedom fighters to have forced the British out. Partly in response to these seemingly chronic structural disabilities in the post-colonial order, a third view became something of a consensus in the 1970s. Many scholars, mostly but by no means exclusively on the left, came to see decolonisation neither as a revolution nor a transfer of power (at most there was a transfer of certain limited aspects of political *authority*) but a transition to neo-colonialism. What occurred was in Frantz Fanon's phrase a 'false decolonisation' achieving merely 'flag independence' and leaving intact the essential features of colonial exploitation: the post-war policies of the colonial powers often being seen as deliberately directed towards this end. As Gary Wasserman puts it, summarising Kenyan decolonisation: 'Independence . . . marked not so much a moving out of the colonial relationship as an enlarging and enhancing of that dependent relationship, with the colonial patterns emerging relatively unscathed.'[16]

This is evidently a more serious and sophisticated historiographical case than the polemical simplicities of revolutionary nationalist and administrative transfer of power accounts. Yet too many of its proponents have rested on unexamined assumptions about the nature of Britain's economic stake in the colonies, have held an almost vulgar Marxist view of economic interest simply and directly determining political calculation, and have virtually bypassed study of the political events of decolonisation in their emphasis on economic continuities. They have tended to assume that independent governments of post-colonial states either have no effective power *vis-à-vis* the metropolitan bourgeoisie (which they often seem mentally to abbreviate to the metrobogey, as John Lonsdale wryly suggests[17]) or that they have exercised such power as they do have in ways not

---

[16] Gary Wasserman, *Politics of Decolonization: Kenya Europeans and the Land Issue* (Cambridge: Cambridge University Press, 1976), 15.

[17] John Lonsdale, 'State and Peasantry in Colonial Africa', in Raphael Samuel (ed.), *People's History and Socialist Theory* (Routledge & Kegan Paul, 1981), 109.

significantly different from that of the colonial state. Furthermore, there is a curious assumption that not only did Britain's rulers seek to adopt a neo-colonialist strategy, but that it was a *successful* strategy.

All this is frequently underpinned by a tacit conceptual slide in the treatment of the state's economic role. The colonial state is seen as a managing agent for metropolitan capitalist interests. It is then argued or assumed, either that the post-colonial state operates in exactly the same way, or else that the *direct* influence of metropolitan capital, rather than an influence mediated through the state, perpetuates neo-colonial underdevelopment.[18] Astonishingly little is said either about the relationships between nationalist politics and the state's economic role or about the perceptions and reactions of metropolitan firms during decolonisation: indeed there remains a perplexing dearth of literature on the latter question.[19] Thus we are left quite in the dark how far this school thinks changes in the form of state like decolonisation have altered or could alter the patterns of economic dependence they describe. At the extreme—as in the theory of which Samir Amin is now the rather lonely eminent exponent—only socialist revolution and complete delinking from the world economy are thought able to do so.[20]

It is not perhaps surprising that theories of neo-colonialism and underdevelopment, so heavily derivative of the Marxist tradition, have had so little success in theorising decolonisation. For the main intellectual problems here are those on which Marxism has been at its weakest: nationalism (aptly described by Tom Nairn as 'Marxism's great historical failure'[21]); the analysis of non-capitalist social formations; the theory of the state; the ideologies and actions of groups who do not readily fall into the simple class categories of classical Marxism—which means that too often they are unceremoniously dumped into a shapeless sack labelled the petty bourgeoisie.

---

[18] To take another East African example, such a conceptual slide seems to operate in E. A. Brett, *Colonialism and Underdevelopment in East Africa* (Heinemann, 1973), esp. 283–311.

[19] The few exceptions include D. K. Fieldhouse, *Unilever Overseas* (Croom Helm, 1976); Josephine Milburn, *British Business and Ghanaian Independence* (Hanover, NH: New England University Press, 1977); A. G. Hopkins, 'Imperial Business in Africa', parts 1 and 2, *JAH* 17 (1976); and a synoptic view of French economic decolonisation unfortunately unmatched for the British case, Jacques Marseille, *Empire colonial et capitalisme français.* (Paris: Albin Michel, 1984).

[20] Samir Amin, *Delinking: Towards a Polycentric World* (Zed Books, 1990), and *Maldevelopment: Anatomy of a Global Failure* (Zed Books, 1990).

[21] Tom Nairn, *The Break-Up of Britain* (Verso, 2nd edn., 1981), 329.

Nor have the more sophisticated attempts at mobilising structuralist Marxist approaches to analyse late colonialism, notably through theories of the articulation of capitalist and pre-capitalist modes of production, helped much. Indeed they have tended to direct attention even further away from politics and from any possibility of explaining the reasons for or effects of decolonisation. One detailed and influential study of central Africa adopting this perspective characteristically brushes aside the whole question of the colonial mode of production and decolonisation as essentially unimportant, relating only to 'transitional', 'secondary', and 'superstructural' phenomena.[22]

Even the colonial state very rarely played the simple instrumental role of managing agent for the metropolitan bourgeoisie. Attempts radically to remodel colonised societies in accordance with some general logic either of capital accumulation or of bureaucratic rationality were, where attempted at all, at best only very partial successes.[23] They can even plausibly be characterised, as they are by Ranajit Guha, as absolute and preordained failure.[24] Still less can post-colonial polities be lumped together in such a totalising and one-dimensional account. Much of the literature on post-colonial societies, and especially that centred on concepts of dependency, unequal exchange, or modes of production has evinced an utterly impoverished conception of the political. The now considerable body of theoretical work on post-colonial state forms, too, whilst it has inevitably confronted political problems more directly, has done so in a highly formalistic and ahistorical manner.[25] In reaction against an earlier period of often hagiographic historiography on nationalist

[22] Pierre-Philipe Rey, *Colonialisme, neo-colonialisme et transition au capitalisme* (Paris: Maspero, 1971). See also the critique of the articulation school in Berman, *Control and Crisis*, 34–41.

[23] For the most extended and detailed British attempt, that made over successive generations in India—and its failure—see Ranajit Guha, *A Rule of Property for Bengal* (2nd edn., New Delhi: Orient Longman, 1982); Francis Hutchinson, *The Illusion of Permanence* (Princeton, NJ: Princeton University Press, 1967); Eric Stokes, *The English Utilitarians and India* (Oxford: Oxford University Press, 1959).

[24] Ranajit Guha, 'Dominance without Hegemony and its Historiography', *Subaltern Studies VI* (Delhi: Oxford University Press, 1989), esp. 272–81. For a less grandiose, more localised, view of the colonial mission as utter failure, see Anne Phillips, *The Enigma of Colonialism: British Policy in West Africa* (James Currey, 1989).

[25] The major debate here was opened by Hamza Alavi, 'The State in Post-Colonial Societies: Pakistan and Bangladesh', *NLR* 74 (1972). Its shortcomings—and many of the wider failures of the Third World Marxism of the 1970s and 1980s—can be savoured at their worst in Yash Tandon (ed.), *Debate on Class, State and Imperialism* (Dar es Salaam: Tanzania Publishing House, 1982).

movements,[26] there has been a tendency almost wholly to discount both the aspirations and the effectiveness of political nationalism. This has become part of a general shift away from perceptions of decolonisation as a watershed: a shift back to focus on the transformations wrought by depression in the 1930s and, more particularly, forward to trace continuities between colonial and post-colonial conditions. Attention moves up to the world system, down to the social history of peasants and labourers. Such sharply opposed tendencies as the Subaltern Studies group and the so-called Cambridge School share here much common ground. Almost all would concur with Anil Seal's characterisation:

by the side of the vast swell of aspiration and rivalry which has hurled it forward, the political readjustments of independence seem of small account. These nationalisms have been merely the swirling surface of the waters; below them pulse the tides of social change.[27]

III. DECOLONISATION, THE METROPOLE, AND THE 'OFFICIAL MIND'

Yet it is evident that the 'tides of social change' in the colonised world cannot alone explain the pattern and timing of decolonisation, the political forms it took and produced. Decolonisation took place in territories with widely varying histories and political economies, with greatly divergent political and economic links to Britain, and with nationalist movements at vastly different levels of development. Yet it happened in them all in about two decades: so compressed a time-scale that to some contemporaries the British government's actions could only be comprehended in terms of betrayal, of loss of nerve or cowardice.[28] This fact alone suggests that however powerfully determinant local conditions may have been, the procedures of, and

---

[26] See the ferocious demolition of this tradition in A. Temu and B. Swai, *Historians and Africanist History: A Critique* (Zed Books, 1981).

[27] Anil Seal: *The Emergence of Indian Nationalism* (Cambridge: Cambridge University Press, 1968), 351.

[28] Such perceptions were of course widespread in and around the right wing of the Conservative Party, but more detached critics also sometimes suggested that the Government had simply lost control. See W. P. Kirkman, *Unscrambling an Empire: A Critique of British Colonial Policy, 1956–1966* (Chatto & Windus, 1966); and J. Darwin, 'The Fear of Falling: British Politics and Imperial Decline since 1900', *Transactions of the Royal Historical Society*, 5th ser. 36 (1986).

pressures on, metropolitan policy-making were decisive in the end of Empire.

As we have seen, a dominant tradition of British scholarship has until recently viewed these in terms of a planned and orderly transition from Empire to Commonwealth, a graceful abdication of power. Almost literally no one believes this any more; and whereas earlier alternative approaches—suggesting either a revolutionary break or a continuity of economic imperialism—mounted external or trans-cendent critiques of it, the availability of new types of evidence including much of the official record has subsequently made possible internal or immanent modes of critique. Much recent work on British decolonisation has taken this form: detailed scrutiny of Colonial Office and other governmental papers in order to evaluate the pro-cesses of policy-making that led up to withdrawal. The central focus has thus been on what was influentially baptised, for an earlier period, as the 'official mind of imperialism'.[29] Now, however, there is a far greater opportunity than in the earlier administrative histories of the transfer of power to ascertain how closely the real determinants and course of policy corresponded to the public proclamations about it. Essentially three types of question have been asked: those of periodisation, procedure, and pressure. *When* were the crucial decisions of decolonisation taken, *how* and *by whom*, and, most broadly, what were the most important *influences and constraints* under which decisions were made?

Very broadly, three views have emerged on the question of periodisation: that which sees the advent of the Attlee Government as the turning-point, and the vital changes of policy as having taken place in the late 1940s; that which centres on the war years; and that which traces significant new directions in policy back to the later 1930s.[30] Judgement on this question will, however, vary according to

[29] Ronald Robinson and John Gallagher with Alice Denny, *Africa and the Victorians: The Official Mind of Imperialism* (Macmillan, 1961).

[30] The case for 1945–51 is presented in D. K. Fieldhouse 'The Labour Govern-ments and the Empire-Commonwealth 1945–51', in Ritchie Ovendale (ed.), *The Foreign Policy of the British Labour Governments, 1945–51* (Leicester: Leicester University Press, 1984); that for 1939–45 in R. D. Pearce, *The Turning Point in Africa: British Colonial Policy, 1938–48* (Frank Cass, 1982); Jane Bowden, 'Development and Control in British Colonial Policy, with reference to Nigeria and the Gold Coast, 1935–1948' (Birmingham University Ph.D. thesis, 1980); and J. M. Lee and Martin Petter, *The Colonial Office, War and Development Policy* (Maurice Temple Smith, 1982); for the 1930s in John Flint, 'Planned Decolonization and its Failure in British Africa', *African Affairs*, 82/328 (1983). The major attempt at synthesis thus far, that of John Darwin, lays its main emphasis on the impact of the Second World War: *Britain and*

which colonies are the focus of attention—if South Asia the decisive moments may well be placed earlier than any of these, if East and Central Africa, rather later—and according to whether the plans for social and economic change pursued from the late 1930s are seen as consciously preparatory to decolonisation (as was retrospectively to be claimed) or on the contrary as intended means of strengthening imperial power.

The discussion on where the most influential sources of decision-making are to be found is in part dependent on the question of periodisation. Those who focus on the post-war years will tend to see the role of senior politicians as central, and strong claims have been made for Attlee himself, for Ernest Bevin, and for Arthur Creech Jones;[31] though another account has stressed the influence in this period of an official, Sir Andrew Cohen.[32] The role of civil servants has, however, been more heavily emphasised in accounts centring on the war years or earlier.

Some interpretations have argued or implied, indeed, that changes in personnel and political complexion at ministerial level had very little effect, and that the vital decision-makers were at every stage the Colonial Office civil servants. Others have stressed—again particularly with reference to the immediate post-war years—the extent to which other Departments, notably Foreign Office and Treasury, impinged upon areas of responsibility which were formally those of the Colonial Office. This was of course especially the case where perceived vital strategic interests were at stake,[33] or where colonial economies were seen as crucial to Britain.[34]

Decolonisation (Macmillan, 1988), esp. 331–5; *The End of the British Empire: The Historical Debate* (Oxford: Blackwell, 1991), 117–22. David Goldsworthy's most recent work, however, depicts British governments still thinking in terms of retaining substantial colonial possessions as well as great-power status well into the 1950s: 'Keeping Change Within Bounds: Aspects of Colonial Policy during the Churchill and Eden Governments, 1951–57', *JICH* 18/1 (1990); 'Britain and the International Critics of British Colonialism, 1951–56', *JCCP* 29/1 (1991).

[31] Kenneth Harris, *Attlee* (Weidenfeld & Nicolson, 1982), esp. chs. 21 and 22; Alan Bullock, *Ernest Bevin, Foreign Secretary* (Heinemann, 1983); Kenneth O. Morgan, *Labour in Power, 1945–1951* (Oxford: Oxford University Press, 1984), ch. 5.

[32] Ronald Robinson, 'Andrew Cohen and the Transfer of Power in Tropical Africa, 1940–1951', in W. H. Morris-Jones and Georges Fischer (eds.), *Decolonisation and After* (Frank Cass, 1980).

[33] Wm. Roger Louis, *The British Empire in the Middle East, 1945–1951* (Oxford: Oxford University Press, 1984).

[34] Michael Cowen and Nicholas Westcott, 'British Imperial Economic Policy during the War', in David Killingray and Richard Rathbone (eds.), *Africa and the Second World War* (Macmillan, 1986).

Similarly, the degree to which Colonial Office decisions were subject to wider forms of external pressure, whether from Parliament, private interest groups, public opinion, foreign powers, or agitation in the colonies themselves, might depend substantially on the importance of the issues felt to be in play in a particular colony. Yet even among studies devoted to the 'official mind' of the Colonial Office and based largely or exclusively on Colonial Office sources, we find a very wide range of views on the importance of such wider pressures—too wide to be attributable to the oddities of the locality, too wide to be subsumed within the hollow generalities of the Commonwealth.

Thus Turnbull's study of British planning for post-war Malaya finds the influence of every interested party outside the Eastern Department of the Colonial Office to have been marginal. Successive Secretaries of State, the War Cabinet, the Malayan Civil Service, Malayan and British public opinion, business and ethnic lobbies: all were trivial in their impact on policy. Only a tiny group of officials really mattered.[35] Yet the most comprehensive studies of British planning for post-war West Africa—which might *prima facie* be expected to have been considered, if anything, less strategically and economically important to Britain than Malaya—have found external pressures of various sorts to have been crucial at every turn in forming the official mind.[36]

These studies of official planning in the early stages of decolonisation and the immediately preceding era have addressed a more restricted range of questions than those raised in the literature surveyed earlier. On a number of crucial points, none the less, they have registered substantial disagreements. In particular, analyses of the official record have differed widely on when, by whom, and under what sorts of external pressure major decisions of decolonisation were made.

It may be doubted whether a mode of analysis directed almost exclusively towards thinking in government circles can in itself answer these questions, any more than can one centred solely on the ideologies of nationalist movements or on the structures of colonial

---

[35] C. M. Turnbull, 'British Planning for Post-War Malaya', *Journal of South-East Asian Studies*, 5/2 (1974).

[36] Bowden, 'Development and Control'. See also Richard Rathbone, 'Introduction', in id. (ed.), *British Documents on the End of Empire: Series B*, i. *Ghana*, 2 vols. (HMSO for Institute of Commonwealth Studies, 1992).

economies. It may be that neither immanent nor transcendent critiques of the dominant transfer of power account are in isolation adequate for a satisfactory alternative explanation. Such suspicions are strengthened when one turns to those points on which a certain scholarly consensus has emerged, and seeks to elucidate their implications.

It is generally agreed that there was some kind of relationship between British economic decline and imperial withdrawal. In this sense all the major explanations of decolonisation are, as B. R. Tomlinson suggests, 'mercantilist'.[37] Growing national weakness and insecurity provided the conditioning context for decolonisation—and this is not a truism, since it is widely argued that much colonial expansion, especially in tropical Africa, was also motivated by feelings of weakness and insecurity. It is further generally agreed that decision-makers aimed to minimise the dangers arising from this position; that they sought to do so at the lowest possible cost; that such calculations of cost themselves implied value-judgements on aims and priorities; that the dominant strand in these judgements believed colonial possessions to be means to other ends (above all the security and prosperity of Britain itself) rather than ends in themselves; and that the most characteristic means of maximising advantage and minimising cost was pre-emptive action, staying one jump ahead of any potential opposition. And it is widely, though not universally agreed that a policy of planned or consensual decolonisation was dictated by these considerations and that the guiding idea of the Colonial Office was, where possible, thus to anticipate or accommodate possible challenges.

Yet very divergent conclusions can be drawn from the recognition that this was the guiding principle of colonial policy (or for that matter, as Paul Kennedy would argue, of post-Palmerstonian British governmental attitudes in general[38]). One view—that of successive governments themselves—is that such a policy was carried through successfully, with the central aim of spreading democratic values and collective security, and with the Commonwealth as its monument. Another stance would agree that the policy was in general successful, but sees the crucial interests preserved by this pre-emptive action as

[37] B. R. Tomlinson, 'The Contraction of England: National Decline and the Loss of Empire', *JICH* 11/1 (1982).
[38] Paul Kennedy, 'Why Did the British Empire Last so Long?', in *Strategy and Diplomacy, 1870–1945* (Allen & Unwin, 1983).

those of multinational capital, and the continuation of capitalist underdevelopment in the ex-colonies as the monument.[39] Others still see here a record of failure, with British attempts to keep the initiative in the post-war years failing time and again to anticipate the speed and strength of nationalist mobilisations. Britain is argued to have proved unable to retain the allegiance of former collaborators or to reconcile conflicting local interests (as in India, Palestine, Cyprus, and the African colonies of white settlement); and even sometimes to have called into existence the very forces it aimed to pre-empt. Thus plans for accelerated colonial economic development are suggested to have brought about vastly increased governmental intervention, especially in the African colonies (the 'second occupation') which in turn stimulated and provided a focus for local political responses from which grew modern nationalism.[40]

Why, then, were plans for rapid colonial development seen as so crucial by British policy-makers, despite these attendant risks? Here again recent studies have drawn a wide range of implications from the record. Some have traced a genuine and deep-rooted belief among officials and Ministers (notably expressed by Andrew Cohen, Arthur Creech Jones, and Lord Hailey) that the development plans pursued were both absolutely beneficial to colonial peoples and the indispensable foundation for political development.[41] Others have taken a far less favourable view. The driving force behind the policy, it is very widely argued, was the financial crisis in Britain itself. In particular, the recovery of Britain's balance of payments position,[42]

[39] Though, as noted above, such 'neo-colonial' interpretations have been rare among the *political* historians of decolonisation. Wasserman's *Politics of Decolonization* and Cowen's work perhaps come closest to it.

[40] Such arguments, building more or less explicitly on Robinson and Gallagher's peripheral theory of colonialism, are found in much recent work. See John Gallagher, *The Decline, Revival and Fall of the British Empire* (Cambridge: Cambridge University Press, 1982); Flint, 'Planned Decolonization'; Darwin, *End of the British Empire*. For my own earlier view, see 'British Decolonization and Malta's Imperial Role', in Victor Mallia-Milanes (ed.), *The British Colonial Experience 1800–1964: The Impact on Maltese Society* (Malta: Mireva Publications, 1988).

[41] John Flint ('Planned Decolonization'), Morgan (*Labour in Power*, 201–2), Lee and Petter (*Colonial Office*), and, at greatest length, S. A. H. Haqqi in *The Colonial Policy of the Labour Government, 1945–51* (Aligarh: Aligarh University Press, 1960), whilst none of them wholly discounting motives of British national self-interest, all stress this view and thus explicitly or implicitly discount allegations that the policy was intended as a 'neo-colonial' one.

[42] Emphasised in Bowden, 'Development and Control'; Fieldhouse, 'Labour Governments'; and Partha Sarathi Gupta, 'Imperialism and the Labour Government of

the attempt to maintain sterling as a major world currency,[43] and to preserve British economic independence *vis-à-vis* the USA,[44] have been cited as the main reasons for espousing colonial development.

Thus we may conclude that, so far at least, far from resolving the conflict between 'colonial revolution', 'transfer of power', and 'neo-colonialist' interpretations of decolonisation, access to large parts of the official record has been held, in different recent studies, to provide fresh evidence for all three. Scrutiny of the official mind has for some scholars reinforced a belief in planned decolonisation motivated largely by concern for the welfare of colonial peoples, for others has suggested a British government forced into ever-greater concessions by the quite unexpected upsurge of mass nationalism (even if British policy may itself have helped call this upsurge into being), and for others again has shown a Britain attempting, albeit with mixed and declining success, to maintain her world position by new 'neo-colonial' means of control. The immanent critique of the official mind has more often than not reproduced the conclusions of the transcendent critique, though usually on a more sophisticated level.

Some of these disputes may possibly be resolved, or at least some new light shed on the presuppositions and behaviour of the protagonists, if a wider view of British politics in the era of decolonisation is incorporated into the picture. In other words, the focus should be widened from the official mind to include parties, pressure groups, business interests, and the currents of public opinion. As we have seen, studies of the inner circle of colonial policy-making have differed on how influential such wider pressures may have been—and as has been argued, the question cannot be answered solely by reference to that inner circle. What is required is, in effect, an attempt to reintegrate the imperial dimension into the mainstream of British historiography. As E. P. Thompson notes: 'Since Namier's time the "imperial problem" and its ever-present pressure upon British political and economic life, has far too often been relegated to

1945–51', in J. M. Winter (ed.), *The Working Class in Modern British History* (Cambridge: Cambridge University Press, 1983), 105–11.

[43] Susan Strange, *Sterling and British Policy* (Oxford: Oxford University Press, 1971); Allister E. Hinds, 'Imperial Policy and Colonial Sterling Balances, 1943–56', *JICH* 19/1 (1991).

[44] Michael Cowen, 'The British State and Agrarian Accumulation in Kenya', in M. Fransman (ed.), *Industry and Accumulation in Africa* (Heinemann, 1982).

specialist studies, and then forgotten.'[45] Nowhere is this relegation
more apparent than in the period of decolonisation. A British political
history in which the imperial dimension is forgotten, or is treated only
as a side-issue irrelevant to the main themes, is mirrored by an
imperial history in which inter- and intra-party conflict within Britain
is radically underestimated or abstracted from any attempt to
comprehend a relationship between such conflict and a wider context
of British politics. The few recent studies of decolonisation which
have seriously engaged with the influence on it of change within
Britain have tended either still to focus heavily on the governing inner
élite (as does John Darwin,[46] arguing that wider public opinion was
successfully innoculated against concern about imperial decline), on
Parliament and party leaders (as does David Goldsworthy in what
remains far the best and most detailed work in the field[47]), or to rely
on sweeping claims about changes in middle-class attitudes (as does
R. F. Holland[48]).

Thus a situation persists in which all three dominant paradigms in
the historiography of decolonisation operate with an essentially
consensual model of British politics as it related to colonial issues.
This model is explicit in such statements as that of a Conservative
politician that 'colonial policy is almost the only field in which there is
a broad identity of aim and purpose between the two parties';[49] or
that of an African historian that 'decolonisation was [in Britain] not a
party or an ideological question, but a national one'.[50]

I shall argue that on the contrary decolonisation and the intertwined

---

[45] E. P. Thompson, 'Eighteenth-Century English Society: Class Struggle without
Class?', *Social History*, 3/3 (1980), 139. See also Thompson's *Customs in Common*
(Merlin, 1991), 26–7, and his splendid discussion on the interaction of British and
colonial notions of property and law, ibid. 164–75.

[46] Darwin, *Britain and Decolonisation*, esp. ch. 4; and *End of the British Empire*,
10–39.

[47] David Goldsworthy, *Colonial Issues in British Politics* (Oxford: Oxford University
Press, 1971).

[48] R. F. Holland, *European Decolonisation, 1918–1981* (Macmillan, 1985), esp.
208–10.

[49] Bernard Braine, MP, in a letter to *The Times* (4 May 1955); quoted in Goldsworthy, *Colonial Issues*, 1.

[50] Olajide Aluko, 'Politics of Decolonisation in British West Africa, 1945–1960', in
J. F. Ade Ajayi and Michael Crowder (eds.), *History of West Africa*, ii (Longmans,
1974), 626. Newer overviews of decolonisation from the 'periphery' reproduce this
lack of attention to internal British politics: the subject is barely mentioned in Gifford
and Louis's two massive volumes on African decolonisation, or in Louis's equally
monumental study of the end of Empire in the Middle East. Prosser Gifford and Wm.
Roger Louis, *The Transfer of Power in Africa: Decolonization 1940–1960* (New Haven,

issues of British attitudes to imperialism and the Third World were ideological questions *par excellence*; and that there were very significant differences of aim and purpose over these questions in Britain. This is not to deny either that colonial issues played a far less dramatic role in British political controversy than they did, for instance, in France;[51] or that there was, at least in some periods, a degree of consensus on many colonial questions between the leaderships of the two main parties.[52] It is to suggest rather that many of the deepest divisions and most important arguments were within rather than between the parties, or were expressed in contexts other than the inner decision-making cliques of government and party. In particular, many of the most interesting of these disputes took place between different varieties of socialists and radicals. Attention to these, I shall attempt to show, not only supplements but in some important respects alters our picture of British decolonisation.[53]

IV. BRITISH SOCIALISTS AND IMPERIALISM: CONTEXTS AND INTENTIONS

This, then, is an exercise in blurred genres: part history of political actors and actions, part history of ideas. It straddles the subdisciplines

Conn.: Yale University Press, 1982); *Decolonization and African Independence: The Transfers of Power 1960–1980* (New Haven, Conn.: Yale University Press, 1988). Only Anthony Low's contribution to the latter volume (pp. 33–72) addresses the issue even in passing.

[51] The contrast, and some possible explanations, are explored in Miles Kahler, *Decolonization in Britain and France* (Princeton, NJ: Princeton University Press, 1984), and in Smith, 'A Comparative Study'. See also, on French anticolonialism, Jacob Moneta (ed.), *La Politique du PCF dans la question coloniale 1920–1963* (Paris: Maspero, 1971); Claude Liauzu, *Aux origines des tiers-mondismes: colonisés et anti-colonialistes en France (1919–1939)* (Paris: L'Harmattan, 1982); David H. Slavin, 'The French Left and the Rif War, 1924–5: Racism and the Limits of Internationalism', *JCH* 26 (1991), as well as the substantial literature on the Algerian question in French politics.

[52] The best account of the origins, limits, and eventual breakdown of bipartisanship in colonial affairs is Goldsworthy, *Colonial Issues*.

[53] The major works dealing with colonial issues in British politics (as opposed to the evolution of official policy *per se*) are Goldsworthy, *Colonial Issues*; Georges Fischer, *Le Parti Travailliste et la décolonisation de l'Inde* (Paris: Maspero, 1966); Dan Horowitz, 'Attitudes of British Conservatives towards Decolonization in Africa, 1957–1963' (Oxford University D.Phil. thesis, 1967); Partha Sarathi Gupta, *Imperialism and the British Labour Movement, 1914–1964* (Macmillan, 1975); A. J. MacKenzie, 'British Marxists and the Empire: Anti-Imperialist Theory and Practice, 1920–1945' (London University Ph.D. thesis, 1978); Barbara Bush, 'Britain and Black Africa in the Inter-

of British and imperial history; and seeks to make, and to exemplify, an argument for the necessity of smudging that boundary. It is also, and perhaps to its author most importantly, a history of political languages: of how a set of key terms (imperialism, colonialism, nationalism, socialism) bent and twisted under the force of circumstances, sometimes wreathing into a cage that imprisoned their users. Or, in the idiom of imperial history, it investigates the 'unofficial mind', or rather a variety of unofficial and oppositional minds, in decolonisation.

Within the Labour Party and trade unions anticolonialism was perhaps the only issue on which the left seemed to score unequivocal victories during the 1950s and 1960s. And not only there; for what had appeared as extreme or utopian rhetoric even within Labour in the late 1940s had, in many instances, become the accepted wisdom of a Conservative government by the late 1950s.

We can still draw only tentative conclusions about the way this transformation took place. In some spheres fairly firm conclusions can be drawn about the influence of radical anticolonialism: on the evolution of Labour Party and TUC policy, attitudes among left-wing Party activists, parliamentary attention to colonial problems, and on some specific issues like Suez, South Africa, the Central African Federation, the Kenyan Emergency, and a range of colonial civil liberties cases. In others, however, rather little can yet be said with any confidence: notably the decision-making processes of Cabinet and Colonial Office and the development of public opinion on colonial questions. For the former, we do not yet have access to much of the documentation which would enable construction of a more complete picture. As for public opinion, the data on which we might base any conclusions are almost wholly absent—and will remain so, for the overwhelming fact about British public perceptions of colonial issues during decolonisation, as earlier, was that of sheer ignorance. There is now a significant literature on both official and mass-media attempts to *influence* public opinion about Empire, and on imperial themes in popular culture.[54] Little if any of this, however,

War Years (Sheffield University Ph.D. thesis, 1986); Paul Rich, *Race and Empire in British Politics* (Cambridge: Cambridge University Press, 1986); and C. J. Sansom, 'The British Labour Movement and Southern Africa, 1918–1955' (Birmingham University Ph.D. thesis, 1982).

[54] See esp. John M. MacKenzie, *Propaganda and Empire* (Manchester: Manchester University Press, 1984); id. (ed.), *Imperialism and Popular Culture* (Manchester:

is able to provide hard information on how these efforts were received or how widely and deeply implanted pro-imperial sentiment became in the public mind.

There are also wider theoretical problems involved in trying to trace the effects of radical and anticolonial ideas in decolonisation. It is clearly unsatisfactory merely to note the existence of such discourses—though some general surveys of decolonisation have contented themselves with this, going no further than to include them in an eclectic checklist of assorted factors possibly influencing decolonisation.[55] Yet their effects are exceedingly difficult to assess, let alone to quantify. The general problem is that of analysing the nature and effects of political languages or discourses; yet until relatively recently this has not often been seen *as* a problem. It has ordinarily been assumed (by most historians) or explicitly argued (especially by Marxists) that political language is in some direct sense a reflection of material reality, or of the material interests of those employing it. Changes in such languages reflect changes in this external reality.

That the matter is not so simple may be indicated by reference back to the 'official mind' in decolonisation. We may begin by noting that there were many 'official minds', exhibiting great variety of experience and outlook. They included former trade union officials such as Ernest Bevin and Arthur Creech Jones as well as senior public servants with pronounced radical sympathies such as Andrew Cohen, Hugh Foot, or that intriguing disciple of Henry George, Charles Temple. And if these varieties of background and world-view were in some sense subsumed, as so many radical critics claimed, within a common and conservative world-view, then still the influence of that variety may not be discounted. For the world-view itself changed, like Britain's place in the world, if perhaps more slowly and often with painful reluctance.

The official mind can never be a fully open mind, nor can the official ear bend with equal eagerness to all voices. The voices are always too numerous, their tales too varied, too complex, for that.

Manchester University Press, 1986); and J. A. Mangan (ed.), *Making Imperial Mentalities* (Manchester: Manchester University Press, 1990).

[55] Such strictures apply with some force to such major general texts as Henri Grimal, *Decolonization* (Routledge & Kegan Paul, 1978); Rudolph von Albertini, *Decolonization* (New York: Doubleday, 1971); Franz Ansprenger, *The Dissolution of the Colonial Empires* (Routledge, 1989); and Holland, *European Decolonisation*.

Procedures for selection from among the voices, filters to cut out some frequencies, some sources, to establish criteria of authority— these are the first requirements of the policy-maker. The primary need is rarely felt to be the acquisition of information, but rather some rationale for rendering the polyphonic chorus of sources of information into a simple melody. Sometimes the selective filters which make this possible are provided by personal predilections; more often they are inscribed in traditions and protocols of official discourse itself. Some voices will thus be excluded altogether, others ranked in established hierarchies according to the perceived status of the speaker. Is it then surprising that what people and institutions hear is often merely the echo of their own speech?

Yet such procedures are not immutable. Often gradually, but on occasion with dramatic rapidity, the filters change. New voices are granted authority, old ones cast out as discredited. And as the procedures are thus transformed, so also are perceptions of reality, of the choices open, the policies to be pursued. The official mind has changed.

Usually the changes are gradual. For instance a tribesman, with a smattering of mission education and an unverifiable claim to speak for the insignificant political organisation of an agrarian people may arrive in London: seeking audiences, drafting memoranda, finding friends among Communists and disreputable radicals. For the official mind, he is to be ignored, granted at best a brief courtesy meeting with a junior functionary. Twenty years later the same man leads tens of thousands of that agricultural people in the same (if renamed) political association. Terrorists claiming his leadership kill settlers, force the commitment of British troops. For the official mind, he is now a serious threat. He is attacked in Parliament; official commissions investigate his activities; he is imprisoned. Ten years later again his following among the agrarian people has shown no signs of diminishing: prison and isolation appear only to enhance his influence. Powerful voices in Parliament, in the press, in foreign capitals, and even among white settlers of the country in question suggest that peace can only return to that country if he is incorporated into the peace-making process. After another decade, the same African is President of a stable, pro-Western regime, an elder statesman, one of the leading moderates on the African scene.

The changes in the way Jomo Kenyatta was officially viewed from Britain may be paralleled for many another process of decolonisation—

for Eamon de Valera, for Mahatma Gandhi, for Kwame Nkrumah (who went full circle, back to being regarded with intense hostility), for Robert Mugabe. Undoubtedly the objects of the official view changed personally. More obviously and more profoundly, the political backgrounds against which they were seen changed. But the process by which the view was formed had its own specificity, its own relative autonomy, its own effects. New voices were added to the chorus to which the governments listened; some voices were amplified, others muted; the nationalists, and their allies and advocates within Britain, came to dominate the chorus.

It is with these allies and advocates that this study is concerned, and a central object of the concern will be their language, for the ordering and filtering of information in both official and unofficial minds took place in and through particular political discourses. As Gareth Stedman Jones points out, we cannot simply decode these discourses in order to ascertain the interests they reflected or the influence they exerted, since:

It is the discursive structure of the political language which conceives and defines interest in the first place. What we must therefore do is to study the production of interest, identification, grievance and aspiration within political languages themselves. We need to map out these successive languages . . . both in relation to the political languages they replace and laterally in relation to rival political languages with which they are in conflict. Only then can we begin to assess the reasons for their success or failure at specific points in time.[56]

Attention to patterns and shifts in language is also, and perhaps more self-evidently, important in discussion of the ways in which ideas of a more general or theoretical sort about imperialism developed on the British left during our period. Just as little of the existing literature on decolonisation has devoted attention to the influence of political activity within Britain, so little of the now considerable body

[56] Gareth Stedman Jones, *Languages of Class* (Cambridge: Cambridge University Press, 1983), 22. It may be noted here that the major influence on my thinking about language and history is the work of J. G. A. Pocock. See in particular *Politics, Language and Time* (2nd edn. Chicago: Chicago University Press, 1989), and *The Machiavellian Moment* (Princeton, NJ: Princeton University Press, 1975). The proliferating body of work on colonial discourse in literary and cultural theory, by writers like Edward Said, Homi Bhabha, and Gayatri Chakravorty Spivak, cannot be addressed here. I attempt to engage with it in *Decolonisations: Postcoloniality, Culture, and the Politics of Identity* (Verso, forthcoming 1993).

of work on theories of imperialism and underdevelopment has sought to place these theories in their political and historical context. Thus, while the genesis of Lenin's *Imperialism* both in the changes he identified in European capitalism and in the polemics against the social-patriots of the Second International have been exhaustively discussed,[57] equivalent investigations of the political determinants of other modern writings on imperialism have barely been broached.

The most obvious lacuna in commentary on theories of imperialism—a lacuna which results from a conception of the development of theory as a linear succession of major figures influenced by one another and apparently by little else—is that the years between 1917, with the publication of Lenin's pamphlet, and 1957, when Paul Baran's *Political Economy of Growth* appeared, are passed over in virtual silence. Even when it is acknowledged that socialist and Marxist writers did discuss problems of imperialism and under-development during these years, their work is widely dismissed as that of 'vulgarisers and dogmatists' labouring under the evil influence of Stalinism.[58] This gaping historiographical hole has opened largely because the history of ideas, in this field, has developed almost independently of political history. A wide range of material has been seen as the proper province of political historians alone—pamphlets, articles in political journals and newspapers, the documents of parties and pressure groups. Yet such documents are often of the greatest importance to the genealogies of political and economic theories.

These would hardly be novel suggestions in most historical fields; but it is striking how rarely histories of ideas about imperialism have adopted such forms of analysis.[59] Where the relationship between political context, intention, and the theoretical text has been scrutinised at all, as in Warren's *Imperialism, Pioneer of Capitalism* and the controversy which this work evoked, the terms of debate have been crudely polarised. Thus for Warren the European left's conceptions

---

[57] Of the many works discussing Lenin's *Imperialism* in its political context, probably the most balanced overview is Neil Harding, *Lenin's Political Thought*, ii. *Theory and Practice in the Socialist Revolution* (Macmillan, 1981), 6–70.

[58] Tom Kemp, *Theories of Imperialism* (Dennis Dobson, 1967), 106. See also, for a similar dismissal, Ken Tarbuck, 'Introduction' to Rosa Luxemburg and Nikolai Bukharin, *Imperialism and the Accumulation of Capital* (Allen Lane, 1972), 42.

[59] Richard Koebner and H. Dan Schmidt, *Imperialism: The Story and Significance of a Political Word* (Cambridge: Cambridge University Press, 1964), fairly comprehensive on 19th-cent. usages, is sketchy in the extreme in treating 20th-cent., and especially radical, views.

of imperialism and its relation to socialism and Third World nationalism are seen as a simple history of unbroken decline and theoretical impoverishment; the left since Lenin has wholly misconceived that relationship, surrendered to 'nationalist mythology and liberal guilt', and thus 'disarmed the working classes of much of Asia, Africa and Latin America'.[60]

I attempt below to provide a somewhat more nuanced account of the way in which the left in Britain viewed these issues and acted on them during the period of decolonisation. Such an account may help to bridge the gap between Hobson and Lenin on the one hand, modern development theory and present British attitudes to the Third World on the other. Anti-imperialism has been one of the central characteristics of the Western left's self-definition up to the present day; and the ideas and activities of anticolonial groups in the post-war years represented a crucial moment of transition between traditional British radical attitudes to international issues and many of the significant themes of British left-wing politics in the 1960s and since.

These campaigns and ideas were also important in shaping the views, and the forms of organisation, both of early black British political groups (many of which started as outgrowths of anticolonial lobbies) and of many future leaders in ex-colonial states. Ian Duffield has aptly described Britain between the 1930s and the 1950s as a 'junction-box' for intellectuals from much of the colonised world: there they could establish contacts and develop common ideas far more easily than in their diverse homelands.[61] The lines of association and of ideological interchange ran largely through London (and Manchester, site of the seminal Fifth Pan-African Congress in 1945) rather than directly between colonial capitals, and within this junction-box it was usually in the organisations devoted to the various causes of colonial freedom that such contacts were made and ideas formed.

Much of this story of contact and of the exchange of ideas between British socialists and colonial radicals, as well as among the latter, is almost impossible to recover. This is because so much of it took place outside the boundaries of formal politics: in private meetings, personal friendships, brief encounters of various sorts, leaving no

---

[60] Warren, *Imperialism, Pioneer of Capitalism*, 128, 5–6.
[61] Ian Duffield, 'History and the Historians', *History Today* (Sept. 1981), 34–6.

written records.[62] From scattered sources including the techniques of oral history some part of this hidden dimension can be glimpsed; but a study such as this cannot hope to reconstruct the pattern as a whole.

[62] The literature in these fields is still scanty. On early black British politics, see Peter Fryer, *Staying Power: The History of Black People in Britain* (Pluto, 1984); Ron Ramdin, *The Making of the Black Working Class in Britain* (Gower, 1987); B. W. Heinemann, Jun; *The Politics of the Powerless* (Oxford: Oxford University Press, 1972); and A. Sivanandan, 'From Resistance to Rebellion', *Race & Class*, 23/2–3 (1982). On colonial *émigré* politics in Britain, relevant references are scanty—in part because of the dearth of adequate biographical studies especially of African politicians. See below, pp. 83–9. Perhaps the most illuminating picture is a fictional one (though a fiction closely based on real events and personalities): Peter Abrahams, *A Wreath for Udomo* (Faber & Faber, 1956).

2

Socialism and Empire Before 1939

I. LABOUR AND IMPERIALISM: ORIGINS AND OVERVIEWS

The modern British left tends to proclaim itself as founded on, and shaped by, a deep-rooted internationalist tradition. Opposition to imperialism is seen as central to this and is traceable as far back as the Levellers of the mid-seventeenth century who opposed Cromwell's subjugation of Ireland. A Leveller pamphlet of 1649 posed three questions which were to be echoed by opponents of colonial conquest throughout the succeeding centuries:

Whether those who pretend to freedom (as the English now) shall not make themselves altogether inexcusable in entrenching upon others' freedoms, and whether it is not the character of a true patriot to endeavour the just freedom of all as well as his own? How can the conquered be accounted rebels, if at any time they seek to free themselves and recover their own?[1]

Continuity for this kind of stance may be seen over the following two centuries; in the support given by some English radicals to the American colonists in their war of independence, in the campaigns for the abolition of the slave trade, in the sympathy shown for revolutionary movements in Latin America and for the rebellion of the slaves in Haiti—an attitude which is most movingly symbolised in Wordsworth's sonnet to Toussaint l'Ouverture. Chartist leader Ernest Jones lauded the Indian Mutiny, and established what was to become almost a tradition of turning the boasts of Empire into bitter aphorisms in commenting that 'On its colonies the sun never sets, but the blood never dries.'[2] (Compare the later Irish Nationalist suggestion that the sun never set on the Empire because God did not trust the British in the dark.) Parts of the Liberal coalition, notably the Free Trade

---

[1] *The Moderate Intelligencer* (May 1649); quoted in H. N. Brailsford, *The Levellers and the English Revolution* (2nd edn., Nottingham: Spokesman, 1976), 502.

[2] 'Notes to the People' (May 1851); quoted in R. Palme Dutt, *The Crisis of Britain and the British Empire* (Lawrence & Wishart, 1953), 320.

group under Cobden and Bright, various forms of nineteenth-century Radicalism, and certain religious groups shared this legacy of hostility to Empire.

The pioneer British socialist groups—the Social Democratic Federation, the Socialist League, and the Independent Labour Party— took up similar themes. At the height of the Scramble for Africa William Morris's Socialist League denounced the invasion of the Sudan as being 'prompted solely by the desire to exploit the country in the interests of capitalists and stock-jobbers . . . who could not exist as a class without this exploitation of foreign nations to get new markets'.[3] The form of this attack, associating colonialism with speculative capitalism, seems to anticipate themes conventionally associated with the name of J. A. Hobson; but in fact these were the common currency of the socialist sects twenty years before Hobson gave them coherent expression.[4]

Even in the thought of the early socialist often seen as the most significant exception to this general picture, SDF leader H. M. Hyndman, a clear anticolonialist strain can be discerned. Hyndman has been viewed by some historians as having become an increasingly avid imperialist from at least the time when, in 1901, he abandoned his earlier opposition to the Boer War.[5] Yet his *England for All*, the most important founding statement of English Marxism, devotes considerable space to the problems of Empire, and the tone is entirely hostile to the imperial mission. In his much later work, *The Awakening of Asia* (1919), he was still urging the 'frank abandonment of the fallacious policy of imperialism'.[6]

Yet the nature and limits of Hyndman's anti-imperialism bear closer examination, for—prefiguring themes which were to be reiterated and extended by British socialists over the next sixty years or more—*England for All* offers sharply different prescriptions for dif-

[3] Morris in the *Daily News* (3 Apr. 1885); quoted in E. P. Thompson, *William Morris: Romantic to Revolutionary* (2nd edn., Merlin, 1977), 387.

[4] Indeed, as Bernard Porter points out, in relating imperialism to overproduction the radical critics were 'only repeating the common view of the imperialists themselves', *Critics of Empire* (Macmillan, 1968), 44.

[5] For the view of Hyndman as straightforward imperialist, see George Lichtheim, *A Short History of Socialism* (Fontana, 1975), 216, or Perry Anderson, 'Origins of the Present Crisis', in id. and Robin Blackburn (eds.), *Towards Socialism* (Fontana, 1965), 24. For the contrary interpretation see Chushichi Tsuzuki, *H. M. Hyndman and British Socialism* (Oxford: Oxford University Press, 1961), and Asa Briggs, in David Rubinstein (ed.), *People for the People* (Ithaca, 1973), 117–18.

[6] H. M. Hyndman, *The Awakening of Asia* (Cassell, 1919).

ferent parts of the Empire. On Ireland, the message seems unequivocal: 'Legislative independence for Ireland is a necessity if we
Englishmen are to continue Parliamentary government.'[7] For India, it
is participation in government rather than independence that is
advocated. The African and other tropical colonies are barely mentioned. And for the white-settled Dominions, for which the term
'colonies' is generally reserved by Hyndman, a bright future is seen
as 'the chief mainstay of Anglo-Saxon domination outside these
islands . . . in permanent union with the more ancient democracy of
England'.[8]

For Hyndman, then, 'imperialism' denoted the exploitation, or
more particularly the military conquest, of subject non-white races;
but the 'colonies' were the younger children of a world-wide family
of English-speaking peoples. It was therefore quite consistent for him
to denounce the former, but regard the latter as an international
commonwealth in support of which patriotic, democratic, and socialist
principles combined. This commonwealth is celebrated also in terms
of an explicitly racial solidarity; whilst Irish Home Rule is valued not
so much for its possible benefits to Ireland, but because British rule
in Ireland damages Britain (or, as Hyndman interchangeably calls it,
England) itself. This, then, is an essentially self-interested or Little
England version of anti-imperialism, uneasily combined with notions
of global mission and of racial solidarity. Hyndman was both, by his
own lights, a committed anti-imperialist; and a man who, as T. A.
Jackson said, 'always had a touch of the jingo in him'.[9]

Such dichotomies mark the attitudes to Empire of most Victorian
and Edwardian radicals; and for most early socialists, for whom
Hyndman was not only an influential but a symptomatic figure. The
view of Empire suggested in the 1649 Leveller manifesto was always
a minority one. It may well have been so among the Levellers
themselves; the document quoted above (known only from a hostile
source, an official journal's attack on it, as the original has not
survived) is almost the only recorded statement opposing intervention
in Ireland on grounds of general principle as opposed, for instance, to
soldiers' pragmatic objections to serving there. Most English Pro-
testants under the Commonwealth, even among the radicals, un-

---

[7] *England for all: A Textbook of Democracy* (1881; ed. C. Tsuzuki, Brighton: Harvester,
1973), 130.
[8] Ibid. 152–68.
[9] T. A. Jackson, *Solo Trumpet* (Lawrence & Wishart, 1953), 69.

doubtedly supported Cromwell's Irish campaigns on both nationalist and religious grounds.[10] There appears to have been no organised or public protest at all against Cromwellian imperialism in the West Indies and elsewhere.

Similar stories can be told for most anti-imperial sentiment in the eighteenth and nineteenth centuries: it was both a minority current, and a limited and conditional stance. British supporters of the American colonists generally argued on grounds of the rights of the 'freeborn Englishman', not some more general right to self-determination.[11] Many eighteenth-century radicals—usually styling themselves patriots—were ardent expansionists like their Cromwellian forebears, as well as being Gallophobe and anti-Catholic.[12] British abolitionists of the revolutionary era rarely moved from opposing chattel slavery to advocating political self-government for the former slaves: few of them were believers in racial equality in any strong sense.[13] And links between abolitionism and domestic British radicalism, though always present, were never conflict free. Many abolitionists opposed Reform; some Reformers saw abolitionism as at best a distraction from the plight of the British poor. The savagery of the *Poor Man's Guardian* towards abolitionist T. H. Buxton was not atypical:

He is one of those erratic philanthropists for whom emancipation has no charms, unless the slave happens to live some thousand miles off, with the additional recommendation of a black hide, thick lips, and a woolly head. Tell him of British children pining in factories, of English adults yoked to gravel carts, or of famished Irishmen striving to sustain nature by sea-weed and raw porpuses, and Buxton's heart is hard as marble;—but tell him of a

---

[10] Christopher Hill, 'Seventeenth-Century English Radicals and Ireland', in Patrick J. Corish (ed.), *Radicals, Rebels and Establishments*, Historical Studies, xv (Belfast: Appletree Press, 1985). It is even possible that the anti-imperialist arguments by Levellers reported in the *Intelligencer* and in *Walwin's Wiles* are opponents' fabrications.

[11] Colin Bonwick, *English Radicals and the American Revolution* (Chapel Hill, NC: University of North Carolina Press, 1977).

[12] Linda Colley, 'Radical Patriotism in Eighteenth-Century England', in Raphael Samuel (ed.), *Patriotism*, i (Routledge & Kegan Raul, 1989); 'Whose Nation? Class and National Consciousness in Britain, 1750–1830', *Past & Present*, 102 (1982); Hugh Cunningham, 'The Language of Patriotism, 1750–1914', *HWJ* 12 (1981).

[13] See, amidst a vast literature, Seymour Drescher, *Capitalism and Antislavery* (Macmillan, 1986); Roger Anstey, *The Atlantic Slave Trade and British Abolition, 1760–1810* (Macmillan, 1975); Robin Blackburn, *The Overthrow of Colonial Slavery* (Verso, 1988).

sleek stupid negro getting a dozen or two of lashes for not doing what he is well fed for doing, and Buxton's eyes are bathed in sensibility![14]

Equally, few of those in Britain who celebrated rebels against the empires of other, rival European powers—admirers of a Toussaint, a Bolivar, or a Garibaldi—extended similar sentiments to revolts against British rule. Ernest Jones's enthusiasm for Indian revolt was exceptional even among his own circle, the most militant wing of Chartism. If Seymour Drescher is right to argue that abolitionism, 'far from deflecting attention away from metropolitan grievances, delivered a message of long-term popular power';[15] and Robin Blackburn correct that 'anti-slavery themes had a resonance within all social classes ... Not only did leading abolitionists support Chartism but leading Chartists articulated their ideas by drawing on the anti-slavery tradition';[16] then these were neither universally recognised affinities nor ones which extended to a shared or widespread anticolonial sentiment.

Blanket opposition to Empire was an even more fragmentary and fugitive presence among early Victorian Liberals. The anti-imperialism of Cobden, Bright, and their followers subsumed a variety of inconsistent, incompatible views. These ranged from hostility to the acquisition of *new* territories (not necessarily entailing the abandonment of existing possessions), through a desire to introduce representative government in colonies of white settlement (but, so far as most Manchesterites were concerned, *only* in these), to generalised claims that Empire was unprofitable, or undesirable because it perpetuated the power of the aristocracy within Britain. Calls for wholesale decolonisation were very rare—though Cobden sometimes made them. And when such calls were heard, they were almost never based on appeal to universalistic principles of democracy or self-determination. Despite the pervasive moralism of much Manchester discourse, especially that of John Bright, their main arguments against Empire were always Little England ones invoking metropolitan self-interest.[17]

---

[14] *The Poor Man's Guardian* (17 Nov. 1832), 609.

[15] Drescher, *Capitalism and Antislavery*, 151.

[16] Blackburn, *Overthrow*, 536.

[17] See James L. Sturgis, *John Bright and the Empire* (Athlone Press, 1969); John Gallagher and Ronald Robinson, 'The Imperialism of Free Trade', *EcHR* 6/1 (1953); Peter Harnetty, *Imperialism and Free Trade* (Manchester: Manchester University Press, 1972); Ewan Green and Miles Taylor, 'Further Thoughts on Little Englandism', in Samuel, *Patriotism*, i; John Morley, *The Life of Richard Cobden* (Chapman & Hall, 1879), esp. ch. 27. The strongest—indeed perhaps overstated—argument for the Little England roots of Manchester anticolonialism is Miles Taylor, 'Imperium

Bentham's disciples, meanwhile, were even less likely to be hostile to Empire *per se* than were Bright's. Their dominant concerns were with cultural diffusion, and with rationalising imperial rule: with good government rather than self-government.[18] The dominant attitude to the latter was classically expressed by John Stuart Mill: that, in the case of 'rude' peoples, 'a civilised government, to be really advantageous to them, will require to be in a considerable measure despotic'.[19]

Thus for Victorian and Edwardian radicals, advocacy of self-determination for white settler colonies could be combined with belief in an imperial civilising mission towards non-Europeans. Conversely, support for the ideas of expansion of the race and of the advantages of closer economic or political relations with areas of substantial British settlement could coexist with opposition to imperialism in the sense of aggression against or rule over territories without such settlement. In so far as social imperialist doctrines gained any substantial foothold in radical circles, it was primarily or only in relation to the settler colonies. And all these arguments were conducted with minimal attention to the desires or rights of the colonised. The primary focus was domestic. Above all, it was on whether or not imperialism was economically beneficial to Britain.

The corner-stone of radical opposition to Empire, in the two decades before 1914 as in the era of Cobden, was thus that Britain as a whole gained very little, or actually suffered, from imperial investment and trade: that this profited only a small clique of financiers. Hobson's was the most famous and powerful formulation of this view:

Aggressive Imperialism, which costs the taxpayer so dear, which is of so little value to the manufacturer and trader, which is fraught with such grave incalculable peril to the citizen, is a source of great gain to the investor who cannot find at home the profitable use he seeks for his capital.[20]

Few even among the early Marxian socialists believed, however, that the critique of aggressive imperialism implied a policy of with-

---

et Libertas? Rethinking the Radical Critique of Imperialism during the Nineteenth Century', JICH 19/1 (1991).

[18] See Eric Stokes, *The English Utilitarians and India* (Oxford: Oxford University Press, 1959).

[19] J. S. Mill, 'Considerations on Representative Government' (1861), in *Utilitarianism, Liberty, and Representative Government* (Everyman edn., 1968), 178.

[20] J. A. Hobson, *Imperialism: A Study* (James Nisbet & Co., 1902), 62.

drawal from territories already occupied.[21] Marx himself, as is well known, had regarded British rule in India as historically progressive despite its brutalities. Although he had strongly supported demands for Irish freedom, he had seen the Raj as 'the unconscious tool of history' in bringing about an economic revolution in Asia.[22] Marx never offered any speculation as to what might be the colonial policy of a future socialist state. Engels, though, had done so; and while he stressed that 'the proletariat emancipating itself cannot conduct any colonial wars . . . [and] can force no blessings of any kind upon any foreign nation without undermining its own victory in so doing' he in no way suggested that colonial nationalist movements might be natural allies of the European proletariat.[23] Neither man showed much interest in nationalisms outside Europe. Many colonised peoples evidently, if implicitly, fell into the category Engels (following Hegel) dismissed as 'non-historical': groups which, 'no longer capable of a national existence, are absorbed by the larger nations.'[24] Marx and Engels were neither cultural relativists nor believers in national independence as a good in itself: it was valuable only in so far as it contributed to social progress. And this meant chiefly progress in the large industrialised states, which they expected to achieve socialism first. Thus Irish independence, for instance, was supported because it would remove barriers to socialist advance within Britain, not for any reason intrinsic to Ireland or Irish opinion.[25] The German socialist exiles reproduced a soi-disant Little Englandism. The Irish case,

---

[21] For general surveys of late Victorian and Edwardian British socialists' views of Empire, see Porter, *Critics of Empire*; Bernard Semmel, *Imperialism and Social Reform* (Allen & Unwin, 1960); Stephen Koss (ed.), *The Pro-Boers* (Chicago: Chicago University Press, 1973); Henry Pelling, 'British Labour and British Imperialism', in id., *Popular Politics and Society in Late Victorian Britain* (Macmillan, 1968); Preben Kaarsholm, 'Anti-Imperialism in England in the period of the South African War', ICS seminar paper (1983); and Richard Price, *An Imperial War and the British Working Class* (Routledge & Kegan Paul, 1972). For comparative perspectives, see Charles-Robert Ageron, *L'Anticolonialisme en France de 1871 à 1914* (Paris: Presses Universitaires de France, 1973); Marcel Merle (ed.), *L'Anticolonialisme Européen de Las Casas à Karl Marx* (Paris: Armand Colin, 1969).

[22] Karl Marx, 'The British Rule in India', *New York Daily Tribune* (25 June 1853); from Karl Marx and Friedrich Engels, *On Colonialism* (Moscow: Progress Publishers, 1959), 41.

[23] Friedrich Engels, letter to Kautsky (12 Sept. 1882); *On Colonialism*, 342.

[24] Friedrich Engels, 'Po and Rhine' (1859), in Karl Marx and Friedrich Engels, *Collected Works*, xvi (Lawrence & Wishart, 1975 et seq.).

[25] See e.g. Marx's letters to Kugelmann (29 Nov. 1869) and to Engels (10 Dec. 1869), *Collected Works*, xliii (Lawrence & Wishart, 1975 et seq.).

however, was seen as *sui generis*. Elsewhere, colonialism and the attendant creation of a unified world market were celebrated by Marx and Engels in so far as they destroyed feudal or oriental despotism, paving the way for modern capitalism and hence eventually for socialism.[26]

Marx and Engels, then, were clearly not anticolonialists in the sense that I have defined that stance. Nor were most British radicals or socialists before the First World War. Hyndman believed that some colonies should be retained even if only as a 'duty'. Hobson, though he felt that British colonial rule had persistently failed to live up to ideals of trusteeship, none the less accepted those ideals themselves. He believed appeals to principles of colonial freedom to be practically meaningless: 'To those who utter the single cry of warning, "laissez faire, hands off..." it is a sufficient answer to point out the impossibility of maintaining such an attitude.'[27] When he listed principles whose observance would make colonial rule legitimate, he did not include the wishes of the colonised among them. His positive prescriptions corresponded quite closely to the ideals of a Lugardian Indirect Rule system, with the addition of some form of international supervision.[28]

E. D. Morel, famous critic of Leopold's rapacious regime in the Congo, was more fulsome in his praise of the Lugardian ethos. British rule in Nigeria was 'entirely creative... a work of which the value can but grow in public estimation... The Southern Nigeria Administration stands for high ideals and good government.'[29]

Such radical approval of the Indirect Rule philosophy may have stemmed from the view, which they shared with official proponents of that mode of colonial administration, that one should interfere as little as possible with indigenous tradition and ways of life. This desire to preserve, and tendency to idealise, tradition—the 'myth of Merrie Africa'—may in turn derive from a romantic anti-capitalist ethos held both by many colonial administrators and by many British radicals.[30]

---

[26] *The Manifesto of the Communist Party* includes the most famous of Marx's hymns to the progressive capacity of capitalism: see *The Revolutions of 1848*, ed. David Fernbach (Harmondsworth: Penguin, 1973), 71.

[27] Hobson, *Imperialism*, 242.

[28] Ibid. 235–97.

[29] E. D. Morel, *Nigeria: Its Peoples and Its Problems* (Smith, Elder & Co., 1911), 136, 259.

[30] On 'Merrie Africa', see David W. Throup, *Economic and Social Origins of Mau Mau* (James Currey, 1987); and Anne Phillips, *The Enigma of Colonialism: British Policy*

Radical-Liberal objections to the exploitation of non-European peoples, and to aggressive imperialism of the sort they saw in South Africa, were thus far from incompatible with acceptance of closer association with the white Dominions or of the necessity of continued British governance over the lower races. And in this sphere as in many others, the characteristic emphases of Radical Liberalism were carried over with little change into early British socialism. The British socialist movement, unlike those of Germany, Austria, or Russia, did not develop an indigenous or distinctively socialist analysis of imperialism. At most there were fragmentary suggestive hints from William Morris and Belfort Bax. Marxist theory, the background from which such an analysis emerged on the Continent, was a sickly transplant on British soil. The Liberal intellectual heritage, by contrast, was vastly stronger there than in central or eastern Europe.

The Fabian Society's dispute over the Boer War crystallised these tensions and limitations. In their first years the Fabians had almost wholly eschewed discussion of international and colonial problems. Only with the outbreak of the second Anglo-Boer War was the Society reluctantly forced into a debate on Empire, which revealed sharp divisions of opinion within its ranks. The dominant view, most stridently argued by George Bernard Shaw and represented in the tract *Fabianism and the Empire*, was favourable towards the imperial mission. The domination of backward races by the more advanced, and of smaller political units by larger, was claimed to be both inevitable and, since efficiency was the prime socialist virtue, desirable. Nationalism was a romantic anachronism, the Empire a step towards its transcendence.[31]

On this view of imperialism, considerations of justice were irrelevant. For Sidney Webb the Boer War was 'wholly unjust but wholly necessary'.[32] Some in the Society could not accept this attitude:

in West Africa (James Currey, 1989)—which suggests strong elective affinities between the theories of Henry George and the preferences of British officials in Nigeria. On romantic anti-capitalism, Martin J. Wiener, *English Culture and the Decline of the Industrial Spirit, 1850–1980* (Cambridge: Cambridge University Press, 1981), is a stimulating—if overpraised—presentation of both conservative and radical thought as deeply imbued with hostility to industrialism. Preben Kaarsholm, 'Imperialism and Romantic Anti-Capitalism' (Kultur og Samfund, Roskilde Universitetscenter, 1983), traces such views in writers on colonialism as diverse as Hobson, Olive Schreiner, and G. W. Steevens.

[31] George Bernard Shaw (ed.), *Fabianism and the Empire: A Manifesto of the Fabian Society* (Fabian Society, 1900).
[32] Quoted in Peter Clarke, *Liberals and Social Democrats* (Cambridge: Cambridge University Press, 1978), 84.

ethical opposition to aggressive imperialism and a belief in the central role of morality in international affairs, which formed so important a part of Radical-Liberal beliefs, were for people like Ramsay MacDonald and Graham Wallas more compelling than the pursuit of efficiency. Those who felt thus abandoned the Fabians either as a direct result of the Boer War controversy or soon thereafter. MacDonald argued against the claims of the 'civilising mission' on the grounds that even 'the lowest form of institution . . . [shows] rational adaptation of man to circumstances'.[33]

Fabianism and the Empire is not primarily concerned with colonial policy or the British Empire as such: it displays neither any particular knowledge of, nor any particular interest in, the actual record of British imperialism. Instead it takes the form of a series of very general, indeed loose, assertions about the progressive potential of imperial expansion, before turning with apparent relief to the more tractable problems of domestic reform. Its stance arose from domestic political calculation: the Fabians were seeking *rapprochement* with the general enthusiasm for imperial conquest which supposedly swept the British public at the turn of the century. The argument, as expressed by Hubert Bland, was that the Society's long-term aims would:

be entirely crippled if we throw ourselves dead athwart the Imperialist, or any other, strong stream or tendency. As we cannot break up those streams, but can only be broken up by them, we should try in our humble, but sometimes quite effective, way, to direct them.[34]

Bernard Porter's judgement thus seems fair: the Fabians 'were imperialists because they did not think foreign affairs mattered to them; hence they were able to barter their support over the South African war to the highest bidder'.[35] Far more questionable is his later, more favourable, and somewhat incompatible suggestion that Fabian imperial proposals 'were at least *constructive*, capable of supporting definite and detailed policies . . . unlike, for example, the dull

[33] J. Ramsay MacDonald, 'The Propaganda of Civilisation', quoted in Partha Sarathi Gupta, *Imperialism and the British Labour Movement* (Macmillan, 1975), 13. On this dispute see also Porter, *Critics of Empire*, 109–23; Patricia Pugh, *Educate, Agitate, Organise: 100 Years of Fabian Socialism* (Methuen, 1984), 73–81; Gordon K. Lewis, *Slavery, Imperialism and Freedom: Studies in English Radical Thought* (New York: Monthly Review, 1978).
[34] Quoted in Norman and Jeanne MacKenzie, *The First Fabians* (Weidenfeld & Nicolson, 1977), 270–1.
[35] *Critics of Empire*, 122.

disinterest [*sic*] of the more typical Labour parochialist, or the single-minded destructiveness of the blanket anti-imperial Little Englander'.[36] Neither *Fabianism and the Empire* itself, nor any associated Fabian writing, embodied such detailed constructive policies. Above all, there is total silence on colonial political development. The great debate over the merits of the Boer War took place virtually without reference to the indigenous peoples of southern Africa. *Fabianism and the Empire* did espouse the necessity of humane treatment and safeguards for the rights of Africans, but in very cursory fashion and without considering that these rights might include any form of political representation.[37] Yet the anti-war Radicals were little, if any, more advanced in this regard.

British socialists inherited from the Radical-Liberal milieu, then, both a specific theory of imperialism and a wider approach. The theory was that associated with Hobson and his disciples, the wider inheritance that of a moralistic, often Little Englandist anti-imperialism. Imperialism, like socialism, denoted a doctrine well before it was widely used to describe a set of practices or structures—and well before 'colonialism' existed at all as a term. Anti-imperialism, likewise, denoted hostility to the doctrine of expansionism, not necessarily to the existing Empire. This hostility might be stung into intensive action by specific colonial crises like the second Boer War. But in its essential negativity it formed a very unstable basis for any coherent or consistent campaign for disengagement from Empire, and was always liable to collapse into a reflex nationalism under any perceived threat to British power. These ambivalences were well captured in 1908 by the most popular socialist writer of his generation, Robert Blatchford:

Britain must defend her Empire, or lose it.

I am a Little Englander. I don't want to rule anybody, or to command anything. The world is welcome to my share of the Empire, any day. But I recognise that to *lose* the Empire, to be attacked and defeated, would be a bloody, a ruinous, and horrible business . . . If you do not believe in defending the Empire, are you willing to give it up? If you are willing to give it up have you ever reflected what an extremely difficult and dangerous policy that would be?[38]

---

[36] Bernard Porter, 'Fabians, Imperialists and the International Order', in Ben Pimlott (ed.), *Fabian Essays in Socialist Thought* (Heinemann, 1984), 59.

[37] *Fabianism and the Empire*, 30–1, 35–7.

[38] Blatchford quoted in Laurence Thompson, *Robert Blatchford: Portrait of an Englishman* (Gollancz, 1951), 210–11.

A third element, to some extent common both to the narrower theory and the wider approach, became particularly evident during the Boer War: a conspiracy theory of imperialism. The view of Empire as serving the interests of a financial cabal who tricked government and public (the latter through the manipulation of 'jingo' sentiments) into supporting expansionist adventures, is strongly present in Hobson and was eagerly adopted by many in the early socialist sects. It has sometimes been suggested that identification of the profiteers as, supposedly, predominantly Jewish led some of these writers, notably Hobson and H. N. Brailsford, to employ a markedly anti-semitic tone. The assertion is still contested, and Hobson himself claimed to deprecate the 'ignominious passion of Judenhetze'.[39] Yet unquestionably the assimilation of a strain of populist nationalism to anti-imperialist rhetoric could lead to a form of radical xenophobia, of which an apparently anti-semitic vocabulary was one of the most unpleasant facets. With or without such racist undertones, the financial conspiracy theory persisted in the Radical and even the later Marxist critique of imperialism; being obsessively reiterated, for instance, in the 1920s *Communist Review* articles of J. T. Walton Newbold.[40]

After 1918, though, the major theoretical influence on the left besides that of Hobson was of course Lenin—whose views on imperialism, often at second or third hand and often conflated with Hobson's, gained assent well beyond the narrow bounds of the British Communist Party and even among many who were far from considering themselves Marxists. Lenin's and Hobson's theories had much in common, the former drawing heavily on the latter as well as on Hilferding and Bukharin. They therefore have major faults also in common, both failing to fit much of the available evidence on the new imperialism of the late nineteenth century and after.[41]

---

[39] Hobson, *Imperialism*, and *The War in South Africa*, 189; H. N. Brailsford, *The War of Steel and Gold: A Study of the Armed Peace* (Bell, 1914). The argument against Hobson is presented in Richard Koebner and H. Dan Schmidt, *Imperialism: The Story and Significance of a Political Word, 1840–1960* (Cambridge: Cambridge University Press, 1964), 226–7, 252; and Lewis Feuer, *Imperialism and the Anti-Imperialist Mind* (Buffalo: Prometheus Books, 1986), 74–6; and with greater care and detail in Colin Holmes, 'J. A. Hobson and the Jews', in id. (ed.), *Immigrants and Minorities in British Society* (Allen & Unwin, 1978). Clarke, *Liberals and Social Democrats*, 92, offer a defence of Hobson.

[40] *Communist Review* (Oct. 1921, Feb., June, July, and Aug. 1922, July and Oct. 1923).

[41] The critical literature on Lenin's *Imperialism* is immense. For its failure to fit the

Lenin's work in particular raises serious problems of terminology, which we shall see dogging left-wing thought on imperialism over the succeeding decades. 'Imperialism' for Lenin and his followers has had a specialised meaning associated with features of monopoly and finance capital, and with a particular historical period commencing around the turn of the century. The lines of demarcation between this use of the term and other definitions have never satisfactorily been established. The Leninist usage is both narrower, in that it refers only to a specific stage in the historical development of capitalism; and wider, in that it may serve as a general descriptive term for all features of capitalist society in that stage, than the non-Leninist.

There are further difficulties with Lenin's definition of imperialism as the 'monopoly stage of capitalism'.[42] As Giovanni Arrighi points out, this can be taken to mean either that Lenin was arguing for a *relationship* between imperialism and monopoly capitalism, or postulating *identity* between the two. If the former, the proposition can be submitted to empirical verification or falsification; if the latter, 'the definition escapes all empirical control'.[43] Arrighi suggests that the ambiguity may have been deliberate on Lenin's part. Whatever might have been Lenin's own intention, it appears that in much of the subsequent propaganda of the Comintern and its constituent parties, including the CPGB, political and polemical considerations subsumed those of explication, the inherent ambiguities of Lenin's discourse became worse confounded, and the interpretation of his definition as a postulate of identity between imperialism and monopoly capitalism became general. The semantic anarchy ensuing from that confusion made the concepts involved intellectually almost valueless; but politically of considerable power and resonance.

That resonance depended, however, on the continuation of a very different understanding of the idea of imperialism, which identified it

facts of colonial expansion (explaining which was not, admittedly, Lenin's or Hobson's main intention), see, for instance, D. K. Fieldhouse, *Economics and Empire, 1830–1914* (Weidenfeld & Nicolson, 1973); for its lack of originality and rigour, Anthony Brewer, *Marxist Theories of Imperialism: A Critical Survey* (Routledge & Kegan Paul, 1980); for its internal ambiguities, Giovanni Arrighi, *The Geometry of Imperialism, The Limits of Hobson's Paradigm* (New Left Books, 1978), and below, pp. 54–63, 162–4, 293–7.

[42] V. I. Lenin, *Imperialism, the Highest Stage of Capitalism* (orig. pub. 1916; quotations are from the 1975 Peking Foreign Languages Press edn.). Lenin's central definition of imperialism is on pp. 104–6.

[43] Arrighi, *Geometry*, 13–20.

with exploitative relations between advanced and backward areas, particularly through armed conquest and formal colonialism. Such an understanding, drawing heavily on the Radical-Liberal legacy, indeed remained the 'common sense' of the international left, not least among Communists themselves. Thus whilst a Leninist interpretation gained almost generalised currency on the left after 1918 it did so primarily in so far as it was understood in terms of, was in fact parasitic upon, an older and more moralistic discourse of anticolonialism.

II. THE IMPACT OF EMPIRE ON THE BRITISH LEFT

We have sketched some of the main early influences on British socialists' attitudes to Empire. What, though, of the other side of the coin: the influence of Empire on the left itself?

Different currents of socialist opinion, and of both socialist and non-socialist historiography, have expressed entirely opposed verdicts on this issue. It is quite possible to argue that such influences were all-pervasive; that the entire thinking of the Labour Party, for instance, was shaped by its failure adequately to confront the problem of Empire—a view expressed with passion and eloquence by Victor Kiernan.[44] Alternatively, histories of the British left can be, and usually have been, written on the implicit assumption that imperial issues were of no substantive importance at all. And these varied attitudes in part themselves reflect equally contrasting judgements on the significance of Empire for the British polity and society as a whole.

To discover the kinds of arguments which have suggested that the impact of imperialism on British socialism was enormous and deeply debilitating, we may turn first to that most powerful socialist critic of socialism, George Orwell. In 1939 he delivered a crushing judgement on the question:

In a prosperous country, above all in an imperialist country, left-wing politics is always partly humbug. There can be no real reconstruction that would not lead to at least a temporary drop in the English standard of life, which is

[44] V. G. Kiernan, 'India and the Labour Party', *NLR* 42 (1967); id., 'The British Labour Movement and Imperialism', *SSLHB* 31 (1975).

another way of saying that the majority of left-wing politicians and publicists are people who earn their living by demanding something that they don't genuinely want... every real emergency reveals instantly that they are shamming... What we always forget is that the overwhelming bulk of the British proletariat does not live in Britain, but in Asia and Africa.[45]

Two years later he returned to the attack, charging that the Labour Party 'has never been able to achieve any major change, because except in purely domestic matters it has never possessed a genuinely independent policy'. Uneasily aware that the prosperity of its supporters as of all in Britain was dependent on colonial poverty, Labour had—so Orwell argued—remained 'hopelessly parochial in outlook', mouthing hollow slogans about Indian independence but terrified of real power which might force it to confront the issue.[46]

Orwell was here expressing themes which the non-Labour left have invoked against the Labour Party, and Third World nationalists against the British left as a whole, throughout this century. The identification of the British working classes as a labour aristocracy benefiting from colonial exploitation; the claim that this position made its leaders constantly prone to hypocrisy, compromise, and fear of power; the belief that implication in imperialism was not merely a symptom of British socialism's failures but its prime cause—all are present in Orwell's work, and all have found a host of other supporters to the present day.

Orwell believed the perpetuation of this state of affairs to be dependent on the existence of the formal Empire.[47] Subsequent writers adopting otherwise similar perspectives, though, saw world inequality, the exploitation of poor countries by rich countries, as sufficient in itself to maintain the quiescence of the advanced countries' working classes, with or without formal colonialism. Thus Arghiri Emmanuel believed that the mechanisms of unequal exchange between states ensured that:

The relative importance of the national exploitation from which a working class suffers through belonging to the proletariat diminishes continually as compared with that from which it benefits through belonging to a privileged nation... Today everything suggests that there is more socialism and inter-

---

[45] George Orwell, 'Not Counting Niggers' (orig. pub. *Adelphi*, June 1939), in *Collected Essays, Journalism and Letters*, i (Harmondsworth: Penguin, 1976), 434–7.

[46] Orwell, 'The Lion and the Unicorn' (orig. pub. 1941), in *Collected Essays*, ii. 113.

[47] See Bernard Crick, *George Orwell: A Life* (Secker & Warburg, 1980), 254–5, 378.

nationalism in the brains of the intellectuals of the Labour party, and perhaps still more in those of some bourgeois liberals, than in the feelings and reactions of the British working class.[48]

An older and perhaps more widely influential group of theories than these, however, has been that which sees not the entire working class of the advanced countries but a privileged portion of it—a labour aristocracy—as having had its consciousness profoundly altered by imperialism. This was the view of much orthodox Marxist thought, building on a notion that had been hinted at by Engels and developed by Lenin. Engels had talked of an 'aristocratic' section of the British working class having been accorded a relatively privileged position and saw this as resulting in their abandonment of radical politics. But although he saw Britain's Victorian position as world economic leader as making this possible, he did not specifically link it to imperialism—in any sense of that term. Lenin, however, did make the connection, associating the phenomenon of the labour aristocracy with the imperialist stage of capitalism and drawing characteristically sharp political conclusions from this: the labour aristocrats had been 'bribed' by capitalism and tended therefore to compromise and divide the working class, becoming the effective agents of the bourgeoisie.[49]

It was these political implications which British Marxists took up during the 1920s, arguing that British capitalism increasingly assumed a parasitic character (as Lenin had predicted) and relied on colonial super-profits to survive. Sections of the working class gained from this parasitic imperial system, and this was held to explain their lack of revolutionary ardour.

As we shall see, the theory of the labour aristocracy was to remain central to Communist discussion of imperialism. Other writers on the left, though, stressed less the economic effects of Empire on the Labour movement than the ideological hegemony of an imperial world-view. The second New Left of the 1960s, in particular, extended the terms of the critique to grant to the legacy of Empire a central place in a negative assessment of British socialism and indeed of British culture and intellectual life as a whole. Thus Perry Anderson

---

[48] Arghiri Emmanuel, *Unequal Exchange* (New York: Monthly Review, 1972), 180–2.

[49] Lenin, *Imperialism*, 9–10, 128–30; *Left-Wing Communism: An Infantile Disorder* (orig. pub. 1920; cited from 1975 Peking edn.), 36–49. See also E. J. Hobsbawm, 'Lenin and the Labour Aristocracy', in id., *Revolutionaries* (Weidenfeld & Nicolson, 1973).

and Tom Nairn argued that imperial power made possible the perpetuation in power of a largely preindustrial patrician élite. By comparison with other countries, Britain's bourgeois revolution was
incomplete. External expansion preserved an anachronistic political
and cultural structure, whilst the international role of British capital
sheltered the domestic economy from the harsh winds of competition.
Imperialism, in both formal and informal guises, therefore generated
a deferential and hierarchical politics, a declining industrial base, an
archaic ruling class, and a complacent, reactionary culture. British
socialism, it is argued, never really challenged this: the imperial ethos
co-opted Labour as it had previously done the industrial bourgeoisie.[50]

Another, related line of argument which suggests that imperialism
was decisive in shaping the attitudes of the British left arises from
concern with race relations in Britain, and sees Empire as having
been above all the incubator of British racism. This perception of the
colonial legacy has been put forward in various forms by writers
associated with the journal *Race Today*,[51] with the Birmingham Centre
for Contemporary Cultural Studies,[52] and with the Institute of Race
Relations.[53] These have all suggested various sorts of structural
relationship between the colonial past and domestic racism: links
anchored in the political economy of Empire. An alternative approach
is to trace more direct connections in the formation of attitudes, as is
done by John Rex. He sees imperialism as having posed a frontal
challenge to the dominant liberal individualist ethos of British left-
wing thought. In face of this challenge 'a minority maintained their

[50] The main works in which this case is put forward are Tom Nairn, 'The English
Working Class', in Robin Blackburn (ed.), *Ideology in Social Science* (Fontana, 1972);
id., 'Anatomy of the Labour Party', *NLR* 27 and 28 (1964); 'The Left Against
Europe?', *NLR* 75 (1972); and id., *The Break-Up of Britain* (2nd edn., Verso, 1981);
Perry Anderson, 'Components of the National Culture', *NLR* 50 (1968), and 'Origins
of the Present Crisis'. Their interpretation generated an enormous critical literature, in
which the most influential polemic was E. P. Thompson, 'The Peculiarities of the
English', *Socialist Register* (1965). During the 1980s, Nairn tended to shift his explanatory emphasis from Empire to monarchy, see *The Enchanted Glass* (Century
Hutchinson, 1988); whilst Anderson reiterated and deepened his original case, notably
in 'The Figures of Descent', *NLR* 161 (1987).

[51] Darcus Howe, 'Bringing It All Back Home', *Race Today*, 6/3 (1974), and
numerous other articles in this journal.

[52] S. Hall *et al.*, *Policing the Crisis* (Macmillan, 1978); Centre for Contemporary
Cultural Studies, *The Empire Strikes Back* (Hutchinson, 1982).

[53] A. Sivanandan, *Race, Class and the State: The Black Experience in Britain* (Race and
Class, 1976); Shirley Joshi and Bob Carter, 'The Role of Labour in the Creation of a
Racist Britain', *Race and Class*, 25/3 (1984).

liberal principles and became radical anti-imperialists. Most, however, either abandoned their liberalism altogether or compartmentalised it, keeping it as a doctrine for domestic consumption only.'[54] When combined with a wider ideological phenomenon, the 'fearful sense of threat and competition with which British men and women faced the people of the Empire',[55] an intolerable strain on socialist attitudes was imposed. And after 1945, colonial immigration to Britain meant that even the earlier compartmentalisation of liberal attitudes was no longer possible. Thus Labour sponsorship of discriminatory practices and immigration laws finally revealed, so Rex argues, that the legacy of Empire had destroyed the ethical basis on which British radicalism had claimed to stand.[56]

I shall be returning to some of these arguments, in more specific contexts, in later chapters. It will be suggested that there were indeed intimate connections between the fate of Empire and the development of British socialism. These, however, will be shown to have been neither as all-embracing as is argued by Anderson, Kiernan, Nairn, or Rex, nor as closely tied to a particular model of formal colonialism as Orwell believed or as labour aristocracy theories sought to demonstrate.[57]

III. THE LABOUR PARTY

For critics of Labour's stance on colonial issues between the wars—and they were many—the party's sins seemed more often those of omission than of commission. Serious thinking, or even active agitation, on such matters before 1914 had been almost exclusively the preserve of the Marxist propaganda sects and of Radical-Liberal intellectuals. A similar situation persisted after the First World War.

[54] John Rex and Sally Tomlinson, *Colonial Immigrants in a British City* (Routledge & Kegan Paul, 1979), 37.

[55] Ibid. 287.

[56] For further variants of this type of argument, see Philip Cohen, 'The Perversions of Inheritance: Studies in the Making of Multi-Racist Britain', in id. and Harwant S. Bains (eds.), *Multi-Racist Britain* (Macmillan, 1988); Peter Fryer, *Staying Power: The History of Black People in Britain* (Pluto, 1984), esp. ch. 11; Paul Rich, *Race and Empire in British Politics* (Cambridge: Cambridge University Press, 1986).

[57] See also the further discussion of these themes in my 'Labour Patriotism, 1939–83', in Samuel (ed.), *Patriotism*, i; also Paul Rich, 'A Question of Life and Death to England: Patriotism and the British Intellectuals, *c.*1886–1945', *New Community*, 15/4 (1989).

Most of the party's leaders, most of the trade unionists who formed the bulk of Labour's parliamentary strength, and most of the Fabians who so dominated its political thinking, were primarily if not exclusively concerned with domestic problems.[58]

Labour's first Colonial Secretary is reported to have introduced himself to his officials with the declaration that 'I've been sent here to see that there's no mucking about with the British Empire.'[59] It is tempting to take Jimmy Thomas's combination of ludicrous bluster and visceral conservatism as emblematic of inter-war Labour attitudes, and some commentators have indeed thus simplified the picture. In reality Labour Party thought on colonial issues was considerably more varied than this would suggest: the very absence of sustained analysis from the party's core left open a space within which a plethora of ideas, interests, and half-articulated assumptions could move.

Both Labour's major early leaders, Keir Hardie and Ramsay MacDonald, took a more than passing interest in colonial questions: though Hardie's was fitful, MacDonald's more considered. Hardie, whilst expressing sympathy for the demands of Congress in India, stopped far short of urging complete independence for India or for any other tropical colony. He felt it necessary to emphasise and re-emphasise the modesty of Indian demands: 'The Congress movement in India is not seditious. It is ultra loyal. Part of it is extreme in its moderation, whilst the other part is moderate in its extremes.'[60] MacDonald, like Hyndman, categorised dependent territories according to an implicit racial hierarchy, with the white Dominions intended to form an ever-closer Commonwealth in association with Britain, India to be 'nursed' towards self-government within an unspecified time-scale, and the tropical colonies to be maintained and developed as a duty and according to what MacDonald called an 'Imperial standard' of 'human liberty and the administration of justice'.[61] His main concern was that such standards be applied uniformly in all territories; and in this respect he was optimistic if not

---

[58] See Ross McKibbin, *The Evolution of the Labour Party, 1910–24* (Oxford: Oxford University Press, 1974); Geoffrey Foote, *The Labour Party's Political Thought* (Croom Helm, 1985).

[59] Gregory Blaxland, *J. H. Thomas: A Life for Unity* (Frederick Muller, 1964), 170.

[60] J. Keir Hardie, 'A Scamper Round the World' (1907), quoted in Emrys Hughes, *Keir Hardie* (Allen & Unwin, 1956), 156. The third sentence appears (moderately, or extremely) meaningless.

[61] J. Ramsay MacDonald, *Labour and the Empire* (George Allen, 1907), 50.

complacent, believing that with the possible exception of South Africa such application need cause no friction.[62] Labour thus espoused a 'socialist imperialism': 'not of the aggressive or the bragging order ... To its subject races it desires to occupy the position of friend; to its self-governing Imperial states it seeks to be an equal.'[63]

MacDonald's and Hardie's approaches set the tone for their party: moral indignation at exploitation in the colonies, but with very little attempt either to trace the causes of such evils or to propose strategies for their removal; eagerness to dissociate oneself from 'seditious' movements (later transmuted into an increasingly obsessive anti-Communism); evaluation of colonial peoples' capacities for self-rule according to a racial hierarchy with white settlers at the top and Africans at the bottom; desire to achieve a bipartisan approach validating Labour's claims to be a responsible party of government. An early Labour MP expressed the fears that underlay the latter aspiration:

One thing has impressed me more than any other in the objections of our opponents to a possible Labour Government, and that is their almost unanimous opinion that under Labour the Empire is bound to come to a sticky end.[64]

The necessity of disproving such fears—one following inevitably from Labour's adoption of a conception of the national interest essentially identical with their opponents'—became paramount, to the detriment if not to the exclusion of plans for colonial reform. By 1937, for Clement Attlee, this necessity had produced the assertion that Labour, far from being destructively anti-imperialist, was a more trustworthy guardian of imperial interests than its opponents, since 'The imperialism of the Conservative Party, so far from preserving the British Empire and the Commonwealth, is calculated to lose the one and break up the other.'[65] Attlee therefore felt it important to explain that Labour attitudes to Empire had changed:

As long as the Socialist movement was only a propagandist body, with no prospect of achieving power, it was possible to take up a purely negative and critical attitude ... Socialists took their full share in denouncing and exposing the exploitation of the black, brown and yellow races ... As, however, the crude imperialism of early years became modified ... it was realised that the

---

[62] Ibid. 53.
[63] Ibid. 108–9.
[64] Jack Jones, *My Lively Life* (John Long, 1928), 181.
[65] Clement Attlee, *The Labour Party in Perspective* (Gollancz, 1937), 232.

relationships between advanced and backward peoples raised problems not easy of solution. The past could not be wiped out.[66]

Indeed it could not. Labour's own past, a complex and contradictory legacy of attitudes to Empire inherited from different traditions within the socialist and liberal movements, weighed heavily on its attempts to grapple with the problem. Attlee's reference to denunciation of exploitation seemed to point in one direction; his assumptions about advanced and backward races held quite different implications. The changes invoked were vague in the extreme. Labour had advanced from being a propagandist body—but towards what? The Empire had altered from an expression of crude imperialism—but into what? Some of the deepest divisions within Labour found early expression on colonial issues: between the rhetoric of class and that of national interest; between the propaganda of opposition and the compromises of government; between 'doctrine' and 'ethos'.[67]

Colonial nationalists learned soon and often with bitterness the force of these contradictions: that the attitudes of the anticolonialist lobby on the party's left might be worlds apart from the policies of the leadership, especially in government. It was not so much a case of Labour gradually changing from a propagandist body to a consensual party of government and of the national interest, as Attlee seemed to suggest, as of the two aspects uneasily coexisting and contending for paramountcy.

Four broad currents of opinion on colonial issues emerged among Labour politicians between the wars. Two of these were within the mainstream of party argument. There were the 'constructive imperialists' who held, with MacDonald, to the doctrine of trusteeship and a perspective of gradual development towards self-government. This was seen as a development which would, for most tropical colonies and most non-white peoples, come only in the far distant future, which would even then be self-government *within* the Empire, and from which some would apparently always be excluded on grounds of size, viability, strategic significance, or ethnic composition. Then there were those who wanted a more positive commitment to

---

[66] Ibid. 228–9.

[67] H. M. Drucker, *Doctrine and Ethos in the Labour Party* (Allen & Unwin, 1979). For Drucker, doctrine denotes the formal policies of the party, ethos its unarticulated assumptions and traditions. The two are always in a state of overt or incipient tension. The years since 1979 have done nothing to alter this perception.

native rights (including acceptance of the paramountcy of those rights in colonies with white settler minorities), social and economic development, and active preparation for self-government. The former view predominated among the party leaders, the latter in the small group of colonial experts who staffed Labour's Imperial Advisory Committee.

Two other stances found expression further to right and left. To the right were the self-designated Empire Socialists: whole-hearted supporters of the imperial idea and of protectionism. To the left were the root and branch anticolonialists who are this book's main subject. These last had as yet very little influence on Labour's leaders, their pressure being felt through the agitation of the Communist Party, of parts of the ILP, of educational bodies like the Labour College movement, and issue campaigns like the League Against Imperialism rather than in Labour's central policy-making circles. And such was the strength of moral opposition to aggressive imperialism, and so close the perceived links between this, protectionism, and Conservatism, that most of the time Empire Socialism too remained a marginal current.

The central debate, then, lay between leaders like MacDonald, Thomas, and Snowden and the more radical lobby advocating gradual but far-reaching reform leading to self-government. The latter group was composed largely of intellectuals rather than professional politicians, was predominantly upper middle class and included few trade unionists, and involved many former liberals, pacifists, and supporters of the League of Nations and the Union of Democratic Control. Nicknamed by contemporaries the Foreign Legion and later by A. J. P. Taylor the Troublemakers, this fairly cohesive fraction mounted consistent but firmly non-revolutionary criticism of all aspects of British foreign and imperial policy.[68] The key figures in this group and on the Labour Party Advisory Committee on Imperial Questions (LPACIQ) were Leonard Woolf (the Committee's Secretary), Sir John Maynard (its chairman), Charles Roden Buxton, Sydney Olivier, Major Graham Pole, H. S. L. Polak; and slightly later Norman Leys, Dr Julius Lewin, and Professor W. M. Macmillan. A wider circle including H. N. Brailsford, J. A. Hobson, E. D. Morel, and H. G. Wells advocated many of the same causes and strongly influenced the Troublemakers' thinking on them.

In the view of such men, their argument with the Labour leaders

[68] A. J. P. Taylor, *The Troublemakers* (Hamish Hamilton, 1957).

was often not so much one between different perspectives on colonial affairs as a clash between knowledge and ignorance. The leaders, it was almost despairingly felt, were complacent about the Empire because they knew too little to appreciate the scale and urgency of the problems and, preoccupied with domestic concerns, seemed not even to want to become better informed. The exception, Woolf later suggested, was MacDonald himself. He 'was not entirely ignorant of the situation and took an interest in what we were doing on the committee' but, alas, 'he was entirely untrustworthy'.[69] The net result was that the LPACIQ 'did an immense amount of work, pouring out reports and memoranda which the Executive Committee accepted, which became "party policy", and were then never heard of again'.[70]

The short-lived minority Labour Government of 1924 witnessed no significant initiatives in colonial policy, but after its fall there was widespread debate on what a socialist colonial policy should be in various left-wing journals: *Lansbury's Labour Weekly*, the *Plebs*, the *Sunday Worker*, and the Glasgow paper *Forward*. From this emerged the explicitly pro-imperialist Empire Socialist current, first articulated by *Forward*'s editor, Clydeside ILP leader Thomas Johnston. He suggested that the Empire, far from being simply an 'engine of exploitation', could be a vehicle for progress and for socialist planning. The anticolonialism of the left, Johnston argued, was merely one of the 'Whig superstitions which our Communists had apparently adopted under the belief that they were "advanced"'.[71]

Support for these views came from some who were normally regarded as on Labour's left wing, notably several Scottish ILP Members who were noted for their radicalism on domestic issues but held orthodox views on, or were wholly indifferent to, international problems. Their attitude was summed up in David Kirkwood's declaration that 'I know that all this interest in foreign affairs is a heritage from Liberalism'.[72] The Empire Socialist group's main

---

[69] Leonard Woolf, *Downhill All the Way: An Autobiography of the Years 1919–1939* (Hogarth, 1967), 224.

[70] Ibid. 235.

[71] In *Forward* (9 Aug. 1924); quoted in Stuart MacIntyre, *Imperialism and the British Labour Movement in the 1920s: An Examination of Marxist Theory* (CPGB 'Our History' series, 1975), 16.

[72] *New Leader* (30 Mar. 1923). This narrowness—a direct descendant of the language of Little England, even if expressed in Scottish accents—was not, however, shared by the Clydesiders leader, James Maxton, nor in the policies of the ILP as a whole.

strength came, however, from right-wing Labour MPs, led by Dr Leslie Haden-Guest (who was shortly thereafter to cross over to the Conservatives). Quite what this strength was is disputed. Haden-Guest somewhat implausibly claimed the adherence of a hundred MPs, while Johnston put the figure at twenty to thirty.[73] The truth would seem to be that this was in no sense a cohesive clique: even the hard core of eighteen who followed Haden-Guest into the Government lobby on 12 June 1925 in support of imperial preference on some foodstuffs were not all clear supporters of his views. George Lansbury, briefly chairman of the group, was never really a protectionist at all; and some seem to have convinced themselves that there were humanitarian and internationalist arguments for protectionist measures, in that they would prevent the import of sweated goods.[74]

As this short-lived revival of imperialist ideas within Labour's ranks fragmented and declined in the late 1920s, so too did other currents of belief on Empire. Equally rapidly dwindling was the strain of romantic anti-capitalism which placed its faith in the survival of traditional village communities in Asia and Africa and saw Britain's duty as the preservation of such communities and the simple virtues they were held to embody. As we have seen, Morel had returned from Nigeria with views akin to these, but their *locus classicus* was India. Josiah Wedgwood, another able but eccentric convert from Liberalism, was probably the strongest advocate of this view of India, but MacDonald, Hardie, and others—including, incongruously enough, Sidney Webb—had expressed hopes that the collective agriculture and communal decision-making they idealistically believed to be characteristic of the Indian village could provide a route to rural socialism without the social costs of capitalist industrialisation.[75]

By the end of the 1920s such expectations seemed increasingly threadbare. It was evident to the most minimally informed that under

---

[73] Leslie Haden-Guest, *Labour and the Empire* (Labour Publishing Co., 1926), 24; Gupta, *Imperialism*, 64–7. Labour had 151 MPs in 1924–5.

[74] Gupta, *Imperialism*, 65; Hugh Dalton, *Call Back Yesterday* (Frederick Muller, 1953), 158.

[75] Josiah Wedgwood, *Essays and Adventures of a Labour MP* (Allen & Unwin, 1924), exemplifies, and Georges Fischer, *Le Parti Travailliste et la décolonisation de l'Inde* (Paris: Maspero, 1966), 60–5, summarises early Labour hopes for Indian communes. The similarity of these views both to certain Gandhian themes and to those of the late Marx on the Russian *mir* is evident. Phillips, *Enigma*, discusses Wedgwood's influence on West African policy.

colonial rule, even in African Indirect Rule systems, rapid social and economic change was under way. Romantic anti-capitalism was far from dead on the British left—we shall see it re-emerging in reactions to 'African Socialism' and in early Marxist debates on underdevelopment—but that version of it premised on the preservation intact of traditional structures could no longer provide inspiration for colonial policy. Debate would necessarily now centre on how to react to social change; and perhaps, increasingly, on how to direct it. It could not be about how to avert it.

Yet at the same time hopes that British radicals could intervene effectively to direct colonial change, even under a Labour Government, seemed to be fading. With Morel's death, the Foreign Legion had lost their leader; whilst the proven ineffectiveness of the League of Nations and the new spiral of European rearmament shattered many of their hopes.[76] Their gradualist version of anticolonialism was coming under increasing challenge from the Marxist one. All this weakened the cohesion and confidence of their thrust to reform imperial policy. More directly damaging was the record of Labour's second Government in 1929–31. This was a far graver disappointment to the colonial reform lobby than its predecessor.

The 1926 policy statement *Labour and the Empire: Africa* had contained a relatively ambitious programme for constitutional change, but the only part of it that came anywhere near fruition was an ambiguous pursuit of the idea of native paramountcy in East Africa. Colonial Secretary Sidney Webb failed to pursue the policies formulated by the Advisory Committee with any vigour even here. Rapidly yielding to pressure from civil servants and from Kenya Governor Sir Edward Grigg, Webb presided over the gradual abandonment of the new doctrine. As Norman Leys complained, 'All over East Africa the news has gone out that the Labour Government has recanted.'[77]

On India too there were new and far-reaching proposals for the devolution of power. But these fell a long way short of what Congress

[76] Taylor, *Troublemakers*, 169, probably exaggerates the effect of Morel's death, saying that it left the dissenters as 'sheep without a shepherd'; but it was a severe blow none the less.

[77] Norman Leys, *A Last Chance in Kenya* (Hogarth, 1931), 141. A detailed study of the Labour Government's Kenya policy is given in Robert Gregory, *Sidney Webb and East Africa: Labour's Experiment with the Doctrine of Native Supremacy* (Berkeley, Calif.: University of California Press, 1962).

demanded, reflected little that could be attributed specifically to Labour initiative, and were overshadowed in many Indian (and British socialist) eyes by Labour's participation in the Simon Commission, the repression of civil disobedience campaigns, imprisonment of Gandhi and Nehru, and the Meerut trials. Thus although two major British initiatives on India took place under Labour, the Simon Commission report and Lord Irwin's 31 October 1929 promise of eventual Dominion status, Labour gained no credit for them among nationalists—and indeed deserved none. Both had been originated under Baldwin; and their main architect was Irwin himself. Congress felt a vague promise of eventual self-government to be valueless: it demanded immediate Dominion status and eventual full independence. And Congress boycotted the Simon Commission and was deeply angered by Labour's participation in it.[78]

The third major innovation, the 1929 Colonial Development Act, had likewise been a Conservative project before Labour took it over. It provided very little development funding (just £1 million per annum), established no effective framework or machinery for planning, and was in any case directed towards alleviating Britain's unemployment rather than fostering colonial development.[79]

After these disappointments—eclipsed, of course, in most Labour circles by the crises of the domestic economy, MacDonald's 'betrayal', and the formation of the National Government—Labour's leaders lapsed into near silence on colonial reform. The LPACIQ under Woolf's direction continued to bombard the leaders with reports and proposals, and these continued largely to be ignored. The 1933 Policy Report was if anything more cautious than those of 1926 and 1929. Not until the end of the decade was there to be any major and public revaluation of Labour's philosophy on colonial affairs. Meanwhile the focus of attention shifted to less official and more radical initiatives.

---

[78] Mesbahuddin Ahmed, *The British Labour Party and the Indian Independence Movement, 1917–1939* (Oriental University Press, 1987), chs. 3 and 4; Fischer, *Parti Travailliste*, part 2; Gupta, *Imperialism*, ch. 7.

[79] Stephen Constantine, *The Making of British Colonial Development Policy, 1914–1940* (Frank Cass, 1984); G. C. Abbott, 'A Re-examination of the 1929 Colonial Development Act', *EcHR* 24 (1971); D. J. Morgan, *The Official History of Colonial Development*, i. *The Origins of British Aid Policy, 1924–1945* (Macmillan, 1980), 44–6, predictably and unconvincingly claims more altruistic motives for the Act.

IV. BRITISH COMMUNISTS AND THE EMPIRE

The history of the Communist Party of Great Britain has been interpreted in three contrasting ways: as an organic part of an indigenous British socialist tradition; as a radical departure from the norms of British Labour movement politics—the 'party of a new type' of its own phraseology; and as a perversion, sterilisation, even a betrayal of the spirit of the Labour movement.

The CPGB itself, and its more sympathetic historians, have opted naturally enough for variants of the first two interpretations. Which of them has been preferred has depended, especially in the rhetoric of the Communist leadership, upon political circumstances. In its first years and again in the isolationist, ultra-left periods of the late 1920s, and 1939–41, the originality and specificity of the CPGB, the factors distinguishing it from other currents on the left, have been stressed. At other times—in the Popular Front period of the 1930s, during and immediately after the Second World War, and again in the party's last years in the 1970s and 1980s—the strength of its indigenous roots, its sense of tradition, and of itself as part of a broad progressive movement, even its commitment to patriotic values, have been the main themes.

Far more influential outside the party itself, however, has been the view of it as an alien growth upon the body of British socialism; whether this is seen as having been the case from the start or as being the result of later degeneration under Stalinism, and whether it is attributed to Marxist theory, Leninist modes of organisation, or, more simply and crudely, to Moscow gold.[80] The problem with these

---

[80] For the official view, see James Klugmann, *History of the Communist Party of Great Britain*, 2 vols. (Lawrence & Wishart, 1968, 1969); Noreen Branson, *History of the CPGB, 1927–1941* (Lawrence & Wishart, 1985); and a critique from within the CP of that view: E. J. Hobsbawm, 'Problems of Communist History', in *Revolutionaries*. For critical histories from the left, L. G. Macfarlane, *The British Communist Party: Its Origins and Development until 1929* (MacGibbon & Kee, 1966), Walter Kendall, *The Revolutionary Movement in Britain, 1900–1921* (Weidenfeld & Nicolson, 1969), and Hugo Dewar, *Communist Politics in Britain* (Pluto, 1976). Neo-Trotskyist perspectives are purveyed in Michael Woodhouse and Brian Pearce, *Essays on the History of Communism in Britain* (New Park, 1975), and James Hinton & Richard Hyman, *Trade Unions and Revolution* (Pluto, 1975). Criticism from further right is exemplified in the only scholarly attempt to survey the party's whole earlier history: Henry Pelling, *The British Communist Party: A Historical Profile* (Adam & Charles Black, 1958). More restricted in scope, but more detached (if broadly sympathetic) and in many ways more

hostile judgements is that they make it very difficult to understand how it could be that Communism in Britain, though never a mass creed, was never wholly marginalised: how a political formation so alien to British traditions, so thoroughly bureaucratised and lacking in internal democracy, so subject to wild zigzags of policy directed from abroad, was nevertheless able to gain the support both of some of the most politically aware sections of the British working classes and, particularly in the 1930s, of a significant part of the radical intelligentsia.

One reason why this has seemed such an enigma is that earlier histories of British Communism, whether sympathetic or condemnatory, investigated it not only in a highly partisan spirit, but almost solely from the perspective of central organisation, with little attention to the wider political culture within which it operated or to the beliefs and activities of the rank and file in local Communist cells.[81] This latter world, despite the leaders' increasingly unquestioning allegiance to Moscow and gradual stifling of internal party debate, drew on a strong sense of spontaneous class solidarity, a warm emotionalism and predilection for moral uplift. Such features found at least echoes in the discourses of party leaders themselves, as any reading of the speeches, journalism, and autobiographies of early Communist leaders demonstrates.[82] This mode of discourse particularly dominated Communist discussion of imperialism.

We have earlier noted the significant differences between Leninist

satisfactory than any of these are Stuart MacIntyre, *A Proletarian Science: Marxism in Britain, 1918–1933* (Cambridge: Cambridge University Press, 1980); id., *Little Moscows: Communism and Working-Class Militancy in Inter-War Britain* (Croom Helm, 1980), and Kevin Morgan, *Against Fascism and War* (Manchester: Manchester University Press, 1989).

[81] More recent work, especially in social/cultural history, has begun to remedy this. See MacIntyre, *Little Moscows*; Jonathan Ree, *Proletarian Philosophers* (Oxford: Oxford University Press, 1984); James Hinton, 'Coventry Communism', *HWJ* 10 (1980); Raphael Samuel, 'The Lost World of British Communism', *NLR* 154, 156, and 165 (1985–7).

[82] It is arguable, indeed in my view likely, that the employment of such warm and emotional language by CPGB leaders may often have been calculated and cynical. This does not significantly affect the argument: what is important is the nature of the language chosen and its intended and putative effect on audiences. There is certainly a general danger that the emphasis on social history from below may lead, as Geoff Eley warns, to 'a history of communism with the Communism left out'—ignoring the specificity (and, I would add, the inhumanity) of Marxist–Leninist ideology. Yet this is, as I shall try to show, a limited and controllable risk in evaluating Communist language. See G. Eley, 'International Communism in the Heyday of Stalin', *NLR* 157 (1986), 92.

and earlier definitions of imperialism, the complex ambiguities in the Leninist definition, and the intermingling of different usages and play upon such ambiguities in much left-wing writing about the colonised world. It has been suggested that the Leninist interpretation was interpreted through, or parasitic on, earlier Radical-Liberal ideas which stressed a more overtly ethical opposition to imperialism. This was clearly the case in early British Communist anti-imperialist discourse. For most CPGB members as for other radicals, imperialism evoked primarily not a theory of capitalist development but colonial injustice: Indian labourers underpaid, Jamaican strikers shot by the police, African peasants expropriated, and, perhaps most emotively of all given the large Irish presence in the early CPGB, the Irish struggle and the Black and Tans.

The tendency of CPGB propaganda to reflect this orientation aroused recurrent concern in Moscow. The party's early concentration on colonial exploitation rather than on imperialism as a world-system, its taste for expressions of moral outrage rather than exegesis on Leninist texts, its reliance on the writings of autodidact worker–scholars like Tommy Jackson and Mark Starr rather than on making available the major Russian works (Lenin's *Imperialism* did not appear in a full English translation until 1926, Bukharin not until 1927), were sharply criticised. The Comintern's Propaganda Department in 1925 deplored the absence of 'theoretical discussion of the question of imperialism' by the CPGB, and urged that it should not confine its treatment of the issues to 'the narrow bounds of the British Empire' [!] but should deal with the problem on a world scale—viewing it, that is, less as a synonym for colonialism and more as equivalent to monopoly capitalism.[83]

The CPGB, unlike most other European Communist parties, emerged from the fusion of several small propaganda groupings rather than from the fission of an existing mass party. These small groups, notably the British Socialist Party and the Socialist Labour Party, had a common heritage of anti-imperialism, and many of the key themes of CPGB agitation on the issue had been anticipated by their publicists like Theodore Rothstein and William Paul.[84] Neither

[83] Quoted in McIntyre, *Imperialism*, 10.
[84] Theodore Rothstein (of the BSP), *Egypt's Ruin* (Fifield, 1910), and *Essays in Socialism and War* (under the pseudonym of John Bryan, British Socialist Party, 1917); William Paul (of the SLP), *Labour and the Empire* (Socialist Labour Party pamphlet, n.d. but *c.*1917).

the BSP nor the SLP, though, had anywhere near the political strength needed to make any impact on public opinion about Empire, let alone to offer any practical assistance to nationalist or radical movements in the colonies themselves. The BSP especially also lacked even minimal cohesion or unity of view on colonial questions. All these deficiencies the CPGB aimed to rectify. It appeared to possess some prerequisites for this, with its far larger membership, greater ideological coherence, stronger reserves of intellectual and journalistic talent, and firmer international commitment through the Comintern.

The Communist Party saw its task in relation to colonial questions as twofold: to break the influence of imperialism in the British working class and especially within the Labour movement; and to develop means of practical aid and solidarity with 'progressive' movements among colonial peoples.[85] Despite the CP's apparent advantages *vis-à-vis* earlier Marxist groups, both tasks looked almost insuperably difficult. Part of the difficulty lay in the effective absence, over most of the Empire, of organised political movements with which links could be forged or sympathy aroused. Even more glaring was the lack of specifically working-class or socialist, let alone Communist, parties in almost all British colonies. Within Britain the initial problem, as posed for a party placing primary importance on having a firm theoretical base for its practical politics, was how imperialism was to be explained to British workers.

Marxist theory, as understood in Britain in the early 1920s, provided few clear answers—and was intermingled with other types of discourse: the Hobsonian tradition, the history of Radical-Liberal ethical condemnation, the Irish experience, and its theorisation by James Connolly and others.[86] In the first years, the party seems to have floundered in search of an approach. Its first policy statement on the colonies, an Introduction to the Comintern's Theses on the National and Colonial Question (themselves the product of heated

[85] R. Palme Dutt, *The Communist Party in the Fight Against Imperialism* (World News pamphlet, 1952).

[86] Both J. T. Murphy and Tommy Jackson noted Connolly's influence on their views of imperialism, whilst a number of other early CP leaders had Irish nationalist backgrounds. Some of Connolly's main writings on the subject are collected in Peter Berresford Ellis (ed.), *James Connolly: Selected Writings* (Harmondsworth: Penguin, 1973). See also David Howell, *A Lost Left* (Manchester: Manchester University Press, 1986), part 1; and Austen Morgan, *James Connolly: A Political Biography* (Manchester: Manchester University Press, 1988), esp. ch. 7 and Afterword.

disagreement between Lenin and pioneer Indian Marxist M. N. Roy), has a somewhat muddled and idiosyncratic air about it. It sees the prime function of Empire as being to supply a source of military force and a training-ground for military repression—something which does not enter Lenin's analysis at all. Stress is laid on the propaganda uses of Empire for the ruling class. It is admitted that British workers gain economic benefits from imperialism, although this means that the 'comparative prosperity of the British working class is built upon a hideous foundation'.[87] Support is urged for 'the broad national liberation movement in the colonies irrespective of whether it is Communist in outlook or not'.[88] Here and in subsequent writings (which came most prolifically from the pen of Tommy Jackson, the liveliest stylist and perhaps the most attractive personality among the early CP leaders), emphasis is placed on the Irish experience as a paradigm of colonial rule, and the approach seems to owe more to such diverse figures as Morel and Connolly than to Lenin.[89]

After 1924–5 a more clearly Leninist analysis began to emerge, as note was taken of the Comintern's admonitions on the subject, as the legacy of the pre-1918 sects was subsumed within a more centralised, disciplined Bolshevik organisation, and as a more orthodox and systematic thinker, the formidable Rajani Palme Dutt,[90] began to dominate the CPGB's theoretical output.

This new orthodoxy started from the idea, quite contrary to Marx's own thought but developed by Lenin, sanctioned by the success of revolution in underdeveloped Russia, and backed by the authority of successive Comintern Congresses, that revolution could come about by snapping the chain of imperialism at its weakest link. Revolution in the colonial countries, where exploitation was held to be at its most intense and nationalist motives for revolt were added to class ones, might pave the way for revolution in the advanced states. Beyond this basic point, however, sharply divergent possible lines of argument lay open.

One available approach centred on the theory of the labour aristo-

[87] *Introduction to the Communist International Theses on the National and Colonial Question* (CPGB pamphlet, Feb. 1921), 4.
[88] Ibid. 8.
[89] See esp. T. A. Jackson, *The British Empire* (CPGB pamphlet, 1922).
[90] For a preliminary if somewhat thin biographical sketch, see John Callaghan, 'The Heart of Darkness: Rajani Palme Dutt and the British Empire—a Profile', *Contemporary Record*, 5/2 (1991); also the hagiographic memoir by PCI leader P. C. Joshi, 'R. P. Dutt and Indian Communism', *Indian Left Review* (July 1971).

cracy.[91] Yet there has been considerable ambiguity in the Leninist tradition as to the identity of this aristocracy. Was it simply the better-paid workers, or those whose employment depended on colonial trade, or the leaders of the Labour Party and trade unions? If the first or second of these, it had no clear correlation with political conservatism, but included many of the most militant sections of the trade union movement—including the CP's own major base of support in the engineering industry. If the third, the political task posed was that of breaking the allegiance of the working class to the Labour Party and unions. That would be an undertaking with little obvious relevance to the phenomenon of colonialism, and in any case one in which the CPGB was having woefully little success. Communist writers made other suggestions too: that in an era of rising unemployment all those who retained their jobs formed a sort of aristocracy, or even that the entire British working class was aristocratic.[92]

Acute political difficulties followed from this uncertainty. With no clear and agreed criteria for distinguishing corrupted pro-imperialists from latently revolutionary workers, and the lurking suspicion that the former might be the majority, the Communists were again left reliant on liberal–humanitarian arguments against imperialism. These could provide neither a distinctively Marxist policy nor pretensions to a scientific analysis, and would be regarded with the utmost suspicion both by the Comintern and by the liberals themselves, as Communist MP Shapurji Saklatvala discovered when Morel sharply rebuffed his attempts at alliance.[93]

The alternative approach was to suggest that, far from gaining benefits, however limited, from Empire, British workers had their own standard of living damaged by imperialism. This had the evident merit of urging a direct self-interest for anticolonialism, and became

[91] There are good critical overviews of the historical debate on this theory in Gregor McLennan, *Marxism and the Methodologies of History* (Verso, 1981), 206–32, and H. F. Moorhouse, 'The Marxist Theory of the Labour Aristocracy', *Social History*, 3/1 (1978). The map of this historical field has, however, dramatically been redrawn by newer work on British working-class language and culture. See esp. Gareth Stedman Jones, *Languages of Class* (Cambridge: Cambridge University Press, 1983), and Patrick Joyce,: *Visions of the People* (Cambridge: Cambridge University Press, 1991).
[92] Argued respectively by Jack Leckie in the *Communist Review* (May 1924) and by Theodore Rothstein in *From Chartism to Labourism: Historical Sketches of the English Working Class Movement* (Martin Lawrence, 1929).
[93] See Gupta, *Imperialism*, 108–11, and Mike Squires, *Saklatvala: A Political Biography* (Lawrence & Wishart, 1990), 165–6.

the main line of argument of the CPGB between 1924 and 1928. It was asserted that British capital export to the colonial Empire tended to stimulate rapid growth of industry in the colonies, especially in India, because lower wages and less intense competition there enabled a return on investment far higher than in Britain. The bribery of a labour aristocracy, characteristic of Britain's period of world economic dominance, was no longer possible. As Tommy Jackson, again presenting the most effective popular exposition of the argument, put it:

every part of the Empire has developed a local capitalism of its own . . . Each part of the Empire is threatened by defeat in commercial competition with every other part . . . The working mass at home in Britain must suffer because any redistribution of capitalist production throughout the Empire cannot fail to begin with a crushing down of their wage standards, and to necessitate a permanent and progressive increase in the numbers of the unemployed.

Indian workers too, it was claimed, would suffer through intensified exploitation of their labour-power in the new industries there.[94] The rhetorical sleight of hand involved in arguing that both investment and disinvestment produce immiseration hardly requires comment. Yet the line of argument served its purpose admirably. It appealed both to the altruism and to the self-interest of its audience. It demonstrated, at least to the CPGB's own satisfaction, the moribund nature of British capitalism and the way in which, while searching for expedients to prolong its life, it continually strengthened the very forces which would inevitably overthrow it, both at home and in the colonies. The thesis was elaborated, with considerable supporting evidence on Indian industrialisation, in Palme Dutt's book of 1927, *Modern India*.[95] From confused and unpromising beginnings the CPGB had evolved an approach to the colonial question which, whatever its logical flaws, was relatively coherent and sophisticated, well grounded in Marxist tradition, and politically appealing. But within a few months events in Moscow were to force a reversal of the entire theory and strategy.

At the Sixth World Congress of the Comintern in July–September 1928 the CPGB's analysis of colonial economic development was

[94] T. A. Jackson, *What Is the British Empire to You?* (CPGB pamphlet, 1925), 5–8.
[95] R. Palme Dutt, *Modern India* (Martin Lawrence, 1927). See also his article in *Labour Monthly* (June 1928).

subjected to full-scale assault by the chiefs of the International. The Comintern Secretariat argued that, contrary to the British party's view, it was in the interests of British capitalism to *retard* colonial industrialisation, and that therefore India was deliberately being kept in a state of underdevelopment.

The CPGB theory was accused of both left-wing and right-wing deviations. It was allegedly right-wing in that, by arguing that Britain was industrialising India, it suggested a coincidence of interests between imperial power and colonies (although the CPGB had explicitly denied that Indian industrialisation would bring real benefits to the Indian people—Karl Marx lay far more open to the charge of this particular heresy than did Palme Dutt!). The left deviation lay in the supposed British suggestion that under such conditions the Indian bourgeoisie was a counter-revolutionary force, and that only the industrial proletariat was a progressive element in India. Again, the CPGB had not in fact argued on this basis. Nor had it stated, as the Comintern charged, that what was taking place in India amounted to decolonisation through the emergence of distinct national capitalisms.[96]

The British delegation, supported by some Indians, attempted to defend their position against this violent and inaccurate criticism—in what was to prove the last time that open opposition was expressed from any quarter within the Comintern. Only twelve votes from the British delegation, plus two Indians, supported the CPGB line when the vote came. Two Britons adhered to the majority Comintern view; and an interesting light is thrown on the unimportance of theory as against sentiment for some leading British Communists by the fact that these two apparently took their stance not for any theoretical reason but out of personal friendship for the British representative on the Secretariat, J. T. Murphy, with whom they shared a background in the Sheffield shop stewards' movement.[97]

The CPGB, having made its protest, now faced the difficulty of

[96] There are several accounts of the debate at the Sixth Congress, which display considerable differences of emphasis and some variance on the facts. For instance both Bill Warren in *Imperialism, Pioneer of Capitalism* (NLB 1980), 107, and Macfarlane, *British Communist Party*, 208, seem to be in error on the voting figures. I have relied primarily on the official Comintern report of the debates, *International Press Correspondence* (English edn., Moscow, 1928), and on the summary and references in Enrico Collotti Pischel and Chiara Robertazzi, *L'Internationale communiste et les problèmes coloniaux* (Paris: Mouton, 1968), 313–41.

[97] J. T. Murphy, *New Horizons* (John Lane, 1941), 286.

selling and applying the new line in Britain. This task was made no easier by the fact that, also at the Sixth Congress, the Third Period alignment of total opposition to all social democratic and reformist parties had been proclaimed. This meant that the CPGB was required not only to denounce the Labour Party, to which it had formerly sought affiliation, but to encourage independent working-class movements in the colonies and undermine bourgeois nationalists like the Indian Congress. It was hard to see how this was consistent with the argument that imperialism was deliberately underdeveloping India, since such underdevelopment made the views that an Indian proletariat was increasingly capable of independent action, and that the colonial bourgeoisie was the natural ally of British capitalism, far less plausible.

The new positions were pushed through—despite protest and without discussion because of an alleged lack of time—at the CPGB's Tenth Congress the following January.[98] They were first presented to the public in the party's 1929 election manifesto, *Class Against Class*. Amid the storm and stress of this document's fierce attacks on the Labour Party, it may have escaped the notice of many readers that in place of previous references to colonial industrialisation threatening jobs, there was now the assertion that:

The Empire is maintained as a vast reservoir of human exploitation and raw materials for the metropolis... The capitalists of Great Britain have taken measures to retard the industrial development of the colonies and to secure the extension of Empire preferences.[99]

Admirable though this was as polemic, it lacked the earlier theory's capacity to appeal to British workers' self-interest against colonialism. This need was met by a theme which was to remain a central plank of Communist anticolonial propaganda for the coming decade. This was the blunt and dramatic assertion that empires led inevitably to war, and that the British working class must scrap the Empire to avoid being massacred in another global conflict.[100] Initial claims that the war threat came from Anglo-American rivalry were of limited plausibility; but the events of the succeeding years in Europe were to make the warning of new imperialist wars seem ever more convincing.

[98] CPGB, *Tenth Congress Report* (CPGB 1929); Macfarlane, *Communist Party*, 209; MacIntyre, *Imperialism*, 15.

[99] *Class Against Class: The General Election Programme of the CPGB* (CPGB 1929), 16.

[100] Ibid. 12, 30.

If the difficulties involved in trying to arouse mass support for anticolonial campaigns in Britain were considerable, those which faced the party in trying to aid liberation movements in the colonies were even more so. Many colonies had no organised political opposition at all. In very few cases were there Marxist-influenced or class-based parties. Strictly Communist parties were rarer still. Even where potential allies did exist, the problem of how best to aid, guide, or support them was a complex one. Direct control of colonial movements by the CPGB, though the British authorities often suspected it, was almost impossible. The Comintern placed on the CPGB the responsibility for co-ordinating Communist groups in the entire Empire (except Canada, for which the US Communist Party was responsible). But quite apart from the inherent difficulties of communication, attempts at British control would undoubtedly be resented by the local leaders, as M. N. Roy came to resent the CPGB's role in Indian affairs. Such intervention would all too closely resemble the very imperialism against which it was supposedly directed.

There was also persistent uncertainty, compounded by changing Comintern directives, as to whether non-Communist nationalists should be supported as the only viable anti-imperialist force, given a provisional and critical support coupled with attempts to strengthen left-wing elements within them, or denounced. Underlying this was the more general question of the alignment and likely development of social classes in the colonies. Attitudes to the peasantry posed especial problems,

The peasants were, on the whole, seen as a potentially revolutionary force, but one which would follow the proletariat's lead rather than play an independent role. At times divisions within the colonial peasantry were emphasised, with rich peasants ('kulaks') seen as reactionary, poor ones as revolutionary.[101] But except for Palme Dutt no Communist addressed the issue in detail—and the agrarian scene was not even *his* main focus. As for rural conditions and movements in colonies other than India, there was total silence and near-total ignorance from British Communists.

Thus, tied to conceptions of political action as Eurocentric as those

---

[101] Before 1928 there was an emphasis on capitalist development and consequent class differentiation within peasant agriculture—see for instance Clemens Dutt, 'Capitalist Exploitation in Indian Agriculture', *LM* (Nov. 1927). Thereafter the main theme was agrarian immiseration, discussed in most detail in R. Palme Dutt, *India Today* (Gollancz, 1940), 181–249.

of the colonial governments themselves, the CPGB never considered that agrarian resistance movements, so widespread throughout the colonial world between the wars, might be a portent of the nationalist future rather than a relic of the pre-colonial past. The main focus of British Communist attention remained on industrial rather than agrarian militancy, 'Westernised' rather than 'traditional' discourses of political struggle. It was inevitable on this score, as well as on account of the sheer size of the subcontinent, its unique importance to Britain, and the balance of expertise among its own writers, that CPGB colonial activity and propaganda before 1939 should concentrate on India and largely bypass the other tropical colonies.

In its formative years, Indian Communism had developed quite independently of Britain: but in 1924 the Comintern, growing impatient with the slow progress and internal squabbling of M. N. Roy and his followers, decided that they required supervision. The CPGB was given this job at the Fifth Comintern Congress; much to Roy's displeasure. The British party thus established a Colonial Department which was intended to work closely both with London-based Indians and with the Communist Party of India (CPI). A series of emissaries began to go out from the CPGB to work in India.[102] The interdependence of the two parties was cemented by Clemens Dutt (Palme Dutt's brother) being made simultaneously a member of the CPI's Foreign Bureau and the CPGB's Colonial Department.

There was, however, no real unity of aims between Roy and the British. Although the attitude of Palme Dutt to the Indian bourgeoisie and to Congress was to be criticised by the Comintern for being too hostile, for Roy it was too favourable.[103] He believed that the CPGB was attempting to force him into an alliance with the middle class

[102] On early Indian Communism and its links with the CPGB, see Sir Cecil Kaye, *Communism in India* (Delhi: Government Publishers, 1926); Gene Overstreet and Marshall Windmiller, *Communism in India* (Berkeley, Calif.: University of California Press, 1959); M. R. Masani, *The Communist Party of India* (Derek Verschoyle, 1954); David N. Druhe, *Soviet Russia and Indian Communism* (New York: Bookman Associates, 1959); A. J. MacKenzie, 'British Marxists and the Empire' (London University Ph.D. thesis, 1978); R. A. Ulyanovsky, *The Comintern and the East*, 3 vols. (Moscow: Progress Publishers, 1978, 1979, 1981); Sibnarayan Ray (ed.), *Selected Works of M. N. Roy*, i. *1917–1922* (Delhi: Oxford University Press, 1987); id., 'In Freedom's Quest: Life of M. N. Roy', *Radical Humanist* (Aug. 1985 *et seq.*); J. P. Haithcox, *Communism and Nationalism in India* (Princeton, NJ: Princeton University Press, 1971); Squires, *Saklatvala*.

[103] For Roy's own militant early views on Indian class polarisation and political prospects, see esp. 'India in Transition' (1918), 'What Do We Want' (1922), and 'India's Problem and Its Solution' (1922), all reprinted in Ray, *Selected Works*, i.

which could end only in surrender to their exploitative interests. Roy wanted to denounce Gandhi without reservation; whilst the CPGB took a more nuanced attitude, which is expressed in a fascinating exchange of letters between Gandhi and Communist MP Shapurji Saklatvala.[104] Saklatvala's intention was to win over Gandhi, or at least his supporters, to the view that the nationalist struggle could only succeed if linked with a class struggle, led by urban workers, and supported by poor peasants. Gandhi, of course, persisted unmoved in his belief that class conflict and capitalist development were both equally alien to India's civilisation. Other Congress leaders, most notably Jawaharlal Nehru, were to prove more sympathetic to the sorts of argument put forward by Saklatvala.

The CPGB meanwhile continued to send out agents and organisers to India, aiming to work primarily within the trade union movement. Most important of these were 24-year-old Cambridge graduate Philip Spratt and engineering worker Ben Bradley. Spratt went about his task with an almost charming ineptitude, as he recalled in his disarmingly entitled memoir *Blowing Up India*. His invisible ink did not work; and his ciphers, involving such pseudonyms as Methodists for the Communist-front Workers' and Peasants' Party and YMCA for the CPI, can hardly have convinced any alert policeman. Bradley, for his part, was travelling as the supposed representative of the remarkably implausible-sounding Crab Patent Underdrain Tile Company. None the less, their energy produced results; and it was in large part through their efforts that the All-India Trades Union Congress (of which Bradley became a Vice-President) came under Communist control.[105]

On 20 March 1929 this activity was brought to an abrupt halt by the arrests of Spratt, Bradley, Lester Hutchinson (another CPGB emissary and later a 'fellow-travelling' Labour MP), and most of the

---

[104] *Is India Different? The Class Struggle in India* (CPGB pamphlet, 1927). Saklatvala's own position, it may be noted, was always more sympathetic to co-operation with Congress than were those of Palme Dutt, let alone of the CPI or the Comintern: and his personal relations with Roy were extremely poor. See Squires, *Saklatvala*, 142–51. Also of interest, though unrevealingly hagiographic, is the privately printed memoir by Saklatvala's daughter: Sehri Saklatvala, *The Fifth Commandment* (Salford: Miranda Press, 1991).

[105] Philip Spratt, *Blowing Up India: Reminiscences and Reflections of a former Comintern Emissary* (Calcutta: Prachi Prakashan, 1955); Overstreet and Windmiller, *Communism*, 86–90, 105–6, 111–12; Masani, *Communist Party*, 25–30; MacKenzie, 'British Marxists,' 35–40; John Saville, 'The Meerut Trial, 1929–1933', in Joyce Bellamy and John Saville (eds.), *Dictionary of Labour Biography*, vii (Macmillan, 1984).

leading Marxists in the AITUC. After protracted court proceedings most of the accused were given lengthy prison sentences. Although the Meerut trials severely damaged the organisation built up by the CPI and CPGB they enabled the accused to turn the court into a public platform for their views. 'The trial...is an education in the economics of Karl Marx, and their revolutionary application by Lenin...enabling newspapers all over India to publish material that under ordinary circumstances would be banned', noted one observer.[106] They won renewed support for the left among more conservative nationalists who resented the Government's heavy-handedness, and they gave British Communists the opportunity to wage an impassioned publicity campaign (ranging from street theatre to a flood of pamphlets) against colonial repression.[107]

For some time the CPGB had been seeking to make mileage at home from its contacts with colonial movements. Indeed activity in this field may have been a partial emotional compensation to party leaders for their failures at home.[108] The election of Saklatvala—the only black British MP between 1906 and 1987—to Westminster was in itself a significant gesture; and his fiery parliamentary performances on colonial issues made it something more than a gesture.[109] There were also several Communist-inspired interventions on colonial issues at TUC and Labour Party conferences. Most successful of these was at the TUC's uniquely militant 1925 Congress, where Arthur Purcell and Harry Pollitt's resolution of blanket condemnation for colonial rule was overwhelmingly carried.[110] As late as the 1960s CPGB publications continued to point to this resolution as an example for the latter-day TUC to emulate (which, however, in

[106] Edgar Snow in *China Weekly Review* (19 Sept. 1931), quoted in Saville, 'Meerut', 86–7; on Meerut see also Overstreet and Windmiller, *Communism*, 135–7, 149–52; Branson, *CPGB* 59–61.

[107] The Meerut case probably inspired more left-wing pamphlet literature than any other colonial issue between the wars: see pamphlet section of this volume's bibliography for a (no doubt incomplete) list of this material. The street theatre production 'Meerut' is discussed and partially reproduced in *HWJ* 4 (1977) and was revived for a historians' conference in Sheffield in 1983.

[108] See for instance Tom Bell's grossly exaggerated claims for the CPGB's colonial influence at the party's Seventh Congress: *CPGB Seventh Congress Report* (CPGB 1925), 76.

[109] Sehri Saklatvala, *Fifth Commandment*, and Squires, *Saklatvala*, provide disappointingly bland accounts of Saklatvala's parliamentary and anticolonial activities. Spratt, *Blowing Up India*, gives a far more vivid sense of personalities, including the tensions between Saklatvala and the Dutts (p. 36).

[110] *TUC Annual Report* (1925), 553.

itself says something about the ineffectiveness of such declarations). Attempts by Communist-influenced constituency parties to introduce similar resolutions at Labour conferences during the 1920s, though, were heavily defeated.[111]

At least equally important were attempts to open contact with students, visitors, *émigrés*, and exiles from the colonies in Britain. The League Against Imperialism (for which see below, pp. 71–7) was the CP's main forum for its attempts to influence colonials in Britain. Apart from students—especially Indians, of whom so many were thus influenced whilst studying abroad that, as Masani comments, 'the aristocracy of the Communist Party, as of other parties in India, is today drafted . . . from the class of people whose parents could afford an expensive foreign education'[112]—the most important source of possible contacts was thought to be colonial seamen in British ports. In 1930 it was reported that the party was working among them in Liverpool, Glasgow, South Wales, and London, and this 'had proved an excellent method of keeping contact . . . the men were generally willing to take literature and distribute it at foreign ports'.[113] As for the students, 'although most of them were of bourgeois extraction, there were some potential revolutionaries among them'.[114]

One African of great future importance, at least, became associated with the CPGB at this time. Jomo (then known as Johnstone) Kenyatta had arrived in London in March 1929 as lobbyist for the Kikuyu Central Association. He opened contacts with various British politicians, Labour people initially predominating, but by late June was seen regularly in the company of Saklatvala and of Elinor Burns of the CPGB Colonial Department. In early 1930 Kenyatta was publishing articles on Kenya in the Communist press, and in 1929 and 1932 made two still somewhat mysterious trips to Moscow.[115] A police report of April 1930 said that he 'has now actually joined the CPGB' and that London Communist Robin Page Arnot was speaking of him prophetically as 'the future revolutionary leader in Kenya.'[116]

[111] See Gupta, *Imperialism*, 108–9; id., 'British Labour and the Indian Left, 1919–1939', in B. R. Nanda (ed.), *Socialism in India* (Delhi: Vikas, 1971).

[112] Masani, *Communist Party*, 47.

[113] 'Secret Report on Communist Party Activities in Great Britain among Colonials'; submitted to Colonial Office by Superintendent E. Parket (22 Apr. 1930), quoting Robin Page Arnot at CPGB meeting, 12 Apr. 1930. (Copy in Hodgkin papers, apparently deriving from Nyasaland colonial archives.)

[114] Ibid.

[115] Jeremy Murray-Brown, *Kenyatta* (Fontana, 1974), 114–27, 352–4; Montagu Slater, *The Trial of Jomo Kenyatta* (Secker & Warburg, 1955), 159.

[116] Parket Report.

The CPGB gained little in the long term from its association with Kenyatta, who was too much an opportunist to be long influenced by any ideology he might have gleaned from, or any gratitude he might feel towards, his London Communist friends. Other relationships with colonial *émigrés* in Britain—some discussed below, others still shrouded in mystery—were to be somewhat more productive. The party's real achievement, though, lay in the fact that colonial nationalists like Kenyatta, seeking help and advice in London, became at least as likely to turn to the relatively tiny CPGB as to Labour. The latter's ambivalent record on colonial issues alienated many nationalists, and it almost wholly lacked machinery for maintaining contact with opinion in the colonies or among colonials in Britain. The CPGB, for all its doctrinal shifts, at least seemed forthright in its anticolonialism; and despite its limited resources it put far more effort into establishing colonial links than did Labour. Few of these brought it concrete or lasting results; but this aspect of Communist involvement in the Empire was to continue arousing both Labour and British Government alarm in the coming years.

V. THE INDEPENDENT LABOUR PARTY

If some commentators have seen the Communist Party as an alien implantation within British socialism, the ILP has been widely regarded as the indigenous socialist tradition's most characteristic incarnation. United, if at all, around emotions rather than theories; evangelical and propagandist rather than systematising or power orientated; always critical of the Labour Party which it had helped to found but for most of its career existing in symbiosis with it; imbued with a strong Marxist strain but at least as heavily influenced by libertarianism, pacifism, and religious thought: the ILP was both the CPGB's main rival to the left of Labour and in many ways its antithesis.

Given this heterogeneity, it is hardly surprising that there was no clear single view on imperialism associated with the ILP in its early years. Most of Britain's major non-Communist left-wing writers on colonial issues between the wars—Hobson, Brailsford, Morel, MacDonald, Woolf, Brockway, Lewin, Leys, Barnes—were at some time associated with the ILP; but their views were extraordinarily diverse. If common themes can be identified at all, these are very broad ones: opposition to colonial economic exploitation and to aggressive imperialism; internationalist, anti-militarist, and often with pacifist leanings. The latter formed the basis for the earliest post-war ILP statements on colonial issues, which centred on British military occupation of Egypt and later on intervention in China.[117]

There was also, inevitably, an increasing interest in the Indian nationalist movement. In 1924 the ILP took the lead in pressing the Labour Government to call a round-table conference of Indian politicians and with them prepare a scheme for self-government 'with a view to immediate application'.[118] Disillusion among ILP activists with the performance of the 1924 Government was the starting-point for the evolution of a more independent, and sharply critical, ILP view of Labour colonial policy. Fenner Brockway[119] complained that Indians had 'looked forward to the coming of a Labour Government as a great opportunity ... They have been profoundly disappointed, and the ILP ought to make it clear to the Indian people that it shared their disappointment.'[120]

The following year the party for the first time established an Empire Policy Committee. Its membership included many of the same Foreign Legion stalwarts who also staffed the LPACIQ, as well as Harold Laski, Fred Longden (former anti-war campaigner and later Birmingham Labour MP), T. P. Sinha (the party's main Indian expert and later secretary of its Indian Advisory Committee), and four MPs. This committee urged that Britain's long-term aim should be a Socialist Commonwealth of self-governing states, but that 'for many races in tropical Africa, self-government, is an ideal which could not be realised for some years'. In the interim, therefore, 'paternal' government should prepare the way with a code of native rights, trade union legislation, land reform, local representation on Legislative Councils, League of Nations supervision, and, above all, vastly expanded educational opportunities.[121]

It was, by the standards of the time, a far-reaching scheme—and

---

[117] 'The Triumph of Socialism', R. C. Wallhead's Chairman's Address to the 1923 ILP Conference (ILP 1923), 5.; *Annual Report of the National Administrative Council* (NAC) to 1925 ILP conference (ILP 1925), 13, 70.

[118] Ibid. 14.

[119] Brockway, then ILP Organising Secretary, was to become a key figure in British anticolonialism. For biographical details see below, 169–73.

[120] ILP Annual Conference Report (1925), 160. See also speeches at this conference by the Revd Campbell Stephen, MP (p. 125), and Walter Ayles (p. 135).

[121] *Socialism and the Empire: Report of the ILP Empire Policy Committee*, submitted to the Annual Conference 1926 (ILP 1926).

indeed the proposals were essentially the same as those which were to form the basis for official government policy twenty years later. Yet on the committee, and in the conference debate on its report, a dissenting voice was raised to query the most fundamental assumptions of its thinking:

> There were only two views that Socialists could take: first, that of refusing to interfere with the rights of natives anywhere, and second, clear-cut co-operation. The report assumed superiority to natives. It said that they [the British] were so superior that they were capable of guiding these natives in the way they should go. God's Englishmen, appointed to guide natives along the lines of self-government! Who were they to do this?[122]

Thus Fred Longden vehemently denounced the paternalist view of socialist colonial policy. Sinha responded with the argument then dominant throughout the non-Communist left: that refusal to interfere amounted to an abdication of responsibility, whilst co-operation as equals with the colonial people was a hope for the future rather than an immediate possibility. A stance like Longden's, he said:

> neglected the duty before them, which was not merely to withdraw, but to reverse their policy. They had to check the doings of the white settlers. Either that, or they must arm the Negroes and the Indians.[123]

This dichotomy, between planning for progress in the colonies on the one hand, identifying oneself with whatever one felt to be the aspirations of the colonised on the other—the former view thinking the latter irresponsible, the latter accusing the former of élitism if not racism—was to be the crux of future divisions on the British left over responses to colonial nationalism. We shall see its terms being replicated throughout the period of decolonisation. In the ILP in 1926, the paternalists won the day: subsequent years were to reverse the verdict.

During the later 1920s the ILP became ever more critical of official Labour colonial policy. Late in 1927 Brockway clashed with Lord Olivier over the Bengal Ordinances, and also sharply condemned Labour's participation in the Simon Commission, which he saw as an 'insult' to India.[124] With the entry into office of the second Labour Government, ILP discontent moved into outright opposition. The Colonial and Indian committees of the party had now been

---

[122] ILP Annual Conference Report, 93–4.
[123] Ibid. 94.
[124] Fenner Brockway, *New Leader* (21 and 28 Oct. and 11 Nov. 1927).

merged into a single imperialism committee—in itself a telling change of title—with Brockway as chairman. At the Executive of the Second International, the ILP representative, John Paton, pressed for a more militant anticolonial policy. The overt paternalism of *Socialism and the Empire* was abandoned, with the ILP now calling at the International's 1929 Congress for greater support for 'the growing movement among the coloured peoples of Africa to claim equality'; and at its own 1929 Conference for colonial self-government as and when the colonised demanded it.[125]

Brockway entered Parliament in 1929 and immediately took on the informal role of ILP spokesperson for colonial affairs. Equally immediately, he identified himself as an impassioned critic of the Labour Government's policy, harrying Sir Oswald Mosley over the Colonial Development Bill and Wedgwood Benn over political imprisonments in India. Challenging the speaker to demand a debate on the latter issue, he was suspended from the House—giving rise to a celebrated incident when fellow ILP Member John Beckett attempted to run away with the Mace.[126] This, with numerous other demonstrative incidents, all added to the dissident ILP group's reputation as parliamentary troublemakers. But behind the disruptive theatricals of the group, led now by the intense and emotional Glaswegian Jimmy Maxton, was something close to despair at the direction Labour was taking, not least in the colonial field.[127]

This process of disillusionment culminated in 1932 with the secession of the ILP from the Labour Party. In making the break, the ILP embarked on a rapid move to the left, but failed to carry many of its former supporters with it into what many members saw as a political wilderness. While large numbers of ILP supporters preferred to remain with Labour, a faction known as the Revolutionary Policy Committee sought fusion with the CPGB; despite some

[125] Report of the NAC to 1929 ILP Conference, 15, 32, 47–8; Agenda for 1929 ILP Conference, 19.

[126] Fenner Brockway, *Inside the Left* (Allen & Unwin, 1942), 198–206.

[127] There is as yet no full published account of the inter-war ILP—by contrast with the several admirable works on its earliest years. R. E. Dowse, *Left in the Centre* (Longmans, 1966) and R. K. Middlemass, *The Clydesiders* (Hutchinson, 1965), tell only part of the story, and are not free from error. Gordon Brown, *Maxton* (Edinburgh: Mainstream, 1986), is a solid but unrevealing biography, notably thin on Maxton's international activities. Knox's and McNair's biographies are equally unrevealing: William Knox, *James Maxton* (Manchester: Manchester University Press, 1987), 86–9; John McNair, *James Maxton: The Beloved Rebel* (Allen & Unwin, 1953), 180–4.

limited cooperation between the parties, this never came close to fruition, however. Later some of the first small groups of British Trotskyists emerged within the ILP, creating further internal divisions. Indeed, as Brockway later recalled, the evolution of the party during the 1930s was a microcosm of all the major currents in European socialism:

at one time approaching the Communist International and at another moving towards the Trotskyist position, at one stage attaching its hope to united fronts and at another reverting to purism, at one period going all out to prepare for Soviets and at another recognising the value of Parliament.[128]

ILP colonial policy reflected both this general drift to the left and the divisions within the party. Its colonial debates had, moreover, an important additional dimension; for a number of colonial radicals moved into association with the ILP during the 1930s, including the West Indian Marxists C. L. R. James (who became chairman of an ILP branch) and George Padmore (who worked on the party's colonial committee).[129]

By 1935–6 the ILP position on colonialism had become unequivocally revolutionary in its language—far more so, indeed, than that of the CPGB now was. The view that there was a necessary interdependence of British and colonial socialist movements, and that both must be revolutionary, was now the guiding theme:

The struggles of the subject peoples of the Empire for national self-determination and the revolutionary struggle of the British workers . . . will inevitably react upon each other . . . British workers must realise the necessity of helping to foster revolutionary movements in the colonies, and the formation of principled united fronts with nationalist movements of a bourgeois character, because these movements represent a step towards the achievement of Workers' power in these countries.[130]

VI. THE LEAGUE AGAINST IMPERIALISM

The most significant attempt to establish an international anticolonial body between the wars was the League Against Imperialism. Formed

---

[128] Brockway, *Inside the Left*, 237.
[129] On these individuals see below, pp. 83–9.
[130] *ILP Policy: The Basic Resolutions Adopted by the Annual Conference 1936*, together with *Supplementary Resolutions* (ILP 1936), 15.

in 1927, the League was primarily a Communist initiative, intended by its architect Willi Munzenberg as a centre-piece of the United Front strategy. As such, for a time it involved a substantial number of non-Communist participants, both European (especially British) and colonial.

The founding conference in Brussels in February 1927 was attended by nearly 200 delegates: supposedly representing 134 organisations from 37 countries—though this claim may well have been inflated. These included a British contingent drawn from a fairly wide range of left-wing groups. Labour MPs George Lansbury, John Beckett, and Ellen Wilkinson were present, with Fenner Brockway (ILP), John Stokes (London Trades Council), Raymond Postgate (Plebs' League and War Resisters' International), S. O. Davies (South Wales Miners), William Brown (Secretary of the Amsterdam Trade Union International), and Harry Pollitt, Arthur MacManus, James Crossley, Helen Crawfurd, and William Rust of the CPGB. The key figure in the British delegation, however, was Reginald Bridgeman, a former diplomat who had been the British organiser of preparations for the conference. Thus at least half the British group (Stokes, Crawfurd, Pollitt, MacManus, Crossley, Rust, and Bridgeman) were members or close supporters of the Communist Party; the remainder came from groups in and around the Labour left, particularly the ILP. Yet this was still a broader-based delegation than those from any other participating country.[131]

What made the conference more impressive, to sympathetic observers, than the presence of European socialist luminaries was

---

[131] Munzenberg's creation went through a bewildering series of name changes. The preparatory body was known as the League Against Colonial Oppression, and the initial title was the League Against Imperialism and For National Independence; though some literature used still other variants. There are several published and unpublished studies of the LAI, but none of these provides a very full account. MacKenzie, 'British Marxists', has the greatest range, but is marred by inaccuracy on points of detail. John Saville, 'The League Against Imperialism, 1927–1937', in *Dictionary of Labour Biography* vii. 40–50, is, despite its brevity, the best account in English. See also Sarvepalli Gopal, *Jawaharlal Nehru*, i. *1889–1947* (Cape, 1975), 100–6; J. Ayodele Langley, *Pan-Africanism and Nationalism in West Africa, 1900–1946* (Oxford: Oxford University Press, 1973), 304–5, 383–8; Marjorie Nicholson, *The TUC Overseas: The Roots of Policy* (Allen & Unwin, 1986), 106–9; Hans Piazza, 'Jawaharlal Nehru und die Antiimperialistische Liga', *Wiss. z. Karl Marx Univ. Leipzig*, 19/3 (1970); id., 'Der Kampf der Komintern für eine antiimperialistische Weltfront', *Beiträge zur Geschichte der Arbeiterbewegung*, 2 (1969); Squires, *Saklatvala*, 170–7; Gupta, 'British Labour', 95–101.

the large number of representatives of colonial movements.[132] For Brockway their attendance made the foundation of the LAI a potential turning-point in world history:

I have attended many conferences which have been described as 'International', but only one of them was international, in fact . . . It was held in Brussels last February. From the platform the conference hall was a remarkable sight. Every race seemed to be there. As one looked on the sea of black, brown, yellow and white faces one felt that here at last was something approaching a Parliament of Mankind.

The League, he suggested, was 'The Coloured Peoples' International', and a major stride towards uniting the world socialist movement: 'it may easily prove to be one of the most significant movements for equality and freedom in world history.'[133]

Brockway's more general prediction for the future significance of colonial nationalism was no doubt correct; but his hopes for the LAI itself rapidly proved to be misplaced. The alliance between colonial movements and different varieties of European socialists seemingly prefigured at Brussels began to fall apart almost immediately. Even at the conference some of the non-Communist speakers, notably Lansbury, had come under attack for their apparently equivocal attitude to decolonising their own countries' empires. The view of the Socialist International's leaders was hostile from the start, seeing the League as a Comintern conspiracy pure and simple. Brockway argued that even if this were so—and he believed that Communist influence within the LAI was relatively slight—'the real issue centres not on the Communists but on the coloured workers'. Socialists could not afford *not* to be associated with so important a movement.[134] The Second International was not convinced, and Brockway was forced to withdraw from the LAI. The Labour Party International

---

[132] Though of course the representative status of some of these was doubtful, as the Socialist International pointed out: Saville, 'League Against Imperialism', 41; Nicholson, *TUC Overseas*, 107–8.

[133] Fenner Brockway, 'The Coloured Peoples' International', *New Leader* (26 Aug. 1927). Twenty years later, Brockway was to greet the founding of the Congress of Peoples Against Imperialism with the same enthusiasm and in almost the same words. See below, pp. 176–83.

[134] Fenner Brockway, 'At the International: War and Imperialism', *New Leader* (16 Sept. 1927). For overviews of Socialist International colonial attitudes in the 1920s, see Michel Dreyfus, 'L'Internationale ouvrière socialiste et les problèmes coloniaux', and Jan Tomicki, 'Sozialistische Arbeiter-Internationale und die Koloniale Frage', papers for Internationale Tagung der Historiker der Arbeiterbewegung, Linz, 1984.

Department too was hostile, and the Labour and ILP leaders withdrew or were expelled from the League in rapid succession. Lansbury, Maxton (who had briefly taken over as chairman of the League's British section), Beckett, Wilkinson, and miners' leader A. J. Cook had all gone by autumn 1929. In November of that year, the Labour Party declared the LAI an 'organisation subsidiary to the Communist Party'; barring individuals from joint membership.

Thus the first three years of the LAI British section's existence were largely devoted to expulsions and resignations, apparently leaving little time for other business. By 1931 the League was an almost entirely Communist body. To that extent Second International and Labour suspicions may be seen as self-fulfilling prophecies. Yet there were at least equally powerful pressures operating from the other side to drive non-Communists out. For in 1928 the Comintern had adopted its 'Class Against Class' policy, repudiating the tactic of united fronts. Co-operation with non-Communists was now frowned upon, and this meant that not only the ILP (now described by the CPGB as 'the most dangerous enemies of the working class', thus usurping Labour's title to that dubious distinction[135]) but most of the colonial nationalists themselves were expelled. In June 1931 the International Executive Committee of the League proclaimed its policy to be not only 'the complete national independence of the colonial and semi-colonial peoples' but also expropriation of all capitalists and landowners. Only those 'honestly prepared to support and fight for these demands' would be admitted by the LAI.[136] As the Report of the League's Secretariat put it:

By publicly condemning the treachery of the social-democratic and national-reformist hangers-on against the cause of national independence and by finally expelling these traitors from the ranks of the League, the Executive Committee has cleared the air and assured the League of the possibility of speedy development.[137]

What they had in reality done was to assure the League of the inevitability of isolation and virtual impotence. Only in Britain did it retain more than a nominal existence after about 1932, and there

[135] Resolutions of the 11th Congress of the CPGB, Nov.–Dec. 1929 (CPGB 1930), 8–9.
[136] 'The Basic Demands of the League Against Imperialism', in *The Meerut Prisoners and the Case Against Them* (LAI pamphlet, 1931), back cover.
[137] *The Colonies and the Oppressed Nations in the Struggle for Freedom* (Berlin: LAI International Secretariat, 1931), 5.

largely through the efforts of Reginald Bridgeman. Bridgeman, born in 1884 in a wealthy, distinguished, and firmly Conservative family, had become a career diplomat but whilst counsellor of the Embassy at Tehran had undergone a conversion to socialist and anti-imperialist beliefs. Whilst never actually joining the Communist Party (he was indeed an active member of Hendon Labour Party and parliamentary candidate for that constituency until expelled from Labour for his LAI activities) he maintained from the early 1920s, as John Saville says, a 'steady and apparently unwavering commitment to the policies of the Comintern'.[138] He involved himself in campaigns for Irish freedom, was secretary of the LAI's British section from the start, and after 1932–3 seems to have run it virtually single-handed.

In November 1933 the International Secretariat also was formally transferred to London, but just how feeble this had become is indicated by Bridgeman himself:

All that was handed over to me on my appointment as the International Secretary of the League was a list of addresses which was not up to date and so of little value. It was necessary to reconstitute the work of the League from the beginning.[139]

Yet however weak the LAI's international wing, and most of the national sections outside Britain, may rapidly have become, in Britain it was for a time not a negligible force. It attempted—albeit with little success—to rally trade union support, played an active role in organising protests over the Meerut trials and established a new front, the Negro Welfare Association, in 1932.[140] Bridgeman seems, despite his generally known Communist sympathies, to have retained contacts, friendships, and some influence among Labour MPs and others interested in colonial affairs but who would otherwise have spurned all co-operation with the Comintern.[141] Thus when, for instance, the West African nationalist I. T. A. Wallace-Johnson came to London in 1937 he contacted Bridgeman for help and advice; and the latter was able in turn to introduce him among others to Labour

[138] John Saville, 'Reginald Francis Orlando Bridgeman', in *Dictionary of Labour Biography*, vii. 30.

[139] Quoted in Saville, 'League Against Imperialism', 45.

[140] MacKenzie, 'British Marxists', 157–64; Saville, 'League Against Imperialism', 44–6.

[141] Julius Lewin, the Labour Party colonial specialist, though wholly hostile to Communism, regarded Bridgeman (together with Palme Dutt) as extremely able and well informed and—unlike all other British Communists—worthy of respect and co-operation (interview with Dr Julius Lewin, 1984).

MPs Reginald Sorensen, Arthur Creech Jones, D. N. Pritt, Sir Stafford Cripps, and George Daggar.[142] Similarly Nehru, at least in 1929–30, appears to have corresponded regularly with Bridgeman and sought his aid rather than that of left Labour MPs.[143]

A fairly large number of colonial students in Britain seem to have become involved with the LAI. In 1930 it was reported that an LSE branch with thirty members had been formed, and that 'many more were anxious to join, but that only those with a definite revolutionary outlook had been accepted'.[144] Under Bridgeman's direction, the League continued to produce literature, including an attack on British colonial policies complete with gory photographs of atrocities in China and India and a contrasting section on 'How the Soviet Union Solved the National Problem';[145] and a protest at the invasion of Abyssinia.[146] Yet with the limited exception of some ILP branches, the League had become an organisation with very little support outside the Communist Party. Even within the CP, Bridgeman was clearly not universally trusted. A police report noted that he 'came in for much criticism. It was stated that he was non-Communist'. Robin Page Arnot, defending him, was reported to have admitted that Bridgeman was 'not all that good politically from the Marxian stand-point' (presumably implying a paucity of the right kind of theoretical awareness), but had stood by the LAI to the sacrifice of his prospects of high office in the Labour Party.[147]

Yet one man, however able and dedicated, could not maintain the League under the conditions of the late 1930s—especially as the Comintern and CPGB themselves, their attention centring ever more on the threat of war in Europe, devoted few resources to colonial affairs and soft-pedalled their critique of the imperial powers. The story of the LAI is one of gradual decline from the very start: its hopes of a broad united front undermined by suspicion and sectarianism, its initially world-wide activities reduced to a single

[142] LaRay E. Denzer, 'I. T. A. Wallace-Johnson and the West African Youth League: A Case Study in West African Radicalism' (Birmingham University Ph.D. thesis, 1977), 148–67.

[143] Gupta, 'British Labour', 100.

[144] Parket Report. Page Arnot replied to this by pointing out that, as the LAI was supposed to be a broad front, even the non-revolutionary students should be accepted. This suggests a less sectarian attitude than the League's Secretariat was by then adopting.

[145] *The British Empire* (LAI pamphlet, n.d. but *c*.1935).

[146] *Abyssinia* (LAI pamphlet, n.d. but *c*.1935).

[147] Parket Report.

country and eventually to the efforts of a single man. When Bridgeman, announcing the disbandment of the League in mid-1937, claimed that its very success meant it was no longer needed, he can neither have believed what he wrote, nor expected to be believed by others.[148]

VII. THE TRADE UNIONS

By comparison with the ideologies of the CPGB and ILP, or even that of the Labour Party—all of which dictated an interest in and action on colonial issues—the focus of attention of British trade unionism was by tradition almost wholly parochial. A persistent complaint of Labour's colonial experts was the enormous difficulty in getting the unions to play any part even in formulating policy on such questions. Yet there were always exceptions to this lack of interest; and between the wars a number of developments gradually drew the TUC, and to some extent individual unions, into greater colonial involvement.

That involvement, however, was of a strictly limited kind and reflected a tightly constraining set of presuppositions—which have, for that matter, often been reproduced in subsequent academic discussion of the growth of colonial trade unionism. Whilst noting that the British TUC never played quite so direct a role in fostering colonial unionism as the CGT did in French colonies, many commentators have seen trade union activity in the colonies as 'imitation of institutions already developed to meet British conditions' and the formation of colonial unions as attributable largely to 'thinking about prospective colonial development . . . in the Colonial Office itself and generally in interested circles in Britain'.[149]

Such a view—a perception of the transfer of institutions directly analogous to that of the transfer of power—necessarily not only undervalues the indigenous contribution to colonial trade union growth, but makes inevitable a distorted picture of its character. Underlying it is a crude kind of modernisation theory, seeing colonial societies as sharply divided between 'traditional' and 'modern' ele-

---

[148] Bridgeman to F. A. Bruce (4 June 1937); quoted in Denzer, 'Wallace-Johnson', 167–8.
[149] Sir Sydney Caine, Preface to B. C. Roberts, *Labour in the Tropical Territories of the Commonwealth* (Bell, 1964), p. ix. Nicholson, *The TUC Overseas*, a more detailed and sophisticated account, still reproduces many of the same dubious assumptions.

ments. Trade unionism is seen as part of the 'modern' sector and believed only to come into existence in association with or following from other aspects of modernisation—industrial development, mass literacy, and the rest.

In contrast to such assumptions, colonial trade unionism often owed as much to 'traditional' as to 'modern' forces. It often grew out of, and intertwined with, other sorts of organisation—local, ethnic, social, political. Its origins and modes of operation were often spontaneous and based on individual charisma rather than formalised and bureaucratic. Memberships, especially in tropical Africa, were typically polyglot and largely illiterate. Unions, often very small and/or without formal membership lists, might take on a wide variety of community functions rather than being solely concerned with wage bargaining. Above all, colonial unionism was almost by definition a political phenomenon: the colonial state was often the major employer; in any case it closely and sometimes repressively regulated employee conditions and all forms of collective action; and almost everywhere unions embraced anticolonialist politics.

British unions found this picture, when they recognised it at all, an unfamiliar and uncomfortable one—despite its many similarities to infant British trade unionism a century or more earlier. They tended to want instead to encourage a more formal structure: one based, in fact, very closely on the British industrial relations model itself. They looked to non-political unionism, which was almost impossible under colonial conditions as well as appearing somewhat hypocritical when British unions were themselves organically linked to political parties. Increasingly, they were prepared to work closely with British and colonial government to attain these ends. Under such circumstances, conflict between British union leaders and their colonial counterparts, and between the British structures and more radical anticolonialist circles in Britain, was inevitable.

The earliest imperial contacts of British trade unions were with movements in the white-settled territories, where unions had often been established by emigrating British workers. Even in Africa the only direct links the TUC possessed before the 1920s were with exclusivist white unions in South Africa and the Rhodesias. There was no communication either with African proletarians or with the nascent Indian workers' movements in east and southern Africa.[150]

[150] Nicholson gives a fairly thorough if uncritical survey of the pattern of TUC colonial contacts, concentrating mainly on India.

Indeed when Clements Kadalie, leader of the rapidly growing black Industrial and Commercial Workers' Union (ICU) of South Africa, asked the British TUC for help in 1926, the response may justly be described as pitiful. William Gillies, secretary of the TUC International Committee, thought it 'hardly the special duty of the British TU officials to establish contact and assist them'.[151] It was left to individuals associated with the ILP to offer Kadalie a platform in Britain, to table parliamentary questions about legal restrictions on the ICU in Southern Rhodesia, and to pay for an adviser to go out and aid Kadalie.[152]

In general, suggestions that the TUC should raise money for colonial unions, or send organisers to help them, fell on deaf ears. In 1927 and 1928 individual unions urged that such aid should be sent to Indian labour organisations, but were rebuffed.[153] There were closer contacts with Indian unions than was yet the case in Africa, but these were neither extensive nor always friendly. Almost all the AITUC leaders were active nationalists, and many were sympathetic to Communism; so the British call for responsible, non-political trade unionism in India met with an understandably hostile response. Visitors from the AITUC to Britain more than once used the fraternal greetings spot at TUC conferences (usually an occasion for internationalist platitudes) to deliver swingeing attacks on British unions for their alleged complicity in imperialism.[154]

When the AITUC split in 1929 over the issue of Communist involvement—which was itself, of course, heavily influenced from Britain through Bradley and his Meerut co-defendants—the TUC supported and made donations to the smaller, anti-Communist break-away All-India Trade Union Federation.[155] The TUC refused to

---

[151] Gillies to Arthur Creech Jones (30 June 1926); quoted in Gupta, *Imperialism*, 122.

[152] Ibid. 125–6; C. J. Sansom, 'The British Labour Movement and Southern Africa, 1918–55' (Birmingham University Ph.D. thesis, 1982); Clements Kadalie, *My Life and the ICU*, ed. Stanley Trapido (Frank Cass, 1970); id. in *New Leader* (30 Sept. 1927).

[153] *TUC Annual Report 1927*, 382; *1928*, 256–9.

[154] See for instance *TUC Annual Report 1927*, 350 (speech by G. Sethi). After 1930, after the split in the Indian movement, delegates to the TUC came from the less militant AITUF, whose speeches were markedly less critical of the British unions—see *TUC Annual Report 1930*, 316–19 (speech by B. Shiva Rao); *1931*, 390–2 (speech by N. M. Joshi).

[155] *TUC Annual Report 1930*, 190–1; Nicholson, *TUC Overseas*, 124–9.

condemn the Meerut trials, which the General Council argued to be a political matter irrelevant to issues of trade union freedom.[156]

Throughout the inter-war period, effective contact by the TUC was with only a limited range of colonial movements. The most important link was through the British Commonwealth Labour Conference, but by 1928 this still included no delegates from black Africa, the Arab world, the Far East, or (with the exception of a white Trinidadian) the Caribbean. Even this unrepresentative gathering split in two: when the Indians walked out in protest over the Simon Commission only Ceylon and Trinidad (significantly the only other representatives of predominantly non-white movements) supported them.[157]

The gradual increase in TUC involvement during the 1930s was in large part motivated by a growing concern that colonial 'sweated labour' was being used to undermine the living standards of British workers. From this fear widely divergent conclusions could be drawn. It might be argued, as it was by Ernest Bevin in 1930, that there ought to be 'some control' over colonial development in order to prevent competition with British industries.[158] Such a suggestion —calling, in fact, for the sort of measures deliberately retarding industrialisation which the CPGB claimed were already being implemented—was particularly popular among textile workers' unions whose members felt threatened by Indian production. Few, though, broke with the Labour movement's dominant free trade tradition and advocated full-fledged protectionism.[159] A more common response was to argue that such fears of competition gave British workers a direct incentive to encourage effective trade unionism in the colonies,

---

[156] *TUC Annual Report 1930*, 189. Nicholson, *TUC Overseas*, 114–15, notes the TUC's 'persistent approaches' to the India Office over the case; but these seem to have been confined to complaining at delays in the trial and asserting that some of the accused were not in fact Communists.

[157] *TUC Annual Report 1928*, 267–74; Gupta, 'British Labour', 97–8; Nicholson, *TUC Overseas*, 109–12.

[158] *TUC Annual Report 1930*, 286.

[159] Though as noted above the Empire Socialist group had done so in the mid-1920s; and in 1932 the TUC, in conjunction with the Federation of British Industries, advocated Empire Free Trade—a formula artfully combining the traditional verbal appeal of the free trade slogan with a protectionist imperial substance. As Gupta points out, so strong did anti-protectionist feeling remain in the labour movement that even Bevin's own union had to defend the TUC proposals as a step towards world economic unity and play down their protectionist implications (*Imperialism*, 153). The idea was in any case torpedoed by the economic nationalism of the Dominions at the Ottawa conference.

which would combat 'sweated labour' there and prevent unfair competition. This argument was made not only by British union leaders but by colonial ones too, as V. R. Kalappa of the AITUC did at the 1929 TUC Conference.[160]

The mould of TUC apathy towards colonial unionism was only fully to be broken, however, at the end of the decade, when events in the West Indies forced an awakening of concern. These developments, the wartime initiatives to which they gave rise, and the anticolonial left's responses to them, are discussed in the following chapter.

---

[160] *TUC Annual Report 1929*, 365–8.

3

The War Years, 1936–1945

It has long been a commonplace that the eventual effect of the Second World War was to weaken, perhaps fatally weaken, the British Empire. There are numerous clear reasons why this should have been so. Yet many would now argue, with John Gallagher, that 'In the short term, the impact of war considerably strengthened the empire.'[1] Strategic demands resulted in the tightening of Britain's military and political grip on the Middle East and the Indian subcontinent. The needs of a war economy meant that large areas of tropical Africa were effectively drawn into the Imperial economic system for the first time, and that the pre-war neglect of the Caribbean was rapidly reversed. Perhaps most important, wholly new tasks were imposed on the Colonial Office and in response to these emerged new and bolder thinking about colonial development. Lee and Petter summarise the effects of this change as follows:

The Colonial Office became both more vulnerable and more confident. It was more sensitive to attacks against its alleged failure to meet the expectations of the colonial peoples and at the same time it was better equipped to apply a more constructive set of policies to the whole range of colonial territories.[2]

Both the increased confidence and the growing vulnerability are important to the understanding of post-war developments in British handling of colonial affairs. The latter in particular is vital to the influence of radical criticism of colonial policy, for it was from the anticolonialist left that allegations of failure to meet colonial expectations came most vigorously. Increasingly, too, their voices were echoed elsewhere; not only from colonial intellectuals but from the United States and other international sources. And they found resonances also within official circles, where the new radicalism of

[1] John Gallagher, *The Decline, Revival and Fall of the British Empire* (Cambridge: Cambridge University Press, 1982), 139.
[2] J. M. Lee and Martin Petter, *The Colonial Office, War and Development Policy* (Maurice Temple Smith for Institute of Development Studies, 1982), 16.

which Sir Andrew Cohen was the most vigorous opponent chimed closely with much Labour Party thought. Far from marking time amidst the distractions of global war, both official and unofficial thinking on colonial affairs took on unprecedented energy between 1939 and 1945. In important respects, indeed, this new thinking can be traced somewhat further back. For already a series of colonial upheavals, in India, Abyssinia, the West Indies, and Central Africa, had introduced fresh alignments and fresh actors to British debates on Empire.

I. BLACK JACOBINS AND FRIENDS OF ABYSSINIA

British socialists had had contacts with Indian nationalist politicians, including very radical politicians, since at least the beginning of the twentieth century. So far as Britain's African and West Indian colonies were concerned, though, such contacts only developed rather later, and were initially with groups who were, as Hardie had said of Congress, 'extreme in their moderation'. The phrase 'bourgeois nationalist' was heavily overworked on the anticolonialist left; but it does not, I hope, belittle the real courage and imagination of the pioneers of modern politics in British Africa to say that the label fits them almost too perfectly. Wealthy, self-improving, constitutionalist, aspiringly faithful replicas of the English gentleman in their tastes, manners, and aims, the leaders of the first significant such group, the National Congress of British West Africa, had as their objective an increased political voice for people of their own class rather than for the population as a whole.

Their main quarrel was with the system of Indirect Rule, with its lack of niches for educated Africans, and with colour bars in government service and the professions rather than with British domination as such. Accordingly, when they decided in 1920 to send a delegation to London, they had no intention of seeking links with the radical left in Britain. Indeed one of the delegates, the Gambian H. N. Jones, advised his fellows that:

For the purposes of the Cause, all intercourse with the Press of the Labour Party should be eschewed as any intercourse or connection with them would prejudice our cases in the eyes of the moderate element among politicians of all parties.[3]

The early West Indian nationalists with British connections were a more disparate group. But they were equally lacking in organised contacts with British left-wing organisations. Only by the 1920s and 1930s did far more radical figures appear among the nationalists forging links with British politicians; and an increasing number of these based themselves in Britain. There they formed, joined, or lobbied various bodies which they believed could aid their countries' struggle for independence.

The Indians remained naturally the largest contingent, including notable activists like Saklatvala, Sinha, and Krishna Menon. There were a few Malayan Chinese and others from South-East Asia, among them some who were to become important leaders of the left in post-war years. There were as yet almost none from East, Central, or Southern Africa: Jomo Kenyatta was virtually the sole significant political figure from those regions in Britain. Most significant for future developments were the growing numbers from West Africa and the West Indies who visited or settled in Britain during the 1930s. Men like Sierra Leonian I. T. A. Wallace-Johnson and Gambian E. F. Small associated with the Communist Party and the LAI, as did a number of other West African radicals.[4] The three most influential figures in the black radical circles of the 1930s and 1940s, however, all came from the Caribbean: C. L. R. James and George Padmore (baptised Malcolm Nurse) both from Trinidad, and T. Ras Makonnen (baptised George Griffith) from British Guiana.

These men and their supporters founded or were involved with a bewildering variety of anticolonialist organisations and had complex, close, but often stormy relations with various sections of the British left. They brought to it a sense of internationalism which was passionately held rather than being, as so often among British

[3] Quoted in J. Ayodele Langley, *Pan-Africanism and Nationalism in West Africa, 1900–1946* (Oxford: Oxford University Press, 1973), 245.

[4] On Wallace-Johnson, the most influential and perhaps the most militant of these early West African socialists, see LaRay E. Denzer, 'I. T. A. Wallace-Johnson and the West African Youth League' (Birmingham University Ph.D. thesis, 1977), and Langley, *Pan-Africanism*, 226–9, 326–48; also Leo Spitzer and LaRay Denzer, 'I. T. A. Wallace-Johnson and the West African Youth League', *Journal of African Historical Studies*, 6/3–4 (1973). On Small, see Langley, *Pan-Africanism*, 137–9.

socialists, a matter of piety and abstract conscience. Padmore and the remarkably prolific and polymathic James were also writers of greater power and originality than were almost any of the British critics of colonialism.

Padmore and many of the others started as Communists (Padmore was a leading official in the Red International of Labour Unions and its offshoot, the International Trade Union Committee of Negro Workers), and James as a Trotskyist; but through disillusionment with existing white-dominated political parties and especially with what they saw as the Communists' preparedness to subordinate colonial liberation to Russian interests, they arrived at an ideology of Pan-African socialist nationalism which challenged the orthodoxies of Soviet as much as of British thought.[5]

What first brought these disparate individuals together was the Italian invasion of Abyssinia, which seemed to them evidence both of the continued virulence of aggressive imperialism and, in the acquiescence of the other powers, of the general culpability of Europe. As the sole significant independent African state Abyssinia also possessed powerful symbolic resonance for them all. The invasion helped turn James's main attention from the Caribbean to Africa; Russia's failure to observe sanctions against Italy precipitated Padmore's and others' break from Communism. To the young Kwame Nkrumah 'it was almost as if the whole of London had suddenly declared war on me personally'.[6] The London *émigrés*— Padmore, James, Kenyatta, Makonnen, and Colonial Seamen's Union

[5] On Padmore, see J. R. Hooker, *Black Revolutionary: George Padmore's Path from Communism to Pan-Africanism* (New York: Praeger, 1967), and his own *Pan-Africanism or Communism?* (Dennis Dobson, 1956). On Makonnen, see his autobiography *Pan-Africanism from Within*, as recorded and edited by Kenneth King (Nairobi: Oxford University Press, 1973). On James, who sadly died with a projected autobiography unwritten, the three volumes of his collected essays are the closest substitute: *The Future in the Present, Spheres of Existence*, and *At the Rendezvous of Victory* (Allison & Busby, 1977, 1980, and 1984); also Paul Buhle, *C. L. R. James: The Artist as Revolutionary* (Verso, 1988); id. (ed.), *C. L. R. James: His Life and Work* (Allison & Busby, 1986); Kent Worcester, *C. L. R. James: A Political Biography* (Lanham, Md.: North & South Press, 1988). On the intellectual background and milieu, see Immanuel Geiss, *The Pan-African Movement* (New York: Africana Publishing Co., 1974); Ivor Oxaal, *Black Intellectuals Come to Power: The Rise of Creole Nationalism in Trinidad and Tobago* (Cambridge, Mass.: Harvard University Press, 1968); Langley, *Pan-Africanism*; John Gaffar LaGuerre, *The Social and Political Thought of the Colonial Intelligentsia* (Mona, Jamaica: Institute of Social & Economic Research, 1982).

[6] Kwame Nkrumah, *Ghana: The Autobiography of Kwame Nkrumah* (Edinburgh: Nelson, 1957), 27.

organiser Chris Jones—formed the International African Friends of Abyssinia with the aim, as Padmore said, 'to arouse the sympathy and support of the British public for the victim of fascist aggression and to assist by all means in their power in the maintenance of the territorial integrity and political independence of Abyssinia'.[7] From this body their activities expanded into a wider group, the International African Service Bureau, and later the Pan-African Federation.

These colonial intellectuals now felt that they must organise independently and, rather than looking to any British political group for salvation, would seek co-operation only with those who were prepared to work with them on terms of equality. This, for Padmore and most in the group, now excluded the 'hypocrites' of the CPGB as well as the Labour leaders with their attachment to 'pettifogging reforms'.[8] It did not, on the other hand, exclude the more militantly anticolonial ILP; though there were sharp differences of opinion between the black radicals (supported by many of the ILP rank and file) and the ILP leaders on the Abyssinian issue.

No one on the left seemed to have any faith in League of Nations sanctions as a means of stopping Italy in Abyssinia; but Maxton, John McGovern, and other ILP leaders felt that socialists should adopt a policy of non-intervention since "the Abyssinian dispute to us is an Imperialist quarrel between Britain and Italy'.[9] Maxton and McGovern also said that Abyssinia was a primitive feudal autocracy which no socialist could defend. James and the IAFA, on the contrary, argued that the last really independent African state must be protected against aggression whatever its internal regime, and that British workers could take effective action to that end by 'blacking' goods destined for Italy. In this they were supported by Brockway, and by a majority of delegates at the ILP's 1936 conference.

Here was a clear and sharp clash, as there had been at the 1926 ILP Conference, between two different conceptions of anti-

[7] Padmore, *Pan-Africanism*, 145.

[8] Ibid. 148–9. Apart from Padmore, prominent Pan-Africanists with CPGB or 'fellow-travelling' backgrounds included Chris Jones (mentioned in the Parket Police Report, see above, pp. 66–7, as the CP's most valuable contact among colonial seamen), Wallace-Johnson, Arnold Ward of the Negro Welfare Association, and Kenyatta. Some black radicals did manage to combine Pan-African beliefs with continued Communist links even after the shocks of the 1930s. Two who certainly remained involved in both circles for some time were Peter Blackman (a Barbadian former missionary active in Caribbean affairs) and Nkrumah.

[9] Quoted in Daniel Waley, *British Public Opinion and the Abyssinian War* (Maurice Temple Smith, 1975), 26.

imperialism: black radicals and a few British socialists feeling that the first duty was the defence of the victims' national sovereignty; with most of the British left seeing the situation as one of rivalry between imperialist powers with Abyssinia itself as an insignificant and somewhat unsavoury pawn. The CPGB meanwhile decried both Italy and the League of Nations, remaining silent about Soviet sanctions-breaking.[10]

In terms of the development of anticolonialism in Britain, the main outgrowth of the Abyssinian affair was the foundation by Padmore, Makonnen, James, and Kenyatta of the International African Service Bureau (IASB). Modelled in part on the lobbying techniques of the India League,[11] this aimed both to unite black radicals in Britain and the colonies around a coherent philosophy of Pan-Africanism and to influence public opinion in Britain. It produced a regular journal, initially entitled *Africa and the World* (and edited by Wallace-Johnson), then the *African Sentinel*, and, from July 1938, *International African Opinion* (edited in its early issues by James). Apart from the leaders of the IASB itself contributors included ILP politicians and a wide variety of anticolonial publicists.[12]

The IASB was fragmented by the coming of war: the leaders had apparently agreed some time before that they would not allow themselves to be caught in Britain when war broke out. James had gone to the USA at the end of 1938. Wallace-Johnson returned to Sierra Leone where he was first imprisoned and then placed under restriction by the colonial authorities.[13] Kenyatta went to live in rural Sussex where he seems to have undertaken little political activity, and Makonnen to Manchester where he ran a successful chain of

[10] See Independent Labour Party, *Italy and Abyssinia: Should British Workers Take Sides?* (Controversy Special Supplement 1, 1936); A. J. MacKenzie, 'British Marxists and the Empire' (London University Ph.D. thesis, 1978), 214–18; Waley, *British Public Opinion*, 25–9, 115; Langley, *Pan-Africanism*, 326–8; Makonnen, *Pan-Africanism*, 112–17. Makonnen gives fascinating—though of course not necessarily reliable—detail on the differing private reactions of himself, James, and Padmore.

[11] Makonnen, *Pan-Africanism*, 117.

[12] Apart from the references cited in n. 3, see Roderick MacDonald, 'The Role of London's Black Press in the 1930s and 1940s' (paper for History of Blacks in Britain conference, London, 1981) and Jeremy Murray-Brown, *Kenyatta* (Fontana, 1974), 195–208.

[13] Though he continued to conduct an extensive political correspondence with Brockway and others in Britain, wrote poems and numerous articles intended for the *New Leader*—only one of which was published, in the issue of 3 Oct. 1942—and prompted considerable agitation in Parliament and elsewhere for his release: see Denzer, 'Wallace-Johnson', 371–426.

businesses.[14] Nkrumah too was in America.[15] Padmore alone remained in London and worked with the ILP. The activities initiated by the IASB did not wholly lapse, but only with the end of the war did they again bear fruit.

James, of course, did not remain idle during his time in the USA, but continued the trajectory of historical and political enquiry he had initiated during the 1930s. His adherence to Trotsky's Fourth International (whose foundation in Paris in 1938 he had attended) became increasingly evidently a marriage of convenience. James had arrived at his views on the colonial question largely independently. These views had little in common with those either of Labour reformers whose paternalism and parochialism he, like Padmore, scorned; or of the Communists whose entire strategy he regarded as both inept and dishonest. (Nor would the latter have tolerated the unorthodoxy of his ideas on literature and culture.) Trotsky's theories were more attractive—or at least offered fewer points of substantive disagreement. But James was developing a position which went much further than that of Trotsky in seeing the anticolonial movement as central to world revolution.

James's hopes for colonial liberation were expressed in a series of writings of the 1930s and 1940s, finding their fullest early formulation in *The Black Jacobins* in 1938. This was a study of the Haitian slave revolution of the 1790s: a major work of historical scholarship but also, obliquely but unmistakeably, a commentary on what its author saw as the immediate future of Africa and the Caribbean.[16] James argued that, not only could the 'backward' colonial countries provide fertile ground for revolution—as Lenin and others had earlier recognised—but that the situation of colonial peoples (and, James soon added, of black workers in the advanced countries) was such that they could lead the way. Their drive for change was greater as their oppression was greater, and out of this they would develop ideas and tactics more advanced than those economically more favoured: 'in a period of world-wide revolutionary change . . . the revolutionary crisis lifts backward peoples over centuries and projects them into the very forefront of the advanced movement of today.'[17]

---

[14] Murray-Brown, *Kenyatta*, 209–24; Makonnen, *Pan-Africanism*, 133–47.
[15] Nkrumah, *Ghana*, 23–9.
[16] C. L. R. James, *The Black Jacobins: Toussaint L'Ouverture and the San Domingo Revolution* (Allison & Busby, 1980; orig. pub. 1938).
[17] C. L. R. James, *Nkrumah and the Ghana Revolution* (Allison & Busby, 1977; orig.

James presented an embryonic version of these ideas to Trotsky during extended discussions in Mexico in 1939, and seemed to win his assent.[18] But, James recalled later, 'the Trotskyist movement accepted it . . . but I don't think they really understood it. At any rate, in 1951 my friends and I broke irrevocably and fundamentally from the premises of Trotskyism.'[19] What James had eventually come to believe was that his theories, based on spontaneity rather than on Leninist modes of party organisation and on cultural and racial rather than purely economic oppression, were incompatible with any orthodox Marxism.[20] He had arrived at an attitude to Leninist ideas of revolution similar to that which Makonnen, never really a Marxist, had come to almost instinctively some years earlier: 'If you are interested in Communism, then buy the book . . . Don't join the club! The Bible is there to buy if you want to know about Jesus. You don't have to join the Catholics.'[21]

Thus the British-based black radicals of the 1930s had begun to formulate a new and independent body of thought on colonial problems. This centred on the proclaimed world-wide unity of peoples of African descent, on the interrelation of socialist and nationalist aspirations, and on the necessity for black political groups to establish their own identity rather than rely on metropolitan socialists. Such developments meant that in the post-war years British anticolonialists would find it increasingly necessary to come to terms with nationalism as an independent force, not only in the colonies but through its representatives in Britain. They were challenged to question much of their own earlier paternalism and to find new ways of working with colonial politicians. Equally, the Communist Party's self-proclaimed monopoly of effective revolutionary theory came under question from newly radicalised Pan-African and other nationalist ideologies.

pub. 1962), 66. James was here summarising what he retrospectively believed to have been the central message of *The Black Jacobins*, though the lesson was not so explicitly drawn in his late-1930s works.

[18] 'Conversations with Trotsky', in *At the Rendezvous of Victory*, 33–64. Indeed at some points Trotsky appears *more* optimistic about the leftist political potential of African-Americans than does James in these discussions.

[19] *Spheres of Existence*, 235.

[20] His ideas on these subjects are most fully developed in *Notes on Dialectics* (Allison & Busby, 1980; orig. pub. 1948). I am indebted to A. X. Cambridge for helping me, through many fruitful discussions, to appreciate the significance of this work.

[21] Makonnen, *Pan-Africanism*, 159.

II. WARNING FROM THE WEST INDIES

In 1935–8 a wave of unrest swept the British Caribbean, engulfing St Kitts, St Lucia, Trinidad, British Guiana, Barbados, and finally, and most severely, Jamaica. Originating primarily as spontaneous protests over wages and labour conditions, they rapidly took on a more directly political and often violent colouring. There were dozens of deaths, hundreds of injuries, and thousands of arrests; and the modern nationalist movement in the region emerged from the upheaval. In the parliamentary debate following the Trinidad labour revolt of 1937, Labour MP William Lunn noted that:

It is a rare thing for any event that takes place in any British colony to get any sort of publicity in this country . . . something really sensational has to happen if anything is to take place in this country with regard to the colonies.[22]

As Lunn went on to suggest, the West Indian disturbances of the 1930s provided such a rare 'really sensational' event. Not since the Governor Eyre controversy of the 1860s had any Caribbean question—or indeed almost any colonial issue at all other than major wars and constitutional crises—called forth as much political attention and activity as did the 1935–8 rebellions. Nor has the Commonwealth Caribbean ever subsequently attracted such notice from British politicians; with the dubious exception of a fitful and often racist concern about why some of its inhabitants should want to migrate to Britain. Before 1937–8, British political debate on colonial issues had concentrated overwhelmingly on India; from the 1940s it centred on sub-Saharan Africa. Only for these few years did the West Indies occupy centre stage.

Yet this relatively brief flurry of activity did have a wider and a longer-term significance. British reactions to the Caribbean labour rebellions marked a vital turning-point in colonial policy, a milestone on the road to decolonisation not only in the West Indies, but also in Africa and Asia. For the British left and the Labour movement, in particular, responses to the risings had an impact well outside the restricted circles of those with a close interest in the Caribbean. Much of the shape of post-war Labour colonial policy, especially in the trade union field, was formed in the mould which the West Indian events produced. And on the other side of the imperial

[22] *HC Deb.* (28 Feb. 1938), col. 766.

relationship, probably nowhere in the Empire were radical movements so heavily influenced by their British counterparts as in the Caribbean.

Labour and nationalist organisations of various kinds in the British West Indies had long sought inspiration from, and sometimes direct links with, British Labour's organisational forms or ideological prescriptions. The most developed case of this before 1937 was Trinidad, where the Trinidad Workingmen's Association, formed in 1897, derived its structure and name from similar associations in Victorian Britain. It established contact with Westminster Labour MPs and adopted (or was adopted by) two of these—first Thomas Summerbell, later Joseph Pointer—as its representatives in Parliament.[23] Later pioneer Trinidadian nationalist Captain Cipriani explicitly modelled his programme on British Labour lines, and developed a close relationship with Labour leaders. He was the only Caribbean representative to attend the 1928 British Commonwealth Labour conference.[24]

This is not to suggest, as is sometimes done, that Caribbean reliance on British Labour models, on a British socialist ideological inheritance, or Caribbean politicians' often inflated expectations of what British Labour would do to help them, amounted either to a (literally?) slavishly derivative ethos or to a wholesale incorporation into the imperial framework. The former view is neatly, and rather absurdly, encapsulated in the Cold War-shaped claims of a 1950s American text:

In Barbados and Jamaica socialism is an important ideology brought to the colonies by middle-class West Indians returning from English universities. Generally, this brand of socialism is mild and intellectual with an emphasis on anticolonialism, and the need for self-government and economic planning. Lip service is paid to Socialist theories but it is generally recognised that socialism is not a practicable approach... Trade union leaders told the writer they called themselves Socialists only because capitalism has such a bad reputation in a colonial area.[25]

---

[23] See Brinsley Samaroo, 'The Trinidad Workingmen's Association and the Origins of Popular Protest in a Crown Colony', *Social and Economic Studies*, 21/2 (1972); B. Simpson-Holley, 'Members for Trinidad', *Journal of Caribbean History*, 6 (May 1973); Richard Hart, *Origins and Development of the Working Class in the English-Speaking Caribbean Area, 1897–1937* (Community Education Trust, n.d.).

[24] See above, p. 80; Bridget Brereton, *A History of Modern Trinidad, 1783–1962* (Heinemann, 1981).

[25] William H. Knowles, *Trade Union Development and Industrial Relations in the British West Indies* (Berkeley, Calif.: University of California Press, 1959), 134–5.

Similarly, to claim as does Bridget Brereton that for men like Cipriani there was a straight choice between reliance on the British Labour Party and 'the politics of the street' is clearly a gross oversimplification.[26] Rather, that reliance presented itself in the first instance as a matter of immediate practicalities. The British model of political and trade union organisation was by far the most readily available one, not only because of historical patterns of culture but in terms of access to literature, sources of advice, and personal exposure. There was a growing knowledge of the American experience, but in the 1930s this was a rather recent and tenuous phenomenon. There was a general awareness that pressure could be brought to bear on colonial governments often more effectively from within Britain—even by relatively marginal opposition forces—than in the colonies themselves.

Thus all parts of the Caribbean political spectrum looked, to some degree, to Britain both for practical aid and for sources of inspiration. There were cultural nationalists like Alexander Bedward or Marcus Garvey with their ambiguous appropriation of certain British imperial ideological themes,[27] authoritarian populists like Alexander Bustamante with his insistence that only British labour relations experience, *not* that of other colonies, was good enough for Jamaica,[28] constitutional reformers like Cipriani or Norman Manley with their intimate ties to the Labour Party, Pan-Africanists like James, Padmore, and Makonnen with their choice of Britain as the most advantageous base for their operations, or early Caribbean Marxists seeking association with and advice from the British Communist Party.[29]

Very few British socialists had any knowledge of, or interest in, the Caribbean before the revolts of the later 1930s. Pre-eminent among the few who did was Sydney Olivier; pioneer Fabian of the 1880s, Labour peer, and former Secretary of State for India. Almost 80 when the revolts broke out, his involvement with the West Indies

[26] Brereton, *Modern Trinidad*, 170.

[27] For instance, the singing of 'God Save the King'—with deliberate ambiguity as to whether the reference was to George VI or Haile Selassie.

[28] See Ken Post, *Arise Ye Starvelings: The Jamaican Labour Rebellion of 1938 and its Aftermath* (The Hague: Institute of Social Studies, 1978), 383.

[29] These links are traced for Jamaica in Post, *Arise*, and id., *Strike the Iron: A Colony at War, Jamaica 1939–1945*, 2 vols. (Atlantic Highlands, NJ: Humanities Press, 1981). These volumes are not only by far the most detailed published account of the labour rebellions and their consequences, but are virtually unique in the literature on British colonialism in giving detailed, scrupulous attention both to colonial and to metropolitan events.

went back to 1896 when he had been Secretary to the Royal Commission on economic conditions there. Governor of Jamaica in 1907–13, he had written two books about the island and had returned as chairman of the Sugar Commission of 1929–30—the second Labour Government's only major policy initiative towards the Caribbean. The other Labour politician who was to be most continuously involved in responses to the risings was Arthur Creech Jones, a former TGWU official who was already establishing himself as one of Labour's colonial specialists, initially through an interest in Southern African labour problems.

The other major British source of information and activity on Caribbean questions was naturally from West Indians resident in Britain. These may loosely be grouped into three circles, each having intimate if sometimes uneasy relations with different sections of the British left. There were those sympathetic to the Communist Party: a much diminished band by 1937–8 since the Comintern's Popular Front policy had led it to downplay anticolonialism and had caused many black radicals to lose faith in it. Most prominent of those still involved were Arnold Ward of the Negro Welfare Association and Peter Blackman, a Barbadian former missionary. The second, larger group was that around the International African Service Bureau, led by C. L. R. James, George Padmore, T. Ras Makonnen, and Chris Jones. These tended to stress the necessity for independence from any British political party; but many of them were members of, or close to, the ILP. Third was the League of Coloured Peoples, founded in 1931 by Dr Harold Moody as a moderate, largely middle-class campaign against racial discrimination and associated with the Fabian wing of the Labour Party.[30] An intriguing absence from the spectrum of responses was that of Marcus Garvey and his followers. Garvey, who in the 1920s had been the most popular political figure not only in the Anglophone Caribbean but throughout the Afro-American world, was resident in London in the later 1930s—but Garveyism seems barely to have figured in responses to the labour revolts. What little Garvey did write or say was startlingly conservative.

Initial British responses to the successive waves of disturbance in

---

[30] Roderick MacDonald, 'Dr Harold Arundel Moody and the League of Coloured Peoples, 1931–1947: A Retrospective View', *Race*, 14/3 (1973); id., 'The Role of London's Black Press in the 1930s and 1940s'; Peter Fryer, *Staying Power* (Pluto, 1984), 326–34; Geiss, *Pan-African Movement*, 340–50; Ron Ramdin, *The Making of the Black Working Class in Britain* (Gower, 1987), ch. 5.

the West Indies were predictably sensationalist. There was little publicity for the first, relatively minor outbreaks in St Kitts, St Lucia, and St Vincent; but when Trinidad erupted in June 1937 the coverage in the British press was extensive and dramatic. As Lord Olivier remarked, the combination of riots and oil provided excellent copy.[31] Eleven months later the Jamaican events gained still more prominent attention. The Labour-orientated press shared fully in the general sensationalism of this coverage, and in the tendency to stress economic conditions rather than political or racial grievances as the cause. In other respects, the divergences between different left-leaning papers' stances were very marked. The Liberal *News Chronicle* discussed land hunger, poverty, and neglect, but went on to explain the risings in blatantly racist fashion:

For the most part Jamaican labour is uncomplaining and peaceful. The people possess something of that inherent African happiness which even the direst poverty cannot dispel. But again, like Africans, they can easily be aroused to a passion that becomes berserk in its rage. It is these passions which certain agitators in the towns are now playing upon.[32]

The two most staunchly Labour papers, the *Daily Herald* and *Reynolds News*, by contrast, placed the main burden of blame squarely upon the Colonial Office. The latter wheeled out veteran anticolonialist H. N. Brailsford to launch a fierce attack on 'The Slavery that is Jamaica', condemning British repression and calling for the common ownership of land and a return of the capital drained from Jamaica by Britain.[33]

The new Labour left weekly *Tribune*, founded by Sir Stafford Cripps, was considerably sharper still, but chose to direct its assault primarily against private capitalist rather than governmental targets. Its front-page banner headline on Trinidad asserted 'How Big Financiers Set Trinidad Aflame', and it argued that British finance capital had long 'had the worker of Trinidad gripped by the throat. Only with the co-operation of British Labour can that grip be effectively broken.'[34] A similar line was taken by the Communist *Daily Worker*, but it was distinctive in placing emphasis on the need for

---

[31] Quoted in Howard Johnson, 'The Political Uses of Commissions of Enquiry: (i) The Imperial-Colonial West Indian Context', *Social & Economic Studies*, 27/3 (1978), 257.

[32] William Makin, 'Why Men Riot in Jamaica', *News Chronicle* (19 May 1938).

[33] H. N. Brailsford, 'The Slavery that is Jamaica', *Reynolds News* (5 June 1938).

[34] 'How Big Financiers Set Trinidad Aflame', *Tribune* (4 Feb. 1938).

constitutional as well as economic reform, demanding 'a government elected by and responsible to the people of the West Indies'.[35]

The first parliamentary reaction to the risings came earlier, in the spring of 1935. Undramatic as it was in itself, it revealed in microcosm many of the features which were to dominate debate—not only on the Caribbean but about other subsequent colonial crises—in the future: a slowness of response on the part of both Government and official Opposition; a demand by an individual Labour MP both for fuller details on what was happening and for a public inquiry into it; evident discomfort, and equally evident lack of information, from the Government side. In later parliamentary exchanges another portent of the future was to emerge: sharp differences among Opposition Members between the advocates of bipartisanship and the emotionally committed anticolonialists. This mould-setting significance makes Westminster reactions to the Caribbean events worth pursuing in some detail.

On 8 May 1935 William Lunn raised the question of the St Kitts riots, demanded a statement on them, and called for a full inquiry. Replying, Colonial Secretary Sir Philip Cunliffe-Lister admitted that he still had no official information on the upheaval, and very little even from unofficial sources (this over three months after the disturbance!).[36] Not much more was heard for over a year, until in the general colonial debate of 9 July 1936 another Labour back-bencher, Lt.-Commander E. F. Fletcher, again raised the St Kitts affair, a 'very ugly feature indeed', and linked it with what seems to have been the first parliamentary reference to the 'very considerable disturbances' in British Guiana.[37] Fletcher went on to speculate about the causes of this first wave of violence, identifying three major themes. First was the plight of peasant agriculture, which he felt should be remedied by schemes of peasant development (a proposal harking right back to the 1898 Commission, over which there had been forty years of inaction).[38] Second was the state of the sugar industry, on which he wanted to know why British sugar beet producers were heavily subsidised whilst the Caribbean producers suffered. Third was lack of progress towards self-government, 'which

[35] Editorial, *DW* (5 May 1938).
[36] *HC Deb.* (8 May 1935), cols. 955–7.
[37] Ibid. (9 July 1936), col. 1516.
[38] cf. Post, *Arise*, 35–44, 58–67, 114–31.

should be the aim and object of our colonial administration'.[39] He did not suggest, however—and very few Labour spokespeople were to do so—that the demand for self-government was a direct cause of the upheavals.

There was still no response from the Colonial Office; and one reason for this became apparent when in March 1937 Walthamstow Labour MP Valentine McEntee enquired, with bitter irony, whether the Colonial Secretary 'still has reason to believe that there are no unemployed persons in the West Indian islands'. The answer was tragi-comic: officials had no idea at all about unemployment figures anywhere except Jamaica, and no detailed statistics even for there.[40] A few months later Lunn returned to the attack, demanding now a general inquiry into West Indian economic and social conditions, and indulging in some heavy irony of his own with the comment that 'wages are low and unemployment is rife, and yet we are told the people are very pro-British, for which, I suppose, we ought to be very thankful'.[41]

But the irony was double-edged, for Lunn like many Labour speakers apparently genuinely believed in the essential imperial loyalty of the West Indian workers and peasants and asserted that this loyalty imposed special obligations on the British Government. Whether the reference was to a specific matter, Trinidad union leader Uriah Butler's war service, or a generality like the high level of literacy on the islands, the claim was that Caribbean peoples were more like 'us' in their attributes, their aspirations, and their political affections than the Government realised (an explicit contrast was often made with Africans); and therefore should be treated more like 'us' in terms of working conditions, trade union rights, and the franchise. The identification was closest when left-wingers like Jimmy Maxton claimed Butler as a political and emotional soul mate.[42] How such claims are judged may depend on taste: instances of cultural myopia and colonial arrogance; or affirmations, rare for their time, of solidarity across racial lines? They were, I suspect, both.

During 1937 Labour MPs Fletcher, Creech Jones, and David Adams continued to call for an inquiry on labour conditions in the islands, and for the establishment of labour departments in the

[39] *HC Deb.* (9 July 1936), col. 1515.
[40] Ibid., *Written Answers* (24 Mar. 1937), cols. 2923–4.
[41] Ibid. (2 June 1937), col. 1036.
[42] Ibid. (28 Feb. 1938), cols. 816–21.

colonial administrations. It was at the end of the year as news of the Trinidadian explosion began to emerge, though, that the temperature in the Commons really rose. Labour left-winger Ellen Wilkinson (another with long-standing colonial interests: she was a close associate of the India League and had briefly participated in the LAI) wondered angrily whether the presence of British troops 'is not being used to overawe people who are making a perfectly legitimate protest against low wages'.[43] The lone Communist MP, William Gallacher, intervened for the first time, aptly pointing out that deaths of members of the security forces were being described as murder, whilst killings by them were never so labelled.[44] The main thrust of Labour pressure, however, came once again on labour conditions; and now the proposals were more specific. Creech Jones suggested official machinery for industrial conciliation, and minimum wage legislation—once more extracting confessions of ignorance from the Government side. New Colonial Secretary William Ormsby-Gore had 'no idea' what the minimum wage in Trinidad might be.[45] Promises of action were, however, finally forthcoming; and Lunn pointed out the obvious but unpalatable truth that only disturbances seemed to force the Government into action.[46]

A full-scale debate on the risings came at last in February 1938, with the publication of the Forster Commission report on Trinidad. Demands for such a debate, and for a wider inquiry into the crisis, had been mounting in the preceding weeks: though still always from the same small group of Labour colonial specialists.[47] Lunn opened the batting for Labour, reiterating the call for a full Commission of Inquiry, stressing economic neglect, labour conditions, and low wages, and referring once more to the 'loyalty' to Britain of the islands. Welcoming the Government's undertaking to enact labour law reform, he raised a question to which others would return when he questioned what exactly the establishment of trade unions on British lines would involve. Ormsby-Gore replied that it meant craft unions.[48]

---

[43] Ibid. (10 Nov. 1937), col. 1775.
[44] Ibid. (10 Nov. 1937), col. 1756.
[45] Ibid. (7 July 1937), col. 332.
[46] Ibid.
[47] Ibid. (15 Dec. 1937), cols. 1149–50; (9 Feb. 1938), cols. 1044–6; (23 Feb. 1938), cols. 334–8: Questions by Ben Riley, Reginald Sorensen, Creech Jones, David Adams, and F. O. Roberts.
[48] Ibid. (28 Feb. 1938), col. 770.

Lunn concluded his speech with a rather tokenistic advocacy of constitutional reform; the need for which, he believed, underlay the 'economic evil'.[49] Creech Jones spoke on similar lines, placing the main burden on the need for economic development, changes in conditions of labour, and the establishment of soundly based trade unionism. More forcefully than Lunn, he raised fears about the consequences of having government-regulated, craft-based unions; citing South African and German parallels.[50] Trade unions 'should enjoy the full rights of trade unionism as enjoyed in this country'. His conclusions were on the need for immediate steps of labour reform, notably the sending out of labour advisers and the creation of a labour department within the Colonial Office.[51] Yet he also felt that economic change must be accompanied by a longer-term programme of political progress including adult suffrage, though 'I do not want to see political agitation submerge the proposals for economic improvement.'[52]

The same themes were further amplified by another trade unionist with Caribbean interests, Ben Riley. His speech, though, was perhaps remarkable primarily for the casualness with which a suggestion that would have reversed the whole direction of British colonial policy was tossed down and then (on the prompting of former Labour leader George Lansbury) picked up again:

RILEY. I do not want to suggest that we should follow the French example of coloured people, living in the West Indies, being members of Parliament.
MR. LANSBURY. Why not?
MR. RILEY. Well why not? . . . Recognition of that kind appeals very much to the people.[53]

The apparent consensus on the Labour benches—developmentalist, paternalist, emphasising economic rather than political change and firmly excluding talk of decolonisation—was then broken by two of the fiercest left-wingers in the House, Aneurin Bevan and Jimmy Maxton. The latter devoted much of his intervention to a hymn of praise for Uriah Butler. He drew comparisons with the issue then at the forefront of most minds: the threat of fascism in Europe. The young Tory MP Charles Taylor, a noted apologist for the sugar and oil interests, Maxton noted, was a supporter of appeasement but saw Butler as a criminal:

[49] Ibid., col. 772.   [50] Ibid., cols. 793–4.   [51] Ibid., cols. 794–5.
[52] Ibid., col. 796.   [53] Ibid., col. 808.

The hon. Member regards Uriah Butler as a criminal because Uriah Butler is an agitator; but Mussolini is a gentleman. There seems to be a curious double standard of judgement in the hon. Member's mind.[54]

Bevan made probably the most forceful attack on the Government's position; from which he distanced himself much more sharply than did most of his colleagues. He intimated that Ormsby-Gore (with whom Wedgwood Benn had just said he had no major disagreements[55]) should resign. He charged that the revelations about West Indian conditions wholly destroyed the claim that Britain was a better and more humane colonial overlord than other European powers. He alleged—in line with the view taken by *Tribune*, the paper with which he was associated—that the real government of the islands was not by Parliament but by the oil and sugar companies. This meant that 'we in this house are not doing our job. And of course, it is impossible that we should do a job of this kind . . . this House of Commons, as proved by this report on Trinidad, is entirely not to be trusted with the stewardship of these areas.'[56] Thus he repudiated the doctrine of colonial trusteeship which was an article of faith for Labour orthodoxy. As for the specific proposals of reform which Lunn, Creech Jones, Riley, and Wedgwood Benn had advocated or welcomed, Bevan thought them useless:

The report suggests that the way is to send out a labour adviser. I have listened to this talk about labour advisers, and I have heard some of my hon. Friends on this side cheering when they heard that a labour adviser was going out, but really these labour advisers do not matter at all . . . The trade unions are to be organised on a craft basis; in other words, the workers of Trinidad are to be organised in a type of union that minimises and not maximises their strength . . . Those unions that are led by good boys will be registered and will negotiate with the employers, and those unions that are led by bad boys, like Uriah Butler, will not be registered at all; in other words, you will have tame unions, unions that the employers want. This is exactly the situation which exists in Germany, and you will have in Trinidad a National Labour Front . . . That is the kind of freedom we are going to bestow on the people of Trinidad. It is an astonishing story.[57]

The debate on the Forster report was, in the event, the only full-scale discussion the House of Commons was ever to have on the Caribbean revolts. The report of the later and more extensive Moyne Com-

---

[54] Ibid., col. 817.   [55] Ibid., col. 840.
[56] Ibid., col. 849.   [57] Ibid., cols. 850–2.

mission should, of course, have provided the opportunity for a wider-ranging encounter; but that report was in effect suppressed. Only a highly abbreviated version was issued in 1940, when its effect was lost amid the traumas of that stage of the war. The full version only appeared in 1945. As events in Jamaica unfolded, Labour MPs continued to press for a debate on them and later for rapid publication of Moyne; but these calls were blocked. In order to trace reactions to the Jamaican and other upheavals, therefore, it is necessary to turn from the Westminster stage and look at other spheres of Labour movement activity.

With the demise of the League Against Imperialism in 1937, no major radical organisation dealing with the whole range of colonial problems existed in Britain. In the absence of such a body, agitation on colonial problems during the late 1930s was mostly carried on by a variety of single issue, often *ad hoc* lobbies. These usually concerned themselves with a particular colonial territory or region; the most active being Krishna Menon's India League and the International African Service Bureau. None dealt specifically with the Caribbean. The IASB, though many of its activists were West Indians, devoted most of its attention to the African colonies and especially to solidarity with recently conquered Ethiopia. Thus there was no ready-made machinery for action on the Caribbean crisis: and, as we have seen, even on an individual level there were few British radicals with prior interest or expertise.

Of the few individual specialists, Olivier rapidly became the most deeply involved. He raised the issue in the Lords, deluged the Colonial Office with letters and comments, drafted suggestions for Commons Questions and speeches, and generally prodded his younger colleagues into action.[58] His first main concern was the behaviour of the security forces: he drew on his Jamaican experience vehemently to deny the racist common sense of Government and press that Caribbean workers were inherently unruly and prone to violence.[59] Later in representations to Ministers and in his evidence to the Moyne Commission he argued the case—which he had been making for more than forty years—for substantial British aid in

[58] See correspondence in Arthur Creech Jones papers (Rhodes House, Oxford: hereafter ACJ); *HL Deb.* (23 Feb. and 2 June 1938); Post, *Arise*, 327, 336–8, 359–63, 442–6; and Francis Lee, *Fabianism and Colonialism: The Life and Political Thought of Lord Sydney Olivier* (Defiant Books, 1988).

[59] *HL Deb.* (2 June 1938), col. 880.

economic development and for trade union rights: though he doubted
the sincerity of the Government's new-found commitment to the
latter, which seemed to him like a 'death bed repentance'.[60] His
attitude to government regulation of industrial relations, however,
was very different from that of left-wing critics like Bevan. Whereas
Bevan saw such regulation as a major threat and invoked Nazi
parallels, Olivier had apparent faith in the capacity of colonial
administrators to act as neutral arbiters checking the power of
capital.[61] This sat a little oddly with his own earlier scorn for the
intellectual capacities and progressive potential of the colonial civil
service.[62]

Another Labour figure with close Caribbean involvements was
Professor W. M. Macmillan, a key member of the LPACIQ. He had
recently returned from a fact-finding tour of the region on which he
had liaised closely with officials; and as a result published in 1936 a
book entitled *Warning from the West Indies*. Appearing as it did just
before the major eruptions, the title alone would have ensured that it
came to be seen as prophetic, and it certainly had an impact both on
official thinking and on the development of Labour's colonial policy.[63]
Its argument stressed the need for centrally directed economic
planning for development; sharing much of Olivier's apparent faith
that the Colonial Office could, if given a different political lead,
become a major force for progress. Yet in a sense the book's subtitle,
A Tract for Africa and the Empire, gave the most accurate indication of
Macmillan's intentions. Like much British discussion of the Caribbean
before and after 1937–8, the primary aim was to use the region as an
example, both for good and for bad, of what might happen on the
larger stage of the African colonies. The West Indies, Macmillan
argued, 'have shown what men of African race can do when given any
opportunity'; but alas in Africa 'the significance of West Indian
experience is completely wasted and warnings go unheeded'.[64]

---

[60] Olivier to Creech Jones (9 Aug. 1938); ACJ 25/6/15–17.
[61] Ibid.
[62] Olivier to Leonard Woolf (30 Apr. 1936); quoted in Partha Sarathi Gupta,
Imperialism and the British Labour Movement, 1914–1964 (Macmillan, 1975), 245–6.
Olivier had stormed that colonial officials were 'mostly third-rate products of the
educational system of our capitalistic society ... incapable of taking a socialist point of
view, or of regarding black people as commensurable human beings'.
[63] W. M. Macmillan, *Warning from the West Indies* (Faber & Faber, 1936; 2nd edn.,
Harmondsworth: Penguin, 1938). See also Mona Macmillan, *Champion of Africa* (Long
Wittenham: the author, 1985), ch. 4.
[64] Macmillan, *Warning*, 17 (1936 edn.).

Arthur Creech Jones, by contrast, had his attention for a time turned almost wholly from African to Caribbean problems by the risings. He established a wide range of contacts, both directly with the islands and with West Indian sources in Britain like Moody and Padmore; and came to act as the main link between them and British Labour circles.[65] Thus he also provided much of the impetus behind the first important association between a major Labour movement organisation, the Fabian Society, and Caribbean affairs. In fact the initial approach had come from the other side and had preceded the disturbances themselves. In 1935 St Lucian Arthur Lewis, then at the LSE, wrote modestly suggesting that if Labour and Fabians wanted information on regional economic conditions he might be able to help. From this tentative idea came the only significant British Labour movement publication on the risings (and for that matter the only general published work on the whole issue before Ken Post's studies): Lewis's pamphlet *Labour in the West Indies*.[66]

Other West Indian political figures in Britain, by contrast, responded to the risings in surprisingly muted fashion. Harold Moody and the LCP, indeed, acted as an important conveyor belt of information—including correspondence from, among others, the Mayor of Kingston—between the islands and Creech Jones; as, to a lesser extent, did Padmore and the IASB. Moody bombarded *The Times* with letters, presided over protest meetings, and, in conjunction with the IASB and the Negro Welfare Association, presented radical recommendations to the Moyne Commission.[67] Yet neither the

[65] See correspondence with Moody, Padmore, Ken Hill, Wallace-Johnson, and others in ACJ, Box 25.

[66] Lewis to John Parker, New Fabian Research Bureau Secretary (12 Mar. 1935), ACJ 25/1A/8; W. Arthur Lewis, *Labour in the West Indies* (Fabian Research series 44, 1939). Correspondence relating to, and successive drafts of, the pamphlet are in ACJ, Box 25, file 1A. The longer-term significance of the ideas first presented there has been ably discussed by Susan Craig in her Afterword to the pamphlet's 1977 republication ('Germs of an Idea', in Lewis, *Labour* (2nd edn., New Beacon, 1977). It will thus not be pursued here except for one general point: which is that Craig's account is heavily coloured by hindsight. Thus she so strongly stresses the cautious reformism of Lewis's stance, and its consonance with the later pattern of dependent development in the region, that one might lose sight of just how radical the same proposals were in the context of 1930s British thinking. Certainly Lewis would, then and later, be placed clearly on Labour's left; and the pamphlet was a revelation for those Labour planners interested in colonial economic policy. See for instance Leonard Woolf to John Parker (5 Apr. 1935), ACJ 25/1A/11.

[67] For instance, Moody to Creech Jones (13 June 1938), ACJ 25/1/22; Creech Jones to Moody (22 July 1938), ACJ 25/1/39; Wallace-Johnson to Creech Jones (14

League nor the Bureau turned its whole attention to this issue: nor is this really very remarkable. The London-based West Indians too were hampered by lack of up-to-date information: they had few contacts among the key actors in the rebellions themselves. And their main preoccupations were elsewhere: for the LCP with the position of black people in Britain itself, for the IASB with Africa. Padmore, James, Makonnen, and the rest had become convinced that the most important developments in the colonial world, and for the future of the peoples in the African diaspora, would take place in Africa. It was an African issue, the Italian invasion of Ethiopia, which had first brought them together. As James later pointed out, even when he was at this time writing on Caribbean history, in *The Black Jacobins*, he was doing so with at least one eye on likely future African developments.[68] Makonnen does not even mention the risings in his autobiography.[69]

More peculiar was the reaction of perhaps the most influential, and controversial, West Indian of his time, Marcus Garvey. Jamaican-born Garvey, spending his last years in London in the period of the rebellions, was already in many ways a broken man. His once massive US-based Universal Negro Improvement Association had collapsed in a welter of incompetence, corruption, and government persecution. And there had always been a strong streak of social conservatism, coupled with vehement anti-socialism, in Garvey's eclectic ideology. None the less his hostile reaction to the 1930s revolts marked a remarkable volte-face for a formerly vociferous anticolonialist—and has proved rather an embarrassment to his subsequent admirers, most of whom have passed over the matter in silence.[70] Garvey's comments on the labour unrest, as on so much else, were inconsistent; but their dominant thread was denunciation of the strikes and riots as the product of 'agitators' and Communists. His pronouncements on

and 16 Feb. and 7 Mar. 1938 and enclosures), ACJ 25/1/142–53; Padmore to Creech Jones (29 Nov. 1938), ACJ 25/5/282. See also Fryer, *Staying Power*, 330.

[68] See the Appendix, 'From Toussaint L'Ouverture to Fidel Castro', in the 1980 edition of *The Black Jacobins*.

[69] Makonnen, *Pan-Africanism*.

[70] The two leading Garvey scholars, Robert A. Hill and Tony Martin, have (at least in their published work so far) almost bypassed the issue: Martin's scattered references to it in *The Pan-African Connection* (Dover, Mass.: The Majority Press, 1983), chs. 4, 5, and 8; and in *Race First* (Westport, Conn.: Greenwood Press, 1976), are apologetic. Rupert Lewis, *Marcus Garvey: Anti-Colonial Champion* (Karia Press, 1987), though generally a near-hagiographic biography, has a fuller and more critical account (pp. 258–73).

these lines during a 1937 visit to Trinidad were greeted with anger and disillusion by many erstwhile devotees.[71]

In the aftermath of the Jamaican revolt, however, an organisation was formed in London to press for change and self-government in the islands. This body, the Committee on West Indian Affairs, began meeting in November 1938. Both its British and its West Indian members spanned a broad political spectrum: the former ranging from Communist sympathisers like Reginald Bridgeman and D. N. Pritt, through Fabians like Creech Jones, to Labour right-wingers like Grenadian-born Dr Hyacinth Morgan; the latter including the militant Peter Blackman as well as the more conservative Moody. Paul Robeson was also drawn in, and offered to stage fundraising concerts for the group,[72] whilst, from Jamaica, both People's National Party leader Norman Manley and left-winger Ken Hill established contact.[73]

The sympathies of the Committee were strongly with the newly formed PNP, which itself embraced views ranging from Manley's moderate constitutionalism to Hill's Marxism. Their contacts were inevitably hampered by communication problems after the outbreak of war, and the Committee's activities seem rapidly to have declined. Some of those involved at the start lost interest, the hitherto ubiquitous anticolonialist Bridgeman among them. Although he lived until 1968 he appears to have abandoned public political activity after the early 1940s. The dominant figures from the British side became Labour MP David Adams, the chairman, and Rita Hinden of the Fabians. Tension soon emerged between these gradualist thinkers and the West Indian Marxists on the Committee, who were now led by Blackman. The latter envisaged the group as a public campaigning body mobilising popular solidarity with the regional nationalist movements, while the British Fabians wanted a more modest role, primarily lobbying MPs and officials.

In May 1943 the British MPs decided to dissolve the Committee, citing both these divisions and the alleged ineffectiveness of the body as their reasons.[74] Blackman responded bitterly to the decision and an acrimonious correspondence ensued, with Adams accusing Blackman of 'ill-founded malice' and saying that it was in any case

---

[71] Ibid. 269–73.
[72] Minutes of Committee meeting (21 Feb. 1939), ACJ 25/1/165–70.
[73] Ibid. (20 Dec. 1938), FCB 2/7/31–3.
[74] Adams to Hinden (7 May 1943), FCB 16/1/85.

'grotesque' to think that the Committee was playing any serious part in bringing about progress in the Caribbean.[75] Both Blackman and Adams expressed their intentions of forming successor committees, each excluding the other's supporters: neither seems to have come to anything.[76]

As this small group faltered and collapsed, others in and around the British Communist Party were taking a growing interest in the Caribbean. The National Council for Civil Liberties, then under a degree of CPGB influence, had responded to the risings by pressing MPs to use their influence in getting a public inquiry instituted;[77] and with the appearance of the Forster report held a public protest meeting condemning both government actions and the report itself, which 'seems openly to encourage shooting as the best means of repressing demonstrations of striking workmen'.[78] Gradually, after 1938, contacts evolved between CPGB colonial specialists and the small group of Jamaican Marxists around Richard Hart. As Ken Post notes, it would appear that some limited moves had already been made: Jamaican labour activist H. C. Buchanan had been in touch with Ben Bradley, the former Meerut treason trial defendant who ran the CPGB's Colonial Information Bulletin.[79] Bradley and four other CPGB members lobbied the Colonial Office and sought association with the Moyne Commission (not surprisingly, they were rebuffed); and at the end of 1938 Harry Pollitt, the CPGB General Secretary, made contact with Hart on a holiday visit to Jamaica.[80] These rather tenuous initial links provided the foundation for a more extensive association between British and Caribbean Marxists after the war, which is discussed in the following chapter.

[75] Blackman to Adams (15 May 1943); Adams to Blackman (24 May 1943), FCB 16/1/92–3.

[76] Blackman to Adams (17 May 1943); Adams to Creech Jones (24 May 1943), FCB 16/1/92 and 94.

[77] Ronald Kidd, NCCL General Secretary, to Creech Jones (15 Dec. 1937), ACJ 25/5/37.

[78] NCCL Press Release and report of meeting at Conway Hall, London, on 3 Mar. 1938 (ACJ 25/1A/15–17).

[79] Post, *Arise*, 358.

[80] Ibid. 358–9; Richard Hart, *Rise and Organise: The Birth of the Workers and National Movements in Jamaica (1936–1939)* (Karia Press, 1989), 148–9. Hart suggests that contact with Bradley came only after, and because of, Pollitt's visit.

III. AGAINST WAR AND IMPERIALISM

Both the Radical-Liberal and the Leninist critiques of imperialism saw it as intimately linked with militarism and war. For the former rivalry over colonial possessions was the prime cause of international tension: the roots of the First World War had lain in Africa and Asia. This view was also developed independently by African-American thinker W. E. B. DuBois, and was adopted after 1918 by the Union of Democratic Control, which argued alternatively for a redistribution of colonies or for their placing under League of Nations supervision as a precaution against new conflicts.[81]

For the Leninist theory, the link between colonial rule and imperialist war was less direct but more inevitable: both were epiphenomena of capitalism in its imperialist stage. Rivalry over spheres of economic influence, itself made inescapable by the 'parasitic, decaying' nature of advanced capitalism,[82] was ineluctably accompanied by struggles for the redivision of the non-European world and thus by inter-imperialist wars.

Yet as the second war with Germany itself came to appear ever more inevitable, only restricted sections of the British left actively pressed either of these views. Events in Europe itself became, especially after the eruption of civil war in Spain, the main focus of attention for both Communist and Labour Parties; to the detriment of even the fitful concern they had hitherto shown for colonial problems. Most, in so far as they invoked imperialism at all as an explanatory category relevant to the threat of war, used the label loosely to describe the policies of the Axis powers.[83]

Within the Labour Party a mixture of pacifism, the UDC legacy, misgivings over the Versailles settlement, and the climate of appeasement led to a widespread discussion on the idea of giving Germany and Italy outlets for their ambitions in the colonial sphere. But except in the wilder imaginings of some pacifists or the wishful thinking of

---

[81] J. A. Hobson, *Imperialism: A Study* (James Nisbet & Co., 1902), and H. N. Brailsford, *The War of Steel and Gold* (Bell, 1914) W. E. B. DuBois, 'The African Roots of War', *Atlantic Monthly*, 115 (May 1915); Martin Ceadel, *Pacifism in Britain, 1914–1945: The Defining of a Faith* (Oxford: Oxford University Press, 1980).

[82] V. I. Lenin, *Imperialism* (Peking: Foreign Languages Press, 1975), 122.

[83] The best contemporary left-wing discussion employing the notion was Franz Neumann's pioneering *Behemoth: The Structure and Practice of National Socialism* (Gollancz, 1942). See esp. part 1, ch. 6, 'The Theory of Racial Imperialism'.

pro-Nazi 'fellow travellers',[84] it could not seriously be believed either that handing over African colonies would resolve European tensions or that a substitution of German for British rule would be other than a change for the worse for the subject peoples. Such proposals never came near to becoming party policy, or indeed that of the Government.[85] They none the less continued, almost to the outbreak of war, to arouse left-wing concern. A conference in July 1939, addressed among others by Creech Jones, Stafford Cripps, and Moody, condemned 'the policy which would redivide the territories inhabited by African peoples as a means of appeasing the Fascist powers'.[86]

From 1934 onward the Communist Party, abandoning the sectarianism of the Class Against Class period, had adopted a Popular Front policy. This advocated a broad alliance of 'democratic' forces against the fascist threat—and co-operation with social-democratic and liberal parties in European countries necessarily implied a muting, if not an abandonment, of calls for the destruction of those countries' colonial empires. This, together with the new concentration on European events, led the Comintern virtually to suspend anti-colonial activity.

Although the CPGB remained verbally committed at least to Indian independence, its position on colonial issues soon appeared little more radical than Labour's. Whilst continuing to see imperialism (now perhaps more vaguely defined than ever before in Communist discourse) as responsible for the threat of war, it regarded the Axis powers as the prime if not exclusive culprits, and joined with most of the Labour left in strongly opposing any redistribution of colonies.[87] The links between Germany's imperial ambitions within Europe and

[84] Richard Griffiths, *Fellow Travellers of the Right: British Enthusiasts for Nazi Germany, 1933–39* (Constable, 1980).

[85] For the debate, see Gupta, *Imperialism*, 237–42; Leonard Barnes, *Empire or Democracy?* (Gollancz, 1939), 13–70; Lionel Birch, *The Demand for Colonies* (League of Nations Union pamphlet, 1936); Labour Party, *The Demand for Colonial Territories and Equality of Economic Opportunity* (Labour Party pamphlet, 1936); National Peace Council, *Peace and the Colonial Problem* (NPC pamphlet, 1935/6). This last includes, intriguingly, a brief contribution by James Joyce. On the seriousness of colonial 'revisionism' in Hitler's foreign policy, see Hartmut Pogge von Strandmann, 'Imperialism and Revisionism in Interwar Germany', in Wolfgang Mommsen and Juergen Osterhammel (eds.), *Imperialism and After: Continuities and Discontinuities* (Allen & Unwin/German Historical Institute, 1986).

[86] Report in *Labour Research*, 28/8 (Aug. 1939), 186.

[87] Ben Bradley, *Colonies, Mandates and Peace* (CPGB pamphlet, 1936).

the British colonial possessions seemed exceedingly tenuous: the latter could no longer be presented as causes of war as they had been after 1929.

For some on the left, though—for the ILP, for most radical nationalists and their *émigré* circles in Britain, and for the small British Trotskyist sects—these connections were still crucial. The coming war, they argued, was a conflict of rival imperialisms, in which neither socialists not colonial peoples should have any part except in so far as it ripened conditions for revolution. Black radicals asserted that it was the merest hypocrisy for Britain—or indeed British Communists—to proclaim opposition to fascism and defence of democracy whilst holding the colonies in a manner which itself amounted to colonial fascism. George Orwell (a former member of, and still close to, the ILP) for a time expressed a similar view: Britain's claim to defend democracy was valid, he said, only with the unspoken proviso 'not counting niggers'.[88] The British-based black radical groups went further: fascism within Europe was simply the reproduction of philosophies and methods of rule long practised on non-Europeans, now arousing condemnation only because for the first time the victims had white skins.[89]

It is unlikely that many nationalists held the view that there was nothing to choose between the Allied and the Axis powers. The stance of Nehru, a passionate pre-war anti-fascist who nevertheless argued that under its threat 'the nationalist position, the question of India versus England, had in no way changed'[90] was far more typical than that of Subhas Chandra Bose, for whom his enemy's enemy was his friend. Yet it was inevitable that some colonial nationalists should react favourably to the Axis leaders' apparent championing of their claims: especially in South-East Asia where the threat to European hegemony came from fellow Asians, and in the Arab world. This was, of course, deeply troubling and embarrassing for British supporters of Arab nationalism; as one such, Reginald Reynolds, wrote to another, Thomas Hodgkin:

[88] George Orwell, *Collected Essays, Journalism and Letters* (Harmondsworth: Penguin, 1976), i. 434–7.

[89] See the Anti-War Manifesto sponsored by various black radical groups (primarily the Padmore–Makonnen axis wearing different hats) and published in the *New Leader* (24 Nov. 1939). This view of fascism was given its canonical formulation by the leading Francophone philosopher of Negritude, Aime Cesaire, *Discours sur le colonialisme* (Paris: Presence Africaine, 1955).

[90] Jawaharlal Nehru, *The Discovery of India* (Meridian, 1946), 379.

It is peculiarly unfortunate for our case that Hitler and Mussolini should have espoused it for their own purposes. They are such melodramatic villains, and our 'Left' public has such a melodramatic mind, that some people seem to find it difficult to believe a fascist can even tell the truth! ... What is really deplorable is that Hitler and Mussolini gain kudos with the Arabs ... while our so-called 'socialists' and 'democrats' are discrediting socialism and democracy by associating these names with oppression.[91]

The most militant anti-war factions in Britain, however, could transcend such agonisings by reducing the impending conflict to the grand simplicity of imperialist rivalries, as an ILP policy declaration of 1938 sought to do:

The threat of World War is due to Capitalism. The Capitalist class in the 'Have' Empire nations cling to advantages won by the sword. The Capitalist class in the 'Have Not' nations threaten to use the sword to win Empires. Their rival Capitalist interests clash.[92]

Overt opposition to the war, when it came, was expressed by only a few small groups within British politics. Although retrospective perceptions of the war years as a period of complete national unity were of course greatly exaggerated, the outspoken expression of fundamental criticism was much constrained by wartime conditions. This applied not least to criticism in the colonial field. Not surprisingly, it was those groups who opposed the war effort itself who also devoted the most continued, harshly critical attention to developments in the Empire. Between 1939 and 1941 the CPGB adopted such an attitude; but, after the German invasion of Russia and the subsequent volte-face by the Communists, only a few far left groups opposed both the war and the Empire. The Independent Labour Party, though undergoing a rapid decline in membership and influence, was the most important of these; but the tiny cliques of British Trotskyists also now emerged as a strident and distinctive voice.

There were in the late 1930s four Trotskyist formations in Britain: the Wicks–Sara group, remnants of the very first British supporters of Trotsky, expelled from the CPGB in 1932; the Militant, a faction within the Labour Party producing a cyclostyled paper of that name;[93] the Marxist League, a clique around C. L. R. James operating within

---

[91] Reynolds to Hodgkin (11 Nov. 1937) (Hodgkin papers).

[92] *Socialist Policy for 1938*, ILP Conference Resolutions (ILP pamphlet, 1938), 3.

[93] *Not* a direct ancestor of the present-day Militant tendency; though as will be seen there are connections between the two.

the ILP and producing the paper *Worker's Fight*; and the largest sect, the Workers' International League, formed by ex-merchant seaman Jock Haston in Paddington in 1936. Only the last had more than a few dozen members, and it was probably no more than 350 strong in 1942.[94]

Ideas about imperialism and colonial revolution occupied as important a place in Trotskyist thought as they did in orthodox Communism, but their theoretical basis was of course rather different. Trotsky's early views had been at least as Eurocentric as those of Lenin, but as with Lenin the revolutions of 1905 and 1917 had stimulated a process of rethinking leading to the view that colonies and 'semi-colonies' might play a key role in world revolution. This conviction arose from Trotsky's theory of combined and uneven development which argued in essence that different regions of the world economy would develop at different paces and in different ways, while remaining interrelated so as to constitute the world capitalist system as an organic whole. Within this system the advanced countries—and hence the revolutionary role of the proletariat in those countries—remained central; but in less developed areas weak links in the chain might break, as had happened in Russia and as, so Trotsky believed, would have happened in China in the late 1920s but for the errors of Stalin. Such colonial revolutions would, however, be primarily the work of the urban workers, *not* the peasantry or nationalist bourgeoisie, of the colonies; and they could succeed only if supported by successful outbreaks elsewhere and particularly in the advanced countries. The view that they could survive alone and the consequent theory of 'socialism in one country' Trotsky saw as Stalin's gravest theoretical mistake.

Equally, revolution could succeed only if it led to a fully-fledged socialist state. This was the theory of the permanent revolution. Even if the initial revolutionary upsurge were led by the bourgeoisie or was

---

[94] On British Trotskyism before 1945 see John Callaghan, *British Trotskyism: Theory and Practice* (Oxford: Blackwell, 1984); Peter Shipley, *Revolutionaries in Modern Britain* (Bodley Head, 1976); Michael Crick, *Militant* (Faber & Faber, 1984); Jim Higgins, 'British Trotskyism, 1938–48', *International Socialism*, 13 (1963); the biographical notes in David Widgery (ed.), *The Left in Britain* (Harmondsworth: Penguin, 1976); *C. L. R. James and British Trotskyism: An interview* (Socialist Platform pamphlet, 1987); and by far the fullest, though pious, accounts: Sam Bornstein and Al Richardson, *Against the Stream: A History of the Trotskyist Movement in Britain, 1924–38* (Socialist Platform, 1986), and id. and id., *War and the International: A History of the Trotskyist Movement in Britain, 1938–1949* (Socialist Platform, 1986).

directed purely towards political independence from a foreign power, it must transform itself into a proletarian socialist revolution. The implications of this were clear: the support given by orthodox Communists to bourgeois nationalists in the colonies, however provisional and critical it might be, was misguided. Success could come only if the correct revolutionary leadership was given. The bourgeoisie might initiate the process, the peasants might play an important supporting role, but only industrial workers under revolutionary Marxist guidance could carry it to fulfilment.

Thus Trotskyism placed greater emphasis on prospects for revolution in the Third World than, by the 1930s, orthodox Communism was doing. It was more sceptical, on the other hand, about a possible progressive role for nationalism (for which Trotsky, the most confirmed internationalist among the Bolsheviks, had an innate distaste), for the peasantry or for the colonial bourgeoisie. It took a considerably more critical view of broad fronts and movements not led by Marxists.[95] It may be doubted, however, how far the tiny groups of British Trotskyists had really assimilated these ideas of their mentor, or the even wider-ranging theories of C. L. R. James, the only one of their number really well informed on colonial movements. Although in 1938 James and others had been able briefly to unite three of the four groups—the Wicks–Sara clique, Militant, and James's Marxist League—into the Revolutionary Socialist League, this soon fragmented and most of its members disappeared back into the Labour Party or ILP, until in 1944 they came together with the larger Workers' International League (WIL) to form the Revolutionary Communist Party.

Between 1939 and 1944, then, independent (or open as opposed to entryist) Trotskyist activity was effectively confined to the WIL. Its journal, *Socialist Appeal*, with an average circulation of about 2,000, was edited by a South African *émigré*, Edward Grant.[96] Grant's

---

[95] For general discussions of Trotsky's views on imperialism and Third World revolution, see Baruch Knei-Paz, *The Social and Political Thought of Leon Trotsky* (Oxford: Oxford University Press, 1978), esp. 86–107, 113–74, 324–31, 358–66; and Ernest Mandel, *Trotsky: A Study in the Dynamic of his Thought* (New Left Books, 1979)—an uncritical account, but perhaps a clearer basic sketch than Knei-Paz's rather disjointed presentation. The standard biography, Isaac Deutscher, *The Prophet Outcast: Trotsky 1929–1940* (Oxford: Oxford University Press, 1963), says little on Trotsky's views of these issues.

[96] Later the main theoretician and long-serving leader of the Militant tendency within Labour.

origins might have been expected to give him a particular interest in colonial affairs, and *Socialist Appeal* did devote considerable space to the subject. Generally, though, this was as an adjunct to its determined denunciation of the British war effort, and little real knowledge of colonial issues was in evidence. The paper's knowing claim that Britain had expelled Italy from Abyssinia only in order to install her own bankers there, for instance, rather forfeited credibility by its misspelling of 'Abbyssinia'—quite apart from the fact that there was no significant British investment in the region.[97]

The WIL did have access to rather more information on India: there was an Indian, Ajit Roy, among its leading members; the Secretary of the Birmingham Indian Workers' Association appeared on WIL platforms; and it took a particular interest in developments in Ceylon where there was a sister party, the Trotskyist Lanka Sama Samaja.[98] The WIL was, naturally, bitterly hostile to the bourgeois nationalists of Congress: in the November 1941 *Socialist Appeal* another leading member, Gerry Healy, denounced them for betraying the Indian masses.[99] The CPI was even more deeply despised: it had, the WIL alleged, adopted 'blackleg' tactics against the nationalist struggle, acting 'under the tutelage of Dutt and Pollitt'.[100] In line with the orthodox Trotskyist prescription for the role of industrial workers, *Socialist Appeal* urged those of India to seize power, free the peasants, and then 'shatter' both British and Japanese imperialism.[101]

The most intensive efforts at publicisation of Indian problems by the WIL, though, came during the great Bengal famine in 1943. This, one of the worst human disasters of the century, resulted in an estimated three million deaths—but received very little publicity in

[97] *Socialist Appeal* editorial (July 1941): 'Abbyssinia Liberated—for Barclay's Bank'.

[98] Sri Lanka was and long remained one of the very few countries with a mass Trotskyist movement, which retained close relations with British Trotskyists. For Roy's reminiscences ('when I think of my faith in those days, I feel very amused'), see Bornstein and Richardson, *Against the Stream*, 262–3; *War*, 8–9.

[99] *Socialist Appeal* (Nov. 1941). Healy later became leader of the Workers' Revolutionary Party, holding near-dictatorial power over his band of followers until his disgrace in 1986 over alleged sexual exploitation of young women party members.

[100] *Socialist Appeal* (mid-Sept. 1943): article by Hakim Mirza. This was the pseudonym of A. C. Bannerji (1895–1967), a former CPI representative at the Comintern, who had broken with the Communists in 1941 and joined the WIL, but who rejoined the CP in the early 1950s. See Bornstein and Richardson, *War*, 135, 156.

[101] *Socialist Appeal* (Aug. 1942): article by Andrew Scott (pseudonym of Andrew Paton, one of the WIL's most prolific publicists; see Bornstein and Richardson, *War*, 13, 54).

the mainstream British press at the time. *Socialist Appeal* and the *New Leader* (and in rather more muted key *Tribune* and the *New Statesman*), by contrast, gave it prominent coverage, linking it with their general attacks on British imperialism and the war effort. The journals of the WIL and ILP both argued that this was in essence a man-made famine, attributable in large measure to government policies: a view which has found support in some significant subsequent scholarly work.[102]

In January 1944 the WIL and the remnants of the RSL—some 400 members in all—merged to form the Revolutionary Communist Party. The amalgamation, undertaken after pressure from the Fourth International, failed to conceal deep divisions of policy between the various groups involved. These centred on whether the new RCP should operate openly and independently, or should practise entryism: the strategy of working within other, larger parties and seeking to take control of or at least win members from them. Initially a compromise was reached; some members would continue to work secretly within Labour and the ILP, others would campaign as an open party.[103]

The factions were united, however, around a remarkable optimism about the imminent prospects of revolution for Britain. In this perspective hopes for the downfall of the Empire were crucial. The RCP's 1945 conference 'envisaged the bloody collapse of British imperialism in India. The consequent loss of "economic tribute", it was argued, would entail a greater rate of exploitation of British workers in order for the bourgeoisie to maintain its position . . . this would create conditions which would be "the most revolutionary in the whole of British history".'[104]

Thus the Trotskyists devoted much attention to Indian and colonial problems during the war, at a time when very few in Britain were prepared to admit either to the economic disasters or to the

[102] *Socialist Appeal* (Feb., Mar., July, Oct., Nov., Dec. 1943; mid–Jan. 1944). Amartya Sen, *Poverty and Famines* (Oxford: Oxford University Press, 1981), argues that the famine was in essence a social rather than purely natural disaster, for which government must bear much of the blame. The CPGB also criticised British handling of the affair, though in far more cautious terms than did the WIL: see Ben Bradley, *India's Famine: The Facts* (CPGB pamphlet, Nov. 1943).

[103] Bornstein and Richardson, *War*, ch. 4 *passim*.

[104] Callaghan, *British Trotskyism*, 30. This messianism was short-lived: soon thereafter the British Trotskyists were to stand out within the International for their relative realism about the prospects for capitalism's survival: Bornstein and Richardson, *War*, 172–80; and see below, pp. 183–8.

extent of the political opposition which wracked India. Yet they were a tiny and isolated group who could have little wider impact. Considerably more important, though in rapid decline and almost equal political isolation, was the ILP, also strongly opposed to the war. It was an opposition which came from diverse sources: some were out-and-out pacifists; some believed that fascism could only be defeated if there were first a socialist revolution in Britain (so that the immediate task was to work for that revolution rather than for the defeat of Germany); others, including Maxton and Brockway, felt that the only solution to the world crisis was a general rising of the workers in occupied Europe, in all the belligerent countries, and in their colonies.[105] For all these views, but especially for the last, the colonial revolution occupied a key place in hopes for the future.

The ILP during the 1940s exhibited a striking variety of political and theoretical influences. In contrast to the rigid orthodoxy of the CPGB's Marxism and to the general ignorance of foreign socialist traditions in the Labour Party, writings by ILP members on imperialism drew on many heretical or forgotten strands of socialist thought. John McNair's *Make Britain Socialist Now!* of 1942 discussed imperialism in terms drawn straight from Hobson.[106] W. L. Taylor's *The Trusts Versus the People* combined a Kautskyite conception of 'ultra-imperialism' with a financial conspiracy theory which would not have been out of place in Walton Newbold's work.[107] F. A. Ridley drew on anarchist ideas, and Bob Edwards on Leninist conceptions of imperialism; both in a book arguing for a Socialist United States of Europe—a slogan drawn from Trotsky.[108] Walter Padley was an enthusiast for the then little-known ideas of Rosa Luxemburg.[109] It was a remarkable mixture to be found within one tiny party: but then one of the ILP's founders, Bruce Glasier, had argued back in 1901 that inconsistency was a great human virtue.[110]

The basis for the ILP's belief that there was very little to choose

[105] The ILP dubbed this idea the 'Third Front'. See Brockway's article in the *New Leader* (13 Feb. 1943).

[106] John McNair, *Make Britain Socialist Now!* (ILP 'Socialist Britain' pamphlet, 1942).

[107] *The Trusts Versus the People* (National Labour Press pamphlet, 1944).

[108] *The United Socialist States of Europe* (National Labour Press, 1944). Ridley had indeed been one of the earliest British admirers of Trotsky, working mostly with Indian and Ceylonese leftist students in London, but had long since broken with Trotskyism. See Bornstein and Richardson, *Against the Stream*, ch. 2 *passim*.

[109] See for instance his articles in the *New Leader* (31 May 1941 and 16 Jan. 1943).

[110] J. Bruce Glasier, 'Tolstoy's Political Appeal', *ILP News* (June 1901).

between the two sides in the world war—a belief founded on its view of the colonial empires—was argued at length by Brockway in 1942:

> Nazism is Capitalist Dictatorship . . . But Imperialism is also a Capitalist Dictatorship.
>
> Under Imperialism the native peoples are denied democratic rights. In that it is similar to Nazism . . .
>
> There is no personal freedom in Germany. Anyone can be put in prison or concentration camp for an indefinite period without trial. This is also a commonplace in India and the Crown Colonies . . .
>
> The Nazis in Germany regard themselves as a superior race and treat the Jews particularly as though they were sub-human animals. This is also the attitude of the white 'Sahibs' towards the coloured peoples . . .
>
> Is it not clear that no Socialist—indeed, no sincere democrat—can identify himself with Imperialism against Nazism, or can be satisfied with an end of the war which would destroy the Nazi form of dictatorship only?[111]

On a more analytical level McNair argued that both underconsumption and the need for raw materials made it impossible for any capitalist state willingly to give up its colonies: these were 'inevitable drives in Capitalist-Imperialism'. Yet retention of the colonies undermined any claim Britain might make to be fighting for democracy.[112]

The ILP made two main demands in the colonial sphere. First, the immediate offer of independence to all colonies, under Constituent Assemblies elected by adult suffrage. Secondly, all economic resources to be returned to indigenous control, 'with an offer of technical assistance on the understanding that the wealth produced should be utilised for educational, social and industrial development'.[113] It was a radical programme, particularly when taken in conjunction with the party's stated belief that it could only fully be implemented by a revolutionary socialist Britain, participating in an eventual United Socialist States of Europe. Without such socialist European unity 'American Imperialism with Britain as its bailiffs in Europe would

---

[111] Fenner Brockway, *The Way Out* (ILP 'Socialist Britain' pamphlet, 1942), 2, 4–7.

[112] *Make Britain Socialist Now!*, 11. It will be seen that Brockway is here using 'imperialism' as synonymous with colonial rule, whilst McNair is employing the term in a sense nearer to Lenin's, but explaining it in Hobsonian style.

[113] 1942 ILP Conference Resolutions reproduced in John McNair, *What the Independent Labour Party Stands For* (ILP pamphlet, 1945), 13.

dominate the world'.[114] But it was inevitably still not radical enough for some within the party's ranks, and particularly not for the small Trotskyist groups who dominated some of its branches.[115] The Trotskyists especially attacked the critical support extended by the ILP to bourgeois nationalist parties. They argued that:

the mass struggle against imperialism . . . would not stop at the struggle for national independence, but would turn against the Indian exploiters as well. That is why the Congress as representative of the Indian landlords and capitalists, has betrayed the national struggle . . . they are incapable of carrying through the national struggle to the end.[116]

Even Nehru, they suggested, 'represents the capitalists . . . he disguises himself behind a cloak of socialist phrases'.

There was a seeming paradox in the ILP's strong support for colonial nationalist movements; for it, perhaps more than any other group on the left at the time, espoused an extreme brand of inter-nationalism and disdain for the whole notion of the nation-state. Nationalism, Frank Ridley argued, was a result of the rise of the bourgeoisie and was now outdated: 'internationalism is, for Socialism, what Nationalism itself was for the Capitalist age.'[117] The party programme said that 'Our final object is the establishment of a World Socialist Commonwealth.'[118] Yet for the ILP as for radical anti-colonialism generally, that long-term aim had apparently to be sought through a more immediate objective of supporting a myriad nationalist and secessionist demands.

Several different arguments could be, and were, adduced to suggest that there was no contradiction here. International unity of a stable and progressive sort, it was claimed, could come only between sovereign states on a basis of equality; so that the transformation of

---

[114] *Final Agenda* of Resolutions for 1944 ILP Conference (ILP 1944), 20; reproduced also in MacNair, *What the ILP Stands For*, 10.

[115] At the ILP's 1943 and 1944 conferences, eight branches seem to have adopted Trotskyist positions—Wallsend, Tooting, Newcastle Central, Birmingham North, Sunderland, Huddersfield, Leeds Central, and Battersea—a judgement based on analysis of conference resolutions and on annotations by a delegate in the copies of conference documents in Nuffield College Library. Of these branches, Tooting was by far the most active: an activism centred on Gerry Healy's wife Betty Russell. See also Bornstein and Richardson, *War*, 81–2, 128–9, 145.

[116] Amendments by Tooting branch to NAC resolution at 1943 ILP Conference: *1943 Conference Final Agenda* (ILP 1943), 31. They were defeated.

[117] Ridley and Edwards, *United Socialist States*, 15–16.

[118] MacNair, *What the ILP Stands For*, 9.

dependencies into self-governing states was a major if apparently indirect step towards that goal. This was a view which could be accepted by many liberals as well as socialists, and later provided for some a radical gloss on the Commonwealth idea. A more specifically revolutionary socialist argument, as put forward by the ILP and others, was that capitalism was the prime cause of international rivalries and that world unity would come—inevitably—with socialism. As struggles for national independence formed a vital first stage towards socialist revolution in colonial countries, and as the end of colonialism was also a precondition for socialism in the imperialist countries, even bourgeois nationalism worked with Hegelian cunning towards proletarian internationalism. Others though argued that nationalist struggles which were not led by socialists, or by the working class, would inevitably fail to attain these wider aims. Still others felt that at least a temporary continuation of enlightened colonial rule, laying the groundwork of economic and social progress for future socialism, might be preferable to conceding the demands of unrepresentative, and unsocialist, colonial élites. And a variant on this notion, citing an idealised post-1917 Soviet parallel, envisaged socialist movements in previously oppressed nations opting voluntarily to forswear independence and reform union with their former rulers. All these arguments, largely theoretical before 1945, rapidly assumed a sharp practical edge thereafter. For no British party were they more problematical than for the Communists.

IV. COMMUNISTS, COMMON WEALTH, AND COALITION

After the closing down of the League Against Imperialism in 1937, there was a period in which the CPGB's anticolonial activities lay fallow. The party leaders said and did little on the issue: the great bulk of what *was* done was undertaken, as had been the case with the LAI in its later years, by one person. That individual was former Meerut prisoner Ben Bradley, who produced a fortnightly *Colonial Information Bulletin* from the address formerly used by the LAI. Bradley was of course a CPGB member, but appears to have run the *Bulletin* on a virtually freelance basis. It seems to have been written almost entirely by him (most articles carried no authorial attribution) and as the name suggests it consisted largely of factual, or purportedly factual, reports on developments in various British colonies rather than explicit pro-Communist propaganda. Continuing agitation by Communists outside London on colonial, especially Indian, issues in the later 1930s—which was apparently most actively pursued among students in Cambridge and Oxford—would appear to have been even more a matter of individual and local initiatives.[119]

The other major source of literature on colonial subjects from Communist viewpoints during the late 1930s was *Labour Research*, a journal for trade unionists issued by the CPGB-dominated Labour Research Department (a quite separate entity from, and spurned by, the Labour Party's own research unit). This had hitherto usually confined its activities to domestic, and mostly industrial, matters;[120] but in the immediate pre-war years it became more international in focus, reporting particularly on colonial economic problems and carrying details of activities by various anticolonial bodies—by no means only Communist ones. It too was primarily descriptive, though highly critical, in its coverage of colonial policy.

This low-key approach, and the adoption of a far more moderate tone than earlier Communist statements on colonial issues, were dictated by the Popular Front policy of unity against fascism. In 1939, however, that policy underwent a sudden change as, with the signing of the Ribbentrop–Molotov Pact, Moscow's stance towards the impending conflict shifted to the claim that this was an inter-imperialist struggle and that Communists in all belligerent states should denounce their governments' participation.

The almost overnight about-turn met with considerable resistance from within the CPGB. At the outbreak of war it expressed its support for the British cause.[121] But within a month, and after intense pressure from Moscow and bitter disputes on the CPGB's Central Committee, the position had swung through 180 degrees to conform with that of the Comintern. Now it said that 'The continuance of this war is not in the interests of the people of Britain . . . The responsibility for the present imperialist war lies

---

[119] Professor V. G. Kiernan, in conversation drawing on his memories of pre-war Communist student circles, has particularly emphasised the continuing nature of such activity despite the lack of encouragement from party headquarters.

[120] Though, in the 1920s, the LRD had produced a series of anti-imperialist pamphlets by Elinor Burns of the CPGB: *British Imperialism in China*; *British Imperialism in Malaya*; *British Imperialism in East Africa*; and *British Imperialism in West Africa* (Labour Research Department, 1926, 1927).

[121] *War! Communist Policy*, CPGB Central Committee Manifesto (2 Sept. 1939).

equally on all the warring Powers.'[122] As a result of this dramatic and unexplained change, CPGB membership plummeted and several of the party's leaders resigned or, as with General Secretary Harry Pollitt, were forced from their posts.[123]

One of those who resisted the change was Ben Bradley. The *Colonial Information Bulletin* of 18 September 1939 strongly supported the war effort: 'Democratic peoples and all anti-Nazis are rallying in order to crush this menace . . . The British people must support every democratic measure to win this war.' The October issue—almost a month after the party's change of line—still backed Britain's cause, and suggested that the Indian and colonial peoples also did so.[124] Shortly thereafter, the axe descended. The following issue, of 30 November, carried the instruction that all enquiries, correspondence, and in particular requests for speakers on colonial subjects should be addressed to 16 King Street (CPGB headquarters) and *not* to Bradley's address. Bradley's one-man show had been closed down, and the *Bulletin* never appeared again. This last issue, like the penultimate, centred on colonial peoples' attitudes to the war—but, in contrast to October, now asserted that they were wholly opposed to it.[125]

This remained the main theme of CPGB propaganda in 1939–41. Renewed concentration on the colonies provided the party's best ammunition for attacking the British war effort (and, as we have noted, exposed a widely recognised contradiction in Britain's claim to be fighting for democracy). Communist speakers argued that the inhabitants of the Empire were united in their resistance to a war which was being fought to further their oppression and was increasing their hardship. Not only was colonial rivalry the 'chief cause of the war',[126] but the colonial peoples now became 'the front-line fighters in the struggle of all the exploited and oppressed to end the capitalist system'.[127] A number of Communists pressing this case on public

---

[122] *Peace or War?*, CPGB Central Committee Manifesto (7 Oct. 1939).

[123] See Kevin Morgan, *Against Fascism and War* (Manchester: Manchester University Press, 1989), chs. 4–6; John Attfield and Stephen Williams (eds.), *1939: The Communist Party and the War* (Lawrence & Wishart, 1984). The latter includes proceedings of a CPGB History Group conference on the issue in 1979, revealing that even forty years later it deeply divided Communist veterans.

[124] *CIB* (18 Sept. and 30 Oct. 1939).

[125] Ibid. (30 Nov. 1939).

[126] Clemens Dutt, 'The Colonial Question and the War', *Labour Monthly* (June 1940), 350.

[127] *The Empire and the War* (CPGB pamphlet, June 1940), 12.

platforms (including Bradley who had evidently either changed his mind or, more likely, been persuaded to swallow his doubts and toe the party line) were fined or imprisoned for such defeatist utterances.[128]

The CPGB argued that the effects of the war on the colonial peoples were disastrous, and that the conflict 'will with extreme rapidity draw remote and backward peoples into the current of the struggle for national independence'.[129] This last prediction was to prove to have had considerable accuracy. Otherwise the very stridency of the tone in which the party denounced the war betrayed its realisation that it was shouting into a void. Few in Britain would now listen to a voice which seemed to be that of a fifth column under-mining the struggle for national survival. The combined forces of British wartime censorship (which closed down the *Daily Worker* in January 1941) and German U-boats in the sea lanes meant that the colonial peoples themselves could not hear. The period in opposition to the war was, in the anticolonial campaign as in other respects, the bleakest era in the life of British Communism. And that campaign was not even accorded the centrality which, by the party's own proclaimed ideology, it should have possessed. Kevin Morgan's suggestion is accurate: it 'remained of fairly marginal concern to most British Communists . . . Communists tended to take up or leave imperialism rather as if it were a certain reactionary policy adopted by the government, like its policies on food or ARP, and not the system that had produced the war and for the preservation of which the government existed'.[130] In other words, the radical notion of imperi-alism as morally reprehensible policy, rather than the Leninist one of imperialism as world system, retained far the greater hold even among CPGB members.

At dawn on 22 June 1941 the isolation was ended. The German attack on Russia instantly transformed the war, for Communists faithfully following the Moscow line, from an imperialist one to one

---

[128] See press clippings on these cases in Richard Hart papers (M 861/1/26). Bradley received a three months' sentence for remarks on 26 May 1940 at an Empire Day meeting. See also Morgan, *Against Fascism and War*, 185–9. It is noteworthy that, even forty years after, those Communists who defended the 1939–41 policy often invoked conditions in Britain's colonies to support their view, whilst those who condemned it referred exclusively to European events: see Attfield and Williams, *1939*, 67, 71, 121, 135.

[129] *The Empire and the War*, 14.

[130] Morgan, *Against Fascism and War*, 187–8.

where the British 'war for democracy' and the Soviet 'Great Patriotic Fatherland War' were united. The CP now yielded to none in its enthusiasm for the war effort, for the National Government, and even for its old enemy Churchill. The party presses issued forth constant exhortations to greater productivity and sacrifice. Membership shot up. In the summer of 1939 it had been about 18,000, and during 1939–41 at least a third of these had left (though there are no reliable figures for this period). By mid-1942, though, 64,000 members were claimed, settling down to about 55,000 over the next three years.[131] As local Labour parties were lapsing into inactivity over much of the country, and Labour Party membership was simultaneously falling to little more than half its pre-war level, this meant that whereas in 1939 the CPGB had been only about one-twentieth of Labour's strength in individual membership, by 1945 Labour Party members outnumbered Communists only by about four to one. The relative political weight of the CP was massively enhanced.

The main thrust of British Communist propaganda after the outbreak of hostilities on the Eastern Front was that the peoples of the world should unite in defending democracy and the Soviet Union against fascism. In this context, what could it say about the imperialism which it had previously blamed for the war; and about the unrest, resistance, and anti-war feeling in British colonies which it had just been hailing with such enthusiasm?

In early June 1941 Harry Pollitt had said that British Communists 'hope that the mighty wave of revolt that is now sweeping [India] ... will succeed in finding the road to complete victory over British imperialism'.[132] A month later, while verbal support for eventual Indian independence had been retained, the other arguments had all changed radically. Self-government was now seen not as a revolution against British imperialism, to be supported in so far as it weakened British power, but as a necessary precondition for the full mobilisation of the Indian people in freedom's battle, not a total break between Britain and India but the means to effective co-operation between them. This meant that any action Congress might take or threaten which would disrupt the war effort was seen as grossly irresponsible: 'The decision of the Working Committee of the Indian National

---

[131] Figures cited in James Hinton, 'Coventry Communism', *HWJ* 10 (1980), 90–1. Morgan, *Against Fascism and War*, 311–18, surveys the fragmentary evidence for 1939–41 in detail and reaches similar conclusions.

[132] Harry Pollitt, 'India—A Call to the British People', *LM* (June 1941), 265.

Congress to threaten a new movement of mass civil disobedience . . . is a disastrous step.'[133]

As for Indian Communists, their British comrades' message to them was now that winning the war must take precedence over all nationalist and class demands. The need to defeat fascism 'is absolute and unconditional, and does not depend on any measures their rulers may promise or concede'.[134] Congress, of course, could never accept such a view. The CPI itself swung only after much reluctance and some bitter internal argument behind the pro-war line. It did so at least in part on CPGB prompting. Most of the CPI's leaders were then in prison, and were, it is claimed, informed of the changed position and the attitude they must now take by messages from Pollitt which the military authorities deliberately allowed to be smuggled in.[135]

While this close and continued, if quite inconsistent, attention was being given to India, the CPGB remained largely silent on developments in, and policies for, the other colonies. In part this reflected the lack of detailed information or expertise available to British Communists on Africa at this time. Their former associates like Padmore, Kenyatta, and Chris Jones had for the most part long since abandoned them.[136] Communication with sympathisers in the colonies was scanty: the small group of Jamaican Marxists, for instance, who had established contact with Bradley and the CPGB in the late 1930s had very little such communication during the war years.[137]

A partial exception lay in the activities of a number of Communists serving in the armed forces in colonial territories. In several cases

[133] Clemens Dutt, 'India and Freedom', *LM* (Aug. 1942).

[134] Rajani Palme Dutt, 'Notes of the Month', *LM* (Sept. 1941), 381. John Callaghan suggests that a 'division of labour came about which enabled Dutt to concentrate his fire against the incompetence of the British government . . . while the CPI took up the harder task of agitating for the pro-war stance' ('Heart of Darkness', 270–1). This is dubious, given the persistent hammering of the pro-war line in Dutt's *LM* and other wartime writings.

[135] Gene Overstreet and Marshall Windmiller, *Communism in India* (Berkeley, Calif.: University of California Press, 1959), 195; David Druhe, *Soviet Russia and Indian Communism* (New York: Bookman Associates, 1959), 210–11.

[136] Padmore spoke of them 'liberating themselves from the eroding influence of doctrinaire Marxism which British Communists operating through certain Negro fellow travellers were trying to impose', *Pan-Africanism*, 147–8. Jones now 'scorned the Communists as opportunists', according to his friend Reginald Reynolds (*My Life and Crimes* (Jarrolds, 1956), 118).

[137] See Post, *Strike the Iron*, and Hart papers.

such British Communist servicemen appear to have established links with local nationalist and socialist circles, often at some personal risk. The full story of such contacts would be almost impossible to reconstruct, but they seem to have been products of individual initiative rather than directed by the CPGB itself.[138]

Bradley's *Colonial Information Bulletin* was briefly replaced by a monthly review of colonial developments produced by the party itself, *Inside the Empire*. This ran from February 1940 until the end of the year when it in its turn was summarily closed down. Apparently export of copies to the colonies was proving impossible and domestic circulation—initially about 2,000—was insufficient to sustain the journal: further evidence of the relative peripherality of the subject to most British Communists.[139] Like its predecessor it contained largely descriptive and factual material, much of it apparently derived from the mainstream British press. It did not, indeed, even announce itself as a Communist Party publication. There were few signs of new thinking or controversial stances in its pages. After its closure the party's coverage of colonial issues was to be sustained by its main discussion journal, *World News and Views*—which in fact concentrated overwhelmingly on the home front and, inevitably, the USSR—and by the nominally independent *Labour Monthly*, edited by Palme Dutt, which did at least give some prominence to Indian events.

The relative silence on the colonies reflected not only lack of information and a certain lack of real interest, but also an acquiescence in the Government's wartime colonial policies which contrasted so sharply with the wild hopes of revolt raised in 1939–41 that, it may be surmised, a low profile on the issue was felt to be tactically necessary. A very favourable welcome was given to the Government's plans for social and economic development in Africa, especially in the field of education.[140] Only as the end of the war

---

[138] See for instance Post, *Strike the Iron*, for such activities in Jamaica; Noreen Branson (ed.), *British Soldier in India: The Letters of Clive Branson* (CPGB 1944), and John Saville, 'The Communist Experience: A Personal Appraisal', *The Socialist Register 1991* (1991), 17–19, for the experiences of such servicemen in India. Richard Kisch, *The Days of the Good Soldiers: Communists in the Armed Forces WWII* (Journeyman Press, 1985), has scattered references, especially concerning Egypt. Mr Tariq Ali, Mr Alec Gordon, and Professor M. Omer Beshir have told me of similar cases elsewhere. This is an important, though difficult, subject for future research.

[139] Morgan, *Against Fascism and War*, 187–8. Files—apparently incomplete—of *ITE* are held by the Marx Memorial Library (which also has a complete run of Bradley's *CIB*), and in the Hart papers.

[140] E. Palmer, 'Colonial Education', *LM* (Apr. 1944).

came in sight did the CPGB return to a rather longer-term, and slightly more critical, view. In a major policy statement, *The Colonies: The Way Forward*, issued by the Executive Committee in 1944, there was a revival of some of the characteristic themes of inter-war anticolonial propaganda: retardation of colonial economic development, the profits made by monopolistic companies, the deleterious effects on British workers' living standards; but all in very much more muted language than before. The positive prescriptions represented only a slightly more radical variant on official Labour policy. There was the same stress on economic as opposed to political development, the same vagueness about timetables for transition to self-rule, even echoes of the doctrine of trusteeship—and not a breath of 'colonial revolution'. The Labour Party was given credit for good intentions in the colonial sphere, relatively gently chided for its continued adherence to arguments that some colonial peoples were not yet fit to govern themselves, and suggested to have had at least in some of its traditions a worthy record of concern for colonial freedom. This was 'the true expression of a Labour outlook and requires only to be developed and put into immediate practical application'.[141] Even in reintroducing its own proposals for accelerated progress to decolonisation, the CPGB clearly had at least one eye on the wartime electoral truce and the prospects for participation in a post-war coalition.

Yet that electoral truce did not remain wholly unbroken, nor were the ILP and the Trotskyists the only ones to seek to break it. From 1942 there developed a remarkable challenge to the Churchill coalition from a new and idiosyncratic party, Common Wealth. This was founded by a Christian Socialist baronet and former Liberal MP, Sir Richard Acland, with the aim of espousing a new communitarian and egalitarian ethic.[142] A number of leading socialist intellectuals dissatisfied with the Coalition flocked to Acland's idealistic banner, which demonstrated its appeal by several striking by-election successes. Of these thinkers perhaps the two most important and interesting were both former Communists, Tom Driberg and Tom Wintringham.[143]

---

[141] *The Colonies: The Way Forward* (CPGB pamphlet, 1944), 55.

[142] Best expressed in Acland's Penguin Special of Feb. 1940, *Unser Kampf* (Harmondsworth: Penguin, 1940).

[143] On Common Wealth see Paul Addison, *The Road to 1945* (Cape, 1975), 159–60, 225–6, 249–50, and Angus Calder, *The People's War* (Cape, 1969),

Both Acland and Driberg were later to play important roles in anticolonial campaigns, as were a number of lesser-known figures associated with Common Wealth like Arthur Carr, its Youth Organiser. Notions of justice for the Empire figured prominently in the party's appeals; though it is more doubtful whether its remarkable if short-lived electoral advance owed very much to these. It proclaimed a strong ethical anti-imperialism as part of its general stance of morally based reform, making freedom for India in particular a major plank of its programme. Here as always Acland scorned appeals to self-interest. In his New International Order:

No financial interests in the 'owning' countries would be allowed to prevent the full resources of the colonies from being developed for the exclusive benefit of the native peoples living there. In the initial stages this process might involve our own people in some reduction of their standard of living... the working people of this country might find that they would have to pay a little bit more for the cheap bananas, cocoa, and rubber which now come to us at such a terrible cost in suffering to the coloured peoples.[144]

And even in the very short term, even in wartime, Acland believed the British Government should make sweeping moves towards colonial freedom. It should immediately 'appoint, as Secretary of State and as Viceroy for India two men who are known to be determined that British economic and political control in India shall end at the earliest possible moment'. Then it should:

summon a conference of the real representatives of the working men throughout the Colonial Empire, including some of those we have put in prison for demanding trade union rights. With them we would discuss how the resources of the Empire could best be developed for their exclusive advantage.[145]

Yet despite the number of Marxists and ex-Marxists in the ranks of Common Wealth, Leninist views of the relationship between capitalism and imperialism did not figure in its propaganda. Indeed, Wintringham had made rebuttal of the CP's ideas on imperialist war a central element in his critique of Communism. He believed the

---

631–40. For Driberg, see his posthumous memoirs *Ruling Passions* (Cape, 1977), Francis Wheen's biography, *Tom Driberg: His Life and Indiscretions* (Chatto & Windus, 1990), and his papers in Christ Church library, Oxford. For Wintringham, see David Fernbach, 'Tom Wintringham and Socialist Defence Strategy', *HWJ* 14 (1982).

[144] *Unser Kampf,* 132–3.
[145] Ibid. 144.

roots of the Second World War to 'relate more to the exploitation of the working class in Europe, and to their revolutionary resistance to exploitation, than they do to the exploitation of colonial peoples'.[146] Whereas Leninist orthodoxy saw colonial freedom as leading inevitably to the collapse of British capitalism (however confusedly, reluctantly, and inconsistently British Communists may have publicised this fundamental idea), Acland saw it as involving only a temporary and necessary economic readjustment: whilst for Wintringham it was not only morally imperative but a precondition for defeating Germany.[147] Driberg, after his 1942 by-election victory at Maldon, made a similar argument for Indian freedom in relation to victory against Japan: 'It is an inevitable preliminary to victory in the Far East that we should enlist the masses of the Indian people on our side.'[148]

V. INDIA AND THE INTELLECTUALS

After the resignation or expulsion of Labour left-wingers from the League Against Imperialism, there were no umbrella anticolonial bodies extant with which Labour people were involved until after 1945. In the interim, however, a number of smaller lobbies concerned with specific colonial issues or territories emerged. The foundation and unhappy demise of one such, the Committee on West Indian Affairs, has already been described. A Friends of Africa Committee, established as a result of contacts between the ILP and Clements Kadalie's ICU, also mobilised both Labour and ILP members.[149] But it was permanently hamstrung for lack of funds, and faded away as the ICU itself did. A number of left-wing Labour MPs also associated themselves with Moody's League of Coloured Peoples and to a lesser extent with the IASB. The LCP had always contained some socialists in its ranks such as Peter Blackman and Arthur Lewis. Moody himself was a close friend of Padmore, and some co-operation between his organisation and Padmore's more radical group was undertaken; though Makonnen, who derided the LCP's

---

[146] Fernbach, 'Tom Wintringham', 78–9, quoting Wintringham's book, *The Politics of Victory* (1941).

[147] See for instance the peroration to Tom Wintringham: *New Ways of War* (Harmondsworth: Penguin Special, Aug. 1940), 121–8.

[148] *HC Deb.* (11 Sept. 1942), col. 628.

[149] See correspondence between Creech Jones and Winifred Holtby, ACJ 6/1/1–36; and Christopher J. Sansom, 'The British Labour Movement and Southern Africa, 1918–55' (Birmingham University Ph.D. thesis, 1982), 148–51.

trust in 'the goody-goody elements in Britain', saw the relationship's value as limited.[150]

After 1939, the LCP began both to take more interest in colonial policy (as opposed to British race relations) and to adopt a less cautious stance. Moody remained a sufficiently respectable figure to be invited to join a Colonial Office advisory committee in 1942,[151] but in 1944–5 the LCP was to involve itself in drafting and publicising very radical proposals for colonial change. A further London-based organisation of colonial peoples which attained some political significance in these years was the West African Students' Union (WASU). Though primarily a social centre, it acted as sponsor or host to numerous political meetings on colonial subjects (despite its name, participants included West Indians and Africans from outside the west coast colonies—and many who were in no strict sense students!) and also produced a journal, *WASU*, which articulated many of the political aspirations of Africans in Britain. Members included a remarkably high proportion of future West African political leaders: among them Kwame Nkrumah, Nnamdi Azikiwe, J. B. Danquah, Milton Margai, Kojo Botsio, Joe Appiah, Samuel Akintola, and H. O. Davies. Since several of Labour's colonial specialists, notably Creech Jones, Haden-Guest, Reginald Sorensen, Ben Riley, and David Adams, were also associates or regular visitors, WASU also functioned as another of the significant informal junction boxes linking British socialists and colonial nationalists.[152]

Ad hoc bodies of various sorts came and (usually very quickly) went. Sometimes their existence seemed to owe more to factionalism within the British left than to any genuine colonial issue—thus, following a clash with CPGB sympathisers over the running of one meeting on colonial affairs, Reginald Reynolds and Dinah Stock 'invented overnight the Colonial Research Bureau, which consisted of three or four people and existed thenceforth solely as a sort of holding company for delegates' credentials and similar occasions'.[153]

[150] Makonnen, *Pan-Africanism*, 126–7.
[151] LCP, *Newsletter*, 38 (Nov. 1942).
[152] See G. O. Olusanya, *The West African Students' Union and the Politics of Decolonisation, 1925–1958* (Ibadan: Daystar Press, 1982).
[153] Reynolds, *My Life and Crimes*, 119. Stock was Assistant Editor of the *Socialist Review* and for a time Jomo Kenyatta's companion. Reynolds describes a loose alliance of ILP, Socialist League, and IASB people, centred around himself, Stock, Padmore, and Chris Jones, operating in rivalry with CPGB groups in London anticolonialist circles in the late 1930s and early 1940s.

Far more purposeful than such ephemeral bodies was the India League. This was the most important of a number of British lobbies on behalf of Indian independence. After the First World War the Indian Home Rule League, founded by Annie Besant, had listed many prominent Labour Party and ILP members among its supporters. A more left-wing body, the Workers' Welfare League of India, mobilised Marxists like Saklatvala, many of whom later joined the CPGB; and for a time acted as London representative for the Indian trade union movement. The Home Rule League disbanded in 1920, to be succeeded by a Commonwealth of India group under Josiah Wedgwood and Graham Pole. This failed to get Labour front-bench support and its aspirations to found a British-model Labour Party in India met with an unsurprisingly stony reception there.[154]

Meanwhile Reginald Reynolds, freshly returned from working with Gandhi in India, started a Friends of India society comprised primarily of ILP members.[155] The most important initiative came from a pupil of Harold Laski at the LSE, V. K. Krishna Menon. He joined the semi-moribund Commonwealth of India League, became Joint Secretary in 1928, and began agitating to transform it into a far more radical and campaigning body. Initially he was resisted by the older British members of the League, particularly as regards his demand that it should fight not for Dominion status for India, but full independence. By the end of 1930 Menon's efforts succeeded; and thereafter the organisation, renamed the India League, was the major lobby in Britain on behalf of Indian nationalism.

The influence of the India League in left-wing circles grew steadily during the 1930s, and its activities reached a crescendo during the war. Many of the British left's leading anticolonialists became associated with it: Brockway, Lansbury, Ellen Wilkinson, Laski, Cripps, Brailsford, and, increasingly important, the Revd Reginald Sorensen (Unitarian minister, Labour MP, fervent anticolonialist, and—another indicator of how small the social world of anticolonialism often was—Brockway's brother-in-law). Close relations were established with the UDC, with Labour's main left-wing faction the

---

[154] For these groups see Partha Sarathi Gupta, 'British Labour and the Indian Left', in B. R. Nanda (ed.), *Socialism in India* (Delhi: Vikas, 1971); and for the WWLI's trade union activities see Marjorie Nicholson, *The TUC Overseas* (Allen & Unwin, 1986), 151–5.

[155] Ibid. 101, 113; Reynolds, *My Life and Crimes*, 57–70.

Socialist League, and with *Tribune* and the *New Statesman*.[156] The centre of activity, however, was always Menon; and in terms of its day-to-day operations the India League seems to have been as much a one-man show as was the LAI under Bridgeman or the *Colonial Information Bulletin* under Bradley. Menon's biographer records him working an eighteen-hour day: completing MA and Ph.D. theses in his spare time, serving as a Labour councillor in St Pancras and as an ARP Warden, rarely eating, and continuing India League work throughout the heaviest raids of the Blitz.[157]

The IL's political orientation was towards the socialist wing of Congress and particularly towards Nehru, who became a close friend of Menon. Its major early coup was to sponsor a fact-finding tour by three sympathetic Labour MPs in 1932. The resulting report appears to have had a major impact on Labour thinking about Indian independence—and was banned in India itself.[158] The outbreak of war inevitably brought about a breach between Menon and some of the League's Labour supporters. Menon, like Congress, could not accept Britain's right to declare war on India's behalf; and this view brought him into tactical alliance with the Communist Party. Menon, though a Marxist of sorts, was not himself a Communist nor in the usual sense a 'fellow traveller'. The CPGB, though, was in 1939–41 wholeheartedly espousing Indian independence when Labour was not, and for him that was all that mattered. He therefore participated in the People's Convention, a CPGB-organised campaign against the war;[159] and wrote for *Labour Monthly* over the next few years.[160]

[156] Gupta, 'British Labour', 108–19; T. J. S. George, *Krishna Menon* (New York: Taplinger, 1965), 51–152. Both the Socialist League and *Tribune* had been established, largely with Cripps's money, to campaign for an anti-fascist Popular Front. The former was short-lived, but *Tribune* survived to become the main house journal of the Labour left. It always maintained a strong anticolonialist editorial line. *New Statesman* editor Kingsley Martin also took an increasing interest in colonial affairs from the late 1930s.

[157] George, *Menon*, 87–93, 120–7.

[158] *Condition of India: Being the Report of the Delegation sent to India by the India League in 1932* (Essential News Ltd., 1933), written by Menon, Leonard Matters, Monica Whately, and Ellen Wilkinson, with a preface by Bertrand Russell.

[159] See Calder, *People's War*, 281–4, and Morgan, *Against Fascism and War*, 201–13, both noting that Menon was among the most popular speakers in the movement.

[160] See Menon's *LM* articles of Aug. 1941, Jan. and June 1942, and Oct. 1943. All, it will be noted, appeared after the CP switched back to supporting the war effort; and they by no means adhered strictly to the Communist line. Thus Menon continued to insist, unlike the CP, that the promise of full independence was a precondition for India's support against the Axis.

This association deepened already existing Labour suspicion of Menon. He had been adopted as Labour parliamentary candidate for Dundee; but the local party executive, apparently under pressure from the NEC, overturned the selection. Labour's National Agent alleged that Menon's primary loyalty to India made him an inappropriate candidate for a British seat—to which he replied that ordinary party members 'do not recognise your frontiers'.[161] The bridges between the IL and the Labour Party were only gradually rebuilt; but many left-wingers had retained their attachment to Menon and to Indian independence during the period of estrangement. Throughout the war a series of pamphlets—protesting at the imprisonment of Congress leaders,[162] pressing for the application of the Atlantic Charter to India,[163] and pressing the general case for independence[164]—issued from the League's offices.

Meanwhile another group, formed by Brockway, Reynolds, and Oxford writer Edward Thompson, established a separate but essentially complementary Indian Freedom Campaign Committee. In the 1930s, Thompson had complained, 'the mere mention of the word "India" is enough to empty the smallest hall in Oxford'.[165] During the war, however, attention and sympathy seemed to have grown. Relations between Labour's leaders and Congress had been extremely strained in 1940–3: the party had strongly condemned civil disobedience, had refused to condemn the detention of Congress leaders, and Labour Ministers in Churchill's coalition had bitterly disappointed those who expected them to use their positions to lobby hard for concessions to India.[166] But pressure from below, orchestrated by the India League, was persistent. In 1944 the party conference overwhelmingly passed a resolution, drafted and lobbied for by the

---

[161] Correspondence between Menon and G. R. Shepherd, Labour National Agent, repr. in Michael Carritt, *India* (CPGB pamphlet, 1941).

[162] India League, *Britain's Prisoner* (IL pamphlet, 1941).

[163] Reginald Sorensen, *India and the Atlantic Charter* (India League, 1942).

[164] V. K. Krishna Menon, *India, Britain and Freedom* (India League, n.d. but late 1941); P. G. Barstow, MP, S. O. Davies, MP, and Alexander Sloan, MP, *India and Victory: Our Immediate Task* (India League, July 1942); Jawaharlal Nehru, *The Cripps Mission* (India League, 1942); id. and A. K. Azad, *India: What Next?* (India League, n.d. but *c.*1943); India League, *Independence* (India League, Jan. 1943).

[165] Quoted by his son, E. P. Thompson, in 'The Nehru Tradition', *Writing by Candlelight* (Merlin, 1980), 140. Thompson senior had been a teacher and journalist in India and was a close associate both of Gandhi and Nehru and of Rabindranath Tagore.

[166] These events are surveyed in detail in Nicholas Owen's forthcoming D.Phil. thesis: I am grateful to him for opportunities to read and discuss his work in progress.

League and moved by the NUR, committing Labour to press for immediate release of all Indian leaders from prison, and for urgent negotiations leading to an Indian National Government.[167] Thus Labour's pledge to Indian independence was reaffirmed in more unequivocal form than ever before. It remained to be seen how it would act on it.

At least as important for the future direction of anticolonialist ideas within Labour as these pressure groups, were the writings of a number of left-wing thinkers during the later 1930s and early 1940s. Among these theorists and publicists, four men in particular may be singled out: Leonard Barnes, Julius Lewin, Norman Leys, and W. M. Macmillan. Their work, and especially that of Barnes, was important in two ways. It helped turn British radical thought on colonial problems away from its earlier heavy concentration on India and towards more systematic engagement with African issues.[168] It also emphasised the significance of the extension of political rights, especially in relation to racial discrimination and to the likely rapid growth of African nationalist sentiment—in contrast to the dominant tendency at the time, even in left-wing circles, to emphasise the priority of economic development and underestimate the prospects for the emergence of mass nationalism.

The especial contribution of Lewin and Leys was to focus attention on colonial race relations, bringing home the salience of colour bars and the attitudes of white settler minorities to colonial problems. Lewin had been secretary of the Friends of Africa Committee and associated with several other anticolonial groups; but his view, at least in retrospect, was that such organisations were of limited value: 'small bodies with few clear ideas: one should emphasise how feeble and cautious these British efforts were.'[169] He believed a more important task to be the general arousal of critical awareness in British political circles: thereafter metropolitan socialists should respond positively to nationalist demands but should not expect to play a significant initiatory role.

Lewin, Leys, Barnes, and Frank Horrabin founded and edited a small, independent anticolonial journal entitled, with ironic intent,

---

[167] *LPACR 1944*, 185–9.

[168] Lewin and Macmillan had been brought up in South Africa; Leys worked as a doctor in East Africa for twenty years; and Barnes, a former Colonial Office official, was a journalist in Southern and East Africa.

[169] Interview with the late Dr Julius Lewin.

Empire. Leys also produced a series of books and articles on the problems of Africa's settler colonies, culminating in *The Colour Bar in East Africa* in 1941.[170] If, to Leys, white settler colonialism was the greatest disaster for Africa, the traditional alternative of Indirect Rule offered no hope either. Only an active developmental policy, stressing agricultural improvement and education, could give British Africa its last chance.[171]

Macmillan's stance was less radical: he appears to have had more faith in the good intentions of the Colonial Office, and less in the emergence of African nationalism, than the others. None the less his *Warning from the West Indies* came to be seen as prophetic when Britain's Caribbean colonies exploded within months of its publication. He played a major role on the LPACIQ from 1937, and had a significant if unacknowledged influence on Lord Hailey's *African Survey*.[172] Macmillan's intellectual background lay in the study of South African history and race relations. This provided him with powerful convictions on the evil of segregation and minority domination. His Caribbean research persuaded him that official complacency and *laissez-faire* economics could be no less malign in their effects. His main positive argument was of the necessity for centrally planned and state financed economic and social development, in which educated elements among the colonised must be allowed to play an active, responsible part. Thus far his thinking was congenial to the emerging left-wing consensus of the 1940s. But Macmillan had little time for the left's standard view that colonialism was primarily economic in motivation: not exploitation but neglect, he thought, was the great colonialist sin.[173] He was also profoundly sceptical about the abilities and motivations of aspirant African successor élites, and thus about the prospects for stable post-colonial democracy—and in this, of course, he parted company with most of the left.

Far more left-wing, and in these years certainly the most widely

[170] Norman Leys, *The Colour Bar in East Africa* (Hogarth, 1941).

[171] Norman Leys, *A Last Chance in Kenya* (Hogarth, 1931).

[172] *Warning from the West Indies*; see also Hugh Macmillan and Shula Marks (eds.), *Africa and Empire: W. M. Macmillan, Historian and Social Critic* (Temple Smith for Institute of Commonwealth Studies, 1989), esp. chs. 9–11; and Mona Macmillan, *Champion of Africa*.

[173] Macmillan, *Warning, passim*; see also W. M. Macmillan, *Africa Emergent* (Faber & Faber, 1938), and 'Freedom for the Colonial Peoples', in Harold Laski (ed.), *Programme for Victory* (Routledge, 1941).

read and influential writer on colonial affairs in radical circles, was Leonard Barnes. His series of accessible, polemical, but well-researched books, *The Duty of Empire* (1935), *Empire or Democracy?* (1939), and *Soviet Light on the Colonies* (1944),[174] together with various pamphlets and articles, amounted to perhaps the most sustained public idictment of British colonial policy yet to come from the left. His central argument was for a revitalisation, and an injection of urgency and of socialist internationalism into the doctrine of trusteeship; accompanied by a major programme of economic reform having as its aim 'establishing one common standard of life for workers at home and for workers in the colonies'.[175]

This radicalised variant of the trusteeship ideal was unusually combined with an underlying Leninist economic analysis: 'imperialism is not a policy which the monopolists happen to have selected from a number of choices open to them, and which they can abandon in favour of some non-imperialist policy... To imagine that any such possibility exists is to assume that the politics of imperialism can be divorced from the economics of imperialism.'[176] Barnes also went against the then Labour orthodoxy in doubting the feasibility or desirability of extending the Mandate system; and undoubtedly played a part in turning socialist intellectuals away from this line of thought.[177] International control of the colonies, he urged, would be no better than rule by a single coloniser, either morally or practically.[178] He hammered home the argument that Britain's colonial role damaged her in her wartime allies' and the world's eyes:

The colonial question... and the British attitude towards the colonial question, are two of the main rocks on which the whole allied effort to win the peace may founder... The people of Britain, never much given to seeing themselves as others see them, do not yet appreciate how deep, and how damaging to ourselves, is the anxiety felt throughout the world, about this continuing dependence.[179]

---

[174] Gollancz, 1935, Gollancz, 1939, and Harmondsworth: Penguin, 1944, respectively.

[175] *Duty of Empire*, 291.

[176] Leonard Barnes, 'The Uprising of the Indian and Colonial Peoples', in *Where Stands Democracy? A Collection of Essays by Members of the Fabian Society* (Macmillan, 1940), 82.

[177] Though John Flint would stress more the influence in this regard of W. M. Macmillan, whose views on international control if not on colonial economics were similar to Barnes's: 'Macmillan as a Critic of Empire', in Macmillan and Marks, *Africa and Empire*, 212–31.

[178] *Empire or Democracy?*, 239–55.

[179] *Soviet Light*, 6–7.

Soviet Light on the Colonies presented this message by describing a fictional tour of Britain's colonies undertaken by a Russian visitor, who repeatedly expresses amazement at the backwardness of the conditions and attitudes he encounters. This literary device was made all the more effective by the strongly pro-Soviet mood of wartime British public opinion. It was a mood shared by Barnes himself: the Marxist strain in his writing, already evident in the language of the 1939 book, deepened in his wartime work. He became—apparently only briefly—a CPGB member during the war, though without severing his Fabian links.[180]

VI. LABOUR PARTY AND TUC: REAPPRAISAL AND RENEWAL

Official Labour Party policy on the colonies had essentially marked time during the middle and later 1930s. With the minor exception of a 1936 pamphlet which centred on fears of new colonial rivalries being engendered by the rising tension in Europe,[181] there was no party policy document or significant published expression of Labour leaders' thinking between 1933 and the outbreak of war. Individuals and groups associated with the party, on the other hand, had not been idle; and their ideas on a wide range of colonial problems were to have a major influence during the 1940s. The TUC, too, had shown reawakened interest in the Empire, largely prompted by events in the West Indies.

In December 1937, alarmed by the Caribbean labour unrest, the TUC finally established a specialist Colonial Advisory Committee, though this was a body largely composed, not of trade unionists, but of the same middle-class experts who staffed the LPACIQ— Roden Buxton, Creech Jones, W. M. Macmillan, McGregor Ross, Drummond Shiels.[182] The TUC General Secretary, Walter Citrine, served on the Royal Commission investigating the disturbances; and came back with both augmented expertise and awakened interest in colonial labour problems. Largely through the efforts of Citrine

---

[180] On Barnes's CP activities, see *Inside the Empire*, 1/5 and 8 (June and Sept. 1940), 3/1 (Mar. 1944).

[181] Labour Party, *The Demand for Colonial Territories and Equality of Economic Opportunity* (Labour Party, 1936).

[182] *TUC Annual Report 1938*, 205–7; Nicholson, *TUC Overseas*, chs. 6–7.

and of TGWU boss Ernest Bevin (these two having long been advocates of greater TUC involvement in international affairs), TUC–Government co-operation in the colonial field grew rapidly. The TUC pressed the Colonial Office to establish specialist bodies to deal with labour issues, and for the British unions to be represented on these bodies. Initially the Government resisted: the Colonial Office set up a Social Services Department in 1939, but hedged on a separate labour relations department.

In 1942 a Labour Advisory Committee was finally established at the Colonial Office, and at the same time it was decided that experienced British trade unionists should be sent out to the colonies as advisers on labour relations to the local administrations. The first two such advisers were appointed in 1942, and after 1945 their number grew rapidly. The TUC meanwhile started a scheme to finance colonial trade unionists to study in Britain at Ruskin College, Oxford.

Thus the years between 1937 and 1945 saw a rapid growth in TUC involvement with colonial trade unionism, which was further to expand in the post-war era. These developments aroused very mixed reactions on the anticolonialist left. Greater interest by the British unions was, in itself, naturally welcomed (left-wingers had, as we have seen, been trying with rather little success to awaken it between the wars). Yet the close ties between TUC and Colonial Office aroused suspicion. To many on the left it came to appear as if TUC activity was often directed more towards imposing the British union leaders'—or even the British Government's—preconceived ideas on colonial unions, to undermine or suppress Communist and radical nationalist unions, and to defuse militancy, than towards aiding the growth of colonial labour movements.[183]

Meanwhile the major thrust of Labour's colonial rethinking was directed towards economic change. The stress on economic development as a precondition for any viable political advance owed much to a further institutional development of the war years. This was the foundation in 1940 of the Fabian Colonial Bureau. Established on the initiative of Rita Hinden, a South African economist, and Arthur Creech Jones,[184] the FCB became the main source of expertise and

---

[183] See B. C. Roberts, *Labour in the Tropical Territories of the Commonwealth* (Bell, 1964), ch. 5; Nicholson, *TUC Overseas*, ch. 6; and D. I. Davies, 'The Politics of the TUC's Colonial Policy', *PQ* 35/1 (1964); also below, pp. 283–8.

[184] On Hinden see Kath Jones, '"A Quiet Fame": A Biography of Rita Hinden'

information on colonial problems for Labour MPs and leaders. It reached the peak of its influence during Creech Jones's period as Colonial Secretary in 1946–50. Yet the FCB did not, as an organisation, advocate immediate or very rapid decolonisation nor identify itself with the demands of radical nationalist movements; though some individuals working with the Bureau, especially in its early years, did so identify themselves. The dominant view of the FCB's officers and leading members was that:

we feel they [the anticolonial groups in and around Labour's left wing] are unrealistic in demanding independence for all territories under colonial rule now. We agree with the policy of the Government which seeks to lead the Colonies towards self-government within the Commonwealth, and appreciate that whereas some Colonies... are almost ready for self-government other Colonies, such as the East and Central African territories, are not.[185]

Indeed by the late 1940s the Bureau was increasingly identified, in radical eyes, with the right wing of the Labour Party and even as a source of apologetics for the Colonial Office.[186] Dr Hinden herself, associated in the 1930s with the ILP and the Labour left, later became a leading figure of the revisionist Labour right and editor of its main journal, *Socialist Commentary*.[187] More generally, however, the change in the FCB's position relative to the wider debates on colonial affairs resulted not so much from shifts in the thinking of the

(Ruskin College, Oxford, Dip.L.S. thesis, 1985). Julius Lewin, in interview, recalled that Dr Hinden's decision to make the Fabian Society her focus of activity on colonial affairs was on his suggestion—though this is only one of several rival claims to parenthood for the FCB. The Bureau will not be considered in detail here; for two reasons. First, its story has been dealt with in some depth in the work of David Goldsworthy (*Colonial Issues in British Politics, 1945–1961* (Oxford: Oxford University Press, 1971), 123–7, 129–44, 255–64, 321–4) and Patricia Pugh (*Educate, Agitate, Organize* (Methuen, 1984), 183–99, 216–17, 222–5, 233–6, 240–1, 250–1); and will be further illuminated in Deborah Johnson's forthcoming research. I am grateful to Dr Goldsworthy, Ms Pugh, and Ms Johnson for much help. Second, as will be seen, the FCB was not strictly an anticolonialist body in the sense used here.

[185] Hilda Selwyn-Clarke to M. M. Carlin (9 Jan. 1951), FCB 4/3/5.

[186] Tony Benn, Lord Brockway, Bob Edwards, Lord Hatch, and Julius Lewin all put forward variants of this criticism in interview with the author, whilst all paying tribute to the FCB's research role.

[187] The fullest expressions of the FCB's philosophy are to be found in its two volumes of essays: Rita Hinden (ed.), *Fabian Colonial Essays* (Allen & Unwin, 1945), and Arthur Creech Jones (ed.), *New Fabian Colonial Essays* (Hogarth, 1959). On Labour 'revisionism' see David Bryan, 'The Development of Revisionist Thought among British Labour Intellectuals and Politicians, 1931–64' (Oxford University D.Phil. thesis, 1984), and Elizabeth Durbin, *New Jerusalems: The Labour Party and the Economics of Democratic Socialism* (Routledge & Kegan Paul, 1985).

Fabians themselves as from a transformation of the general political situation, and related changes in what defined a left- or right-wing position on colonial issues. The Fabian insistence on gradual change with priority given to economic and social structures remained fairly static and consistent, but was rapidly outflanked by the growing demands for the recognition of nationalist aspirations.

All these new influences—of a revitalised Fabianism, of newly aroused trade union interest, of the writings of Barnes, Lewin, Leys, and Macmillan, of the various single-issue campaigns like the India League, and of the Colonial Office's new-found enthusiasm for planning—were in varying degrees reflected in the attitudes which Labour brought to its first majority in 1945. In September 1941 Leonard Woolf drafted a new policy statement which took into account at least some of the arguments of Lewin, Leys, and Barnes. It urged that emphasis be placed on the elimination of colour bars in colonial employment, and that imperial grants-in-aid should go only to colonies which had taken steps in that direction.[188] Otherwise little change in thinking on colonial development was in evidence in this document: the view that the tropical African colonies would not be able to stand by themselves for some considerable time to come persisted.

At the 1942 party conference these assumptions were dramatically challenged. The surprising figure of Leslie Haden-Guest, last encountered advocating Empire Socialism, who had thereafter sojourned for a time with the Conservatives but had moved sharply back towards the left during the late 1930s,[189] moved an amendment proposing a Charter of Freedom for Colonial Peoples. This concept, a colonial counterpart to the Atlantic Charter, had initially been floated in a lecture by Lord Hailey, had been taken up by Rita Hinden, and had been the subject of a conference sponsored by the FCB and the League of Coloured Peoples.[190] The notion of such a charter had, indeed, been mooted in left-wing circles even earlier; George Padmore and the ILP had suggested it in 1940; and WASU put forward rather similar proposals in 1941.[191] The version of

---

[188] LPACIQ Memo no. 236 (Sept. 1941) (Labour Party papers).

[189] Under the influence, apparently, of his son David, who was killed fighting for the Republicans in Spain.

[190] See FCB 46/4/2–3 (Hailey's speech and pamphlet); 46/4/8–9 (Hinden's draft); 46/4/15 (report of conference, 15 Nov. 1942).

[191] 'A Magna Carta for the Subject Empire', *Left* (Aug. 1940). A very similar document, 'A Charter for the Colonies', appears in Nancy Cunard and George

the Charter passed at Labour Party Conference went considerably further than anything in the official party proposals, and was also more radical than those suggested by Hailey or Hinden. It embodied five main demands: full equality of social, political, and economic rights for all colonial peoples; the abolition of colonial status itself and its replacement by Dominion status for all dependent territories; democratic systems of government in all colonies; nationalisation of mines and other resources and communal ownership of land; and the establishment of a Council for Commonwealth Co-operation.[192] This programme was widely taken to indicate a considerable spontaneous enthusiasm for decolonisation among Labour's rank and file; but, in a manœuvre familiar in the history of Labour conference management, the leadership, though accepting the principle of the Charter, had it referred to a committee of the NEC. When the latter reported to the 1943 conference, little of the substance of the original resolution remained.[193]

The policy statement issued by the party in 1943, then, carried few echoes of these bold political demands. It drew much from Woolf's draft of 1941, and was prepared by a committee on which Creech Jones was the dominant figure. The major proposals of this document—which, in the absence of substantive colonial policy proposals in Labour's 1945 election manifesto, served as the main public indication for Labour policy in government—were thus directed towards social and economic development. In this sphere it was more comprehensive and far reaching than anything the party had hitherto sponsored. It was striking in the positive role it envisaged for private capital investment in colonial development; thus breaking sharply with the assumptions of Leninist and Hobsonian traditions on the inherently exploitative nature of capitalist imperialism.

More striking still, though, was the extreme caution on the issue of political change. There was a reiteration of the principle of trusteeship,

Padmore, *The White Man's Duty* (W. H. Allen, 1942), 37–48. Organisations like the LCP and the National Council for Civil Liberties continued to make the Charter idea central to their campaigns: see LCP, *Newsletter*, 10/59 (Aug. 1944); 11/61 and 62 (Oct. and Nov. 1944), and Overseas Subcommittee of the NCCL, *Civil Liberties in the Colonies* (NCCL pamphlet, Apr. 1945). On WASU's ideas see Olusanya, *West African Students' Union*, 53–63.

[192] *LPACR 1942* 154–6.
[193] *LPACR 1943* 207–8. For the arts and crafts of fixing Labour Party Conference the classic study is Lewis Minkin, *The Labour Party Conference* (Manchester: Manchester University Press, 2nd edn., 1980).

an expression of the conviction that local government would provide
the best training ground for the exercise of self-rule, and of
the opinion that the latter would not be possible in Africa for 'a
considerable time'.[194] Here there was neither a detailed blueprint nor
any break with tradition. In the political sphere, the only development
that was even arguably innovative was the final laying to rest of faith
in Indirect Rule: and on this Labour had moved little if any more
rapidly than had the Colonial Office itself. Colonial Office experts
were indeed delighted with the statement's closeness to their own
ideas: 'it is remarkable how extensive is the area of agreement',
commented Sir Sydney Caine.[195] Neither the views of Labour's
anticolonialist left nor the incipient upsurge of colonial nationalism
had been taken significantly into account. As David Goldsworthy
points out: 'the new policies could be implemented only within the
traditional framework of unchallenged British authority, and colonial
political developments were very soon to demonstrate that the old
authority was no longer Britain's to command.'[196]

VII. THE GLOBAL CONTEXT

It was not only a changed political landscape in the colonies themselves, plus shifts in British thinking, that were weakening the
old ethos of colonial authority. Pressures from outside the imperial
framework also impacted increasingly on British policy. Among these,
two in particular stand out: the policies of South Africa and, more
crucially, of the United States. For the defence of East, Central, and
Southern Africa Britain had been forced from 1940 to rely heavily on
the South African Government. This was regarded as the most
difficult of Britain's Commonwealth allies (there was, after all, a
strong pro-Nazi current amongst Afrikaners) and great emphasis was
therefore placed on good relations with Prime Minister Jan Christian
Smuts, the man seen as Britain's surest friend there. Yet Smuts's co-
operation could not be taken for granted: it became evident that he
would demand a price for it in the shape of South African control
over the High Commission territories and increased influence in East

---

[194] *The Colonies: The Labour Party's Post-War Policy for the African and Pacific Colonies*
(Labour Party, 1943).
[195] Quoted in Lee and Petter, *Colonial Office*, 159.
[196] *Colonial Issues*, 122.

Africa and the Rhodesias—where it was feared that the white settlers would be all too willing to fall in with such schemes.[197]

The Dominions and Colonial Offices stood firm against Smuts's overtures; and this resistance, despite the political advantages to be gained from concessions, has been seen as testimony to the reality of their commitment to trusteeship ideals.[198] No doubt this was so, but awareness of the prospect of uproar from MPs and others—involving a strange alliance of left-wingers concerned for African rights and Tories determined to defend the boundaries of Empire—clearly played its part. Already MPs as diverse as Communist Willie Gallacher, Labour's Ben Riley, and Conservative Lt.-Col. Sir Thomas Moore had fired warning shots in the House over the issue.[199] Strong feelings of insecurity over South Africa's ambitions in the region had, all the same, been aroused in the Colonial Office; and this was to be one of the most contentious of post-war colonial problems.

Even more important than South African pressures were those from the USA. There was deep anticolonial sentiment in American political circles and this exercised a considerable influence on US–British relations during the war, despite the widespread British feeling that American criticism of British colonial rule was ignorant, hypocritical, or self-interested. As Louis says, 'The anti-colonial attitude of the United States gave powerful impetus to the decolonization of the European colonial empires.'[200] And this impetus first became crucial with Britain's wartime dependence on US military and financial support.

The emerging American view of the post-war fate of Britain's colonies, particularly in its enthusiasm for the idea of international trusteeship, evidently ran closely parallel with the attitudes of Labour's colonial policy-makers. When the US Government's Advisory Committee on Post-War Foreign Policy received a copy of Labour's

[197] See Ronald Hyam, *The Failure of South African Expansion, 1908–1948* (Macmillan, 1972), esp. 163–83; also Sansom, 'British Labour Movement', 175–9, 233–5, 259–63.

[198] Hyam, *Failure*, 183; Ronald Robinson, 'Andrew Cohen', in W. H. Morris-Jones and Georges Fischer (eds.), *Decolonisation and After* (Frank Cass, 1980), 55–6.

[199] *HC Deb.* (24 May 1944), cols. 750–1 (Gallacher); (20 Apr. 1944), cols. 415 (Riley) and 473 (Moore).

[200] Wm. Roger Louis, *Imperialism at Bay* (Oxford: Oxford University Press, 1978), 3. See also Christopher Thorne, *Allies of a Kind* (Oxford: Oxford University Press, 1978), and Robert M. Hathaway, *Ambiguous Partnership: Britain and America, 1944–1947* (New York: Columbia University Press, 1981). For a view more critical of US aims, Gabriel Kolko, *The Politics of War* (Weidenfeld & Nicolson, 1969).

colonial proposals, two of its members commented that this was 'extraordinarily interesting since, quite independently, we have reached exactly the same point of view'.[201]

This is not to suggest that Labour's colonial experts necessarily always welcomed the American pronouncements: members of the FCB, in particular, regarded much US criticism as ill-founded and deplored its lack of understanding of the positive initiatives in colonial policy already undertaken by progressive elements in Britain. Many on the British left, too, were already expressing fears lest the diminution of British imperial power to which they looked forward would merely result in its replacement by American hegemony. Marxists especially would naturally tend to anticipate a US global imperialism as a consequence of her growing economic power,[202] but Fabians too had given thought to the prospects of a post-war American imperialism. Creech Jones had proposed writing a book or pamphlet on the subject:

I have excellent things to say—America in the West Indies, Hawaii, Philippines, and America's westward expansion in the United States—not to mention her internal race problem!!!!![203]

Of the wartime manifestations of the Anglo-American alliance which had repercussions for British anticolonialists, the most immediate and far reaching in its effect was the Atlantic Charter of 1942. Article III of this included the statement that the Allies 'wish to see sovereign rights and self-government restored to those who have been forcibly deprived of them'.[204] In response to enquiries—eager ones from nationalists and British anticolonialists, anxious ones from colonial Governors—the War Cabinet expressed the view that this referred only to the nations under Axis occupation and not to the British Empire, and Churchill stated in the Commons that the Charter had no application to the colonies.[205] Attlee, however, immediately went on record as saying that the Charter's sentiments, so far as he was concerned, *did* apply to the 'coloured races' also.[206]

---

[201] Quoted in Louis, *Imperialism at Bay*, 174.

[202] See below, pp. 290, 301–4.

[203] Creech Jones to Rita Hinden (18 Sept. 1943), FCB 18/2/1–5.

[204] For the evolution of the Charter, see Louis, *Imperialism at Bay*, 121–33; on the divergence between British and US war aims *vis-à-vis* the subject peoples, see also Thorne, *Allies*, chs. 3, 7, 8, 12–14, 19–21, 26–8.

[205] See D. J. Morgan, *The Official History of Colonial Development* (Macmillan, 1980), v. 1–9.

[206] Louis, *Imperialism at Bay*, 125.

In any case the relevance of the declaration to the colonies seemed self-evident both to colonial nationalists and to their sympathisers in Britain.[207]

[207] See, for instance, Reginald Sorensen, *India and the Atlantic Charter* (India League pamphlet, 1942).

4

The Labour Governments, 1945–1951

I. LABOUR IN POWER

For radical anticolonialists, previous experience of Labour Governments' handling of colonial affairs hardly fostered confidence in Attlee's prospects. The 1924 and 1929 Governments, with Colonial Secretaries distinguished neither by radicalism nor expertise, had undertaken few positive initiatives in the field. On India, the party had since moved gradually to an advocacy of self-government, although in ways and at a pace which made each of its shifts too little, too late for Congress or for its own left-wing critics. Proposals on Africa too had become bolder since the 1920s, but whilst by 1945 they were far reaching in their ideas on economic progress they remained almost silent on political change.

Labour came to power in 1945, then, with a commitment to Indian independence but with cautious and modest proposals for the other colonies. The election manifesto itself, *Let Us Face the Future*, contained no details on these proposals; and for many members of the new Cabinet and Parliamentary Labour Party this was evidently a peripheral subject. Thus after 1945, as in the 1920s, Labour policy would develop less as the expression of a coherent and consistent philosophy of colonial affairs than in a fragmented, complex, often *ad hoc* fashion. And as in the earlier period, though under very different conditions, an absence of sustained analysis at the level of the party leadership would leave space in which a variety of conflicting assumptions and pressures, official and unofficial, could interact.

A major element in this complex of ideas was the notion of bipartisanship in colonial affairs. This notion was itself conditional. Labour spokesmen did not argue (especially not when addressing Labour movement audiences) that their colonial policy was identical with that of the Conservatives—though the latter were inclined to emphasise continuity between their own and the more 'responsible' of the Labour policies. Rather, Labour leaders spoke of a constructive colonial policy opposed both to old-fashioned Tory imperialism, seen as damaging to Britain's long-term overseas interests; and to purely negative anti-colonialism, which was identified particularly with the Communists. Creech Jones suggested that the continuity and bipartisanship were indicative more of Conservative liberalisation than of any rightward shift on Labour's part:

> We have witnessed a much more liberal attitude on the part of the British public, a desire to get the content of imperialism changed, and the application to the colonial peoples of a progressive policy which recognises their inherent rights as human beings and their claims to freedom, liberty and economic justice. Therefore, instead of Labour Members endorsing the sentiment that the policy of the Labour Government is just the continuity of previous policies, they should rejoice that, at last, our propaganda has succeeded in converting the Tory benches to a much more human and liberal approach to these problems.[1]

This commitment to a constructive colonial policy was argued to mean that imperialism as a system either of military aggression or of economic exploitation was a thing of the past. Thus Ernest Bevin could claim in 1948 that 'We have ceased to be an Imperialist race: we dominate nobody.'[2] The Labour Party *Speakers' Handbook* for 1948–9 could suggest, apparently without a trace of intended irony, that 'In all the areas under our control, we have abandoned the old type of capitalist imperialism . . . Imperialism is dead, but the Empire has been given new life.'[3] Amidst this rhetoric of new beginnings, Herbert Morrison's famous reference to Labour being 'great friends of the jolly old Empire' was thoroughly embarrassing to the reformers.[4]

The abandonment of concepts of capitalist imperialism opened the way for the belief that economic development of the tropical colonies could only be beneficial. The characteristic presentation of the development plans was in terms of Britain's 'enlightened self-interest'—a phrase of which Creech Jones was inordinately fond. Ideas about development were typically both unilinear—envisaging monetisation of 'backward' economies leading to increased cash-crop and export production, thus eventually generating a surplus for industrialisation—and strongly technocratic.[5] They were open to

---

[1] Creech Jones, *HC Deb.* (9 July 1946), col. 343.

[2] Quoted in R. Palme Dutt, *The Crisis of Britain and the British Empire* (Lawrence & Wishart, 1953), 332.

[3] *Labour Party Speakers' Handbook, 1948–9* (Labour Party, 1948), 143–5.

[4] *The Times* (12 Jan. 1946).

[5] For an acute critique of Fabian developmental assumptions—though one which arguably overstates both their continuity over time and their agrarian bias—see Michael

criticism from those who wished to place more stress on political change and progress towards self-government, as well as from those who argued that their form was dictated by a thoroughly *un*enlightened pursuit of the self-interest of the British national economy: though, as we shall see, such criticism was slow to develop within Britain.

The pressures of post-war British economic reconstruction, and the desire to maintain or rebuild British economic independence *vis-à-vis* the USA, imposed substantial constraints on colonial development plans. Such pressures, spearheaded by Dalton and then Cripps at the Treasury, intervened on several fronts. There was the argument that Britain simply could not afford to spend money on the colonies. There was the desire that any colonial planning must be very closely tied to the needs of the domestic economy. This could be in terms of raw material production, pushing Colonial Development and Welfare plans towards the creation of export-orientated monocultures, with dangerous long-term results, as well as leading to the fiasco of the Groundnuts Scheme. Additionally protecting home-based industries could imply hostility to import-substituting industrialisation in the colonies. Perhaps most damaging of all, there was the imperative to protect sterling.

This last, through the workings of the Sterling Area dollar pool, the sterling colonial exchange standard, and a variety of physical controls on trade, exploited the major primary product exporters among the tropical colonies in order to subsidise British reconstruction and the attempt to use sterling as a major means to the perpetuation of British world power. The whole amounted to what may well have been the most oppressive form of economic imperialism yet seen in British tropical colonies, carried out with a combination of self-interest, myopia, and liberal good intentions.[6]

Cowen and Robert Shenton, 'The Origin and Course of Fabian Colonialism in Africa', *Journal of Historical Sociology*, 4/2 (1991). See also Ronald Hyam, 'Africa and the Labour Government, 1945–1951', *JICH* 16 (1988).

[6] Generally approving accounts of the Attlee Governments' colonial development record are given in Kenneth O. Morgan, *Labour in Power, 1945–1951* (Oxford: Oxford University Press, 1984), 200–2, 228–30 (a summary marred by apparent confusion between the Colonial Development Corporation and the Overseas Food Corporation); Henry Pelling, *The Labour Governments, 1945–51* (Macmillan, 1984), 155–9; J. M. Lee, *Colonial Development and Good Government* (Oxford: Clarendon Press, 1967), ch. 3; D. J. Morgan, *The Official History of Colonial Development*, iii (Macmillan, 1980); and S. A. H. Haqqi, *The Colonial Policy of the Labour Government, 1945–51* (Aligarh: Aligarh University Press, 1960). More critical views include Jane Bowden, 'Development and Control in British Colonial Policy' (Birmingham University

Pressures of a different sort came from the Foreign Office. Ernest Bevin was perhaps the only senior Cabinet member who was a genuine enthusiast for Empire, envisaging for it both limitless possibilities of economic development and a key strategic role.[7] His was truly an imperialist Foreign Office, seeking constantly to extend its influence over other departments: and the Colonial Office, especially over the issue of Palestine and other territories where major strategic interests were involved, was a prime target. The subordination of Colonial Office to Foreign Office was also influenced by the facts that Creech Jones was a former subordinate of Bevin's in the TGWU; that his integrity and expertise were not matched by forcefulness in Cabinet or in the House; and that Attlee had little faith in him. Creech Jones, Attlee considered, 'had not appeared to have a real grip of administration in the Colonial Office. He was bad in the House and contributed nothing in Cabinet.'[8] The first charge was blatantly unjust; the others had a certain truth. Yet even without these personal factors, strategic considerations would have laid a heavy hand on the future of many colonies.

It was already apparent by the later 1940s that two types of colonial territory would pose particular problems: those with substantial white settler populations and those of strategic importance to Britain and/or the USA. Labour's failure, despite the efforts of Leys and Haden-Guest, to grasp the nettle of racial discrimination helped ensure a troubled future for the former. The advent of the Cold War after 1947 sharpened the dilemmas over the latter.

To an extent hardly matched before or since, decisions in the colonial field were taken under the Attlee Government, in all cases where vital British interests were felt to be at stake, not by the Ministers directly responsible but by the Cabinet's dominant figures:

Ph.D. thesis, 1980); D. K. Fieldhouse, 'Labour Governments', in Ritchie Ovendale (ed.), *The Foreign Policy of the British Labour Governments, 1945–51* (Leicester: Leicester University Press, 1984); Partha Sarathi Gupta, 'Imperialism and the Labour Government', in J. M. Winter (ed.), *The Working Class in Modern British History* (Cambridge: Cambridge University Press, 1983); R. D. Pearce, *The Turning Point in Africa* (Frank Cass, 1982); and Cowen's crucial work on the Colonial Development Corporation. The most crucial official papers on the period are now available in Ronald Hyam (ed.), *British Documents on the End of Empire: Series A*, ii. *The Labour Government and the End of Empire, 1945–1951*, 4 vols. (HMSO for Institute of Commonwealth Studies, 1992).

[7] See Alan Bullock, *Ernest Bevin, Foreign Secretary* (Heinemann, 1983); Pearce, *Turning Point*, 94–5; Gupta, 'Imperialism and the Labour Government', *passim*.

[8] Quoted in Pearce, *Turning Point*, 92. See also Kenneth Harris, *Attlee* (Weidenfeld & Nicolson, 1982), 446.

Attlee, Bevin and Morrison, Dalton and Cripps. Only in the spheres of social and constitutional development in tropical Africa did Creech Jones and Cohen have something of a free hand; and here their cautious, long-term plans were soon overtaken by the rising pressure of nationalist political demands, breaking out first in the Gold Coast with the riots of February 1948.

Labour's colonial Ministers did, however, at least enjoy for a time relative freedom from attack by their own party. During the 1945–50 Government the Labour left did not mount any significant challenge to the colonial policy of George Hall and Arthur Creech Jones. On one level this quiescence merely reflected the general lack of open dissent with the Labour Party at a time when Attlee's Government was seen to be implementing so many long-cherished socialist plans. Yet whereas the Government's domestic policy was, at least in 1945–7, sufficiently radical to win the approval of much of the left its colonial policy was in large measure a bipartisan one—and that bipartisanship was more explicit in colonial than in foreign policy, and this did draw substantial left-wing criticism.

Furthermore aspects of the colonial development strategy might, as noted above, have been expected to incur the wrath of those traditionally attuned to the denunciation of economic imperialism. Equally the lack of evidence that the Government intended to pursue the sort of rapid political change for which the Party Conference had called in 1942 seemed a natural target for left-wing attack. There was to be little such criticism forthcoming, however, from the back-benches or the party activists.

A number of reasons for this state of affairs suggest themselves. There was a general lack of concern for colonial issues as compared with the urgent domestic tasks of post-war reconstruction, nationalisation, and extending welfare provision. The tendency to view these in terms of raising working-class living standards and rectifying the still freshly recalled privations of the 1930s may have blinded many to the overseas side-effects of the means adopted. The combined forces of party loyalty, party discipline (far stricter in the 1940s than today), and approval of the Government's record in other spheres of course stifled overt expressions of dissent. And in the colonial field itself, the granting of independence to India, Pakistan, Ceylon, and Burma overshadowed lack of progress in other territories.

The Labour left lacked a clear-cut colonial issue around which opposition might centre (for reasons which we shall discuss below, the crises in South-East Asia and Palestine did not provide such an issue). It lacked a parliamentary leader in the field until Fenner Brockway re-entered the House in 1950. It lacked an organisational focus for an alternative policy: the FCB may not have had a monopoly of Labour interest in colonial affairs, but in the 1940s it seemed to have a near-monopoly of *informed* interest, and its officers were strongly disinclined to offer any fundamental criticism of policies and Ministers which they regarded in some sense as their own. Thus the left also lacked adequate sources of information on colonial developments, and a coherent political philosophy linking attitudes on colonial issues with socialist policies in other spheres. Marxism-Leninism claimed to offer such a philosophy, but its appeal within the Labour Party was necessarily very limited—and decreasing, as the Cold War deepened and fellow travellers in Labour's ranks were expelled. Nor did the old Radical-Liberal moralism provide the analytical tools necessary to grasp the post-war situation: a mode of critique appropriate to Red Rubber in the Congo could have rather little to say about the Colonial Development Corporation. Labour back-bench protests seemed more like a wistful desire for an alternative policy than the articulation of one.

During the early 1950s all these prerequisites for a vigorous left wing came slowly to be available. In the meantime debate and dissent concentrated on the two major colonial crises faced by Attlee's first Ministry: the conflict in Palestine and the transfer of power in South Asia.

II. PALESTINE AND THE MIDDLE EAST

There has been no single international issue on which British social-ists, and indeed socialists in all countries, have been more deeply divided than the question of Palestine. Attitudes to Zionism and to the contending claims of Jews and Palestinians have cut across most of the conventional distinctions of left and right.[9] Debate on this question in Britain, as elsewhere, naturally reached a climax in 1945–8;

---

[9] There is a massive literature on international attitudes to the Middle Eastern conflict, both during the period of decolonisation and thereafter. The only detailed study of the views of British socialists in the Mandate era, however, is Joseph Gorny, *The British Labour Movement and Zionism, 1917–1948* (Frank Cass, 1983), which concentrates overwhelmingly on party leaders and takes a strong pro-Zionist standpoint.

and during these final years of British rule in the region it became a colonial debate in a more direct sense than ever before, since the outcome of the Arab–Jewish conflict seemed directly dependent on the nature and timing of Britain's withdrawal.

Yet this did not make it by any means a simple argument between colonialists and anticolonialists. There were strong historical links between the Zionist lobby (many of whose leaders were themselves socialists) and the British labour movement. There was widespread sympathy for Jewish national aspiration on the left, compounded by admiration for the socialist experiments undertaken in the kibbutzim, the Histadrut (Jewish trade union federation), and Mapai and Mapam (the Zionist labour parties). Such feelings, generally stronger on the left than among Labour right-wingers, were given great impetus and urgency by the Shoah and the post-war plight of European Jewish refugees.

On the other hand, Zionism was itself in a literal sense a colonialist movement, establishing settlements in and claiming hegemony over a territory already inhabited by another people.[10] Some on the left believed the Zionist project to be in essence a tool of imperialism, encouraged by international finance capital (it will be recalled that the British anticolonial tradition included a strain of attacks on Jewish financiers which shaded into overt anti-semitism). There was also within the British left a current of support for Arab nationalism. Indeed where Egypt or Iraq or Syria were concerned such support was a necessary consequence of anticolonialist beliefs. In Palestine, however, support for Arab self-determination came into direct conflict with Jewish claims: two movements, each invoking principles central to the anticolonialist ethos, appeared irreconcileable. No wonder that Fenner Brockway, ordinarily more prone even than most British anticolonialists to see decolonisation as a simple matter of right and wrong, confessed himself bemused by the Palestinian issue: 'To most problems one can apply general principles, but to Palestine—no. By no other question have I been so puzzled.'[11]

British socialists placed much hope in the prospects for a coming together of Arab and Jewish working-class movements; and some in

---

[10] Some at least of the early Zionist leaders themselves explicitly saw their project as part of the European colonial mission. For a powerful polemical statement of the case for seeing Zionism primarily in this light, see Edward W. Said, *The Question of Palestine* (Routledge & Kegan Paul, 1980), esp. 7–37, 56–82. See also David Vital, *Zionism: The Formative Years* (Oxford: Oxford University Press, 1982).

[11] *Inside the Left* (Allen & Unwin, 1942), 291.

the 1930s and earlier 1940s claimed to discern a growing trend towards unity in Palestinian trade unions and other bodies. The Communists, in particular, believed that the struggle against British colonialism would itself cement such unity.[12] Yet the extreme weakness of intercommunal organisations could not realistically be denied through this kind of wishful thinking; and as the debate on British withdrawal intensified Communists turned to the inconsistent but equally utopian argument that only the presence of the British fomented disunity; and that once Britain's tactics of divide and rule were removed Arab and Jewish workers would find ways to live happily together.[13]

The ILP too had entertained high hopes for the evolution of working-class unity in Palestine, and in the late 1920s had sponsored a Jewish–Arab Committee to Combat British Imperialism.[14] Increasingly during the 1930s the ILP's stance became sympathetic to Zionism. Its leader, James Maxton, had initially been hostile, but gradually shifted his position. John McGovern and Campbell Stephen (the former previously neutral, the latter anti-Zionist) had returned from a trip to Palestine in 1937 full of enthusiasm for Jewish settlement. Their view gained general support within the party during the war; though there were vociferous dissenters led by Reginald Reynolds, who resigned from the ILP over the issue.[15] Brockway remained ambivalent, but for him too meeting the plight of the Jewish refugees was now the prime consideration.[16] The *New Leader* adopted an editorial line strongly sympathetic to Zionist claims during the war.[17]

[12] See for instance CPGB, *Palestine: Terror or Peace* (CPGB pamphlet, 1938).
[13] See for instance Communist MP Willie Gallacher's speech, *HC Deb.* (31 July 1947), cols. 1037–44—a contribution derided by subsequent speakers for its utopianism—and the reports by Jewish and Arab Communist leaders S. Mikunis and E. G. Touma in CPGB, *We Speak for Freedom* (CPGB pamphlet, 1947). On Palestinian–Israeli Communism, see Joel Beinin, *Was the Red Flag Flying There? Marxist Politics and the Arab–Israeli Conflict in Egypt and Israel, 1948–1965* (I. B. Tauris, 1990).
[14] Gorny, *British Labour Movement*, 158–9; Brockway, *Inside the Left*, 292–3.
[15] Reginald Reynolds, *My Life and Crimes* (Jarrolds, 1956) 165–6. Reynolds thought Zionism a 'racket', had close contacts with Arab nationalists, and attributed the ILP's stance to unthinking Clydeside support for McGovern, whom Reynolds thought an anti-Arab racist.
[16] See Gorny, *British Labour Movement*, 154–9; Brockway, *Inside the Left*, 291–3; and his *New Leader* articles of 10 Mar. 1938 and 10 July 1943. Miles Kahler's statement that Brockway was 'anti-Zionist' (*Decolonization in Britain and France* (Princeton, NJ: Princeton University Press, 1984), 250) is thus somewhat misleading.
[17] See Douglas Rogers's articles, *NL* (30 Dec. 1944 and 6 Jan. 1945).

This attitude was shared by most of the Labour left. *Tribune* and those closely associated with it, led by Nye Bevan and Jennie Lee, gave very extensive coverage to the Palestinian issue from a consistently pro-Zionist standpoint. The *New Statesman*'s treatment of the issue was less prominent and more cautious; but it too adopted a pro-Zionist stance as it had done throughout Kingsley Martin's editorship. Both journals blamed Ernest Bevin for the crisis and the violence, seeing him as having been duped by reactionary Arabist opinion in the Foreign Office. *Tribune* was particularly bitter:

> the Labour Government—our Labour Government—has set out on a road along which the milestones will be the graves of innocent British soldiers . . . It gave the most extravagant and categorical undertakings to the Jews and it has broken them with cynical disregard for consequences.[18]

Bevan pressed for the acceptance of partition in Palestine (the course at that time accepted by the Zionists but rejected by both Arabs and Foreign Office) and contemplated resignation over the issue.[19] During the war Labour had moved—substantially on Hugh Dalton's initiative—to a position which not only backed the Jewish claims but went further than the Zionist leadership in urging Arab population 'transfer' out of Palestine.[20] In office this was rapidly reversed, as priority was given to maintaining British influence in the Arab world.[21]

In general the sharpest parliamentary criticism of the Government's about-turn came from left-wing (and often Jewish) Labour back-benchers, led by Sydney Silverman, William Warbey, Ian Mikardo, and Maurice Orbach. These critics included individuals who on some other foreign policy issues attacked Bevin from positions near to that of the CPGB. But on Palestine, whereas the Communists and their close supporters within the PLP were predominantly anti-Zionist this left-wing group of MPs wholeheartedly supported partition and the Jewish demands.[22] Others on the left, though, were by now

[18] Editorial, *Tribune* (25 Apr. 1947).

[19] See Michael Foot, *Aneurin Bevan*, ii. *1945–1960* (Granada, 1975), 87; Gorny, *British Labour Movement*, 205, 207, 220–1; Bullock, *Bevin*, 364, 476; Morgan, *Labour in Power*, 209–15. Bevan's pro-Zionism was supported in Cabinet by Hugh Dalton, Creech Jones, Manny Shinwell, and, guardedly, by Herbert Morrison.

[20] See Ben Pimlott, *Hugh Dalton* (Cape, 1985), 388–90; Gorny, *British Labour Movement*, 164–85.

[21] For the most detailed account thus far, see Wm. Roger Louis, *British The Empire in the Middle East, 1941–1945* (Oxford: Oxford University Press, 1978), *passim*.

[22] See the speeches and Questions of Silverman (*HC Deb.* (11 Oct. 1945), cols. 403–5; (2 Nov. 1945), cols. 785–9; (21 Feb. 1946), cols. 1366–73; (12 Dec. 1947),

having second thoughts. The ILP's paper had backed Jewish claims essentially because Palestine seemed a desperately needed refuge from the Nazis. As Zionist territorial claims were perceived to become more ambitious and Arab opposition more militant, the *Socialist Leader*'s Douglas Rogers decided that Palestine would prove not a refuge but a 'death-trap' for the Jews. The attempt to establish a Jewish state there resembled 'the last mad gamble of desperate men and women'.[23] The ILP reverted to its pre-war aspiration for 'a bilingual socialist movement in Palestine, leading ultimately to the bilingual Arab and Jewish socialist state'.[24] If there had ever been a time for such a dream, by 1948 it was far too late.

Thus the Palestinian question divided the left on unfamiliar lines. The majority was swayed primarily by emotional sympathy with the sufferings of the Jewish people, by admiration for the socialist convictions of many Zionists (as opposed to the conservatism of much of the Arab leadership), and by the conviction that British opposition to Zionism stemmed from the desire to maintain British power in the region and from racism in the Foreign Office. These feelings outweighed suspicions aroused by US support for the Zionist cause, the exclusivist nationalism of the latter, concern for Palestinian Arab rights, and by the belief that British support for Zionism stemmed from the desire to maintain British power in the region and from racism in the Foreign Office.

Others, particularly within the CPGB, conversely argued that Zionism was itself a tool of US regional imperial ambitions and a barrier to working-class unity. Yet the CP itself was clearly unhappy with this position. Fearful of appearing to make concessions to anti-semitic feeling, challenged by many of its own Jewish members, and hampered by the uncertainties of the USSR's view, it took refuge in the facile claim that colonial status was the root of all the problems and in unrealistic hopes for socialist unity across racial and religious boundaries.[25] After the establishment of the state of Israel and the

cols. 1329–41), and Warbey's, Mikardo's, and Orbach's contributions to the debate of 11–12 Dec. 1947 (cols. 1251–7, 1403–8, and 1411–14).

[23] Douglas Rogers, *SL* (24 Aug. 1946).

[24] Editorial, *SL* (8 May 1948).

[25] The uncertainty is reflected in the fact that the party's Executive Committee proposed only an extremely vaguely worded resolution on Palestine for its 1947 Congress. Even this came under criticism for its evasiveness on Zionism and was eventually dropped altogether. See *WNV* (7 Dec. 1946—original resolution—and 4 Jan. 1947—critique from L. Martin); and *Nineteenth Congress—Resolutions and*

subsequent growth of radical Arab nationalism, the CPGB's position—following that of the USSR—hardened: by the early 1950s Israel was being described as 'in practice a semi-colony of American finance-capital'.[26] The independent left was more openly and interestingly divided. Soon after Israel's declaration of independence and military victory over her Arab neighbours, F. A. Ridley in the ILP's *Socialist Leader* was expressing fears that this presaged a new 'Zionist Imperialism' which was 'destined finally to eclipse the now setting sun of British Imperialism in the Middle East'. This, he felt, would be a 'road to disaster' for the Jews.[27] The only desirable alternative, he suggested a little later, was a 'peaceful Middle Eastern Commonwealth of Semitic Nations'.[28] For Reginald Reynolds, predictably, the fact that Ridley opposed not Israel's existence *per se* but only an expansionist Israel amounted to giving 'justifications of Jewish imperialism'; whilst Barnet Litvinoff equally predictably lambasted Ridley from the other side.[29] A mould had been set, of bitter left-wing discord over the Middle East, which was to persist at least into the 1990s.

III. SOUTH AND SOUTH-EAST ASIA

In terms of the significance of the decisions made and of the sheer numbers of people involved, the most important colonial issue under the Attlee Governments was the independence of Britain's South Asian colonies. By comparison with other moments in decolonisation, however, the debates leading to self-government for India, Pakistan, and Ceylon aroused relatively little passion or disagreement within the British left. The general argument for Indian independence had long since been won within the Labour Party, despite the apparent temporary backtracking of 1941–3; whilst Ceylon's sedate decolonisation attracted scant attention. Its conservative nationalist leaders had few close friends among British left-wingers and the details of the transfer of power evoked little dissension. Burma, where the nationalist

---

Proceedings (CPGB, 1947), 14–19 (for the eventual colonial resolution with Palestine references wholly expunged).

[26] R. Palme Dutt, 'The Way Forward', in CPGB, *Allies for Freedom* (CPGB pamphlet, 1954), 9.

[27] F. A. Ridley, 'Britain, Israel and the Middle East', *SL* (22 Jan. 1949).

[28] *SL* (9 Apr. 1949).

[29] Letters in *SL* (11 and 18 June 1949).

movement was far more radical and the transition to independence far more conflictual, produced correspondingly deeper concern from British anticolonialists. Elsewhere in the region the Attlee years witnessed a brief but intense crisis over Britain's role in reimposing French and Dutch colonial rule in Indo-China and Indonesia respectively, and the opening rounds of the long struggle in Malaya.

Burmese nationalism differed from that of the Indian subcontinent (and indeed from that of most Anglophone African and Caribbean colonies) in two important respects. First, those who emerged as its leaders in 1945 were avowedly Marxist, and expressed anti-British sentiments far more vehement than the sorts of love–hate attitude towards Britain characteristic elsewhere. The key figures in the main nationalist party, the Anti-Fascist People's Freedom League (AFPFL), Aung San and Than Tun, had for some time collaborated with the Japanese. Second, all the major nationalist leaders were locally educated, and few had travelled widely outside Burma before 1939. Conversely, hardly any British left-wing politicians or intellectuals knew Burma at first hand (George Orwell was, of course, the most notable exception). Thus there was, in Burma, none of the history of personal contact and political co-operation between nationalists and British socialists so important elsewhere.[30] The British socialists were extremely ill-informed about the situation in Burma and the demands of the AFPFL.[31]

This absence of information and contact was remedied almost solely by one Labour MP, Tom Driberg. Driberg, who had been first elected as an Independent, joined Common Wealth, and then transferred his allegiance to Labour in 1945, visited Burma in the summer of that year. He established friendly relations both with members of the British occupation forces—from Lord Mountbatten down to junior officers and NCOs who were later to prove valuable

---

[30] See Fransisco Nemenzo, Jun., 'Revolution and Counter-Revolution. A Study of British Colonial Policy as a Factor in the Growth and Disintegration of National-Liberation Movements in Burma and Malaya' (Manchester University Ph.D. thesis, 1964), 27–32, 36–57, 88–113, 121–47; Hugh Tinker (ed.), *Burma: The Struggle for Independence*, i. *From Military Occupation to Civil Government*; ii. *From General Strike to Independence* (HMSO, 1983, 1984); id., 'Burma's Struggle for Independence: The Transfer of Power Thesis Re-examined', *Modern Asian Studies*, 20 (1986).

[31] For instance, as Nemenzo notes ('Revolution', 83), British left-wingers opposed the administrative separation of Burma from India, under the impression that in so doing they were championing the wishes of Burmese nationalists and unaware that in fact all currents of Burmese opinion welcomed the move.

sources of local news—and with the leaders of the AFPFL.[32] Returning to London, Driberg became in effect a one-man solidarity campaign with the Burmese cause, working closely with Maung Ohn, the AFPFL's London representative, lobbying Ministers, and at times virtually monopolising parliamentary Questions on Burmese affairs.[33]

British officialdom was deeply split over post-war plans for Burma. There was general agreement on the need for moderate nationalists who would keep Burma in the Commonwealth and safeguard British economic interests; but some wanted an all-out attack on the position of Aung San and the AFPFL; some (including the Governor, Dorman-Smith) suggested a five to seven year interim period of direct British rule during which the pre-war economy could be reconstructed and an amenable nationalist coalition built to counter the AFPFL; whilst yet others (apparently including Mountbatten) hoped to exploit divisions within the AFPFL and isolate the radicals.[34] Driberg and Maung Ohn devoted themselves to the task of convincing Government and Parliament that none of these options was practicable.

The AFPFL, Driberg urged, was the only significant expression of Burmese nationalism, commanding 'overwhelming support'.[35] He said it was not an extremist organisation, but 'a real united front', and spoke of its leaders' 'integrity and incorruptibility'. Aung San was a leader of 'great intelligence . . . the hero of the younger generation in Burma today'.[36] (Meanwhile Conservative colonial expert David Gammans was calling the AFPFL 'neo-fascists' led by a 'traitor and murderer'.[37] Attempts to crush or split the AFPFL, according to Driberg, would be disastrous: Britain's only realistic and democratic course was to work with its leaders.[38] As for British plans to reconstruct the economy on the pre-war model, these would be resisted by all strands of nationalist opinion. They wanted instead a socialist

[32] See the extensive correspondence and documentation in the Driberg papers, file S3. *Ruling Passions* (Cape, 1977), 213–27, has Driberg's vivid reminiscences of the trip. Francis Wheen's entertaining biography, *Tom Driberg* (Chatto & Windus, 1990), adds little except on Driberg's personal relations with Mountbatten.

[33] His major source was Maung Ohn, but he also corresponded with Mountbatten, with Aung San and other nationalists, and extensively with Lt. W. D. Mackenzie (a Royal Artillery officer in Burma) and Flt. Lt. David Crook of the RAF there.

[34] Nemenzo, 'Revolution', 93–113, 121–61.'

[35] Driberg, *HC Deb.* (4 Feb. 1946), col. 1347.

[36] *HC Deb.* (2 Nov. 1945), cols. 802–3.

[37] Ibid. (7 June 1946), cols. 2318–23.

[38] Driberg to Arthur Henderson, Under-Secretary of State for India and Burma (3 Apr. 1946) (Driberg papers S3).

economy, and a Labour Government should have no part in reintroducing the monopoly firms and Indian money-lenders who had previously impoverished Burma.[39] His concern that, unless the British made substantial concessions, the impasse would degenerate into bloodshed was genuine—and realistic. In June 1946 Aung San wrote to him to warn that:

If blind prejudice and stark policy of bureaucratic intransigence is pursued then I hope you will understand us for any action we may be compelled to resort to . . . Still, I will try hard to control the situation at the risk of my popularity and being considered weak.[40]

Driberg pressed urgently for AFPFL demands on the timing and form of independence to be met: submitting, for instance, a series of amendments suggested by the AFPFL to the Burma Legislature Bill.[41] At the end of 1946 the nationalist movement did split, with Than Tun's Burmese Communist Party moving away from Aung San. Driberg was very worried by this, and attempted to mediate,[42] but the AFPFL retained overwhelming popular support; and the schism may actually have made the transfer of power easier in that when Attlee finally met Aung San in January 1947 he could now see him not only as a militant nationalist but as a potential ally against Communism. The blood-bath Driberg had feared was averted. Although the fact that Britain eventually agreed to transfer power to a party initially viewed as unacceptably extremist was clearly brought about primarily by the AFPFL's demonstrated capacity to make it impossible for the British to govern, Driberg's efforts to educate British Labour about Burmese nationalism undoubtedly contributed to the outcome. The end, though, was not happy for him. Aung San and his colleagues were massacred by rivals on 19 July 1947. Driberg bitterly alleged that the assassins' leader, U Saw, had been incited by the British Conservative Party, and that it must bear the moral guilt.[43]

Between the end of the war and midnight on 15 August 1947 there were no major disagreements within the left on the principle of Indian independence, which was generally accepted. Even those who

[39] Driberg to Arthur Henderson (3 Apr. 1946) (Driberg papers 53) and Driberg, *HC Deb.* (5 Apr. 1946), col. 1538.

[40] Aung San to Driberg (12 June 1946) (Driberg papers S3).

[41] Maun Ohn to Driberg (18 June 1946); Driberg to Will Whitely, Labour Chief Whip (26 June 1946) (Driberg papers S3).

[42] Driberg to Aung San and to Than Tun, both 22 Nov. 1946 (Driberg papers S3).

[43] *HC Deb.* (21 July 1947), cols. 866–7.

had previously argued that premature autonomy would merely leave Indian workers and peasants at the mercy of a capitalist-dominated Congress were silenced by the sheer force of Indian nationalist mobilisation: though such arguments were still to recur for numerous other colonies. Yet there were still sharp controversies in 1945–7 over the timing of independence, constitutional arrangements, the economic legacy of British rule, and, of course, over Partition. The most outspoken criticism came, as might be expected, from the Communist Party and the small group of Labour back-benchers closely associated with it. These appeared to doubt the Attlee Government's willingness to transfer power until the very last moment. Earlier others had expressed doubts also. Reginald Sorensen of the India League returned from a tour of India in February 1946 describing the situation as 'explosive, demanding urgent action'. The LPACIQ accordingly urged the Government radically to speed up the transfer of power, recommending the immediate declaration of elections, a new All-India Cabinet, and the cessation of European recruitment to the Indian Civil Service.[44] Such demands indicate that still at this late stage Labour's Friends of India continued to fear that Attlee would deny Indian claims. As the ILP's paper noted: 'In this country there is a feeling that the Labour Government is proceeding reasonably, if cautiously, towards the extension of full self-government for India . . . In India itself, however, there is the feeling that things are getting worse rather than better.'[45]

In general, despite these fears, Labour MPs did not attack the main lines of the Government's India policy but engaged in criticism of detail, particularly on civil liberties and continuing restrictions on left-wing political activity in India. (Though Peter Freeman, whose multi-purpose championing of good causes embraced both colonial freedom and animal rights, also waxed indignant about cruelty to lambs under the Raj[46]). The threat of Partition and intercommunal violence engaged increasing attention, but only the CPGB was inclined to place the whole blame on Britain. Here, as in Palestine, the Communists appeared to suggest that once colonialism was removed

---

[44] Minutes of LPACIQ meeting (27 Feb. 1946) (LP papers LP/CSC/46/3).

[45] Editorial note, *NL* (5 Jan. 1946).

[46] *HC Deb. Written Answers* (4 Feb. 1946), cols. 312–13. Freeman, whose activities included holding office at various times in the India League, the Council on African Freedom, the MCF, the RSPCA, and the Vegetarian Society of Great Britain, was to continue his lonely championing of animal rights in the colonies for many subsequent years.

local conflicts would solve themselves. 'Come out of India. That is all we have got to do, and the Indian people will sort things out', suggested Willie Gallacher.[47]

The debate on the Indian Independence Bill itself, a largely self-congratulatory occasion, indicated the range of views within the PLP. Sorensen presented a moving affirmation of the anticolonialist ethic, expressing the hope that Partition would eventually be ended and that the princely states would adopt democratic systems. He concluded that:

I think we should register a note of profound gratitude to those great lovers of freedom who for many years have striven for the liberation of India, not merely for the benefit of India but for the benefit of Britain as well. Indeed for Britain to be released from the embarrassing position of a conqueror is a service to Britain.[48]

Former Meerut prisoner Lester Hutchinson emphasised economic neglect under the Raj: 'we are leaving India in more or less the same condition as we found it.' India must, he argued, adopt radical economic policies; these would help solve the communal problem and the resulting economic growth would, through increased trade, benefit Britain also.[49] Thomas Reid, by contrast, said Britain could be proud of her record in India. She had done all she could to unite it; and, he believed, the princely states were not undemocratic. Reid, a former Ceylon civil servant and probably the most right-wing of Labour's colonial specialists, thought India's problems were religious rather than economic: 'This new-fangled idea of explaining everything as an economic problem is a travesty of human nature.'[50]

Gallacher, for the Communist Party, scorned British self-praise on independence: the Indians, he said, had forced them out. The British working class had never had anything to do with ruling India, and the capitalists had made a very poor job of it. India's disabilities were Britain's fault: 'While our traders were taking great fortunes out of India, we were deliberately holding back the economic development of that great country. That is why the caste system is there.' Perhaps most surprisingly, he called Congress the only hope for India's future, and made no mention at all of the CPI.[51]

---

[47] *HC Deb.* (12 Dec. 1946) col. 1409.
[48] Ibid. (10 July 1947), col. 2490.
[49] Ibid., cols. 2494–8.
[50] Ibid., cols. 2506–9.
[51] Ibid., cols. 2526–8.

Despite Gallacher's rhetorical contempt the Labour Party felt entitled, then and later, to self-congratulation over Indian independence. Even Nye Bevan, the most outspoken senior critic of the party leadership, had unstinted praise for Attlee's actions in Asia:

Of all the acts of the Labour government, the one which most surely establishes its place in history for its wisdom, vision and courage was the granting of self-government to India, Pakistan, Ceylon and Burma ... it was the natural consummation of at least two decades of Labour Party history. Attlee had become part of that process as well as one of its senior architects.[52]

Far less to the anticolonial left's taste was the Government's committal of British troops to enable the Dutch to regain control of Indonesia. An unusual and temporary alliance of left-wingers such as Driberg, Mikardo, and Michael Foot with normally loyalist party figures such as James Callaghan and Sir Hartley Shawcross combined to protest about this and the parallel deployment of British troops to re-establish French rule in Indo-China.[53] As so often, however, the only public protests were from the Communists and the ILP.[54] More serious still from the point of view of the Government's critics was the degenerating situation in Malaya, which in 1948 erupted into full-scale guerrilla war between the British and Communist groups. It was on this issue that CPGB denunciation of Labour colonial policy was most bitter; for by 1948 the Communists had effected another about-turn, from enthusiasm for the Labour Government to savage condemnation of it.

IV. THE CPGB, THE LABOUR GOVERNMENT, AND THE COLONIES

Labour's landslide victory in 1945 was greeted by the British Communist Party with acclamation, even though it had itself earlier pressed for a continuation of the wartime coalition. As well as Labour's

---

[52] Aneurin Bevan, *Tribune* (16 Dec. 1955). The *New Statesman* echoed the judgement: 'Mr. Attlee's greatest single service to Britain and the world was his post-war decision ... that Britain should "quit" India and Burma' (13 Oct. 1951).

[53] 'Statement on the Situation in Indo-China and Indonesia' (drafts, signatures, and copies in Driberg papers S3), signed by 68 Labour MPs and 3 peers. The original signatories were Driberg, Callaghan, Konni Zilliacus, and Hutchinson (note in Driberg's hand, ibid.).

[54] See for instance *NL* (19 Jan. 1946).

massive Commons majority, two Communist MPs were returned to Parliament, William Gallacher and Phil Piratin—and five or six of those who sat on the Labour benches had few significant disagreements with Communist Party policy.[55] The CP leadership regarded Attlee's Government as likely to make major strides towards socialism in Britain; although already dissenters in the ranks were grumbling that such sanguine hopes were a departure from true Leninism.[56] This endorsement of gradualist Labour policies was extended also into the colonial field. During the later 1940s, however, the Communists moved from this 'moderate' position and adopted a far more critical attitude towards Labour colonial policy.

There were several reasons for this change, all relating to the advent and deepening of the Cold War. Growing hostility between Britain and the USSR, especially from early 1947, was inevitably reflected in the CPGB's stance. The introduction of Marshall Aid and the foundation of the Cominform, also early in 1947, meant that the CPGB was again, as it had not been since the disbandment of the Comintern, under close pressure from the international Communist movement to go on to the offensive. At the end of the year the Zhdanov line was declared, proclaiming that there were now only two camps in world affairs. Neutrality and the search for a third way between the USSR and imperialism were impossible. This declaration was aimed especially at Asian Communist Parties, and shortly thereafter several of them, including the Malayan CP, launched armed insurrections.

Quite apart from these outside stimuli, there is no doubt that many British Communists were already deeply disillusioned with Labour's record, especially in foreign and colonial policy, and eager to attack it more openly. The party began to engage itself more actively in colonial affairs, campaigning vigorously on a number of specific issues (most strident was the coverage of the Malayan war), holding conferences of Communists and sympathisers from various colonial territories, producing substantial quantities of literature on the subject,

---

[55] Again one must note the imprecision of the label 'fellow traveller'; but at a minimum four of the five MPs expelled from Labour for pro-Soviet views may be thus described: John Platts-Mills, L. J. Solley, Lester Hutchinson, and D. N. Pritt. The fifth, Konni Zilliacus, was a quirkier character, perhaps best labelled a Titoist rather than a Stalinist.

[56] Edward Upward's autobiographical novel, *The Rotten Elements* (Heinemann, 1969), gives an acute fictionalised portrayal of these doubts and divisions.

and attempting, with mixed success, to renew its contacts with, and influence on, colonial *émigrés* in Britain.

Yet in the post-war years, almost for the first time, Communists had to contend with a direct challenge to their very conception of imperialism, and one of a peculiarly irritating sort. Since its foundation, the party had pointed repeatedly to the Soviet Union as the example of how a nation could break completely with imperialism and solve its own national and colonial question. Now Attlee and his Ministers were claiming that under their administration Britain had made a decisive departure from imperialist policies and instituted a doctrine of partnership; the USA was an avowedly anticolonial power; it was now the USSR, they said, which was showing itself to be the real imperialist in Eastern Europe and elsewhere. Gallacher's attempt to rebut Attlee's charge evidently carried little conviction in the Commons:

Imperialism is capitalism in the stage of monopoly. [Laughter] Oh, yes; it is capitalism in the stage of monopoly, when the export of capital is absolutely essential to the maintenance of its economy. That is a definition of imperialism which will be borne out by the close and valuable study of Hobson, and I challenge anyone to give a better definition. If we accept that definition, then Russia is ruled out as an imperialist power.[57]

When he avoided such pseudo-academic bluster, Gallacher's parliamentary performances on colonial issues were often effective, making good use of information gathered by the CP's few colonial experts to expose and attack denials of civil rights to Communists and trade unionists in India and elsewhere. He was regularly supported in this by a number of dissident (and in some cases 'fellow-travelling') Labour back-benchers: most closely by John Platts-Mills and Lester Hutchinson. The other Communist MP, Phil Piratin, less quick on his feet and even more verbose than Gallacher, fared less well. Both, however, directed their assaults primarily towards issues of political rights. In common with other left-wing critics of Labour's colonial strategy, the Communists showed little grasp of the changed pattern of economic relationships between Britain and her colonies. Some of the factors which hampered Labour left criticism in this sphere also applied to the CPGB: sheer lack of knowledge and up-to-date information on colonial economic conditions (the detailed work on

[57] *HC Deb.* (22 Jan. 1948), col. 481.

Kenya by two Communist economists being the major exception);[58] a desire, at least in the honeymoon period of 1945–6, not too greatly to embarrass a Labour Government for which the CP retained high hopes. The weaknesses centred, in addition, on a threefold deficiency in the CPGB's stance on imperialism: its moralism, its simplistic Leninism, and its intermingling with the rhetoric of radical patriotism.

It was in analysing patterns of economic change that the weakness of an essentially moralistic critique of colonialism was most clearly to be seen. This was compounded by the simplistic association of imperialism with an earlier stage of capitalist development. Such an association seems to have enabled many of Attlee's Ministers to convince themselves that what was imperialism when undertaken by a private company under a reactionary government was development when done by a public corporation under a socialist administration. The association equally disarmed their Leninist critics. Gallacher's invocation of Hobson (though of course the proposition he was advancing was Lenin's, not Hobson's) to a sceptical House showed that critical tradition at its most threadbare. Further, the post-war years saw the CPGB staking its claim to be the truly patriotic party, defending the British national interest against those who would betray it to the USA and a cosmopolitan bourgeoisie. In so far as colonial development strategy was designed to maintain British economic independence against the USA, and to protect British working-class living standards, Communists found themselves in difficulties arguing against it.[59]

The analytical deficiencies were smoothed over by an almost limit-less optimism about the post-independence possibilities for development in colonial economies. Just as internal political problems in Palestine and India were argued by Communists to be consequences of colonialism which independence would infallibly solve, so it was asserted that only colonial ties held back Asian and African economic progress. The colonial system, it was argued, 'restricts and strangles economic development'.[60] In agriculture, merchant capital in the colonies was held to produce monocultural dependence and indebted-

---

[58] S. Aaronovitch and K. Aaronovitch, *Crisis in Kenya* (Lawrence & Wishart, 1947).
[59] On post-war CPGB and Labour left patriotism, see my 'Labour Patriotism, 1939–83', in Raphael Samuel (ed.), *Patriotism*, i (Routledge & Kegan Paul, 1989).
[60] R. Palme Dutt, 'The Way Ahead', in CPGB, *We Speak for Freedom*, 20.

ness, making 'astronomical' profits thereby.[61] The export of capital led to a process of 'undermining and unbalancing the economy . . . The original relationship between industry and agriculture was broken down, but no new relationship replaced it.'[62] Colonial rule strengthened 'the worst reactionary and monopoly elements in Britain'.[63]

The other side of the coin was the putative effect of decolonisation on the British economy and especially on the British working class; and this proved to be a perennially contentious issue. Although the argument that Britain's colonies, once freed from the imperial shackles, would undergo rapid economic growth was intended to suggest that Britain too would benefit from the expanded markets thus created, not all Communists were convinced. A lively debate on the contemporary relevance of the labour aristocracy thesis opened in 1946–7 and was revived several times thereafter.

In the discussion section of the CPGB's weekly journal for members, *World News and Views*, two party members attacked the analysis of economic imperialism for lack of clarity and realism. The party, they said, had not come to grips with the fact that 'our working-class is maintained in a falsely privileged position . . . is it understood that the militancy of the colonial peoples against imperialist exploitation means either the lowering of our own privileged standard of living, or our increased hard work, or the use of our new conscript army against them?'.[64]

A range of critical responses to this pessimistic view soon appeared. D. G. Priscott argued that the labour aristocracy thus privileged had always been only a small minority of the British working class and that the position even of this minority had been progressively undermined since the First World War. Inter-imperialist rivalries and colonial resistance meant that the colonial tribute available for this bribery was now insignificant.[65] J. Paul concurred: the critics' view would be correct only if capitalism were always able to make up a loss in one place by a gain elsewhere. In fact, to the contrary: 'The anti-imperialist struggle of the colonial peoples does not mean that the

---

[61] Sam Aaronovitch, 'Agriculture in the Colonies', *Communist Review* (July 1946), 21–3.

[62] Desmond Greaves, 'Industry in the Colonies', *Communist Review* (Aug. 1946), 11.

[63] Sam Aaronovitch, contribution to Congress discussion, *WNV* (25 Jan. 1947), 45.

[64] John Rashdall and Graeme Shankland, *WNV* (14 Dec. 1946), 408.

[65] *WNV* (11 Jan. 1947), 19.

capitalists get "more vicious" at home, but that they get weaker.'
Otherwise, one might as well argue for keeping the colonies under
British control, since *someone* would exploit them anyway.[66] Joe Bent
agreed that the pessimists' views 'lead inevitably to a policy of "doing
nothing yet"' about colonialism. The whole economic argument, he
thought, was merely a diversion from the urgent battle for political
independence.[67]

Yet the optimists' position, it will be noted, was itself implicitly
reformist. If working-class and colonial struggles were gradually
weakening imperialism, and could be expected to continue doing so,
then a peaceful rather than revolutionary transition to socialism was
on the cards. This prognosis 'virtually abandoned Marxism', according
to a youthful Hertford Communist, Eric Heffer. He reiterated, with
many pious quotations, Lenin's view that: 'Imperialism is not a policy
preferred by this or that group of capitalist politicians, but is a
definite stage of capitalism.'[68] Émile Burns, for the party leadership,
responded sardonically that Heffer and his co-thinkers might be well
advised to extend their reading of Lenin to his *Left-Wing Communism,
an Infantile Disorder.*[69]

The most important initiative undertaken by the CPGB in the
colonial field during this period was to convene a conference of
Communist Parties of the British Empire in London in February
1947.[70] This was the first occasion on which the CPs of the Empire
had met to exchange information and develop strategy. But the make-
up of the delegations exposed the weakness of the Marxist left in
Britain's colonies. There were representatives from Australia, Burma,
Canada, Ceylon, Cyprus, India, Ireland, Malaya, Palestine, South
Africa, and Syria: eleven countries, four of them self-governing and
five on the verge of independence. There were no black Africans or
West Indians. The reports on South Africa and on 'East and West
Africa and the West Indies' were delivered by a white South African
and a white Jamaican.[71] Indeed, as Jamaican Marxist Richard Hart

---

[66] Ibid. As we shall see, some British Communists later did indeed seem to endorse
this view.

[67] Ibid. (21 Jan. 1947), 45.   [68] Ibid. (1 Feb. 1947), 57.

[69] Ibid. 57–8. See Heffer's reminiscences of these debates and his subsequent
expulsion from the CP in *Never a Yes Man: The Life and Politics of an Adopted
Liverpudlian* (Verso, 1991), 32–41, 56–7.

[70] The main reports and statements from this are reproduced as CPGB, *We Speak
for Freedom.*

[71] D. du Plessis and Desmond Buckle, ibid. 72–7.

pointed out in an unpublished critique of the CPGB's position, the British Communists appeared to know little about the African or Caribbean colonies:

To state that our political demands should be for 'popular legislative assemblies based on universal suffrage' (which several colonies already have won) and not to appreciate that this demand is meaningless without the addition of a Cabinet or Executive Council *responsible* to the legislature is an unforgiveable omission. Not to know that the Caribbean Colonies demand a Federal Dominion, or what the West African colonies are now demanding is gross negligence.[72]

The conference, and in particular the lengthy statements by Palme Dutt which opened and closed it, stressed four main themes: the rapid development of colonial liberation movements themselves; the deepening crisis of the British Imperial system, which the Labour Government's policy was mistakenly trying to resolve through repression and through growing dependence on the USA; the threat to world peace posed by Britain's decline and America's bid for hegemony, which the colonial peoples could avert if they allied themselves with the 'progressive and democratic peoples of the world' led by the USSR; and the possibilities of mutually beneficial partnership between Britain and her ex-colonies.[73] The first and last themes were to prove the most controversial within the left, for it appeared that the CPGB was evading a number of important issues. First, the conference made no clear distinction between colonies and self-governing Dominions on the one hand (CPs from both participated) or between independence and Dominion status on the other (Palme Dutt seemed to speak as if these were interchangeable demands).

Second, the CPGB hoped that close economic and political association between Britain and the former colonies would persist after decolonisation; such co-operation being both mutually advantageous and a necessary bulwark against American aggression. Although it professed that such links would be purely voluntary and reiterated its recognition of the right of secession, suspicions were aroused in some minds that this represented in reality an attempt to sneak the old Labour notion of constructive imperialism in through the back

[72] Richard Hart, 'A Criticism of Certain Weak Points of the Report of the British Empire Communist Parties Conference' (MS in Hart's hand, n.d. but *c*.1947, Hart papers 4/5—emphasis in original).
[73] *We Speak for Freedom*, 4–30, 88–91.

door—or that it looked forward to a 'partnership' like that between the Soviet Union and Eastern Europe.[74] When Palme Dutt cited the USSR's commitment to the right of secession for its own national minorities, or Pollitt later lauded the relationship between the USSR and the Warsaw Pact states, as models for the attitude of a socialist Britain to her ex-colonies, few informed observers can have felt reassured.[75] There was also a marked differentiation between the CPGB's prescriptions for different colonies. Although claiming to repudiate 'all racial theories which seek to separate mankind into "higher" and "lower" races', it demanded immediate independence for the Asian and Middle Eastern colonies whilst saying of the African territories only that: 'The essential first step forward must be the establishment of full democratic and civil rights so as to facilitate the advance of popular organisations as the basis of advance to full freedom.'[76] Palme Dutt rhetorically enquired whether in making this distinction 'we are not abandoning the equal rights of all peoples? Are we not adopting the conception of higher and lower peoples—those who are ripe and those who are not ripe for self government?'[77] Unsurprisingly, he concluded that they were doing no such things. Others were less convinced.

By the end of the year the CPGB had moved to wholesale condemnation of Labour's record, which was now portrayed as unmitigatedly imperialist. Announcing this change, Pollitt echoed the Zhdanov two-camp thesis:

When the world is clearly divided into an imperialist and an anti-imperialist camp, with a Labour Government an active partner in the imperialist camp, and carrying through a capitalist solution to the crisis, it is necessary that important changes in the policy of the Communist Party to meet this situation should be made.[78]

Prominent among these was a more outspoken assault on Labour colonial policy. This, the CPGB now charged, 'resorts to every variation of the old imperialist tricks. It allies itself with the compro-

---

[74] Hart complained that in this respect the CPGB's position of 1947 was less progressive than had been that of its 1944 document (Hart, 'Criticism').

[75] Palme Dutt, *We Speak for Freedom*, 29; Pollitt, *WN* (10 July 1954), 544. In 1956–7 this became a sharply contentious issue within the party—see below, pp. 297–9.

[76] Palme Dutt, *We Speak for Freedom*, 16, 18.

[77] Ibid. 28.

[78] Pollitt's report to CPGB Executive Committee (13 Dec. 1947): *WNV* (20 Dec. 1947), 584.

mising section of the national bourgeoisie, granting nominal concessions in order to maintain its hold, as in India.' (Indian independence, so long a bright banner in the CP's parade of slogans, was now a nominal concession!) As for Labour's colonial development schemes, 'every one of these measures serves neither to help Britain nor the colonial peoples, but to increase their financial difficulties to speed-up the process of tying their economies more firmly to that of the US'.[79]

This accusation that the main effect of British imperial policy was to subordinate both Britain and the colonies to American imperialism became the most persistently reiterated theme of CPGB anticolonial propaganda in the succeeding years. This subordinating alliance, it was suggested, threatened to precipitate a third world war, and thus the anticolonial campaign was linked with the most important single subject of Communist agitation during the 1950s: support for Soviet 'peace' initiatives and opposition to Anglo-American 'warmongering'.[80] Armed conflicts in the colonies themselves were seen as potential catalysts for a global war: that in Malaya, which the British Government was held to have provoked, was especially emphasised, and argued also to be a very damaging drain on British resources. The cost of the war, the CPGB Executive alleged, 'has resulted in severe cuts in the housing, health and social services and in wages'.[81]

V. ATTACK FROM THE LABOUR LEFT, 1950–1

In 1953 an anonymous African reviewer of George Padmore's *Gold Coast Revolution* wrote that:

in pre-war years an African politician had to convince men of the *necessity* of action, in post-war years that necessity was conceded, and political agitation became a discussion of the form of action.[82]

[79] John Horner, 'Colonial Liberation', in *Communist Policy to Meet the Crisis: Report of the CPGB 21st National Congress* (CPGB, Nov. 1949), 43–4.

[80] The use of inverted commas here should not be held to imply any particular judgement on responsibility for the Cold War, but merely indicates the rather specialised meaning attached to the term 'peace' in post-war Communist discourse.

[81] CPGB Executive manifesto, 'Stop the War in Malaya', *WNV* (21 Jan. 1950). See also *Stop the War in Malaya* (CPGB leaflet, Sept. 1948); Jack Woddis, *Stop the War in Malaya* (CPGB pamphlet, May 1950); Harry Pollitt, *Malaya: Stop the War!* (CPGB pamphlet, Jan. 1952); and numerous *World News* and *Daily Worker* articles of this period with a similarly imaginative range of titles.

[82] Quoted in J. R. Hooker, *Black Revolutionary* (New York: Praeger, 1967), 117.

By the time those words were written, this had become the case also for debate on colonial policy within Britain. Before the war and, for many colonial territories, during the 1940s also, critics of Government policy had had to concentrate their efforts either on arguing a general case for progress towards self-government, or on issues of liberal principle like the colour bar. Increasingly after 1950, by contrast, attention was directed towards the pace and form of a political decolonisation whose eventual necessity was very widely conceded.

Under these changed conditions, the site of differences of opinion on the colonies inevitably changed also. The major shifts came in attitudes to political development. Before the war, questions about what type of political system should replace British rule in the tropical colonies could be discussed in an almost abstract manner and on the assumption that British initiatives would always set the pace; except in India nationalist pressures had till then made little impact. By the early 1950s, such pressures were challenging British rule almost everywhere. The preferences of British reformers had perforce to come to terms with, measure themselves against, and establish their attitudes towards the policies, plans, and ideologies of actually existing nationalisms. The spectrum of attitudes to Empire on the British Left was transformed by the addition of this overridingly important new variable.

Thus the growth of African nationalism helped radicalise Labour left-wingers' colonial attitudes. The left's calls for a socialist foreign policy in the later 1940s often seemed to sound in a void, rendered utopian by the absence of strong international forces to which such a policy could relate.[83] In the colonial sphere, by contrast, the presence of articulate nationalist movements, most of them claiming adherence to some form of socialism, gave the Labour left some leverage; or at worst an object on to which to project its hopes. The initial stirrings of this were expressed by the dissident Keep Left group of the PLP. Their first pamphlet, *Keep Left* (1947), had argued for a 'Third Force' in world affairs, escaping the polarisation of Soviet Communism and American capitalism. The prospect of basing such a force on any imaginable grouping of the existing states faded as the Cold War

[83] For Labour left views of foreign policy under Attlee, see Bullock, *Bevin*; Morgan, *Labour in Power*, ch. 6; M. R. Gordon, *Conflict and Consensus in Labour's Foreign Policy, 1914–1965* (Stanford, Calif.: Stanford University Press, 1969); and, above all, Jonathan Schneer, *Labour's Conscience: The Labour Left, 1945–51* (Unwin Hyman, 1988), chs. 2 and 3.

intensified; but linked to the emergence of new nations from colonial nationalism the concept could be revitalised. *Keeping Left*, in 1950, made the connection.[84]

If the rapid growth of nationalist movements and the belief that their success offered the prospect of a new form of socialist internationalism provided pull factors for a more active Labour anticolonialism, there was a subsidiary but important push from developments within the Labour Party itself. To many on the left, Attlee's administration seemed to lose impetus and water down its socialist commitments after 1947–8. In April 1951 Nye Bevan resigned from the Cabinet over Health Service charges, and became the rallying-point for left-wing opposition. Bevan himself was a committed anticolonialist, but no expert in the field. He had, it is true, expressed interest in the Colonial Secretaryship in 1950, but, according to Hugh Dalton, 'he couldn't be trusted there (a) not to waste money (b) not to be carried away by his colour prejudice, pro-black and anti-white'.[85] But at the same time a parliamentary leader for the anticolonial left did emerge, with Fenner Brockway's election for Eton and Slough in 1950. Brockway has already appeared several times in these pages; but from this point onward he becomes a central figure and the best-known British anticolonialist. His views on the subject thus require some analysis here.

Archibald Fenner Brockway (1888–1988; from 1964 Lord Brockway) had been born in Calcutta, the son and grandson of missionaries. He was raised in a Nonconformist and Radical-Liberal tradition like so many British opponents of imperialism. As a journalist in his early twenties, he was converted to the pantheism of the Revd R. J. Campbell's New Theology Movement and the socialism of the ILP. Imprisoned as a conscientious objector during the First World War, he thereafter became Joint Secretary of the British Committee of the Indian National Congress, ILP representative on the Executive of the Second International, sat as MP for East Leyton in 1929–31, and became Chairman of the ILP in 1931. He had plunged into every vicissitude of that party's multivalent and declining course over the

---

[84] See *Keep Left* (*New Statesman* pamphlet, 1947), and *Keeping Left* (*New Statesman* pamphlet, 1950).

[85] Diary entry (30 Oct. 1950); see Ben Pimlott (ed.), *The Political Diary of Hugh Dalton, 1918–40, 1945–60* (Jonathan Cape, 1986), 490. Dalton's claim must be read in the context of his own rather open anti-black racism.

following fifteen years, until rejoining Labour with most other remaining ILP members in 1947.[86]

Brockway claimed that his views on colonialism were formed far less by reading and theoretical argument than by personal experience: that they were indeed 'almost instinctive'.[87] As with many socialists from Nonconformist (and arguably also many from Jewish) backgrounds, he retained the ethical impulses of an inherited tradition whilst rejecting its theological content. I have argued that for most British socialists anticolonialism was seen always in essentially moral terms, with the role of theory decidedly secondary: theories of imperialism and of economic underdevelopment were supplements to a moral case in the light of which the theories themselves were understood. Of no one was this more true than Brockway—even one of his most bitter critics, Kenyan settlers' leader Michael Blundell (who regarded him as an apologist for African barbarism), called him 'a sincere, emotional, rather muddled thinker, who felt in some way that he could resolve the conflict . . . by some great and humanitarian gesture'.[88] Brockway's judgement was often doubted; his sincerity and disinterested concern for justice very rarely. His successor as chairman of the Movement for Colonial Freedom suggested that there was an essential distinction between the anticolonialism of the pre-war generations, based on an indignation at injustice; and that of people whose ideas were formed after 1945, for whom—although the moral aspect might retain an important place—considerations of the long-term economic effects of imperialism were more important than before.[89] On this account, Brockway was the emblematic representative of the earlier generation.

Brockway's socialism remained religiously based despite his abandonment of orthodox belief: 'The Christian ethic—service inspired by love—is the highest one can know . . . Our present economic system stands condemned because it does not reflect this ethic.'[90] In his view imperialism was trebly condemned by this standard, for not only did it export and universalise the demeaning profit motive, but

---

[86] As a party the ILP gradually ceased to exist: but as a current of opinion within Labour under the name Independent Labour Publications it retains a vestigial presence today.

[87] Interview with the author (1982).

[88] Sir Michael Blundell, *So Rough a Wind* (Weidenfeld & Nicolson, 1964), 108.

[89] Interview with Stan Newens.

[90] *Outside the Right* (Allen & Unwin, 1963), 185.

brought in its train national rivalries and war; and fomented racism, the deepest possible degradation of the human spirit. It was in this sense, rather than that of Lenin, that Brockway spoke of imperialism as 'exported capitalism'. Although he shared the general socialist view that modern colonialism was primarily economic in motivation, his use of the term 'imperialism' was clearly not Lenin's. For Brockway, it usually implied any form of interference by one nation in the affairs of another. It was not confined to capitalist systems:

the term imperialism is often held to mean only the occupation of under-developed countries by industrialised nations. The later Marxists identified it specifically as exploitation by monopoly capitalism. This is increasingly true in modern circumstances... But we reject the Marxist limitation historically and also in immediate terms. Not only did the exploitation of peoples begin before capitalism, but... national liberties may be overrun by communist countries.[91]

Unless Marxism is to be taken merely as a synonym for left-wing socialism, Brockway was never really a Marxist. He recalls that during the 1920s he found himself 'accepting a good deal of Marxism but not its materialism'.[92] He worked with Communist Party members on various campaigns during his career, but more on the basis of shared short-term political goals than of common ideological perspectives. The major intellectual influences he acknowledged in shaping his view of imperialism were Hobson and Brailsford, H. G. Wells (as an exponent of internationalism and the ideal of world government), Keir Hardie, Nehru's prison writings, and Padmore's Pan-Africanism.[93]

For Brockway, national self-determination was a first-order good, and there could be no morally acceptable case for its being delayed or compromised in pursuit of other goods. Thus when the problems of decolonisation were phrased, as they often were both by British policy-makers and by groups like the FCB, as a trade-off between self-rule and good government, or self-rule and economic development, basic liberal ethics demanded that one opt for self-rule. Only

---

[91] *The Colonial Revolution* (Hart-Davis, MacGibbon, 1973), 14. The 'we' is intriguing: indicative of a self-consciously programmatic claim, or a quotation from one?

[92] *Inside the Right*, 182.

[93] Interview with Lord Brockway. Brockway evidently read widely throughout his life; but he read for information rather than perspectives and was never essentially a theoretical animal.

the colonised themselves were entitled to decide when and how independence should be attained.

In any case, he did not accept that such a trade-off was at issue. Without necessarily sharing the view sometimes proposed by the CPGB that all economic and social problems were the result of colonialism, Brockway believed that the colonial relationship inevitably distorted and hampered the development of subject territories. Real progress could come only with the co-operation of fully self-governing states, arranged through the UN and other international agencies; and political independence was thus its absolute precondition. In this he fully shared the extreme optimism of almost all of the left about prospects for post-colonial development. He was not wholly blind to the possibility of conflict between the right to self-rule and other values: he noted it, for instance, in relation to the status of women in African societies.[94] But he tended to see—or at least publicly to acknowledge—only good in aspirant nationalist leaders. This led him into some striking errors of judgement about individuals, as with his lauding of Guinea's Sekou Toure as the 'Nehru' of French Africa;[95] and as 'a winning personality... modest... an intellectual... a socialist'.[96] It led him also into breathtaking assertions such as claiming for all 'self-reliant' Asian and African nationalist movements that 'Their one desire is to serve the cause of human freedom and peace.'[97] Brockway was close to being a genuine example of that usually mythical beast, the inverted racist who is blind to all human flaws in people of colour.

Finally, Brockway saw opposition to colonialism not only as a great moral challenge, but as potentially the greatest turning-point in world history—and here the almost messianic optimism of his character took full flight:

it is not too much to say that the history of the world until this century has been a record of successive empires... only since the Second World War has the imposed occupation of the territories of others—the essence of colonialism—been generally adjudged wrong in practice. Empires have fallen before, but this is the first time that the conscience of man has repudiated the actual existence of empires. We are thus witnessing more than the end of

[94] See for instance Brockway, *African Journey* (Gollancz, 1955), 94, and his *PN* column of 19 Sep. 1958.
[95] *PN* (8 Nov. 1957).
[96] Ibid. (17 Oct. 1958).
[97] Ibid. (7 June 1957).

an age; the whole course of human relations over many thousands of years of history has changed.[98]

It was thus inevitable that it should be Fenner Brockway who, at the 1950 Labour Party Conference, should call for a transformation in Labour policy towards the African colonies. This took the form which was to become the characteristic demand of the anticolonialist left during the 1950s: that firm target dates should be set for the independence of all colonies. This demand was linked with the ideas of world peace and of the Third Force colonial revolution:

> I want to suggest that, in consultation with the organisations of the African people we should fix a target date and aim, at that target date, at creating such conditions that full self-government may be possible for those people. If we do that, the Indian revolution will be succeeded by an African revolution, and that in turn will serve not only the cause of liberty but also the cause of peace.[99]

Yet the relative lack of involvement of most constituencies and trade unions was still obvious at this Conference. Only nine resolutions, all from CLPs, made reference to colonial affairs. Of these, five related to the threatened take-over by South Africa of the southern African Protectorates and one to the future of Namibia. Three resolutions, then, made more general statements about colonial policy. One, from Salford East, did so in the context of a blanket demand for more radical policies on all fronts, calling for 'immediate and unconditional freedom to the colonial people' with the aim of 'the securing of allies among the common people of the world' for socialism. Another demanded that the Government convene a conference of African representatives 'to discuss their urgent political, economic and racial problems'. The third, from Paddington South, was phrased in terms obviously deriving from the influence of the Congress of Peoples Against Imperialism (see below, pp. 176–83), urging 'an International Socialist Conference to meet representatives of the Colonial peoples in order to work out a common socialist colonial policy'.[100] The first stirrings of a new radical anticolonialism in the constituency parties could faintly be discerned.

[98] *Colonial Revolution*, 13.
[99] Brockway, *LPACR 1950*, 124.
[100] Resolutions submitted to Labour Party Annual Conference 1950 (Labour Party, 1950), 18, 29–30. The only other major Conference contribution on colonial affairs was an eccentric speech by Trotskyist Gerry Healy, accusing British colonial policy of being merely a tool of the USA (*LPACR 1950*, 117).

During 1950–1 the major and growing cause of back-bench Labour concern was that the Government seemed to left-wingers to be tending towards surrender to the demands of white settler minorities in East, Central, and Southern Africa. This concern focused on three issues: South Africa's claims on the Protectorates, the proposed Central African Federation, and the Seretse Khama case. They were not causes specific to the left of the Labour Party—and indeed some Liberal and even Conservative MPs joined the left-initiated campaigns over Khama and the Protectorates. Nor was there as yet overt criticism of the Labour leadership, except concerning the decision to exile Seretse Khama, the heir apparent to the chieftainship of the Bamangwato people in Bechuanaland. Seretse had married a white woman, Ruth Williams, thus arousing both intense dissension within the Bamangwato and the ire of white South Africa. It was widely believed on the left that British action against Seretse was motivated by the desire to appease South Africa; and Acland, Driberg, Foot, Jennie Lee, Mikardo, and Woodrow Wyatt voted against the Government on the issue.

Keep Left and FCB MPs combined in an Early Day Motion of 26 February 1951 which, under the guise of reaffirming support for the policies of James Griffiths (who had succeeded Creech Jones as Colonial Secretary) and Patrick Gordon Walker (the Dominions Secretary), warned that there must be no concessions to the doctrine of white supremacy. Only sharp exercise of party discipline by Attlee and the Whips enabled the Government to survive a critical motion on the Khama issue brought by Liberal leader Clement Davies. One of the left-wingers thus cowed into voting with the Government, Michael Foot, called this 'the worst vote I ever cast in the House'.[101]

A new consideration which may have discouraged full-scale revolt by the anticolonialist left both in this affair and in the 1950–1 session generally was the feeling that the Opposition was cynically inciting

[101] On the background of the affair, see Michael Dutfield, *A Marriage of Inconvenience* (Unwin Hyman, 1990); Mary Benson, *Tshekedi Khama* (Faber & Faber, 1960); Michael Crowder, 'Professor Macmillan Goes on Safari', in Hugh Macmillan and Shula Marks, *Africa and Empire* (Temple Smith, 1989); Ronald Hyam, 'The Political Consequences of Seretse Khama: Britain, the Bamangwato and South Africa, 1948–1953', *Historical Journal*, 29 (1986); and Michael Scott, *A Time to Speak* (Faber & Faber, 1958). For the parliamentary incidents: *HC Deb.* (28 Mar. 1950), cols. 357–60; (11 June 1951), cols. 1190–318. Foot quotation from Benson *Tshekedi Khama*, 240. See also Philip Norton, *Dissension in the House of Commons, 1945–74* (Macmillan, 1975), 82–3; David Goldsworthy, *Colonial Issues in British Politics, 1945–1961* (Oxford: Oxford University Press, 1971), 157–62; Brockway, *Outside the Left*, 75–6.

Liberal and Labour left dissent in order to embarrass Attlee and Griffiths whilst themselves maintaining a front of bipartisanship. After the 1951 election, Conservatives were increasingly to accuse the Labour leadership of a similar duplicity.

5

The Left Outside Parliament, 1945–1954

This chapter discusses the various anticolonial pressure groups operating between the end of the Second World War and 1954, when many of their activities merged into a single umbrella body, the Movement for Colonial Freedom. Some of these organisations were based on particular tendencies within British socialism—the most important of these being the Congress of Peoples Against Imperialism, established by members and ex-members of the ILP. Some took as their *raison d'être* agitation about a particular colonial territory or problem. Some, like the Union of Democratic Control, saw their role as primarily educational; some sought to influence the colonial policy of the Labour Party, TUC, and other bodies; some, so far as one can judge, had no significant influence on anyone. The chapter deals first with the sectionally based organisations, then the issue based, and concludes with an evaluation of the left's activities on colonial issues within the Labour Party.

I. THE CONGRESS OF PEOPLES AGAINST IMPERIALISM

Amidst their myriad anti-war and anticolonial campaigns of the 1940s, Fenner Brockway and others in the ILP retained the hope of redeeming the failed promise of the League Against Imperialism: building a broad-based international anticolonial movement which would unite European socialists with colonial nationalists. The first limited move in this direction was the establishment of a British Centre Against Imperialism. Initially founded in 1937 in parallel with a similar French Centre, it had held anticolonial exhibitions in London and Glasgow; but the outbreak of war led to a virtual cessation of its modest activities and only late in 1945 was a serious effort made to relaunch it.[1] Its

---

[1] See *Annual Report of the NAC* to 1939 ILP Conference (ILP 1939); Workers' Empire Exhibition Committee, *Come and See the Empire by the All Red Route* (National Labour Press pamphlet, n.d. but *c*.1937); Arthur Ballard, Fenner Brockway, and Frank Horrabin (for BCAI) to FCB (1 Dec. 1945), FCB 3/2/265.

proclaimed objective was 'to link up the anti-Imperialist movements in this and other Metropolitan countries, and the anti-Imperialist movements in the Colonies'.[2] It claimed contacts with such movements in France, Holland, the USA, Burma, Ceylon, India, Indonesia, Iraq, Kenya, Lebanon, Malaya, Sierra Leone, Syria, and the West Indies.[3] Many of these links must have been tenuous in the extreme; primarily operating through the personal networks of Brockway, Padmore, and Kenyatta.[4] There is no record of the BCAI having undertaken any activity beyond holding a single 'Annual Conference' in February 1946 and, in conjunction with the Pan-Africanists, attempting to publicise Kikuyu grievances over land rights in Kenya.[5]

By 1947 this small organisation had renamed itself the British Centre for Colonial Freedom, and was engaged in a rather wider range of activities. A report at the end of that year indicated that, as well as the Kenyan protests, the Centre had lobbied the Colonial Office, held public meetings, or aided delegations on Indian, Burmese, Ceylonese, Indonesian, Nigerian, Sudanese, Cypriot, and other issues.[6] It lamented, however, that whilst several of these actions had gained wide press publicity in the colonies, they had not done so in Britain. Its political base within the British left remained rather narrow. Though eleven MPs and intellectuals such as Harold Laski and Vera Brittain were among the sponsors, the organisations represented on the committee were all small: the ILP (then in its last stages of decline as a distinct party); the Peace Pledge Union (a formerly important pacifist group, now also in reduced circumstances);[7] Common Wealth (to which the same sad story again applied); the Labour Pacifist Fellowship; Victory for Socialism (a loosely knit faction of former ILP members in the Labour Party); and the Socialist Vanguard Group (another small Labour body inspired by socialist refugees from Nazi Germany). All were high-minded congregations of the libertarian and pacifist left, but hardly influential; and of course several of them

[2] BCAI circular announcing relaunching Conference (3 Feb. 1946), FCB 3/2/266, and conference report in *NL* (2 Feb. 1946).
[3] Letter of 1 Dec. 1945 and circular of 3 Feb. 1946.
[4] Interview with Lord Brockway.
[5] See clipping from the *African Standard* (10 May 1946), FCB 3/2/271; and Evelyn Denington, Organising Secretary of BCAI, to Hinden (4 July 1946), FCB 3/2/270.
[6] Report of Activities of British Centre for Colonial Freedom; Douglas Rogers, Hon. Sec. of BCCF, to FCB (15 Dec. 1947), FCB 3/3/273. Additional details from interviews with Lord Brockway and Lord Hatch.
[7] See the PPU's house history: Sybil Morrison, *I Renounce War* (Sheppard Press, 1962).

were the same people wearing different hats. The colonial associates, apart from the ILP's old Pan-Africanist friends represented on the Centre's committee by Padmore and Peter Abrahams, were mostly African, Asian, and West Indian students' groups in London.

A far more ambitious initiative towards an international anticolonial front was undertaken by the ILP and its French associates in 1947-8. After preliminary meetings in London and Paris, a major conference met at Puteaux to form a Congress of Peoples Against Imperialism (COPAI). This grew initially out of the desire of various European left-wing groups—the ILP, the French Section française de l'Internationale ouvrière (SFIO) and various smaller French socialist parties, the exiled Spanish Pertido Obrero de Unificacion Marxista (POUM), the embattled Eastern European socialists, and others—to associate colonial political organisations with the campaign for a United Socialist States of Europe.[8] As the ILP announced:

There is a danger that Russian Communism might steal the anti-imperialist platform; aided, as it undoubtedly is, by the imperialist attitude of many right-wing social-democrats. This Paris Congress seeks, above all, to unite the 'third force' of libertarian Socialism with the anti-imperialist uprising of the colonial peoples.[9]

The African and Asian socialists invited to the conference soon made it clear, however, that they were not interested in being mere auxiliaries to a European movement. The struggle for the end of colonial rule must, they insisted, come first. Only then could they, as independent states, plan for co-operation with Europe.

The colonial, and especially the African, delegates at Puteaux were therefore highly critical of aspects of the bulky Political and Economic Reports prepared by the COPAI's organisers.[10] Abderrhim Bouabid of the Moroccan Istiqlal party said that 'We give our adhesion and that on one condition. That we be treated on the basis of equality, and that there be granted to us the respect as towards a country

---

[8] The idea of the USSE was, as we have noted, particularly associated with Trotsky's legacy, and the Trotskyist parties of various European countries were involved in the COPAI. They were, however, all very small: the dominant groups were the French SFIO and various groups from the inter-war 'Two-and-a-half International' tradition. The Asian representatives at the conference too were mostly from left-wing socialist parties; but the Africans included several of the broad-based and ideologically inchoate nationalist congresses.

[9] *SL* (19 June 1948).

[10] The Reports (as amended at Puteaux) are reproduced in *Congress of the Peoples of Europe, Asia and Africa* (COPAI 1948), 69-123.

enjoying its own sovereignty and liberty.'[11] Peter Abrahams of the Pan-African Congress similarly warned that 'We do not desire to be reduced to the simple role of students of European Socialism. Against this attitude we are compelled to protest.'[12] The Trotskyists present also dissented, though on grounds of the Reports' supposed reformism rather than their paternalism.[13]

The Political Report, drafted by Brockway:

> was based on the idea that Europe itself is in danger of becoming colonised by American economic power and Russian totalitarianism, and put forward the object of establishing a Third Force which would unite the peoples of Europe, Asia and Africa for national freedom, democratic socialism and peace.
>
> This conception was endorsed by the Socialists from Asia and by the few democratic socialists who attended the Congress from Africa; but representatives of the nationalist movements in Africa would not have it.
>
> They were concerned only with gaining the independence of their countries ... They did not want to be on record as in favour or against America or Russia ... As for the Third Force, they identified it with the Coalition Government in France, and that Government was guilty of maintaining imperialism.[14]

With the Europeans grudgingly agreeing to drop the Third Force and anti-Soviet aims and concentrate on the anticolonial ones, the conference approved an ambitious series of proposals for decolonisation and economic development, and established a permanent structure to pursue them. There was to be an International Committee with eight representatives each from Asia, Africa, and Europe, chaired by Brockway and with Jean Rous as General Secretary, and with centres of activity in London and Paris. Yet soon the COPAI's story, like that of the LAI before it, was one of decline and fall from its original high hopes. Neither the International Committee, with its members scattered across the world, nor the Paris Centre, hamstrung by the internal dissensions of the French left and by political restrictions on its activities as the crises in Indo-China and North Africa deepened, seems ever to have functioned effectively. The London organisation had rather greater success, but never broadened into the kind of international anticolonial crusade to which Brockway had aspired. It

[11] Congress proceedings, ibid. 29.

[12] Ibid. 31.

[13] See speech by Pierre Frank, ibid. 56.

[14] *SL* (3 July 1948): Paris report 'By Our Special Correspondent'—undoubtedly Brockway.

remained reliant on the ILP for funds and for most of its active personnel, although a wide range of left-wing Labour MPs and others gave their names as sponsors. Thus its political base in Britain was, if not as restricted as that of the BCAI, still fairly narrow even after most of the ILP activists returned in the later 1940s to the Labour Party.[15]

The COPAI's programme for decolonisation had four main elements. Most important was the demand for recognition of a universal principle of national self-determination, involving the rejection of all proposals for interim development, trusteeship, dominion status, and schemes like the French Union; and the setting of target dates for the independence of all colonies. If the colonial power refused immediately to set such dates, the United Nations should do so. In the meantime European workers should engage in action, including strikes and boycotts, to prevent the use of military force against colonial uprisings; whilst intellectuals should establish a world-wide 'tribune of the conscience of the peoples where the colonials can freely express themselves'.[16]

Second, the Congress called for a far-reaching programme of economic and social development for a post-colonial world. Starting from an analysis of colonialism which saw it in primarily economic terms—though not a Leninist one since the COPAI stressed the search for and control over markets rather than fields of investment[17]—it suggested that the effects of the Second World War were already producing the initial stages of an economic decolonisation. The problem for socialists now was 'to seek means for a possible co-operation on the lines of economic interdependence: and . . . to reconcile this close economic co-operation with the principle of absolute political equality.'[18] Criticising all the then current plans for

---

[15] For the composition of the London Centre, see M. R. Turner (Organising Secretary) to FCB (1 July 1949), FCB 4/3/136, periodic reports of COPAI activities in *SL* and *PN*, and documents in Africa Bureau, FCB, and Labour Party files. Additional information from interviews with Lord Brockway and Bob Edwards. The papers of the COPAI itself do not seem to have survived.

[16] Political Report in *Congress of the Peoples*, 110. This summary of COPAI's philosophy is drawn from these founding Political and Economic Reports; from the Manifesto of the later Conference on the Colonial Peoples and War; and the COPAI documents *Charter of the Congress of Peoples Against Imperialism* (COPAI 1948) and *The Colonial Peoples' Appeal to the United Nations* (COPAI 1952).

[17] Reflecting, no doubt, the Luxemburgist influences on Bob Edwards, who drafted the Puteaux Economic Report.

[18] Economic Report, 71.

economic development, including Labour's Colonial Development and Welfare programme and the Marshall Plan, the Congress asserted the need for a 'general comprehensive economic plan' which would combine a primary emphasis on the satisfaction of local needs with an increasingly strong framework of democratic international co-ordination. Within underdeveloped economies, stress was to be placed on agricultural development and this was to be accompanied by rapid improvement of health, educational, and other social services.

Third, the COPAI envisaged European socialists and colonial liberation movements together forming a new democratic power bloc independent of both US and Soviet spheres of influence and, by exerting pressure on the superpowers, capable of averting the risk of a third world war.[19] The issue of attitudes to the USSR remained contentious within the Congress. When at its second Conference, on the Colonial Peoples and War, European delegates sought condemnation of Soviet imperialism, African representatives made 'impassioned objections' and threw the resolution out.[20]

Fourth, there was a reassertion of the classical anticolonialist belief in the interdependence of all socialist struggles, of the necessity of decolonisation for the building of socialist democracy in former colonising as well as former colonised countries, and of the long-term aim of a World Constituent Assembly and eventually a World Political and Economic Federation.

The resources of the Congress were of course quite inadequate to these grandiose tasks, and even to mounting an effective propaganda campaign in their pursuit. Thus Labour's newly appointed Commonwealth Officer, Edward Farmer, though complaining that COPAI speakers 'give a widely [wildly?] distorted picture of the Labour Government's policy and achievements' and thereby 'cause some difficulties', rather dismissively concluded that 'it is doubtful whether they are of sufficient importance to justify any action against it by the Labour Party'.[21]

Twenty-one Labour MPs joined the sponsors of the Puteaux conference—others included Gandhi and Prasad of Congress, Awo-

---

[19] This hostility to the USSR, apparently smuggled back in despite some of the African representatives' objections, naturally led to the COPAI being denounced by the CP; see R. Palme Dutt, 'Britain and the Colonies', *WN* (9 Jan. 1954), 26.

[20] Conference report, *SL* (22 Oct. 1949).

[21] Memorandum by Farmer for Commonwealth Subcommittee of NEC, Jan. 1951: 'Note on South East Asia Committee and Congress of Peoples Against Imperialism', LP papers CSC/50/20.

Iowo and Azikiwe of Nigeria, Senghor (who attended), Wallace-Johnson, Leon Blum, and, remarkably, South Korean dictator Syngman Rhee. Eighteen sponsored a 1949 COPAI conference on the Colonial Peoples and War; and sixteen a petition on the Kenyan land problem; but of these only Brockway and Leslie Hale, Labour MP for Oldham West, seem to have borne the brunt of Congress work and been at all regularly active in it.[22] The key figures in the organisation's day-to-day activities were three South African socialist *émigrés*, anthropologist Mary Klopper, Doctor Leon Szur, and his wife Rolene, together with Douglas Rogers (Brockway's former assistant as editor of the *New Leader*), Dick Beech of the Chemical Workers' Union, Arthur Carr of Common Wealth, and Trotskyist Betty Hamilton, secretary of the Westminster CLP.

The range of colonial associates was rather wider, including Nkrumah's CPP in the Gold Coast, the Sudanese Umma, Tunisian Neo-Destour, and Kenyatta's KAU in Kenya as well as those listed above. By 1953 COPAI affiliates included seven parties in British colonies, four French, and two from newly independent states. Seven of these thirteen organisations could claim to be the main nationalist groupings of their territories.[23] Brockway was, over thirty years later, 'still astonished at the prestige of the Congress in ex-colonial states'.[24] Unlike those anticolonial lobbies which sought primarily to influence opinion in Britain, the COPAI saw its role as being to encourage and provide aid for the nationalist movements. This seems to have had rather limited practical expression beyond the level of individual contacts, except for links with Kenya and Central Africa, which are discussed separately below.

By 1953–4 Brockway and the organisers of the Congress were becoming increasingly dissatisfied with its work. This discontent, which with other pressures led to the creation of the Movement for Colonial Freedom, was for three main reasons. First, hopes of co-ordinating a Europe-wide campaign were becoming ever more difficult to realise, as the problems already caused by the attempt to run the COPAI simultaneously from London and Paris were compounded by

[22] Broadsheet on COPAI conference, 'The Colonial Peoples and War', FCB papers 4/3/139–41; COPAI petition on Kenya land issue (copies in Africa Bureau papers 29/14/4–5 and Benn papers).

[23] See listing in *PN* (26 June 1953).

[24] Interview with Lord Brockway. See also Fenner Brockway, *The Colonial Revolution* (Hart Davis, MacGibbon, 1973), 38, and id., *Towards Tomorrow* (Hart Davis, MacGibbon, 1977), 152.

the increasing inactivity of the French members.[25] Second, dissension had grown within the London committee as Trotskyist involvement on it became significant. Entrist former members of the Revolutionary Communist Party within London Labour Parties, with Betty Hamilton as their most active spokesperson, produced recurrent factional in-fighting. 'They were not a constructive presence', as Brockway mildly recalled.[26] And to the old argument over whether to attack Soviet as well as Western imperialism was added a new one: divided attitudes to armed struggle. Moves by British pacifists at a London COPAI conference in September 1953 to commit the movement to non-violence were defeated—and the voting figures, 27 against and 22 for the pacifists, indicated not only a divided organisation but a shrunken one.[27] One may, however, doubt whether these divisions were the main reason for the Centre's having 'outlived its usefulness', as has been suggested.[28] Far more important would seem to have been a third and more general consideration.

The activities of the COPAI had been almost exclusively directed outward, towards establishing links with nationalist movements. In the new circumstances where mass nationalism was emerging in almost all colonies, in which debate was shifting to the forms of British response to these movements, and in which (so it was believed) public awareness of colonial conflicts was growing, there was a felt need to shift focus. Mobilising anticolonial opinion in the Labour movement and more generally within Britain now took priority; and a broader-based movement was wanted to conduct this.

II. THE TROTSKYISTS AND THE EMPIRE

In 1945 British Trotskyists, for the first and thus far last time, were united in a single organisation, the Revolutionary Communist Party (RCP). This had somewhat fraught relations with the Secretariat of the Fourth International, world Trotskyism's governing body, which wanted the RCP fully to enter the Labour Party. The majority of the RCP, led by Jock Haston, Ted Grant, and Tony Cliff, wished to

---

[25] Interviews with Lord Brockway and Bob Edwards.
[26] Interview with Lord Brockway.
[27] Conference report in *PN* (2 Oct. 1953).
[28] David Goldsworthy, *Colonial Issues in British Politics, 1945–1961* (Oxford: Oxford University Press, 1971), 276.

remain a separate party, though they had factions operating within both Labour and the ILP; a minority, led by Gerry Healy, shared the Secretariat's pro-entrist view.

Arguments about this issue persisted throughout the RCP's short life, supplemented by debates over Yugoslavia and especially over the USSR; with Cliff developing his (or rather Max Shachtman's) analysis of Russia as State Capitalist and leading the so-called State Capitalism group which was eventually to become the International Socialists and later the Socialist Workers' Party. Healy's pro-entrist group, with the reluctant approval of the majority, moved into the Labour Party in 1948. In the following year the remainder of the RCP dissolved the party and also entered Labour's ranks.[29]

Disputes over foreign affairs were the stuff of the RCP's incessant internal debates, expressed in lengthy, verbose, and often vitriolic position papers; and of its attempts to recruit from the CP. Analyses of Stalinism and endless selective exegeses on texts of Lenin and Trotsky—the latter always referred to as 'The Old Man'—dominated here. Public campaigning, by contrast, was overwhelmingly concentrated on domestic, and especially industrial, issues. Colonial themes were far less prominent: but since in principle the colonial revolution was supposed to be central to Trotskyist hopes for the future, they received intermittent polemical and more rarely theoretical treatment in RCP writings.[30]

For the RCP, unlike the CPGB, there was no honeymoon with Labour in office in 1945. Within a month of the 1945 election, *Socialist Appeal* was predicting that Labour's Indian policy would be no different from that of the Conservatives.[31] The use of British troops in Indonesia was perceived to confirm prognoses of Labour imperialism; and the RCP appealed to other left-wing bodies to join it in a campaign against the intervention. Only the ILP even bothered

---

[29] This account is based primarily on publications and internal documents of the RCP and its successors held by Nuffield College, Oxford; plus Sam Bornstein and Al Richardson, *War and the International* (Socialist Platform, 1986); John Callaghan, *British Trotskyism* (Oxford: Blackwell, 1984); Jim Higgins, 'British Trotskyism, 1938 –48', *International Socialism*, 13 (1963); Peter Shipley, *Revolutionaries in Modern Britain* (Bodley Head, 1976); and David Widgery (ed.), *The Left in Britain, 1956–1968* (Harmondsworth: Penguin, 1976).

[30] It is in a sense surprising that the RCP did not give more attention to colonial subjects, since all three of its leading theorists came from parts of the Empire-Commonwealth: Healy from Ireland, Cliff (originally Ygael Gluckstein) from Palestine, and Grant from South Africa.

[31] *Socialist Appeal* (mid-Sept. 1945).

to reply, and it gave a firm refusal.[32] The Trotskyists bitterly attacked both Labour and Communists for apathy on the colonial question, which the RCP called 'the touchstone of the sincerity of any party that claims to stand for socialism'. Communist support for Labour colonial policy, it asserted, 'will come as no surprise to those who are acquainted with the Stalinist abandonment of the revolutionary struggle of the colonial masses'.[33] Yet the main public demand of the Trotskyists in the colonial field, as expressed by the paper of their Labour Party entrist group, *Militant*, was not so very different from those of the CP or the Labour left:

The immediate granting of the right of self-determination to all colonial and subject peoples and the withdrawal of British forces from their territories; this to be accompanied by the offer of a defensive alliance between a Socialist Britain and such liberated peoples should the latter desire this.[34]

The language, and especially the notion of a post-decolonisation socialist alliance, differed from the CPGB's programme after 1947 only in making no apparent distinction between colonies immediately ready for self-determination and those which were not.

A major problem for the RCP's anticolonial activities was that, weak though Trotskyism may have been in Britain, in the colonial world it was still more so. In June 1947 Natalia Trotsky reported only Indo-China, Palestine, Egypt, Cyprus, and South Africa as having Trotskyist parties. Those of Indo-China and South Africa were estimated to be about 300 strong; the others had only about 50 members each.[35] None the less the RCP had great hopes for colonial support, particularly in Egypt where it saw the socialist movement as 'developing to the Left of the ideology of the bankrupt parties of the Second and Third Internationals. They have much in common with the policy for which the "Militant" stands.'[36] India too was seen as hopeful, and it was noted that former RCP member Ajit Roy had

[32] *SA* (Dec. 1945); letter from John McNair, ILP, to Jock Haston (21 Nov. 1945).

[33] R. Ralph, *SA* (mid-July 1946).

[34] *Militant* (May 1945).

[35] Natalia Trotsky, 'The Fourth International in Danger' (RCP internal mimeo, June 1947); this and subsequently cited RCP internal documents are from the Nuffield Trotskyism collection). It is evident that the Indian subcontinent is for some reason excluded from this list: also that nowhere without a Communist party developed a Trotskyist one, though the converse was not the case.

[36] *Militant* (Apr. 1946). This view of Egyptian nationalists as proto-Trotskyists seems to have been based solely on wishful thinking. See Joel Beinin, *Was the Red Flag Flying There?* (I. & B. Tauris, 1990).

won a place on the executive of the Bengal Socialist Party.[37] In general, though, RCP propaganda could not be built around solidarity with specific colonial socialist groups, for the simple reason that there were almost none of which it approved. It had rather to take the form of a general argument that British imperialism was in a process of rapid, inevitable dissolution, together with the claim that the working class was coming to the fore in the colonies and would eventually turn towards the only correct leadership: that of Trotskyism.[38]

The RCP's analysis, like the CP's, placed great emphasis on the idea that British imperialism was increasingly coming under the control of the USA: 'Desperately, Britain attempts to maintain the Empire, and at least a secondary status in the world. But she is compelled to play a vassal role to American imperialism.'[39] Lacking either the economic or the military force to control mass colonial unrest, the Empire was collapsing from within. New stratagems of divide and rule were being attempted to stem the tide, but were doomed. British capitalism could neither maintain the Empire nor survive without it. Therefore decolonisation must be posed as a 'transitional demand': one which the existing order was incapable of fulfilling, so that its demonstrated failure to do so would turn the masses towards a revolutionary solution.[40]

If the capitalist world order was incapable of carrying through decolonisation, the parties of the non-Trotskyist left were equally so. The RCP scorned indiscriminately the 'fake policy of colonial liberation' of the Labour Party,[41] the compromises and about-turns of the CPGB,[42] the 'pacifists and sectarians' of the ILP.[43] As for the COPAI, in which Trotskyists did participate, they seemed more interested in the manœuvrings of the far left groups within it than in the ostensible aims of the organisation. The Fourth International Secretariat's Report on the second conference of the Congress (that in October 1949 on the Colonial Peoples and War), though noting

---

[37] 'The Case for the Open Party', RCP Internal Bulletin (Feb. 1949).
[38] See for instance RCP Central Committee, 'Theses on Problems of the Colonial Revolution', conference documents (June 1947).
[39] Central Committee resolution for 1946 RCP conference.
[40] Minority Group statement, 'The Turn to Mass Work', Internal Bulletin (1946; month not given).
[41] RCP Central Committee, 'Theses on Problems of the Colonial Revolution'.
[42] 'Communism and the Colonies', *Socialist Appeal* (Mar. 1947).
[43] Internal Bulletin (Oct. 1945). (A sectarian is, of course, a member of a sect other than one's own.)

that this was 'the most representative colonial congress held since the war', devoted itself almost entirely to the vexed question of who among the delegates was and who was not a true Trotskyist. The reporter noted that 'several colonial delegates were confused' by such manifestations of European left sectarianism.[44] This was hardly surprising. far more to be wondered at was the myopia of the Europeans' squabbles. It was the story of the LAI repeated, but this time as farce; for the groups involved were minute, the disputes metaphysical.

On the dissolution of the RCP in 1949 its members, or such as remained, resurfaced in three small groups within the Labour Party. Largest of these was The Club, led by Gerry Healy and publishing *Socialist Outlook*, which presented itself as a broad-based paper of the Labour left and temporarily gained the support of many non-Trotskyist left-wingers through the pressure group, the Socialist Fellowship, which it sponsored. Far smaller (fewer than fifty members and with a circulation of about 350 for its paper, *Socialist Review*) was Tony Cliff's Socialist Review Group. More insignificant still was Ted Grant's Revolutionary Socialist League—though this was to weather the subsequent storms better than its rivals and become the core of the powerful Militant tendency within Labour.[45]

The core of The Club was probably not more than forty activists; but it had a strong and usually controlling influence on *Socialist Outlook* (edited by a Club member, John Lawrence) and a major though not always directing role in the Socialist Fellowship; which at its peak had several thousand supporters and thirty-nine local branches.[46] *Socialist Outlook* devoted little attention to colonial affairs, even though a number of the non-Trotskyists associated with it were active anticolonialists, including MPs Brockway, Stephen Swingler, S. O. Davies, and Zilliacus. Its major campaign on the international front was in opposition to the Korean War, which it sought to present as essentially an issue of colonial freedom.[47] Here as on most foreign policy questions, Healy and his supporters adopted an uncritically pro-Soviet position despite their deep theoretical differences with the Communists—to the point of welcoming Soviet nuclear weapons as 'the workers' bomb'.

[44] Fourth International Political Secretariat Newsletter (2 Nov. 1949).
[45] See Callaghan, *British Trotskyism*, 67–76, 90–101, 163–77; Michael Crick, *Militant* (Faber & Faber, 1984), 37–44; Bornstein and Richardson, *War*, 209 ff.
[46] Mark Jenkins, *Bevanism: Labour's High Tide* (Nottingham: Spokesman, 1979), 91–112; Jonathan Schneer, *Labour's Conscience* (Unwin Hyman, 1988), 127–30.
[47] See *Socialist Outlook* editorial (Apr. 1951).

Militant, similarly, had little time for colonial issues; though later close links were to be forged with a small number of Trotskyist groups in developing countries, especially Sri Lanka. The Socialist Review group was more determinedly internationalist. Its external preoccupations were heavily centred on expounding Cliff's ideas about the USSR; but in the *Review*'s pages David Taylor provided apparently well-informed coverage and sharp criticism of Labour policies on Southern and Central Africa.[48] The Labour leaders' stance on British Guiana and Kenya was also savaged, and by 1954–5 a talented young economist, Michael Kidron, was contributing analyses of colonial economies to the *Review*.[49]

III. PAN-AFRICANISM AFTER 1945

The culmination of the work of the black radical anticolonialists in Britain was the Pan-African Congress held in Manchester in October 1945. It was also in a sense the swan-song of that work, for within the following few years most of the main participants dispersed to their homelands, there to play leading roles in the various nationalist movements. This congress was the fifth in a much-broken series, but essentially a new departure in that it was far larger, more representative of the emerging nationalist movements, and more militant in tone than its predecessors. It also marked a coming of age for African and West Indian nationalists' organisational independence, for it was an almost entirely non-white affair: few British socialists, and few of the black Americans who had dominated previous congresses, were present.[50] Though it addressed an Open Letter to Attlee welcoming the election of the new Labour Government and expressing high hopes for what it would do in the colonial sphere, the main theme of the Congress was the demand for an independence which could be won, it was proclaimed, only by the colonial peoples' own efforts.

[48] 'South Africa Today', parts 1 and 2, *Socialist Review* (Apr.–May and June–July 1952); 'Oppose the Central African Federation', *SR* (May 1953).

[49] 'Kenya and the Mau Mau', *SR* (Dec. 1952–Jan. 1953); 'Forced Labour in Keyna', *SR* (Feb.–Mar. 1953); 'White Terror in Kenya' and untitled article on Guiana, *SR* (Nov. 1953); 'British Guiana', *SR* (Dec. 1953); 'Ape-like, Bestial Brutes?' (on Mau Mau), *SR* (Mar. 1954)—all unsigned; Michael Kidron, 'The Gold Coast', parts 1 and 2, *SR* (Apr. and May 1955).

[50] Though Bob Edwards, Idris Cox, and John Hatch were by their own accounts all in attendance (interviews with Edwards and Hatch, personal communication from Cox).

The immediate occasion for the Congress was the World Federation of Trade Unions (WFTU) conference held in London in February 1945. To this, for the first time, a large number of delegates from colonial unions were invited, some of whom already had contacts with the Pan-Africanists. They were brought to Manchester for discussions with Makonnen, Padmore, Kenyatta, and others, and there the idea of the Pan-African Congress was mooted.[51] In part because of the presence of such representatives of working-class organisations, the Manchester Congress gave more attention to economic problems than had previous Pan-Africanist bodies, and in general adopted more militant positions. British proposals for constitutional reform in West Africa, for instance, were decried as 'pretentious' and 'spurious'.[52] There was far greater scepticism than hitherto about the benefits of working through British socialist groups; though on this issue the Pan-Africanists were divided still.

A few still associated with the Communists, notably Nkrumah who seems briefly have joined the CPGB between his move from the USA to Britain in 1945 and his return to the Gold Coast in 1947.[53] More important were continued links with Brockway and the ILP, in which Padmore remained particularly active. Others, though, were now hostile to any such co-operation: their objections expressed with characteristic pungency by Makonnen:

I felt that George Padmore was really seeing too much of the ILP office ... To me this was almost as treasonable as working for the British Communist Party. And personally I took some pride in knowing that Brockway probably did not even know my face ... This was the trouble with a lot of the Africans who hung about Brockway's place. To me it seems a bit like the mentality of the typical house slave of the American plantations, passing on titbits of news to the master.[54]

The organisers of the Congress established what was intended to be a permanent organisation, and from January 1947 produced an ambitious journal, *Pan-Africa*. Both organisation and magazine

---

[51] See George Padmore (ed.), *History of the Pan-African Congress* (orig. pub. 1947; repr. Hammersmith Bookshop Ltd., 1963); J. R. Hooker, *Black Revolutionary* (New York: Praeger, 1967), 83–8; LaRay E. Denzer, 'I. T. A. Wallace-Johnson' (Birmingham University, Ph.D. thesis, 1977), 462–74; T. R. Makonnen, *Pan-Africanism from Within* (Nairobi: Oxford University Press, 1973), 163–7.

[52] Congress Resolutions in Padmore, *History*, 55.

[53] This membership is tacitly admitted in Kwame Nkrumah, *Ghana* (Edinburgh: Nelson, 1957), 42–52, 65.

[54] Makonnen, *Pan-Africanism*, 179–80.

were short-lived; the latter appearing for just eleven issues. Padmore attributed its premature demise to the fact that it was subjected to persistent banning and censorship attempts by colonial authorities; though Roderick MacDonald speculates that in fact its expensive format made it uneconomic.[55] The Congress itself suffered from internal schisms, primarily between the separatists like Makonnen and those who desired continued co-operation with British socialists or Communists. The former dominated the main Pan-African Federation, the latter the offshoot (or in Makonnen's view breakaway) West African National Secretariat.[56]

While the Pan-African idea itself was very far from dead, its British-based manifestations were of limited significance after the major participants dispersed in the late 1940s. The main focus for anticolonial lobbying by Africans in Britain thereafter was in groups like the MCF and, to a lesser extent, African students' organisations. Separatist bodies of other sorts remained in existence, but were primarily orientated towards particular colonial territories. Broader British black political groups only re-emerged during the 1960s, now primarily concerned with attacking internal British racism rather than colonialism—though often they still argued for an intimate connection between these things.

The CPGB's influence among Africans in Britain in the post-war years, though difficult to assess with any precision, seems to have become weaker in the post-war years than in the 1930s; with the partial exceptions of mostly white South African Communist exiles and some West African, especially Nigerian, trade unionists.[57] Whilst the party ran an Africa Committee from 1950 onwards, rather few of its members seem at any time actually to have been Africans.[58] The party's two major colonial conferences, in 1947 and 1954, were notable for their lack of African representation. The former had no delegates at all from black Africa; the latter received a report from

---

[55] George Padmore, *Pan-Africanism or Communism?* (Dennis Dobson, 1956), 152; Roderick MacDonald, 'The Role of London's Black Press in the 1930s and 1940s', paper for History of Blacks in Britain conference (Institute of Education, London, 1981), 19–20.

[56] Makonnen, *Pan-Africanism*, 261–3; Denzer, 'Wallace-Johnson', 512–15; Nkrumah, *Ghana*, 45–52.

[57] For the CPGB's Nigerian contacts, see *Africa Newsletter* produced by the CPGB Africa Committee, *passim*; also Robin Cohen, *Labour and Politics in Nigeria, 1945–71* (Heinemann, 1974), and Peter Waterman, 'Communist Theory in the Nigerian Trade Union Movement', *Politics & Society*, 3/2 (1973).

[58] *Africa Newsletter*, and personal communication from Idris Cox.

the Sudanese Movement for National Liberation and heard a speech from a pro-Communist Nigerian, but nothing from the other African colonies.[59]

After the departure of most of the Pan-Africanists from Britain in 1946–8, by far the most prominent black radical still active was George Padmore. Indeed he was to all intents the *only* significant such figure between the late 1940s and his own move to Ghana in 1957. Moody had died in 1947. An indigenous black British political leadership had not yet emerged; perhaps its first significant stirrings were to be the founding by Trinidadian Communist Claudia Jones of the *West Indian Gazette* in 1958, David Pitt's parliamentary candidacy in 1959, and the growth of Indian Workers' Associations from the late 1950s. And Padmore himself did not continue his earlier intensity of creating and running anticolonial organisations. Although he remained active in ILP circles, wrote regularly for the *Socialist Leader*, and participated successively in the BCAI, COPAI, and MCF, he was increasingly engrossed in Gold Coast affairs and in the three books he produced between 1949 and 1956.[60] The unique partnership of British, African, and West Indian anticolonialists forged in London in the 1930s gradually dwindled away. Padmore's move to Accra marked its real end: his return to London to die in 1959 merely wrote a sad coda to it.

IV. THE UNION OF DEMOCRATIC CONTROL

The UDC had been founded to campaign for world disarmament and to support moves for the peaceful regulation of international affairs. In pursuit of these very broad aims it had become involved to some extent between the wars in agitation against European intervention in China and elsewhere. Leading figures within it in the 1930s, such as *New Statesman* editor Kingsley Martin and his com-

[59] CPGB, *We Speak for Freedom: 1947 Conference of Empire Communist Parties Report* (1947); CPGB, *Allies for Freedom: 1954 Conference of Empire Communist Parties Report* (1954).

[60] *Africa: Britain's Third Empire* (Dennis Dobson, 1949); *The Gold Coast Revolution* (Dennis Dobson, 1953); *Pan-Africanism or Communism?* (Dennis Dobson, 1956). Among Padmore's more important articles in these years were the 5-part 'Trusteeship —the New Imperialism', *NL* (2 Feb. 1946 *et seq.*), and 'Crisis in Buganda', *SL* (19 Dec. 1953). For his activities and views over this period see Hooker, *Black Revolutionary*, 99–132.

panion Dorothy Woodman, had also taken an interest in Indian and Burmese problems and co-operated with the India League and other like-minded bodies. After the Second World War, however, the UDC began to feel keenly that it had lost much of its earlier influence and sense of direction. Its new General Secretary, Basil Davidson, pointed out in 1950 that the UDC had in the past exercised most authority when it had concentrated on a specific issue, and suggested that it should now 'narrow the rather wide field of its present activities' and should focus its attention on colonial, and especially African, affairs. It had received a grant for research and work on Africa from the Foundation for World Government, and a number of individuals associated with it already had interests in the field.[61]

Davidson's own African interests had, as he recalled to an Italian journalist thirty years later, evolved almost by accident. He had intended to specialise in Eastern European affairs, but soon found that he would not be allowed to travel in the region. Whilst still pondering his future, he received an invitation from trade unionist Solly Sachs to visit and write about South Africa. 'I didn't really want to go, I wasn't interested, but it seemed perhaps a useful thing to do. Of course when I got there ... I was "captured".'[62] A lifelong involvement had begun.

Therefore from 1950 the UDC devoted itself primarily to African issues. Davidson sketched out three general principles to which the Union's African activities should subscribe. These were recognition of the desirability and inevitability of independence for all African colonies; the belief that self-government in itself was not enough but must be accompanied by social and economic development and the attempt to avoid a reactionary white settler nationalism producing an equally narrow reactive black nationalism; and the need for progressive opinion in Britain to press for decolonisation and co-operation with African movements. The programme of action was to be primarily educational: 'to create a two-way channel of communication between

---

[61] Draft Statement of Policy by Basil Davidson, for UDC Executive Committee (25 Aug. 1950) (Hodgkin papers). Davidson, a *New Statesman* journalist who had formerly worked for *The Times* and as a wartime British Intelligence liaison officer with the Yugoslav partisans, began writing on African affairs from mid-1950. Dismissed by the *NS&N* in Dec. 1952 for supposedly 'fellow-travelling' views, he thereafter became a full-time writer on African history and politics.

[62] Basil Davidson, interviewed by Antonio Bronda, *Crossroads in Africa* (Nottingham: Spokesman, 1980), 23.

the various African bodies ... and forward-looking opinion in this country.'[63]

In pursuit of this aim Davidson sought to enlist the aid of the FCB and of various interested individuals in Britain. Most important of the latter was Thomas Hodgkin, a socialist academic who had formerly been a colonial official in Palestine and was now, as Secretary of the Oxford Extra-Mural Delegacy, turning his attention towards African affairs. Through the Delegacy's involvement in programmes for African educational development, Hodgkin had travelled widely on the continent and became involved both in historical research and in political activity there. Two other tutors with the Delegacy, Henry Collins and Tony McLean, sharing Hodgkin's African interests and left-wing views, became, with him, actively involved in the UDC.[64] Plans for co-operation between UDC and Fabians were initially ambitious. Rita Hinden expressed the hope that 'a combination of our two organisations should make a considerable impact on public opinion in this country'.[65] The relatively wealthy UDC subsidised the funds of the impecunious FCB;[66] and in return the Fabians offered advice on African contacts. This centred on warning against work with those the FCB thought extremists: for instance, the Bureau strongly, and no doubt wisely, counselled against the UDC's co-operation with Ugandan Semakula Mulumba, who had recently expressed himself to Labour Ministers in the following thoughtful tones:

We scorn you like the drippings of a privy: rage, you English thieves, white swine, burst if you want ... you English are liars, thieves, drunkards, idlers, who drain away the money of the black folk.[67]

Avoiding association with the apparently deranged, as opposed to the merely eccentric or impatient, was a constant problem for both

---

[63] Davidson, Draft Statement of Policy.

[64] Hodgkin papers and author's interviews with Dorothy Hodgkin.

[65] Hilda Selwyn-Clarke to Basil Davidson (22 June 1950), quoting Rita Hinden's verbal comments, FCB 4/4/34.

[66] Rita Hinden to Basil Davidson (1 Aug. 1950); Davidson to Hinden (2 Aug. 1950), FCB 4/4/38–9.

[67] Telegram from Mulumba to Attlee and others, n.d.; copy sent by Hilda Selwyn-Clarke to Basil Davidson (16 June 1950), FCB 4/4/32–3. Mulumba was the Ugandan Bataka Party's London representative, and was also involved with the Kenya Committee (see below, pp. 205–6) and as an alleged instigator of the 1949 disturbances in Uganda. John Stonehouse, who knew him as an LSE student around this time, described him as a 'pet' of the London Communists: *Prohibited Immigrant* (Bodley Head, 1960), 15.

British anticolonialists and colonial nationalists in establishing working relations with one another. But ideological screening of colonial contacts had different connotations for the cautiously gradualist FCB than for the more radical Davidson and Hodgkin; and the two organisations soon drifted apart. Davidson, indeed, seemed more preoccupied with the need to ensure that the British participants in UDC activities were like minded. As he told Hodgkin, he was concerned that 'control remains in the right hands' on the UDC's Africa committee. There was a danger that it might become unmanageably large, padded out with people unwilling to undertake real work. The main point, though, was ideological: Davidson wanted the committee and the journal he hoped to establish to be clearly focused around the ideal of 'socialism and self-government': 'not, that is, "socialist self-government" (which would certainly be going too far), nor simply Socialism nor simply self-government (which would be either unrealistic or not going far enough).'[68]

Something of what Davidson meant by this was elaborated in his first major African book. Here he emerged as a sharp critic of Labour as well as of official British attitudes to Africa. Indeed, like many anticolonialists, he expressed doubts over whether these were really such different things anyway:

The differences between Conservative and Labour policy have been differences of interpretation rather than of principle: it is far from easy to know how far even the interpretation has really differed . . . The most that can be said is that Labour Government has obstructed less severely the processes of political change. On the processes of economic change, specifically Labour policy has had nothing of importance to say.[69]

Africa, Davidson argued, was in the throes of dynamic social and economic as well as political transformation. The growth of local industries and urban centres and the increasing power and political ambitions of white settlers meant that 'the old imperialism at long range has given way or is giving way to a new imperialism at short range'.[70] There were new opportunities for political and economic progress; but urgent danger that these would be stifled by a declining British imperialism—and a rising US one—pursuing a short-term conception of national economic interest while relinquishing political

---

[68] Basil Davidson to Themas Hodgkin (21 Sept. 1950) (Hodgkin papers).
[69] *Report on Southern Africa* (Jonathan Cape, 1952), 257–8.
[70] Ibid. 270.

power to the settlers. The latter could lead only to ever more bitter conflicts with insurgent nationalism; but the former required more than political self-government. In his early 1950s writings Davidson urged, cautiously, only that it would require social *reform* and modernisation.[71] Later he argued with increasing sharpness that it would necessitate the building of a specifically African social*ism*: indigenous capitalist development was impossible 'except at an exceedingly slow and inefficient rate'.[72]

Yet even in an argument seeking to demonstrate the practical necessity to Britain of an enlightened policy for decolonisation, Davidson's final appeal was the classic anticolonialist's moral one, calling on the British to 'conclude their imperialist epoch with honour' rather than 'serve notice on the world of their own blindness, their own political and moral bankruptcy'.[73]

Davidson and the UDC failed, in the event, to establish either a permanent liaison organisation between British and African anticolonialists or a regular journal on African affairs devoted to these principles. Yet they did succeed in holding a series of conferences on Africa which drew together a remarkable range of politicians, academics, and African nationalists.[74] At least equally important were the individual efforts of Davidson and Hodgkin: the constant flow of books, articles, and pamphlets which both produced after 1950 on African subjects. These were significant not only in drawing British attention to contemporary developments but in establishing the proposition (still a novelty in most European political and scholarly circles in the 1950s) that Africans had rich and complex histories, cultures, and civilisations on which the nationalist movements sought to build.[75] In this sense, the educational role which the UDC had set for itself was fulfilled with considerable success.

[71] e.g. ibid. 272–4.

[72] *Tomorrow's Africa? A Report on some New Trends* (MCF/UDC pamphlet, 1962), quotation from p. 7; *Which Way Africa?* (Harmondsworth: Penguin, 1964).

[73] *Report on Southern Africa*, 274 (the book's last sentence).

[74] Thus those attending the Oct. 1950 conference included, on the British side, Barnes, Brockway, Selwyn-Clarke, Ritchie Calder, Driberg, Arthur Lewis, Thomas Balogh, Michael Foot, Sorensen, Brailsford, J. D. Bernal, and Kingsley Martin; among the Africans Seretse Khama, Charles Njonjo, R. R. Amponsah, and Bankole Timothy.

[75] See Thomas Hodgkin's memoir of this period, 'Where the Paths Begin', in Christopher Fyfe (ed.), *African Studies since 1945: A Tribute to Basil Davidson* (Longmans, 1976). The first major product of this effort was Davidson's *Report on Southern Africa*; perhaps the most important Hodgkin's *Nationalism in Colonial Africa* (Frederick Muller, 1956).

V. CENTRAL AFRICA

Of all colonial issues, that which attracted most controversial attention in the early 1950s was the fate of Britain's Central African territories. Two interlinked issues dominated discussion here: the case of Seretse Khama and the proposed Central African Federation.

The former assumed, as has already been noted, a massive symbolic importance for British anticolonialists; indeed John Hatch, who became the Labour Party's Commonwealth Officer in 1954, believed that until Seretse's fate was settled the British left's ideas could make no headway anywhere in Africa.[76] There were several reasons for this symbolic role. Seretse's exile had come about as the result of hostile reactions to his racially mixed marriage; attaining justice for him was therefore seen as emblematic of a wider fight for racial equality. It had been induced by South African pressure, and therefore opposition to it symbolised resistance to the Union's apartheid policies and regional ambitions. The exile had been ordered by a Labour Government, and was thus viewed as a blot on the good name of British socialism. Seretse himself established friendly relations with many British radicals and seemed a leader of enlightened, modernising views, whilst his rivals within the Bamangwato were depicted (rightly or wrongly) as reactionaries; therefore the case came also to symbolise the drive for social progress within Africa.

The issue was not, all the same, by any means clear-cut. Although Seretse and his uncle Tshekedi Khama had common opponents in the policies of British and South African governments, they were also in dispute with one another. Supporters of Tshekedi in Britain, led by the Revd Michael Scott, believed that Seretse's advocates damaged hopes for a peaceful resolution to the dispute. Scott castigated the role he thought was being played by:

Well-meaning champions of freedom for colonial peoples and professional public relations experts ... Left-wing socialists and anti-Imperialists were strongest in urging Seretse not to abdicate or compromise his position as chief.[77]

Scott's chief suspects were of course Brockway and his associates; and from these circles emerged two small campaigning bodies proclaiming their allegiance to Seretse's cause. First to appear was a

[76] Interview with Lord Hatch.
[77] Michael Scott, *A Time to Speak* (Faber & Faber, 1958), 273.

Seretse Khama Fighting Committee, founded in March 1950 with West Indian cricketer Learie Constantine as chairman. This soon changed its name to the Seretse Khama Campaign Committee, and Monica Whately (the former Labour MP and India League veteran) took over the chair. The organisation would seem, behind the scenes, to have been dominated by the Communists, and Seretse himself kept his distance from it.[78] More important, gaining more mainstream Labour Party support and working more closely with Seretse, was an offshoot of the COPAI, the Council for the Defence of Seretse Khama and the Protectorates. Brockway chaired this group, with Liberal MP Jo Grimond as vice-chairman, Arthur Carr and Mary Klopper of the COPAI as secretaries, and Anthony Wedgwood Benn as treasurer. Council members included ten Labour MPs, mostly but not all left-wingers, and the usual selection of members of the liberal establishment. Its main activity was the collection of signatures for a petition urging that the Bamangwato be allowed the chief of their choice. The Council also held a number of public meetings—almost always with Seretse as the main speaker—lobbied Ministers, and sponsored parliamentary Questions on the issue by Brockway and others. The case, it urged, 'is a challenge to our democratic faith, and to our moral principles, both Christian and humanitarian'.[79] The Council was in regular contact with one of Seretse's most prominent supporters in Bechuanaland, L. D. Raditladi, who provided its main source of information from there.[80] The petition, which gained 10,839 signatures, was presented to Parliament by Brockway on 22 March 1954.[81] Thereafter the Council merged into the MCF.

If the dispute over the Khamas was in large measure of symbolic significance, that over the Central African Federation was of more extensive and material consequence. The Labour Government had,

---

[78] See Seretse Khama Campaign Committee, *Seretse Khama and the Bamangwato People* (SKCC pamphlet, n.d. but *c.*1951), and report on Committee public meeting at Holborn Hall in CPGB, *Africa Newsletter*, 5/3 (May 1952). The latter lists Whately, Percy Belcher of the Tobacco Workers' Union, and Elizabeth Allen of the NCCL as speakers at the meeting. Both Belcher and Allen co-operated closely with the CPGB. Billy Strachan, a CP member active in West Indian affairs, was the Committee's secretary.

[79] Council for the Defence of Seretse Khama and the Protectorates; circular appeal for support, n.d. but late 1952 (Benn papers).

[80] See e.g. Raditladi to Arthur Carr (29 Sept. 1953); Carr to Fenner Brockway (7 Oct. 1953) (Benn papers).

[81] Petition text and notes on presentation (Benn papers). See also Goldsworthy, *Colonial Issues*, 275.

in 1950–1, given cautious support to the idea of a Federation of Northern and Southern Rhodesia and Nyasaland. There were believed to be strong economic arguments for such an arrangement, which would also simplify administration and perhaps counteract South African influence in the region. But African opinion was overwhelmingly opposed to the idea. It would, educated Africans feared, cement and extend the predominance of white settler interests and destroy any hopes of progress towards African majority rule.[82] Labour leaders agreed, at first, with the Conservatives in accepting the pro-Federation arguments. The left, by contrast, believed African objections to be the paramount consideration and opposed Federation on principle. In this they were joined by much non-party liberal and religious opinion. The Fabians also, abandoning their usual loyalism towards Labour Government policy, opposed Federation; though the basis of their objections was rather different. The FCB thought African opinion to be the 'weakest possible' basis for rejection: Federation should, in their judgement, be opposed rather because it would undermine the Government's long-term plans for African development.[83]

A proliferation of bodies arguing the anti-Federation case sprang into activity. The FCB naturally took a close interest; but it believed that, since the FCB was neither intended nor equipped to act as a public agitational body, the main burden of campaigning activity on the issue should be undertaken by the newly formed Africa Bureau. This was a non-party (though broadly centre-left and liberal) organisation founded by Michael Scott and others in March 1952. The Bureau, though seeing its role as the general encouragement of informed debate on Africa rather than the pursuit of particular political objectives, took a strong public stand on Federation. It sought to publicise African objections through the press, the Churches, and other non-party media. Divisions rapidly opened up between this approach and the more explicitly political thrust of the left-wing anticolonialists; for whom, predictably, Brockway and the COPAI once more entered the lists against Federation.

[82] The best general study of the debate on Federation is still Patrick Keatley, *The Politics of Partnership* (Harmondsworth: Penguin, 1963); see also Goldsworthy, *Colonial Issues*, 214–30, 258–64, 306–10. On British pressure-group reactions, Harris B. K. Sandashi, 'The Politics of the Voice' (York University M.Phil. thesis, 1981), gives further detail, though it adds little of importance to the published accounts.
[83] FCB attitudes to Federation are fully discussed in Goldsworthy, *Colonial Issues*, 228–9.

In May 1952 the COPAI established a Central Africa Co-ordinating Committee. This soon evolved into a new body formally distinct from the Congress, the Central Africa Committee. Participants were, all the same, drawn from the same nexus of Bevanite, ex-ILP, pacifist, and colonial student groups who supported the COPAI and Seretse Khama Council, including Leslie Hale, Richard Acland, George Craddock, Mary Klopper, Leon Szur, and Dick Beech.[84] Brockway gave the impression at the Committee's founding session that the Africa Bureau had granted its approval for the COPAI to take the initiative in running a campaign against Federation. The Bureau strongly denied having done so; and the new Committee's relations with the Bureau and the FCB—which in any case disliked Brockway's general approach and doubted the utility of another new anticolonial body—became frosty in the extreme.[85] Indeed Marjorie Nicholson of the FCB spoke of campaigners 'cutting each other's throats' by setting up rival or overlapping organisations.[86] In a letter to Labour MP James Johnson she went further, suggesting that the COPAI and UDC 'do infinite damage to the African cause' by the stridency of their approach and their supposed carelessness about facts.[87] Leslie Hale, who became chairman of the new Central Africa committee, was clearly beginning to feel overwhelmed by the proliferation of anticolonial groups. In response to an appeal for support from the Africa Bureau, he lamented that:

I have today also had a similar letter from Racial Unity . . . I am literally bombarded with correspondence from the Congress of Peoples Against Imperialism.

[84] Fenner Brockway to FCB (30 May 1952), giving details of Central Africa Co-ordinating Committee inaugural meeting, FCB 7/1/164–5. See also reports in *PN* (10, 16, and 30 Jan. 1953) on meetings organised by the Central Africa Committee and Africa Bureau for visiting Central African chiefs to protest against Federation.

[85] Mary Benson to Fenner Brockway (8 June 1952), FCB 7/1/166; Mary Benson to Leslie Hale (24 June 1952), FCB 7/1/20; Brockway to Lady Pakenham, Africa Bureau Secretary (12 June 1952), AB 29/6/1; Michael Scott to Hale (24 June 1952), AB 29/6/4; Donald Wade, MP, to Scott (3 July 1952), AB 29/6/7; Hale to Scott (11 July 1952), AB 29/6/10. Since Brockway's Committee and the Africa Bureau later co-operated closely on meetings against Federation, e.g. *PN* (16 and 30 Jan. 1953), it may be surmised that the hostility came mainly from the Fabians—though Michael Scott in his autobiography was to speak in vague but disgruntled terms of the MCF seeking to 'co-ordinate', or take over, the Bureau (*A Time to Speak*, 271–2).

[86] Marjorie Nicholson to Mary Benson (4 June 1952), FCB 7/1/22.

[87] Marjorie Nicholson to James Johnson (12 June 1952), FCB 18/1/63. Oliver Lyttelton too had accused the COPAI of 'wild and inaccurate' attacks on British policy; but then he was hardly a disinterested witness.

I am chairing a committee of the National Peace Council; I am on the Campaign Committee of the Association for World Peace; I am a member of the World Council of the People's World Assembly; I am a member of the Fabian Society International Committee and a member of the council of the Union of Democratic Control. I am also a member of the House of Commons Africa Committee.

This is really getting to the stage where the same sort of questions . . . are being dealt with time after time through the same members. I keep urging for some sort of co-ordinating committee.[88]

It is impossible not to sympathise with Hale's feeling that the situation was absurd. There were, none the less, a number of clear reasons for it, among which the inherently fissiparous tendency of the British left was only one. Different allegiances in anticolonial campaigns in part reflected factional alignments and backgrounds among British socialists: the centre and right wing of the Labour Party represented on the FCB, the Bevanite left in the COPAI and its offshoots—themselves very diverse, and with former ILP members forming a distinct tendency within their ranks; the Communist and 'fellow-travelling' left; and the largely non-party religious and academic figures drawn to the Africa Bureau. None of these found it easy to work with the others. Then there was the very variety and complexity of the issues involved, ranging from the grandiose ethical aims of the National Peace Council or the People's World Assembly (among whose worthy if woolly objectives colonial freedom was but a part) to the defence of a single individual like Seretse Khama. Perhaps most important, there was the deep, if not always clear-cut, difference between the views of those like Brockway who espoused demands for the immediate recognition of political rights in all colonies and those like the FCB who regarded such an aim as quite unrealistic and preferred a gradualist, perhaps paternalist, approach. Even where they shared an end, as with opposition to Federation, it was for quite different reasons and with quite different strategies for its attainment.

VI. KENYA

Ngugi wa Thiong'o's fine novel of the Kenyan Emergency, *A Grain of Wheat*, centres on Mugo, a Mau Mau detainee who became a local celebrity because 'he organised the hunger-strike in Rira, an action

---

[88] Leslie Hale to Michael Scott (24 June 1952), AB 29/6/32.

which made Fenna Brokowi raise questions in the British House of Commons'.[89] 'Fenna Brokowi' gained near-legendary stature among the militant African nationalists of Kenya. To the activists of KAU in the early 1950s, still hoping for some redress to their grievances by constitutional means even as some of them prepared for armed struggle, he was the outstanding symbol of the sympathetic European. More than that, as the Corfield Report said, there were widespread hopes of 'the millenium which would result shortly from these associations' with Brockway and other British supporters of African rights.[90] Probably in no other case did the activities of British anti-colonialists gain such a hold on the imagination of colonial nationalists as in Kenya.

Conversely, few passages in the process of decolonisation aroused so much public controversy in Britain as did the Kenyan Emergency— perhaps only Suez brought forth more passion. The phenomenon of Mau Mau became the subject of a lurid, indeed on occasion virtually hysterical, press coverage; whose tone had aptly been described as that of 'the pornography of violence'.[91] The trial of Jomo Kenyatta and other nationalist leaders on charges of managing Mau Mau was an occasion for bitter exchanges, as were the later revelations about the methods adopted by security forces in attempting to suppress the rebellion; culminating in the anguished post-mortem on the Hola massacre. And the backdrop of these events—if not the bloodiest, then certainly among the most traumatic, of the conflicts attendant on British decolonisation—loomed menacingly behind the later phases of constitutional talks and progress to self-government.

The anticolonialist left was naturally at the centre of these storms. In other contexts they were frequently accused of being extremist, unrealistic, of pleading the cause of demagogues, Communists, or incipient totalitarians. In relation to Kenya even more emotive charges were levelled. If Mau Mau atrocities represented to much British opinion a uniquely horrible and primitive barbarism, British supporters of Kenyan nationalism could be seen as apologists for, if not actual sponsors of, that savagery. When Anthony Wedgwood Benn, appearing

---

[89] Ngugi wa Thiong'o, *A Grain of Wheat* (Heinemann, 1967), 56.

[90] F. D. Corfield, *Historical Survey of the Origins and Growth of Mau Mau*, Cmd. 1030 (HMSO, 1960), 221. Many of Corfield's judgements, marked as they are by his bitter hostility to, and conspiratorial interpretation of, African nationalism, are now seen by scholars as unreliable. This one, however, is attested by many other sources.

[91] Jeremy Murray-Brown, *Kenyatta* (Fontana, 1974), 273.

on the BBC's *Any Questions*, criticised Kenyan settlers and British policy, his post-bag included sentiments like the following:

Your words travel instantly to millions, and in a few hours, no doubt they are known and made use of in Nairobi; and later another of the 'hated' white settlers will lie in his—or worse, her—death agony.

What right have you to interfere with and screech about the white residents in Africa. You are sitting on your well padded bottom like that exotic Leslie Hale in safety in this country. If the pair of you along with whining voiced D. N. Pritt were sliced up with Kikuyu and Masai spears and knives it would be a good riddance of dangerous rubbish.[92]

Views like these were of course in no sense necessarily representative— and Benn's mail also included warm endorsements of his stance—but may provide some indication of the emotions aroused in Britain by Mau Mau. When Brockway and Hale visited Kenya in 1952 they received death threats from settlers; and later Brockway experienced what he believed was a narrow escape from murder at the hands of a white Kenyan in Britain.[93]

Brockway first visited Kenya, on KAU's invitation, in September 1950. This trip aroused relatively little attention in Britain, though it did result in an extension of the existing links between British anticolonialists and KAU leaders. On Kenyatta's suggestion, KAU affiliated to the COPAI.[94] Brockway's and Hale's visit two years later, this time after the Mau Mau insurrection had already broken out, was a considerably more fraught affair. In Kenya itself it incensed the settlers, alarmed the colonial authorities, and encouraged the nationalists. In Northern Rhodesia settler leader Roy Welensky suggested that 'confirmed racialists' [!] like Brockway 'could do no good in Africa, and might cause a great deal of trouble', and demanded that he 'and others of the same type' be excluded.[95] The accusation was that the tour, intended to discover the facts and encourage racial harmony,[96] would in fact provide propaganda material for the militants

---

[92] Brigadier Rogers to Wedgwood Benn (12 Dec. 1952); Mr Stephens to Benn (14 Dec. 1952) (Benn papers).

[93] Fenner Brockway, *African Journey* (Gollancz, 1955), 135–6; id., *Outside the Right* (Allen & Unwin, 1963), 108–9, 113; id., *Towards Tomorrow*, 195–6.

[94] Corfield, *Historical Survey*, 57–8; Brockway, *Outside the Right*, 55–62; id., *Towards Tomorrow*, 183–7.

[95] *The Times* (30 Oct. 1952).

[96] Statement by Brockway and Hale, ibid. (22 Oct. 1952); Brockway, *African Journey*, *passim*.

in KAU. It may well have had some such effect: as a Mau Mau veteran recalled, the MPs' presence was:

used as evidence assuring people that Mr. Peter Mbiyu Koinange, KAU's delegate to the British government, had been successful in presenting the case . . . and that the return of the alienated land would be announced soon after their return to England. This propaganda, which looked true, encouraged people to have more faith in the movement.[97]

The main outcome of these visits within Britain was that the COPAI, in conjunction with KAU, organised a petition on the Kenya land issue, calling for a ban on white immigration, the restoration of African land ownership rights in all parts of the country, and radical measures of agricultural development planning.[98] After a very lengthy period of circulation in both Kenya and Britain it was presented to Parliament in July 1953, carrying the signatures of 16,434 Britons and 158,642 Africans.[99] Brockway and Hale also argued for an end to wholesale arrests and detentions in Kenya, for lifting the ban on public meetings, the immediate holding of a conference with representatives of all communities, and rapid moves to abolish racial discrimination. Only thus could Mau Mau—which, they insisted, they too wholly condemned—be brought to an end.[100] The roots of violence were primarily economic, secondarily social: Britain had destroyed the traditional Kikuyu way of life and not replaced it, so 'parts of the tribe, denied community democracy, have reverted to the bad in its own past'.[101]

Both the COPAI and UDC brought out pamphlets asserting that land hunger was the main reason for the war, and COPAI announced that it was organising funds and legal representation for Africans facing political charges in Kenya.[102]

[97] Donald N. Barnett and Karari Njama, *Mau Mau from Within* (MacGibbon & Kee, 1966), 129.

[98] Petition text in AB 29/14/4–5. Launched in Jan. 1952, the petition was backed by fifteen Labour MPs, though Lennox-Boyd refused to meet them about it (*PN* (25 Jan. 1952)). Initially KAU and the COPAI had expected far wider support. Douglas Rogers proclaimed that 'Africans are signing it in hundreds of thousands and the sponsors are sure of at least a million signatures in the first stage' (*PN* (18 Jan. 1952)).

[99] *HC Deb.* (15 July 1953), cols. 2029–30.

[100] *The Times* (10 Nov. 1952), Brockway's and Hale's statement on leaving Kenya; (29 Nov. 1952), Brockway's speech at Holborn Hall protest meeting; (6 Dec. 1952), letter from Brockway and Hale.

[101] Fenner Brockway, 'The Social Causes of Mau Mau', *PN* (27 Feb. 1953).

[102] Fenner Brockway, *Why Mau Mau?* (COPAI pamphlet, 1953); Mbiyu Koinange, *Land Hunger in Kenya* (UDC pamphlet, 1952).

The view espoused by Brockway and the COPAI rapidly became the dominant one on the left: that whilst Mau Mau was a barbaric and deplorable movement, its roots lay in economic deprivation, settler racism, and the errors of British policy. The solution must be sought through granting the legitimate demands of the constitutional nationalists. British policy, it was persistently argued, fomented Mau Mau violence by suppressing moderate opinion. 'The only effective way to meet the menace of violence was to give men like Odede, Awori and Murumbi the opportunity to go among the people—as they were willing to do—and to urge them not to touch Mau Mau', thought Brockway.[103] The Government was 'not destroying Mau Mau' but 'making' it, by repression.[104] It 'has done everything possible to alienate' the African population.[105] Whereas official discourse at this time presented Kenyatta and KAU as the masters of Mau Mau, most of the left distinguished sharply between them. They were concerned to defend those they saw as responsible nationalist leaders from the charge of complicity in violence: a defence culminating in former Labour MP D. N. Pritt leading the legal team which appeared for Kenyatta and others at Kapenguria.[106]

Not all on the left shared this high regard for Kenyatta. Both Kingsley Martin and George Wigg, for instance, without necessarily accepting the charges that he was the manager of the guerrilla movement, placed their faith in a new and more moderate generation of African leaders supplanting Kenyatta's 'old guard'.[107] Martin followed Brockway to Kenya in late 1952, rapidly concluded that he had earlier greatly underrated the Mau Mau threat, and, whilst directing sharp criticism at official policy, also reported moderate Africans' 'disappointment' with Kenyatta's leadership and argued that 'Kenyatta must have known about the Mau Mau plans for the campaign of

---

[103] Brockway, *African Journey*, 129.

[104] Fenner Brockway, *PN* (5 Dec. 1952).

[105] Douglas Rogers, *PN* (31 Oct. 1952).

[106] Though in the end Communist-dominated circles spearheaded this effort: see Montagu Slater, *The Trial of Jomo Kenyatta* (Secker & Warburg, 1955); D. N. Pritt, *The Autobiography of D. N. Pritt*, iii. *The Defence Accuses* (Lawrence & Wishart, 1966). Slater was a member of the CPGB, Pritt a close supporter. Brockway's belief in Kenyatta's innocence was evidently not without qualms. 'Was Jomo sincere or was he deliberately bluffing me [?]', he wondered in print; eventually deciding he was sincere (*African Journey*, 89–90). He found the charges against Kenyatta 'difficult to believe', on the rather shaky grounds that the Kenyan leader was 'civilised and cultured' (ibid. 167).

[107] See Martin's reports from Kenya in *NS&N* (Nov.–Dec. 1952) and Wigg's letter, *NS&N* (15 Nov. 1952).

violence and tacitly accepted it: certainly, he offered no constructive alternative.'[108]

In Britain meanwhile, besides the major campaign on KAU's behalf being undertaken by Brockway and the COPAI, another body had come into existence to agitate against Britain's Kenya policy. This was the Kenya Committee, launched at a London conference on 19 July 1953. The conference was attended, according to a Communist Party report, by some ninety people including delegates from a number of trade unions and CLPs as well as Koinange and other Kenyan representatives, other Africans (among them apparently the vociferous Mulumba), and former Labour MPs Monica Whately and John Platts-Mills.[109] 'Virtually unanimous' in seeing the Kenya situation as a genocidal war by Britain against the African people, the conference established a continuing organisation which produced several leaflets on the crisis, ran a news service collecting press reports on developments in Kenya, and held numerous public meetings.[110] Despite the presence in its ranks of various Labour Party groups and individuals, the Committee was clearly dominated by the CPGB. Unlike the majority of the Labour left, the Committee refused to condemn the guerrillas' activities. Arguing that Africans had been forced to enter the forests and resist, it made no mention of atrocities by Mau Mau and called Dedan Kimathi 'the commander of the resistance'.[111] Its publications, not surprisingly, were banned in Kenya.[112]

The line of support for the guerrillas was shared by the Communist Party itself:

We are presented by the newspapers and Tory leaders with the picture of a government trying to maintain law and order against the attack of 'barbaric terrorists'. That is always the imperialist picture of colonial people fighting for their rights.[113]

British Communists bitterly condemned the sentences passed on Kenyatta and his co-defendants, demanded the immediate withdrawal of British troops, the release of all prisoners, and 'recognition of the

[108] Martin's report from Kenya, *NS&N* (22 Nov. 1952). Prior to the visit, Martin had given high praise to Kenyatta; see 'London Diary', *NS&N* (25 Oct. 1952).
[109] CPGB, *Africa Newsletter*, 6/6 (n.d. but Aug. 1953).
[110] Publications and files of the Kenya Committee news service are in the Marx Memorial Library.
[111] *Kenya—Who are the Terrorists?* and *Kenya—We Must Make Peace* (Kenya Committee leaflets, n.d. but 1953/4).
[112] *The Times* (15 Mar. 1955).
[113] Philip Bolsover, *Kenya: What Are the Facts?* (CPGB pamphlet, May 1953), 3.

right of the people of Kenya to freedom and independence.'[114]
Whereas Labour left-wingers almost always accompanied their similar
demands with condemnation of Mau Mau excesses, the CPGB never
did so. Mau Mau was seen as a 'pretext' for repression, the real cause
of which was argued to be Britain's actual or planned military bases
in Kenya.[115] The CPGB thus linked the Kenyan conflict with the
more general campaigns against Western Cold War strategy by stress
on the supposed strategic importance of East Africa for NATO.

The non-Communist left, meanwhile, left no stone unturned in its
search for congenial, non-violent Kenyan resisters.[116] This could
lead it into startling naïvety: thus the anticolonial pacifist journal *Peace
News* carried at length, and apparently in all seriousness, Hollywood
press agent Paul Clarke's report of his clandestine meeting with the
'second in command of Mau Mau', one Olekisio, who spoke of his
desire for peace. 'Olekisio', of course, if he existed at all, was a
hoaxer.[117] More rational approaches could also backfire. The MCF's
Mary Klopper sought the release of Achieng Oneko from detention—
and received a reply from the prison-camp medical officer asking her
to use her influence on Oneko to get him to confess to Mau Mau
activities![118]

The most consistent theme of the left's statements on Kenya,
however, was the allegation—clearly often justified—that the security
forces were adopting extremely repressive methods in their attempt to
crush Mau Mau. In this regard, both CPGB and the Labour left
made use of revelations by British soldiers who had served in Kenya
and been horrified by what they saw;[119] and the latter also publicised
the allegations of Eileen Fletcher, a Quaker who exposed conditions

---

[114] Statement by the Political Committee of CPGB, 'End the Terror in Kenya',
WNV (18 Apr. 1953).

[115] Desmond Buckle, 'Imperialist Terror in Kenya', *WNV* (22 Nov. 1952), 541–2.

[116] See e.g. *PN* (8 June 1956).

[117] 'My Meeting with a Mau Mau Leader', *PN* (22 Oct. 1954). *PN* also apparently
expected readers to believe that Clarke's companion, Edward Botolph, thereupon
signed up as a volunteer with the Mau Mau forces!

[118] Articles by Klopper and reprints of correspondence, *PN* (9 Apr., 18 May, and
1 June 1956).

[119] See for instance *CPGB: Allies for Freedom*, 124–5, a muddled, emotional, but
compelling statement by David Larder, a former British Army Lieutenant court-
martialled and cashiered, as he claimed, for refusing to carry out atrocities, and Peter
Benenson (ed.), *Gangrene* (John Calder, 1959), which includes John Stonehouse MP's
account of meetings with former soldiers who spoke of massacres in Kenya. *PN*
(18 Mar. 1955) carries a letter sent to Brockway from an anonymous British officer in
Kenya who spoke of 'Gestapo methods' which made him 'ashamed to say I am British'.

in the detention camps.[120] As we shall see, such accusations also soon produced major storms in Parliament.

VII. THE CARIBBEAN

After the explosion of unrest in 1937–8, the transition to independence in most of Britain's West Indian colonies was far smoother, less conflictual, and less violent than in East and Central Africa. Broad-based constitutional nationalist parties emerged on most of the islands and were greeted with a relatively conciliatory response from the colonial authorities. The British Labour Party established close relations with a number of these parties, especially where—as in Jamaica, Trinidad, and Barbados—they modelled their organisation and ideology in large part on those of British Labour.[121] A minor exception was Grenada, where the domination of the nationalist movement by the charismatic but unstable and eventually dictatorial Eric Gairy—a domination pregnant with tragic future consequences for the island—aroused early concern from Labour's colonial experts.[122]

A far more important exception to the picture of consensual decolonisation, at least at the time, was British Guiana. There a radical socialist party with Marxist leanings, the People's Progressive Party (PPP) led by Cheddi Jagan and Forbes Burnham, became the majority nationalist force. Reactions to the PPP, and to the British Government's response against its electoral success, were deeply to split the Labour Party in Britain. In many eyes, the 1953 Guiana crisis became the most crucial of all tests to Labour's commitment to

[120] Eileen Fletcher, *Truth About Kenya* (MCF/*PN* pamphlet, 1955). See also Fletcher's reports in *PN* (4 May, 11 May, and 18 May 1956), and her 'reply to critics', *PN* (8 June 1956).

[121] See Labour Party Commonwealth Department and Subcommittee (hereafter LPCD and LPCSC respectively) papers, *passim*, *Annual Reports* of Jamaican PNP, etc. For general accounts of British West Indian decolonisation, see Gordon K. Lewis, *The Growth of the Modern West Indies* (New York: Monthly Review, 1968); Trevor Munroe, *The Politics of Constitutional Decolonization: Jamaica 1944–62* (Kingston, Jamaica: Institute of Social and Economic Research, 1972).

[122] See for instance John Hatch's report on West Indies tour, July–Sept. 1957 (LP/CSC/57/25) warning that Gairy was 'tarnishing' the name of Labour in the West Indies by his association with it; and Reginald Sorensen's report of visit in the summer of 1960 (LP/CSC/59/43) urging that British Labour sponsor a soundly based Grenadian Labour Party in opposition to Gairy, 'elaborate a suitable economic policy for it and press for substantial economic aid'.

colonial freedom. In May of that year the PPP under Jagan won a general election based on a new constitution which gave a large measure of self-government. In less than five months the Governor and the Colonial Office had suspended the constitution, alarmed at the new government's radicalism and arguing that the PPP was a crypto-Communist party intent on establishing a one-party state. The PPP Ministers were dismissed and British forces despatched to keep order. Naturally enough, Jagan and Burnham appealed to the British left to protest on their behalf, and themselves set out for London to press their case. This presented the Labour leadership with a dilemma. On the one hand the abrogation of a newly granted colonial constitution, the sacking by a Governor of democratically elected ministers, and the exercise of gunboat diplomacy (literally so when the cruiser *Superb* and two frigates were sent to Guiana) were affronts to everything they claimed to stand for. If all this had happened just because a colonial government was trying to introduce socialist policies that only made it worse. But if it were true that Jagan and his supporters were closet Communists aiming to build a totalitarian system, Labour could hardly identify itself with them.[123]

Initially the Labour front bench contented itself with a call for more information substantiating the Government's case against the PPP. It came under pressure from the TUC General Council, from opposition parties in Guiana, and from other West Indian politicians, to repudiate Jagan. The anticolonialist left reacted very differently. Tom Driberg alleged that the real reason for the Government's actions was defence of the British-based multinationals which dominated Guiana's economy and which felt threatened by a socialist government there. Both he and Brockway asserted that the suppression of an elected government on the grounds that it might harbour secret totalitarians was itself a totalitarian act, and was more likely to create support for Communism in the colonies than to prevent it.[124] *Tribune* and the COPAI jointly held a London meeting to protest, and to underline the left's view that the PPP was a legitimate socialist party.

The CPGB naturally did not employ this kind of distinction

---

[123] The PPP's version of these events is given in Cheddi Jagan, *Forbidden Freedom* (Lawrence & Wishart, 1954), and id., *The West on Trial* (Michael Joseph, 1966). For British reactions see Goldsworthy, *Colonial Issues*, 230–41.

[124] See Driberg's Foreword to Jagan, *Forbidden Freedom*, and Goldsworthy, *Colonial Issues*, 232–3.

between socialist and Communist views; but nor did it explicitly claim the PPP as an ally or assert ideological kinship with it. As Idris Cox cautiously put it: 'There is no Communist Party in British Guiana. What does exist is a broad and progressive political movement led by courageous Socialist leaders, in particular Dr Cheddi Jagan and Janet Jagan.'[125] The Communists placed even more stress than did the Labour left on the argument that the protection of capitalist profits was the main reason for British actions; and with more than a touch of hyperbole Harry Pollitt claimed that: 'The Tory government's attack on the people of British Guiana is the most shameful outrage in the long and bloody history of British imperialism.'[126]

In the first major parliamentary debate on the crisis most Labour speeches were cautious in the extreme. James Griffiths admitted that some of the charges against the PPP leaders might well be true, and that Britain had to take some action, but deplored the suspension of the constitution.[127] Other Labour speakers echoed this, though at least one, erstwhile Clydeside ILP left-winger John McGovern, believed the suspension to have been justified. No speaker from the anticolonial left was heard; though Jagan, who having arrived in Britain a few days earlier was present at the debate, claimed many were eager to intervene.[128] In the subsequent day's adjournment debate, however, Emrys Hughes, a pacifist left-winger active in various internationalist causes, was able to express his wholesale denunciation of British actions, which he described as exhibiting 'the Iron Hand and the Wooden Head'.[129]

It was clear that Labour was deeply divided over its attitude to the affair; and Jagan's and Burnham's visit brought the divisions into the open. They met with the Shadow Cabinet on 21 October, and Jagan with the NEC on 3 November. He attempted to gain a public labour endorsement for his stance; the Labour leaders sought to probe his political views and the truth of the charges against him. It seems they were by no means satisfied, for following the second meeting General

---

[125] Idris Cox, 'British Guiana, Kenya and Malaya', *WNV* (24 Oct. 1953). The phraseology indicates a degree of support or endorsement beyond that generally given to parties of the 'progressive national bourgeoisie' in the colonies; and, of course, an especial warmth towards the Jagans. US-born Janet Jagan was widely viewed as the real Communist hardliner in the partnership.

[126] Harry Pollitt, statement of 7 Oct. 1953; *WNV* (17 Oct. 1953).

[127] *HC Deb.* (22 Oct. 1953), cols. 2180–95.

[128] Jagan, *Forbidden Freedom*, 66–7.

[129] *HC Deb.* (23 Oct. 1953), cols. 2393–2401.

Secretary Morgan Phillips issued a circular to all local parties and affiliated bodies stating that:

The National Executive committee … regards it as inadvisable for local parties to provide a platform for Progressive People's Party speakers or to co-operate with other bodies (which may well be Communist-inspired) in supporting them. If local parties wish to organise meetings on the crisis in British Guiana, they should engage speakers who will present the Labour Party's point of view.[130]

This evoked a storm of protest. During the next few weeks Labour headquarters received no fewer than 87 resolutions—75 from CLPs, the remainder from other local party bodies—deploring this advice; as against just two supporting it. A further 48 resolutions attacked the Government's actions in various ways. In the following month a further 77 motions, all sharply critical of the Government and many also of the Labour leaders, came in; and an additional trickle of CLP protests continued well into the summer of 1954.[131] The official party hostility to Jagan was widely ignored on the left: Nye Bevan hosted a party for him, Ian Mikardo organised meetings for him, and the COPAI, UDC, and Caribbean Labour Congress all followed suit.[132] Neither Jagan nor Attlee and the NEC could be in any doubt that the Labour leaders' policy was repudiated by at least a third of CLPs as well as by the parliamentary Bevanites and the anticolonialist pressure groups. The NEC's decision to censure Mikardo over the affair did nothing to restore fraternal unity.

British Guiana was not the only Anglophone Caribbean territory where the nationalist movement included Marxists, even if they were uniquely powerful there. Elsewhere in the region Marxist groups, though small, included individuals who were to emerge as key political figures in the 1960s and later. Their main focus of support within Britain was in the London branch of the Caribbean Labour Congress. The parent body, the CLC itself, was a broad association of Labour parties and trade union movements in the area, founded in

---

[130] Circular from Morgan Phillips (Nov. 1953, no day given): copy in FCB 61/1/52.

[131] Monthly analyses of resolutions received on colonial affairs, LP/CSC papers, Nov.–Dec. 1953 and subsequent months. This casts doubt on Goldsworthy's view that 'on the whole the [NEC's] advice was effective' (*Colonial Issues*, 239). Miles Kahler, *Decolonization in Britain and France* (Princeton, NJ: Princeton University Press, 1984), 244, notes the hostile reactions but greatly understates their number.

[132] Jagan, *Forbidden Freedom*, 92–6; for notices of meetings, see *Tribune* (Oct.–Nov. 1953), *passim*.

Barbados in 1945.[133] Its main aim was to press for the establishment of an independent Federation of the West Indies; but some important members, notably Richard Hart, its Secretary from 1947, wanted it also to pursue radical social change. This latter current of opinion was dominant among the CLC's London supporters, many of whom were also close to the CPGB. For these reasons they were eventually repudiated by the more conservative parent organisation.[134] What precipitated the split was the division in the world trade union movement in January 1949. The London-based group, with Jamaican Marxists such as Hart and Ken Hill, and Jagan's PPP, supported the Communist-dominated WFTU. CLC President Grantley Adams of Barbados and most of the Congress's affiliates, such as the British TUC and Labour Party, backed the new anti-Communist ICFTU.[135]

Contacts between the CPGB and Marxist groups in the West Indies, especially Jamaica, had as we have seen been established in the late 1930s. In the war years two Communists serving in the British armed forces in Jamaica, Dr David Lewis and Captain R. H. Nichols, had associated with the local left; and they remained active after 1945 in anticolonialist circles concerned with the Caribbean.[136] The most active such circles were two closely interlocking bodies: the CLC London branch and the West Indies Committee of the CPGB. Somewhere between the two ideologically and forming the link between them was a small inner group of left-wingers in the CLC, who worked closely with the CP without necessarily all being members. This group, which also maintained constant contact with Hart in Jamaica, consisted essentially of the two ex-servicemen Lewis and Nichols, and three West Indians: Billy Strachan, Secretary of the London CLC, also Secretary of the Seretse Khama Campaign Com-

---

[133] See Richard Hart, 'Trade Unionism in the English-Speaking Caribbean: The Formative Years and the Caribbean Labour Congress', in Susan Craig (ed.), *Contemporary Caribbean: A Sociological Reader*, ii (Port of Spain, Trinidad: the author, 1982), and Jeffrey Harrod, *Trade Union Foreign Policy: A Study of British and American Trade Union Activities in Jamaica* (Macmillan, 1972).

[134] The London branch gave its version of the split in *Federation and Self-Government Now or Colonialism and Slavery for Ever* (CLC pamphlet, 1951).

[135] For a summary of the WFTU schism, see J. P. Windmuller, *The International Trade Union Movement* (Deventer: Kluwer, 1980), 45–59; for the British dimension, see Peter Weiler, *British Labour and the Cold War* (Stanford, Calif.: Stanford University Press, 1988), chs. 2 and 3; for the Caribbean implications, see Harrod, *Trade Union Foreign Policy*.

[136] Ken Post, *Strike the Iron* (Atlantic Highlands, NJ: Humanities Press, 1981), ii. 429–57; and Hart papers, *passim*.

mittee and a CPGB member, Forbes Burnham, then a student in London, later President of the Guiana PPP, founder and leader of the People's National Congress, and from 1964 until his death in 1985 Prime Minister of Guyana, and Michael Manley, then also a student, son of PNP leader Norman Manley, later himself to lead the party and serve as Jamaican Premier in 1972–80 and 1989–92.

Lewis, in correspondence with Hart, was candid and more than a little cynical about the intention to ensure left-wing control of the London CLC:

The reason for such a large committee was to allow plenty of right wing[er]s to be voted on and thus satisfy their supporters. There would then still be enough left wingers to do the work.[137]

Hyacinth Morgan, the Grenadian-born Labour MP who had previously been involved with the ill-fated West Indies Committee, became the chairman—to Lewis's malicious glee:

He is ideal I think. So right wing that the Colonial Office will be delighted and such a fool that he can only discredit right wing opinions among the organisation.[138]

An attempt was also made to enlist the support of prominent West Indians in Britain: of George Padmore (a useful frontman even though he was 'not a friend of the Party', as Nichols confided),[139] Arthur Lewis, and Learie Constantine. Constantine became for a time a Vice-President of the London CLC, and Padmore offered advice on its constitution; but neither remained involved, presumably dropping out because of the Communist connection.[140] Arthur Lewis was wholly hostile: 'He very curtly remarked that it was strange for the CLC to have a branch in London . . . Similar to the TUC in Paris registering individuals!'[141] Nor was the CPGB itself as supportive as might have been expected: 'quite candidly it's difficult to get help from the Party, except good advice, although the Colonial Department wholeheartedly support our proposals.'[142] Hopes for financial or organisational assistance from that source were slim, as

[137] Arthur Lewis to Richard Hart (24 May 1948), Hart 6/168.
[138] Arthur Lewis to Richard Hart (22 May 1948), Hart 6/165.
[139] 'Nick' (R. H. Nichols) to Richard Hart (30 Nov. 1947), Hart 4/10.
[140] Lewis to Hart (22 and 24 May 1948).
[141] Billy Strachan to Richard Hart (14 July 1948), Hart 6/177.
[142] Nichols to Hart (30 Nov. 1947).

CPGB officials lamented their own problems of lack of funds and overwork.[143] The aim of establishing the London CLC as a major anticolonial front organisation came to little. By August 1948 it still had fewer than seventy members. Morgan soon resigned as chairman: 'His given reason was that the London Branch was becoming materialistic.'[144] By 1950 it was a rump, largely kept going by Strachan's efforts, and bitterly denouncing its former parent body.[145] Its importance really lies only in the subsequent careers of some of its members; and as a vivid microcosm of the ways in which the CP sought to influence anticolonial movements.

The Communist Party itself continued for a number of years to produce a *West Indies Newsletter*, containing reports and polemics on both Caribbean and wider colonial affairs—almost always anonymous, though it may reasonably be surmised that Strachan, Lewis, and Nichols were the major contributors. Offering unstinted praise for the London CLC and the Guiana PPP, it gave more guarded support to Norman Manley and the Jamaica PNP, and was bitterly critical not only of British Labour leaders but of Brockway and other left-wingers.[146] The schism in the world union movement was predictably greeted with sharp denunciation of the ICFTU and its Caribbean supporters, who were alleged to be trying to 'buy' West Indian trade unionists.[147] Equally predictably, there was praise for the Soviet-backed World Peace Movement, with prominence given to the signing of its petition by Caribbean personalities like Constantine,[148] and for the USSR itself: 'Enslaved, plundered and insulted by Imperialism, the West Indian people are no longer turning in despair to the skies. Inevitably, they take stock of the might and glory of the *Soviet Union*.'[149] More intriguing is the sardonic contempt poured upon

[143] Ibid. Also R. H. Nichols to Richard Hart (28 June 1947 and 8 Feb. 1948), Hart 4/11 and 4/9, Michael Carritt of CPGB Colonial Department to Richard Hart (2 Dec. 1947), Hart 4/22, Carritt to 'Harry' [Arthur Henry?] (5 June [1946?]), Hart 4/13.

[144] Minutes of CLC London Branch 2nd AGM (22 May 1949), Hart 6/148.

[145] CLC, *Federation and Self-Government Now*; Billy Strachan to Richard Hart (17 Apr. 1949), Hart 6/186.

[146] *WIN* 2/9 (Sept. 1950), attacks Brockway over Korea: 'Brockway, an erstwhile supporter of colonial freedom, does not like coming face to face with reality.' (Files of the *Newsletter* are in Hart papers 6/80.)

[147] *WIN* 1/3 (Sept. 1949); 2/2 (Feb. 1950: erroneously dated 1949).

[148] Ibid. 2/9 (Sept. 1950).

[149] Ibid. 3/11 and 4/1 (Dec. 1951–Jan. 1952). Emphasis in original.

Labour anticolonial statements, like the following portrayal of Tom Williams:

The Minister of Agriculture put on a good act in his most cultivated accent. He was ashamed of the criticisms fired at Britain's colonial rule; he was pained; he regretted; he thought something should be done; he had learnt a lot at this wonderful gathering and he wanted better things for the colonial people. The mystery still remains whether the applause which followed was for a good act or because the audience believed he was sincerely interested in colonial welfare.[150]

Sectarian though such mockery was, there can be little doubt that it reflected an attitude to Labour Party rhetoric on the colonies which was increasingly widespread among colonial radicals by the early 1950s.

VIII. MALAYA

A further, and final, major colonial crisis of the early 1950s which aroused strong, conflicting reactions among British radicals was the guerrilla war in Malaya.[151] The activities of the British left on this issue centred around two types of organisation, between which there was a degree of overlapping membership and ideology; though quite how large an overlap was at the time, and has remained, an uncertain and controversial question. One was the association between the CPGB and the Malayan Communist Party, together with the operations of Malayan *émigré* and student circles in Britain sympathetic to the MCP. The other was the nexus of British and *émigré* Malayan individuals involved with the Malayan Forum, the Britain–Malaya Committee, and, later, the South-East Asia Committee of the Movement for Colonial Freedom. In each case the central activists were Malayan-born, Cambridge-educated Marxists resident in Britain in the post-war period and prominent first in Malayan, then in British anticolonialist politics.

---

[150] Ibid. 3/1 (Jan. 1952).

[151] The fullest account of the war is Anthony Short, *The Communist Insurrection in Malaya, 1948–1960* (Frederick Muller, 1975), which is the only study thus far to be based on access to official records. On the controversial issue of the MDU, its relations with the MCP, and the role of John Eber, the most detailed study is Cheah Boon Kheng, *The Masked Comrades: A Study of the Communist United Front in Malaya, 1945–48* (Singapore: Times Books International, 1979). The provenance of this, however, arouses inevitable questions about its objectivity.

For the CPGB–MCP connection, the key figure was Lim Hong Bee, who had become involved in left-wing politics while studying law at Cambridge in 1937–8.[152] In 1946 he helped found, and was briefly Secretary of, the Malayan Democratic Union—a short-lived but temporarily very important and lastingly controversial nationalist party. Also involved with the MDU was John Eber, a Eurasian lawyer who had also attended Cambridge during the later 1930s,[153] but who had only become politicised by his experiences as a prisoner of the Japanese during the war. The MDU, of which Eber became Vice-President and by all accounts its leading strategist, was the major force in Singapore and Malaya pressing for self-government and social reform in the immediate post-war years. As short-term aims, these were not incompatible with the objectives of the powerful Malayan Communist Party; and there was a degree of co-operation between the MDU and the MCP during the period before the outbreak of guerrilla war. What is far less easy to determine is the nature and extent of this co-operation. Students of modern Malayan history have expressed views ranging from that of the MDU as essentially a moderate, social-democratic party subject either to limited infiltration by, or an equally limited desire to co-operate with, the MCP, to that of the MDU as the creation of, and respectable front for, the Communists.[154]

Whichever of these versions may have been nearer the truth, interaction between the parties was virtually inescapable, since in post-war Malaya 'it was almost impossible for any group which wanted to start a political party with mass appeal and with a programme of social and economic reform not to come to terms with the Communists'.[155] None the less, a distinction can be drawn between

---

[152] Cheah, *Masked Comrades*, 75–6; John Drysdale, *Singapore: Struggle for Success* (Singapore: Times Books International/Allen & Unwin, 1984), 19–20.

[153] Ibid. Mr Eber, last known living in retirement in London, did not wish to be interviewed for this study.

[154] See Cheah, *Masked Comrades*; Drysdale, *Singapore*; Fransisco Nemenzo, Jun., 'Revolution and Counter-Revolution' (Manchester University Ph.D. thesis, 1964); Gordon K. Means, *Malaysian Politics* (Hutchinson, 1965); Yeo Kim Wah, 'A Study of Three Early Political Parties in Singapore, 1945–1955', *Journal of South-East Asian History*, 10/1 (1969); Pang Cheng Lian, 'The People's Action Party, 1954–1983', ibid.; David Marshall, 'Singapore's Struggle for Nationhood, 1945–1959', *Journal of South-East Asian Studies*, 1/2 (1970); Charles B. McLane, *Soviet Strategies in Southeast Asia* (Princeton, NJ: Princeton University Press, 1966).

[155] Cheah, *Masked Comrades*, 57. Even Lee Kuan Yew, subsequently a vehemently anti-Communist leader, said in 1955 that no Singapore politician could afford to be

those in the MDU who were secret members of the MCP, and those who had many points of political agreement with the Communists, and who were prepared to work with those whom they knew to be MCP members without wholly identifying themselves with them. Lim Hong Bee would seem to fall into the first category, John Eber into the second. Such differences were not of urgent importance whilst the MCP retained hopes of a peaceful transition to independence, as it did in 1945–7; after the turn to confrontation in 1948 they became fraught with dangerous significance.

Lim Hong Bee had returned to Britain in May 1947, partly to resume his legal studies, partly to act as London representative for the AMCJA-PUTERA Alliance.[156] From 1948, however, he became increasingly openly the London spokesman of the MCP and worked very closely with the British Communists. He founded the *Malayan Monitor*, a bulky but badly produced monthly journal which he edited (and apparently wrote almost single-handed) from late 1947 onwards.[157] This became the main forum in which support for the Malayan Communist guerrillas was expressed in Britain, whilst Lim also wrote regularly for various CPGB publications: *Labour Monthly*, *World News and Views*, and the *Daily Worker*. The themes were consistent throughout this prolific output—and consistently reiterated during the eighteen or so years in which the *Monitor* appeared. The Malayan war was presented as being the result of aggression and provocation on the part of the British. That the MCP had taken a conscious decision to abandon peaceful protest and undertake armed struggle, whether under provocation or not, was never admitted. Nor was the generally known fact that support for the guerrillas came overwhelmingly from Malaya's Chinese community, with the indigenous Malays lukewarm at best towards them. Nor, for that matter, was it in general openly stated that the MCP led the guerrillas, whose nationalistic aims and background of opposition to the Japanese were far more strongly emphasised than their ideological bent.

anti-Communist if he wished to succeed (quoted in Pang, 'People's Action Party', 143).

[156] The united front of the All-Malayan Council of Joint Action and the Pusat Tenaga Ra'ayat; each of which was itself an alliance of a number of smaller parties. The MCP was not formally associated with either group, but had supporters active in both. Eber drafted the Alliance's constitution and programme.

[157] I have been unable to trace a complete file of this journal. The Marx Memorial Library has an incomplete run.

The 'bourgeois' nationalist parties were subject to varying degrees of vituperation: vehement in the case of the conservative United Malays National Organisation, muted for the more radical People's Action Party in Singapore. The successive British proposals for federation and transition to self-government were denounced, as they appeared, as neo-colonialist tricks. The costs of the conflict to the British taxpayer were constantly stressed, as contrasted both with the profits of the companies on whose behalf the British were alleged to be fighting and with the benefits to be expected from trade between Britain and an independent Malaya.[158] By the mid-1950s, there had come to be greater emphasis on the need for a negotiated end to the fighting, including an amnesty for the guerrillas; in fact it would appear that Lim's report on behalf of the MCP to the 1954 Empire Communist Parties' conference was the first indication given anywhere that the MCP now favoured a peaceful solution and was prepared to make substantial concessions in order to get it.[159]

As well as his activities with the CPGB and the *Monitor*, Lim helped found the South-East Asia Committee in October 1950, intended as a 'broad-based organisation on a permanent basis to further the aims of the Cominform', according to a Labour Party report on its activities.[160] It does not appear to have had any real impact, being cold-shouldered by the main colonial students' groups—its natural constituency of support—and soon fading from view.[161]

Eber, meanwhile, had been detained by the authorities in Malaya in January 1950, charged with being an undercover associate of the MCP, and held without trial for three years.[162] He vigorously denied the charges, but his demands that he be brought to trial to face them were ignored. On his eventual release he migrated to Britain, where he immediately became involved in Malayan *émigré* and British anticolonial politics. He became Secretary of, and later he and his

---

[158] See *Malayan Monitor, passim*; also, *inter alia*, articles by Lim in *WNV* (1 Dec. 1951, 13 Dec. 1952, 10 Jan. 1953, 10 July 1954, 8 Jan. 1955, 29 Jan. 1955). Lim also spoke frequently at CPGB meetings, and at the party's 1952 National Congress (*WNV* 26 Apr. 1952), 188–9).

[159] *Allies for Freedom* (CPGB pamphlet, 1954), 35–52; Short, *Communist Insurrection*, 459.

[160] Edward Farmer, memo on South-East Asia Committee and COPAI, LP/CSC/50/20.

[161] Ibid. I have found no reference to activities by this Committee after 1951, though members clearly remained active in other groups.

[162] Cheah, *Masked Comrades*, 108–12; Means, *Malaysian Politics*, 82–3.

supporters were for a time the dominant force within, the Malayan Forum, a non-party political association of Malayans in Britain. The Forum's committee was indeed almost a family affair: its Chairman was Eber's brother-in-law Wan Abdul Hamid, its Treasurer Gladys Lim, the cousin of MDU founder Lim Kean Chye, and another of Eber's brothers-in-law also served.[163] All these were, in their opponents' eyes, secret Communists or fellow travellers. In 1955–6 a bitter little struggle for power took place between them and the anti-Communist Malayan nationalists in Britain who were led by PAP supporter Goh Keng Swee. This ended with the Eber group being ousted from control of the Malayan Forum, its journal *Suara Merdeka*, and the Malayan Students' Union.[164]

Eber also founded, and was Secretary of, the Britain–Malaya Committee. This was ostensibly intended as an association of 'persons of all shades of opinion' who accepted its very broad aims; which were to press for a peaceful settlement of the war, an end to the Emergency, a recognition of Malaya's right to independence, and 'friendship and mutually beneficial trade on equal terms between the two countries'.[165] On this basis it gained the endorsement of such worthies as the Bishop of Birmingham.

The Committee itself, however, was very small, initially consisting of Eber, two other left-wing Malayans (one of them being Wan Abdul Hamid), and two military men, Lt.-Col. Nicholas Read-Collins and Commander Edgar Young (Retd.). The views of this pair may perhaps be surmised from the fact that they were respectively Vice-President of the Britain–China Friendship Association and Vice-Chairman of the British–Rumanian Friendship Association, both organisations proscribed by the Labour Party.[166] Later Reginald Reynolds and Basil Davidson also became members, but both resigned after a brief period.[167]

The Committee published a journal, *Britain-Malaya*, carrying news of political developments in the colony and commentary, mostly from the pen of Eber; and a pamphlet, *Malaya's Freedom is Vital to Britain*,

---

[163] Drysdale, *Singapore*, 136.

[164] Ibid. 135–8.

[165] John Eber, *Malaya's Freedom is Vital to Britain* (Britain–Malaya Committee pamphlet, 1954), endpapers.

[166] See 'Notes on the MCF South-East Asia Committee and Britain–Malaya Committee', LPCD papers, not attributed or dated, but presumably by John Hatch and *c*.Nov.–Dec. 1955.

[167] Ibid.

also by Eber. The arguments in these were similar to those of the *Malayan Monitor* and other pro-MCP publications, though without overt solidarity for the Communists, with less harsh criticism of the other national parties, and with more emphasis on the search for a peaceful settlement.[168] The activities of Eber and his associates were viewed with intense disfavour by Transport House, and by more conservative Malayan *émigrés* and students in Britain. This antagonism gained importance after 1956, producing a major confrontation between the anticolonialist left and the Labour Party.

IX. THE LEFT IN THE LABOUR PARTY

Well before the defeat of the Attlee Government in 1951 many Labour left-wingers had, as we have seen, become deeply disenchanted with its colonial policy. This disillusion was reflected in slowly awakening dissent among back-benchers and some local party activists, and also among some of the NEC's own colonial experts. By the end of 1949, Charles Greenidge was telling Arthur Lewis that 'My impression is that [the] Colonial Policy of the Party is now less progressive than it was in 1943';[169] and Lewis was dolefully replying that 'I wonder if it is worth all the trouble, since a Labour Colonial Secretary seems to do just as his officials please, without reference to the documents we write.'[170]

The 1951 Labour Party Conference was little more than a pre-election rally, so that colonial affairs were not debated other than in the context of somewhat anodyne references to the relevant sections of the Manifesto. The left was on this as on other issues overcome with the usual pre-election concern for a public façade of unity. The 1952 conference in Morecambe, by contrast, saw both an unusually lengthy debate on Empire and the first real post-war expression of widespread interest—and of clear left-wing attitudes—in this sphere at CLP level. Yet the left's major victories at this conference, which marked the appearance of Bevanism as a significant force in the constituency parties and the unions, were not as yet extended to

[168] Incomplete files of *Britain–Malaya* are in Marx Memorial Library and MCF papers.
[169] C. W. W. Greenidge to W. Arthur Lewis (27 Oct. 1949), Greenidge papers 12/9/122.
[170] Lewis to Greenidge (15 Nov. 1949), Greenidge 12/9/123.

the colonial debate. A resolution from Edinburgh West calling for 'immediate independence to all British colonies and dependencies' and the withdrawal of troops and bases from Malaya, Egypt, and the colonies was overwhelmingly defeated; and one demanding militant opposition to the Central African Federation, including extra-parliamentary agitation, was remitted.[171] The day was still carried by the views of Gordon Walker, who spoke of Labour understanding the 'nature and realities of the Commonwealth better than the so-called Empire Party', and of Griffiths, who said that 'all those delegates who talk about leaving [the colonies]: if you leave, what do you leave behind? We could leave, and when we leave there is a vacuum.' But such arguments were already clearly on the defensive, and Griffiths's remarks were greeted with 'cries of "Why?"' from delegates.[172]

The 1953 Conference had before it an unprecedented twenty CLP resolutions on colonial affairs, with fifteen of them calling for independence to be made an immediate priority; as did clauses in three more general foreign policy motions. Three of the resolutions supported the idea of target dates and others used phrases such as 'urgent necessity' or spoke of Mau Mau as 'a direct consequence of resisting the natural aspirations of the Kenyan people'. Whilst some stressed racial justice and economic development the majority were couched, in contrast to the Fabian approach of the 1940s, in terms of Britain recognising the demands of the colonial peoples rather than of its planning for their welfare. In the constituencies at least, Fabianism and paternalism were being replaced by support for radical nationalism.[173]

Meanwhile in the *New Statesman* Basil Davidson was offering faint praise and damning criticism of the colonial sections of Labour's new policy document, *Challenge to Britain*—and doing so from the newly influential perspective of an intimate relationship between economic exploitation, political and racial injustice in the colonies, and the prospects for socialism in Britain. Davidson brought together most of the main lines of socialist critique in colonial affairs into a synthesis which was to dominate left-wing thought during the 1950s. He warned of the danger of 'more and more murderous colonial wars'.

---

[171] *LPACR 1952*, 137–8.

[172] Ibid. 128, 141. Ironically, the phrase about leaving a vacuum behind one had originally been used by a number of left-wingers in criticising the Government's Palestinian policy.

[173] Labour Party Conference Agenda (1953), 40–2, 46–8.

He attacked the effects of capitalist investment in the colonies and the profits made there: 'the profits are large because this labour is exceedingly cheap.' He argued that the benefits of this exploitation were increasingly not even accruing to Britain, but to the USA. He criticised the assumption that 'we'—the British people as opposed to minority capitalist and militaristic cliques—had an interest in the continuation of the colonial Empire. He suggested an alternative economic policy of planned 'real development' in the colonies: Britain must stop sucking out capital, and set up secondary and processing industries leading to the emergence of 'balanced capitalist economies upon which the foundations of Socialism could be laid'.

A partial solution to Britain's economic problems, too, would be to turn British industry to the task of 'producing the capital goods which our colonies need in order to cease to be colonies'. *Challenge to Britain*, he argued:

fumbles this alternative. It speaks of the Sterling Area as a means of economic support which the United Kingdom may take for granted. It fails to face the harsh fact that we are living, as a country, off the fruits of African and Asian labour . . . An alternative and a prosperous relationship—prosperous for the majority, not the share-owning minority—between Britain and her liberated colonies is a real possibility: otherwise Socialism would be a drab and dismal imposter.[174]

There was very little that was original in this argument. It restated some of the classic themes of Hobson, suggested prospects for future development which had become commonplaces of Communist economic thought and, increasingly, of orthodox development economics,[175] and partook of the left's now-familiar ambiguities as to whether 'we . . . as a country' or merely as a parasitic minority gained from colonial exploitation. But these ideas were now, it seemed, listened to as never before within the Labour Party.

The 1954 Party Conference may, in this context, be seen as the real turning-point in Labour discussion of colonial policy. There were twenty-two resolutions on the subject—including, for the first time since the war, a radical colonial resolution from a major trade union, USDAW. A full morning's debate was devoted to it, and

---

[174] Basil Davidson, *NS&N* (27 June 1953), 764–5.
[175] For the convergence of Marxist and orthodox thinking on prescriptions for development in the 1950s, see Tony Killick, *Development Economics in Action: A Study of Economic Policies in Ghana* (Heinemann, 1978).

contributions from the floor were more numerous, showed more signs of knowledge of the issues, and were expressive of more radical attitudes, than ever before. The Movement for Colonial Freedom, itself founded five months before and responsible for inspiring many of the colonial resolutions tabled, had a team of volunteers in Scarborough for the conference, lobbying delegates, and 'flooding Scarborough with MCF literature'. A fringe meeting organised by the Movement, at which Brockway, Benn, Jennie Lee, Joe Murumbi, Solly Sachs, Claude Bourdet, and Syrian Socialist Party representative Clovis Maksoud spoke, had been packed out and filled overspill rooms.[176]

In the conference itself not only the contributions of Brockway and of USDAW leader Walter Padley,[177] but also those of several constituency delegates, showed the clear influence of MCF-type radical anticolonialism. In place of the simple opposition between constructive colonial policy and condemnation of imperialism, or for and against target dates for independence, seen at previous conferences, the argument now was on the *nature* of the target dates. The NEC's statement referred to dates for the transfer of power being fixed 'as soon as the development of each territory makes it practicable'.[178] A composite moved by Padley for USDAW (which had itself, at its own delegate conference in April, had a debate on colonial affairs which was remarkable by the previous standards of the British trade union movement for the level of interest and knowledge displayed[179]) was obviously MCF inspired, reflecting closely the wording of the MCF's own policy statement. It sought to commit the next Labour Government to calling conferences with all colonial nationalist movements jointly to fix dates for independence. An amendment was moved demanding that these dates be established in the first session of a Labour Government.[180] A separate resolution seconded by the ETU sought the addition of a commitment to the withdrawal of all British troops from foreign and colonial soil (a long-standing CPGB demand; and the ETU was of course a Communist-

---

[176] MCF Head Office Report (17 Dec. 1954) (Benn papers); and *PN* reports (1 Oct. and 8 Oct. 1954), which give the audience figure as 400.

[177] Who was, as may be remembered, an old ILP associate of Brockway.

[178] *LPACR 1954, NEC Statement of Policy: From Colonies to Commonwealth* (1954), 199.

[179] USDAW, *Report of Proceedings at the Eighth Annual Delegate Meeting* (18–20 Apr. 1954), 72–81; *LPACR 1954*, 126–7, 128.

[180] Ibid. 126–30.

dominated union). Another left-wing resolution reintroduced for the first time in some years the idea of nationalising industries and mines in colonial territories.[181]

In the event the differences between the emerging left-wing view and that of the leadership were not pushed to an open breach. The USDAW and nationalisation motions were remitted with the consent of their proposers, the 'first session target dates' amendment withdrawn, and the troop withdrawal resolution defeated. The MCF, and the left generally, were more concerned at this stage to consolidate support than to confront their party leaders, especially since official Labour policy was seen as having already moved some way in the right direction. But some observers had noted that:

The veiled disagreements which exist inside the Labour Party are at least as large as those overt disagreements about colonial affairs which divide the two front benches. So long as its spokesmen keep to the generalities of anti-government propaganda sufficient for platform oratory, the Labour Party appears united on colonial affairs. But how superficial that unity is, might very soon be revealed if a Labour Minister were to replace Mr. Lyttelton.[182]

The opening up of disagreements did not have to await that long-delayed eventuality. Indeed over the issues of Central Africa and, more explosively, British Guiana it had already occurred. It was to be repeated on other colonial problems a number of times before the end of the decade; and these matters are discussed in a subsequent chapter. Having charted the shift to the left at Party Conference, we must now turn to investigate how opinion was moving in the constituencies themselves.

In January 1951 the NEC decided that henceforth its subcommittees should keep records of resolutions on their subject areas sent in by local parties and affiliated organisations.[183] These records provide an interesting light on party opinion about colonial questions; though not a full or entirely reliable picture. Not all CLP resolutions would be forwarded to the NEC, so that the latter's records are not a complete account of CLP opinion; and the analyses of resolutions prepared for the Commonwealth Subcommittee appeared at somewhat irregular intervals, so that a precise breakdown of changes over time is difficult to reconstruct. Further, the variety of their

[181] Ibid. 130.
[182] Editorial, 'Waging Peace in the Colonies', *NS&N* (26 Dec. 1953), 809.
[183] Morgan Phillips to Denis Healey (27 Jan. 1951) (LP: unfiled).

subject-matter makes any neat categorisation by subject problematic. None the less, a rough guide to degree of interest among local activists, its changing level, the subjects on which it was expressed, and the general tenor of opinion on these subjects may be obtained, as can be seen in Tables 5.1, 5.2, and 5.3.

Perhaps the most surprising thing about the figures in these tables is the fluctuation in numbers of resolutions over time. Deducing from the level of pressure-group activity on colonial affairs, the numbers of colonial resolutions at Party Conference, and attention to these issues in the socialist press and among left-wing MPs in Parliament, one might have expected to see a gradually rising level of CLP activity in the early 1950s, peaking in 1953–7, and falling away in the later 1950s. Yet whilst the increase in 1951–3 is indeed rapid, thereafter the level of CLP involvement falls away rather sharply, revives somewhat in 1956, collapses again, and undergoes a final upsurge, less intense than that of 1952–3, in 1959–60. Three possible explanations for this might be suggested. The first is that it might reflect the distraction of CLPs' attention by other issues. This does not seem to be the case: the pattern shows no obvious relationship to other major political events, internal or external. For instance, one of the two General Election years during the period, 1955, has far fewer colonial resolutions than those preceding and succeeding it; the other, 1959, has more—though of course in both cases the election period itself produced few resolutions. There may, however, be a correlation with periods of generally increased CLP left-wing activism: in the early 1950s with the rise of extra-parliamentary Bevanism, in 1959 –60 with CND and the controversy over Gaitskell's leadership.

A second possibility is that the pattern of resolutions reflects specific campaigns by interested groups to get their views adopted by CLPs. This can be only a very partial explanation. Both the timing and, in many cases, the wording of resolutions on Kenya, Central Africa, and South Africa after 1954 follow campaigns by the MCF on these issues, but this accounts for a relatively small proportion of the total; whilst very few resolutions (with the notable exception of those from the ETU) reflect the campaigns of the CPGB on questions like the withdrawal of British troops or the call for a general amnesty in Malaya. The FCB and other relevant pressure groups never attempted serious local-level lobbying.

Far more important would seem to be a third and simpler explanation: a very considerable proportion of the resolutions (most

TABLE 5.1. *Resolutions on colonial subjects received by the Labour Party National Executive Committee*

Dates	Number of resolutions received				Notes
	CLPs	Unions	Others	Total[a]	
April–May 1951	6	—	—	6	
November–December 1951	2	—	—	2	
January 1952	10	—	—	10	SA: protests at Malan's visit
February 1952	3	1	—	4	
April 1952	7	—	—	7	
May 1952	9	1	—	10	
June 1952	3	—	—	3	
July–October 1952	28	4	—	32	16 SA, 8 Malaya, 4 against CAF
November 1952–January 1953	46	—	3	49	32 Kenya, 5 against CAF
January–February 1953	5	3	3	11	4 Kenya, 5 CAF
February–March 1953	31	—	—	31	22 CAF, 5 Kenya
April–June 1953	29	2	—	31	17 CAF, 9 Kenya
June–July 1953	8	—	—	8	
July–August 1953	11	—	—	11	5 Kenya
November 1953	122	1	17	140	135 Guiana (87 anti-NEC)
December 1953	88	—	3	91	77 Guiana, 8 Kenya
January 1954	8	—	2	10	7 Guiana
February 1954	6	1	1	8	
May 1954	4	1	—	5	
June 1954	6	1	1	8	
July–August 1954	11	—	—	11	
October 1954	3	—	—	3	
December 1954	4	—	—	4	
January 1955	2	—	1	3	
February 1955	5	—	—	5	
March 1955	4	—	—	4	

Table 5.1. *Continued*

Dates	Number of resolutions received				Notes
	CLPs	Unions	Others	Total[a]	
Summer 1955	3	1	—	4	
October 1955	4	—	—	4	All Kenya
November 1955	3	—	—	3	
December 1955	2	1	—	3	
January 1956	8	1	—	9	8 Cyprus
February 1956	6	1	—	7	6 Cyprus
March 1956	12	1	—	13	11 Cyprus
April 1956	6	1	1	8	7 Cyprus
May 1956	6	3	—	9	6 Cyprus
July 1956	9	2	—	11	
August 1956	9	3	—	12	
September–October 1956	3	2	—	5	
November 1956	1	1	—	2	Not including Suez resolutions
December 1956	4	—	—	4	
January 1957	8	1	—	9	
February 1957	4	—	—	4	
March–April 1957	1	1	—	2	
May 1957	1	1	—	2	
July 1957	2	1	—	3	
September 1957[b]	1	1	—	2	
September 1958	13	1	—	14	5 Cyprus, 2 Kenya, 2 CAF
November 1958	7	—	—	7	5 Cyprus[c]
January 1959	2	—	—	2	
February 1959	2	—	—	2	
March 1959	29	—	—	29	27 CAF
April 1959	15	5	1	21	18 CAF
June–July 1959	18	3	—	21	8 CAF, 7 Kenya
August–October 1959	11	3	—	14	5 Kenya
December 1959	26	2	—	28	19 SA, 7 CAF
January 1960	2	—	—	2	

TABLE 5.1.   *Continued*

Dates	Number of resolutions received				Notes
	CLPs	Unions	Others	Total[a]	
February–March 1960	26	4	11	41	All SA—Sharpeville
April 1960	17	2	—	19	All Sharpeville
May–June 1960	10	2	—	12	10 SA
July 1960	3	—	—	3	
August 1960[d]	1	—	—	1	

[a] Unions are nationally affiliated trade unions, CLPs Constituency and District Parties, Others include youth sections, trades councils, ward parties, the Co-operative Party, etc.

[b] During the following year only a small trickle of resolutions was reported, e.g. three during the summer of 1958.

[c] Eleven CPs also wrote calling for an NEC statement on racism.

[d] After the summer of 1960 colonial resolutions again dwindled to a tiny trickle.

Source: analyses of resolutions of colonial subjects (taken by NEC to include South Africa, but exclude Suez) compiled by Commonwealth Officer (Eddie Farmer 1951–4, John Hatch 1954–61) for CSC (LPCSC/CD).

TABLE 5.2.   *Annual totals of resolutions received*

Year	CLPs	Unions	Others	Total
1951	8	—	—	8
1952	106	6	3	115
1953	294	6	26	326
1954	40	4	4	48
1955	23	2	1	26
1956	64	15	1	80
1957	17	5	—	22
1958	23	1	—	24
1959	103	13	1	117
1960	59	8	11	78

TABLE 5.3.   *Totals of resolutions broken down by subject*

Subject	Resolutions received	Notes
British Guiana	226	
South Africa	164	Mostly boycott calls and Sharpeville protests
Central African Federation	129	Mostly attacking Federation
Kenya	115	Mostly protests at repression
Cyprus	69	Mostly protests at repression
Malaya	16	Mostly protests at repression
Seretse Khama	8	
General policy	51	Mostly calling for more rapid decolonisation, or urging more vigorous attack on Government policies

obviously those on British Guiana, and also many on the Kenya and Cyprus conflicts, the Nyasaland disturbances, and the Sharpeville massacre) were in direct response to well-publicised colonial crises. CLPs on the whole, as opposed to specifically interested minorities within them, were moved to express opinions on colonial matters, and to communicate them to the NEC, when particularly dramatic events caught their attention; especially when these involved repressive actions by British troops. Their activists' newspapers and TV screens, one may surmise, were more important in arousing such responses than intra-party channels of communication.[184]

The other, and perhaps more obvious, conclusion to be drawn from analysis of these resolutions is that the vast majority of them adopted positions implicitly or explicitly more radical than those of the Labour leadership. A large proportion overtly criticised the party's official policies from a radical anticolonialist perspective; a tiny handful expressed right-wing views.[185]

[184] This accords with the conventional wisdom of academic studies of political party activists in the 1950s and 1960s; more recent work on Labour's political culture since the 1970s suggests more intensive internal lines of communication. See Patrick Seyd and Paul Whiteley, *Labour's Grass Roots* (Oxford: Oxford University Press, 1992).

[185] Precise accounting is impossible, given the variety and frequent vagueness of the resolutions; but I would estimate that at least 70 per cent of them were clearly more left-wing than official party policy, less than 5 per cent to its right.

A final indicator of change in the anticolonialist left's influence within the Labour Party is worthy of note; that of personnel in Transport House itself. In 1954 the key job in this sphere, that of the party's Commonwealth Officer, was taken by a man clearly on the left of the party. John Hatch was, like so many of Labour's anticolonialists, a veteran of the ILP, whose National Organiser he had been in 1944–8. Thereafter he had taught at Glasgow University for five years, establishing contacts with Nyerere and others whilst there, and visiting South Africa in 1950. He worked briefly for the Africa Bureau, but became dissatisfied with the 'paternalism' of Michael Scott's attitude to Africans.[186] He began writing extensively on African affairs at this time, including a pamphlet for *Tribune* which took a strongly left-wing stance.[187]

With such a background, and with a conviction that he had a mission to help radicalise Labour colonial policy (which, in his view, meant little more than to bring it to recognition of the new situation in the colonies themselves), it was hardly surprising that he should experience some hostility from the more conservative of Labour's bureaucrats including General Secretary Morgan Phillips. Like some of his predecessors on Labour colonial committees, he came to believe that the most important division within the party was simply between those who knew something about colonial affairs and those who did not. The former were almost by definition on the left, for they appreciated the importance of the pressure for decolonisation and the necessity of working with rather than against it.[188]

Hatch was by no means a lone warrior within the apparatus: by the mid-1950s the NEC's Commonwealth Subcommittee was becoming something of a left-wing enclave within an executive generally dominated by the party's right wing. From 1956 Labour's leading left-wing dissident, Nye Bevan, became Chairman of the Subcommittee, whose members also included prominent Bevanites Barbara Castle, Tom Driberg, and Anthony Greenwood. Both Commonwealth Department and Subcommittee, though by no means always satisfying the party's left-wing critics, were evidently more open to radical influences than were their equivalents in most other areas of Labour policy-making. No wonder that even Brockway felt by 1957 that even

---

[186] Interview with Lord Hatch. See also his part-autobiographical *Two African Statesmen: Kaunda of Zambia and Nyerere of Tanzania* (Secker & Warburg, 1976).
[187] *The Intelligent Socialist's Guide to Africa* (Tribune pamphlet, 1953).
[188] Interview with Lord Hatch.

if the Labour right wing had won the internal battles on most policy fronts, the left had the high ground on colonial affairs.[189] 'During the period in Opposition, Labour's policy in regard to the colonies has advanced more than on any other subject.'[190] But, he warned, public opinion still had to be made 'ready to support bold action. The education of the people to a belief in colonial freedom is a first task for us in Britain during the short period before a Labour Government comes to power.'[191] And by this time Brockway believed that there was, finally, an organisation capable of doing this.

[189] Fenner Brockway, *PN* (11 Oct. 1957).
[190] Ibid. (14 June 1957).
[191] Ibid. (21 June 1957).

6

The Movement for Colonial Freedom, 1954–1964

The formation of the Movement for Colonial Freedom in 1954 may be regarded as the culmination of active opposition to colonialism in Britain—the point at which anticolonial feeling on the British left found its most unified, coherent, and forceful organisational expression, and its widest base of support. During the first ten years of its existence the MCF was, in terms of range of supporters and contacts and scope of activities, among the most important post-war British political pressure groups. This chapter traces the evolution of this movement, its origins, structure, membership, and activities, its parliamentary role, relations with the Labour and Communist Parties, the trades unions, and the nationalist movements.

I. ORIGINS AND FOUNDATION

The MCF's foundation was, in the first instance, the result of discussions between the officers of three anticolonialist lobbies; the British Centre of the Congress of Peoples Against Imperialism, the Council for the Defence of Seretse Khama and the Protectorates, and the British Guiana Association.[1] The stimuli leading to the establishment of the new organisation were various.[2] The most straightforward was that expressed in a circular letter announcing the inaugural conference of the proposed Congress for Colonial Freedom:

---

[1] The former two are discussed in Ch. 5 above. The British Guiana Association, the least important of the three, had been founded by Brockway and Sir Leslie Plummer in late 1953, but had undertaken little if any activity. I have been able to trace no publications or records of this group.

[2] The few published accounts are sometimes misleading on this point. Gupta attributes the MCF's foundation solely to the Guiana crisis, Lee to the Khama case: Partha Sarathi Gupta, *Imperialism and the British Labour Movement, 1914–1964* (Macmillan, 1975), 360–1; J. M. Lee, *Colonial Development and Good Government* (Oxford: Clarendon Press, 1967), 71.

There is disquiet throughout the country, but at the moment it finds no adequate channel of expression. The numerous organisations concerned with these questions tends to create overlapping and confusion.[3]

There was also a feeling (for reasons noted above, pp. 182–3) that the most important of the existing anticolonialist bodies, the COPAI, was inadequate to the task posed by new developments in Britain and the colonies.

If the existing extra-parliamentary groups were felt to be insufficient in scope and excessive in number, a further stimulus was provided by changes in the Parliamentary Labour Party. In 1953–4 an informal group of left-wing MPs interested in African affairs had begun meeting regularly in the House.[4] Almost all of these were of broadly Bevanite sympathies; and although they were not in any strong sense the colonial committee of the Bevan group there was a link between Bevanism and the parliamentary anticolonialists beyond the fact of joint membership. Bevan had in effect dissolved his group in October 1952; but a number of the leading members had continued to meet informally and without taking minutes. At a meeting at Richard Crossman's house in November 1953, it was agreed that the Bevanites should set up a number of informal specialist committees, for which Brockway's African group would act as the model. Brockway suggests in his memoirs that the foundation of the MCF was in part prompted by this decision by the Bevanites to expand the scope of their activities.[5] Thus the MCF's genesis was seen as complementary to the strategy of the Bevanite left within the PLP. The Labour left was, of course, by no means confined to parliamentary Bevanism. It has convincingly been demonstrated that this group was supported by a very considerable body of constituency and trade union opinion; the high tide of which was somewhat later than that of the parliamentary caucus, but

---

[3] Circular signed by Benn, Brockway, Douglas Rogers, and others (n.d. but Mar. 1954) (Benn papers).

[4] Apart from Brockway the regular members were Wedgwood Benn, Geoffrey Bing, Leslie Hale, Ian Mikardo, Reginald Paget, and Sir Leslie Plummer (interview with Tony Benn).

[5] Fenner Brockway, *Towards Tomorrow* (Hart Davis, MacGibbon, 1977), 165; Richard Crossman, *The Backbench Diaries of Richard Crossman*, ed. Janet Morgan (Hamilton & Cape, 1981), 271–2; interview with Lord Brockway. The Bevanites had made some effort to establish colonial contacts as a group; see Harold Wilson to Driberg (7 Oct. 1952); Driberg to Wilson (9 Oct. 1952), concerning Driberg's meetings with the then Mahdi, Abdel Rahman: 'it would, of course, be a good thing on general principles that he should meet you [Wilson] and Nye and one or two others of our group.' (Driberg papers, S3).

whose dimensions were far greater than those of the latter.[6] The constituency and trade union support which the MCF gained might therefore be seen in part as reflecting this tide of extra-parliamentary Bevanism, and indeed as being among its strongest institutional expressions: although adherence to the MCF extended, as we shall see, well beyond this particular current.

The MCF's founding conference, held at the Waldorf Hotel on 11 April 1954, was attended by delegates from 38 CLPs, 22 trade union branches and 3 national trade unions (the FBU, USDAW, and AUEW), 7 Trades Councils, and a wide variety of other organisations including the ILP, UDC, Victory for Socialism, NALSO (the Labour students' organisation), WASU, the Uganda National Congress, Indian Socialist Group, Youth Congress of Nigeria, NCNC London branch, and seven other colonial peoples' organisations. The high level of politicisation still present in the Co-operative movement during the 1950s was underlined by the presence of delegates from some twenty Co-op organisations; as was the continued, if by this time residual, presence of pacifist bodies of pre-war vintage—the Peace Pledge Union, the Crusade for World Government, and War Resisters' International were represented.[7]

II. AIMS AND IDEALS

Initial mobilisation for the conference had been conducted under the title of the Congress for Colonial Freedom; but this was changed immediately before the launch itself to the Movement for Colonial Freedom. The change of name was in itself symptomatic of the belief now gaining ground that the time was ripe for anticolonial agitation to transcend its previous lobbying and advisory role and seek to create a popular movement—if possible, a mass movement. Thus far we have stressed the new opportunities for such a movement in the mid-1950s. There was also a darker side: a new sense of alarm and urgency created by the increasing tempo of crises in colonial territories and by the seemingly increasingly repressive response of the Government. This alarm centred above all on Kenya. Benn, the treasurer of

---

[6] Mark Jenkins: *Bevanism* (Nottingham: Spokesman, 1979); see also Jonathan Schneer, *Labour's Conscience* (Unwin Hyman, 1988), chs. 6–8.

[7] List of organisations sending delegates to MCF Founding Conference in Benn papers.

the new organisation, struck the note of urgency at the Waldorf conference: 'Unification for the common good is now a condition of our survival as a world. We have to telescope 1700 years of history into a few years.'[8] And a few months later Kingsley Martin was saying with characteristic gloom that: 'The Kenya situation is so bad that most people here now try not to think about it'—and then, equally characteristically, promptly contradicted his own fatalism by suggesting that it was this feeling of desperation over Kenya which aroused support for the MCF.[9]

The tone of alarm was, however, subordinated to that of the crusade. The MCF's appeal was couched, at least as much as that of any previous British anticolonial movement, in ethical terms. Benn's inaugural speech centred on this emphasis, comparing the movement against colonialism to Chartism (a favourite reference point for Benn throughout his career), and saying that the quality most needed by the MCF was imagination: 'to bridge the enormous gap between ourselves—you and me—and the African miner on the Copper Belt or the Malay worker on the rubber estate.'[10] Similarly the first Policy Statement, moved by Jennie Lee, although detailing a range of proposals for political, economic, and social change, gave pride of place to a change of heart: 'Our immediate object must be to create a psychological revolution throughout the colonies.'[11] When the MCF came later to elaborate a more extended statement of aims, the same stance predominated:

We believe that there is no more important or challenging factor in world politics today than the upsurge of millions of members of the human race for political, social and economic equality . . . This is the greatest moral issue of our time.[12]

Elsewhere Benn, in a fund-raising circular, described the ending of Empire as 'a moral challenge parallel with the moral challenge of slavery in the last century'.[13] And if Brockway was launching the

---

[8] Benn's speech notes for inaugural conference (Benn papers).

[9] Critic, 'London Diary', *NS&N* (16 Oct. 1954).

[10] Benn speech notes.

[11] Draft text for policy statement to inaugural conference (Benn papers). See also *The Times* report on the conference (12 Apr. 1954).

[12] *A Policy for Colonial Freedom* (MCF pamphlet, 1955). The style and tone are characteristically Brockway; and in interview, he and Benn confirmed that he wrote this text.

[13] Circular from Benn as treasurer (n.d. but early 1954) (Benn papers).

Movement in the spirit of a moral crusade, he believed that the response was in the same spirit. At the end of 1954 he was writing to MCF supporters that 'I've never known anything make such progress in so short a time ... This is the spirit which I knew in the pioneer days, nearly fifty years ago. It's with us again because our Movement is stirred by a great moral impulse for human equality and Freedom.'[14]

The MCF was not presenting a theory of imperialism to its target audiences, as for instance both the League Against Imperialism and the Pan-African Congress had done, in programmatic form, at their foundations. Nor did it represent merely a slightly more impatient variant on an established Labour Party pattern, as it has sometimes been seen as doing.[15] The MCF was clearly an organisation of the left, but initially it refused to define its aims in specifically socialist terms (a matter which was later to occasion some internal dissension); and its points of reference were neither primarily to the Marxist tradition of analyses of imperialism nor to the colonial policy of the Labour Party, but rather to the familiar set of ideas drawn from the radical-liberal heritage.

Brockway suggested that, whilst as a socialist he naturally had a closer 'fellow-feeling' and more intimate association with those colonial leaders who themselves espoused democratic socialist ideas, he and his colleagues 'were above all democrats' and therefore sought co-operation with, and championed the cause of, all legitimate movements of national liberation. He pointed, for instance, to Bourguiba of Tunisia, whom he had helped (and who had indeed presented him with the Order of the Republic of Tunisia for his part in the independence negotiations), although he had never felt the slightest sympathy for Bourguiba's politics.[16]

The MCF's initial position was thus that 'the support of the Movement should go to any bona fide nationalist group'.[17] Where rivalries existed between such groups a body like the MCF could naturally find its situation somewhat difficult. Its leaders seem to have made genuine attempts to hold the ring: thus, with the emergence of deep division between the FLN and MNA in Algeria, 'It was agreed

[14] Fenner Brockway: 'Report from Head Office', MCF circular (17 Dec. 1954) (Benn papers).
[15] Gupta, *Imperialism*, 361; Lee, *Colonial Development*, 71. Goldsworthy's account (*Colonial Issues* (Oxford: Oxford University Press, 1971), 324–6) is much fuller and more reliable, but also rather oversimplifies the sources of the MCF's ideas.
[16] Interview with Lord Brockway.
[17] MCF South-East Asia Committee minutes (27 Oct. 1954) (Benn papers).

that we should continue to keep in touch with both these bodies despite their intense hostility to each other.'[18] Yet the stance of total neutrality might become impossible. By late 1957, in the Algerian case, although the point was reiterated that 'It is not the function of the MCF to choose between rival groups inside the national movements of colonial territories' it was felt that the MNA was 'non-active' and 'non-representative'. Effective contact was maintained only with the FLN.[19]

Similarly on the Movement's West Africa Committee:

it was pointed out that our only representative from the Gold Coast, George Padmore, necessarily and rightly took a view which was close to or identical with the view of the existing Government. Several members [of the committee] thought that we ought to have on the Committee a representative of the Gold Coast taking an independent and at times possibly a critical view of Gold Coast Government policy.[20]

No such representative was immediately forthcoming. The MCF was to continue a close association with Nkrumah's government—to which it was linked by apparent ideological affinity, personal relationships, and Ghana's symbolic status as the first independent black African state—until its overthrow.

The principle of impartiality between different and rival nationalist movements simply could not be maintained in practice. The complexities and often bitter internal conflicts of nationalist choices forced choices on sympathisers in Britain. The persistent assumption of British anticolonialists, as of much nationalist rhetoric itself, that there was or should be a single national liberation movement in each territory was quite unrealistic. The choices, which might necessarily have to be made on the basis of very imperfect information, would reflect prior patterns of personal contact as well as ideological considerations heavily coloured by British experience and alignments. This in turn meant that patterns of access to European languages, travel, education, and political ideas among colonials heavily determined their relations with British anticolonialists. Thus the associates of the MCF and similar groups were predominantly, for instance,

[18] MCF North Africa Committee minutes (25 Oct. 1956) (Benn papers).
[19] MCF Mediterranean and Middle East Committee minutes (16 Dec. 1957) (Benn papers).
[20] MCF West Africa Committee minutes (13 Oct. 1954) (Benn papers). See J. R. Hooker, *Black Revolutionary* (New York: Praeger, 1967), ch. 8 *passim*, for Padmore's increasingly uncritical attitude to Nkrumah and the CPP in this period.

followers of Nehru rather than of Jinnah; of southern rather than northern Nigerians; of Greek rather than Turkish Cypriots; of Israeli Jews rather than Palestinian Arabs. A common denominator in these antitheses was the dearth of links with Moslem politicians and parties in the colonies.

More obviously elective affinities would also, and increasingly, come into play. A number of different criteria might be invoked: which among the rival nationalist movements was more programmatically socialist, apparently more democratic, more representative, more progressive in its aspirations? For those among British anticolonialists either strongly sympathetic or bitterly hostile to Communism other considerations might perhaps prevail: what was the attitude of this nationalist party or leader to the USSR, to the USA, to non-aligned policies, to trade and aid relationships with one or other power bloc? Sniffing out Communist sympathies, whether it was done with eagerness or with suspicion, came to dominate much of the interchange. Initially at least, though, the ostensible basis for the support extended by the MCF to colonial movements was that of a broad set of shared anticolonial principles and a perception of shared emancipatory aims, rather than any specific political programme. Equally, therefore, the Movement was able to draw support from people with a wide variety of views within Britain: Liberal and Communist party members, churchmen of various denominations, groups whose primary motivation was of a pacifist, internationalist, or anti-racist nature. The vast majority of the founders, members, and supporters were, however, members of the Labour Party. It was on the basis of Labour and trade union support that Brockway felt able to boast that the MCF was 'a *mass* organisation'.[21]

III. MEMBERSHIP, PERSONNEL, AND STRUCTURE

For much of its life the MCF could count over three million members. Much of this strength, however, came from the affiliation of major national trade unions; and since some of these might not play a very active role in the Movement (and it is very questionable what proportion

---

[21] Fenner Brockway, draft for Egyptian newspaper *al-Akhbar* (Sept. 1966): Emphasis in original (MCF papers).

of the AEU's 800,000 members, for instance, even *knew* that they were affiliated to the MCF), a high proportion of this was a purely paper membership. Individual members at national level never numbered above a thousand. Both figures—3,000,000 and 1,000—are misleading. The real level of participation was of course much nearer the lower figure; but the MCF was a federal organisation, and many of those involved became so as representatives of affiliated or sympathetic bodies rather than as individual members. The Movement's local organisations, the Area Councils, also had their own memberships. There is no reliable means of knowing how many people may have been actively involved throughout the country at any one time.

The affiliated membership encompassed a wide variety of Labour movement organisations: CLPs, trade union branches, and district committees as well as national trade unions, Trades Councils, Co-operative organisations, ILP branches (in the few areas where these still existed), Labour youth and student groups, and a number of British-based colonial associations. MCF was probably unique among issue campaigns at the time in gaining adherents on such a scale from all sections of the Labour movement: certainly no other received such a degree of trade union support. The Movement's predecessors like the COPAI and Seretse Khama council had been on a far smaller scale, while factional organisations of the Labour left like VFS and the Socialist Fellowship had had far narrower bases of support and very little trade union backing. The Campaign for Nuclear Disarmament offers the nearest point of comparison: it achieved, of course, far higher levels of individual membership, but did not in its earlier incarnations have a structure involving formal affiliation.

Later, groups campaigning on issues like the Vietnam War and Anti-Apartheid were to adopt structures and approaches similar to these of the MCF. In some respects MCF was a pioneer here; and indeed the Anti-Apartheid Movement began as a spin-off from its offices. During the 1960s the child outgrew the parent, while movements like CND achieved vastly more mass activism and public attention than the MCF ever did. Despite Brockway's initial optimism, the 'crusade' against colonialism never captured the imagination of the politically uncommitted as did that against nuclear arms. In part, this resulted from the very success of most of the nationalist causes which the Movement espoused. It was, on the whole, seeking to push the Government and major British parties further and faster down a road on which they were already travelling. The moral disarmament of imperialism identified by Ronald Robinson, already proceeding apace by the 1940s, thus served also to weaken the sense of urgency felt by imperialism's opponents.[22] The End of Empire had been proclaimed in many quarters long before the fact of decolonisation. By the early 1960s, the MCF felt that it was suffering from a widespread though in its view erroneous belief that 'imperialism is dead'.[23] It also often felt itself to be damaged by lack of attention from the media to its activities and to colonial affairs generally. There was always a sharp contrast between the paucity of coverage by British newspapers for anticolonial campaigns—with the partial exceptions of the left-wing press and of especially emotive issues like Mau Mau and Suez—and the very close attention given by the African and Asian press to British opinion on colonial affairs. This disparity was reflected in the coverage given to the MCF.[24] Apart from its own newsletter—initially and oddly entitled *Prod*, later *Colonial Freedom News*—leaflets, and pamphlets, the most reliable domestic outlet for its views was the veteran pacifist paper *Peace News*. This became in effect the Movement's house journal, carrying a weekly column by Brockway and having Rogers, Hale, and other prominent anticolonialists as regular contributors. Indeed from the late 1940s to the early 1960s *Peace News* consistently gave more space to colonial issues than to its original primary concern with disarmament. But with a declared circulation of only 11,000–12,000 during the 1950s, it was no substitute for Fleet Street—and with the rise of CND it too shifted attention away from colonial themes.

The very scope and complexity of the issues the MCF addressed may also have hampered it: much of the energy which it aroused became directed into causes which began as offshoots of its work like Anti-Apartheid, War On Want, or the Vietnam War protests. Under

[22] R. E. Robinson, 'The Moral Disarmament of African Empire, 1919–47', *JICH* 7/1 (1979).

[23] Jack Woddis, draft for policy statement 'The Way Ahead' (n.d. but 1964) (MCF papers).

[24] MCF Central Council minutes and Annual Reports contain persistent expressions of concern at this problem, sometimes attributing it to deliberate suppression of unwelcome information by the 'capitalist press'. *The Times*, for instance, devoted less attention to the MCF's own activities over the years than to the regular violent disturbances caused by the League of Empire Loyalists at MCF meetings. Only the left-wing press gave the Movement consistent attention; especially the *Daily Worker*, *Tribune*, and the ILP's *Socialist Leader*, to a lesser extent the *Daily Herald*, *Manchester Guardian*, and *Observer*.

these circumstances, the MCF's officers bemoaned their failure to attract young people as CND was so dramatically succeeding in doing.[25] Short of a major colonial war such as was to mobilise American youth against their government's Vietnam policy, imperialism as an issue was too diffuse, distant, and apparently abstract to arouse widespread commitment outside the ranks of the already politicised. After the early phase of rapid growth, then, the MCF saw its trade union support continue to swell but, from the late 1950s, there was a parallel fall in numbers of individual members and local affiliations sustained a rapid turnover. Overall levels of active involvement seem to have peaked in 1959–60 and thereafter dropped: gradually until 1964–5, rapidly in the mid-1960s.

General explanations for the trends shown in Table 6.1 are fairly obvious. As the Movement's established status and network of contacts grew, so it was able to gain increasing support from cautious national union officials. Its ability to gain local affiliates reflected a growing awareness of colonial issues on the left during the 1950s, but later suffered from the widespread attitude that colonialism was now an issue of the past. As organisational support widened and decolonisation itself proceeded, with the dramatic colonial crises of the mid-1950s seemingly resolved, some of the momentum—especially at the level of individual commitment—fell away or was transferred to CND. Increasingly, as we shall see, with Labour supporters and the non-aligned dropping out, Communists and their allies filled the gap. This happened especially after 1964–5, hastened by the election of Wilson's Government in that year. The MCF had taken its place in the political scene primarily as an outspoken critic of Conservative administrations' colonial policies. Many of its supporters, the majority of them Labour Party members, would be distinctly less ready to attack a Labour Government in the same way. And there was in any case a belief, shared by Brockway himself, that there would be no need to do so: that, under Labour, policy towards what remained of the Empire and towards the underdeveloped world would be transformed.

The central organisation of the Movement was always on a fairly modest scale. It operated from a succession of London offices: initially in rooms loaned from the ILP and the Chemical Workers' Union and

---

[25] See for instance John Eber, 'Memorandum on Future of MCF', for Executive Committee meeting (27 Oct. 1960) (MCF papers).

TABLE 6.1. *MCF membership and affiliates, 1955, 1959–60, and 1964–5*

1. National trade union affiliates (with numbers of affiliated members)

1955		1959–60		1964–5	
AEU (engineers)	767,430	NUM (miners)	674,000	AEU	980,639
ETU (electricians)	205,429	NUR (railwaymen)	355,000	NUM	501,643
USDAW (shopworkers)	191,252	USDAW	353,000	USDAW	354,701
CEU (construction)	21,054	ETU	230,000	NUR	282,801
FBU (firemen)	20,000	Boilermakers	95,000	ETU	271,912
CWU (chemical)	13,650	ASLEF (train drivers)	65,000	Boilermakers	119,517
TWU (tobacco workers)	7,235	AESD (draughtsmen)	63,000	NUTGW (tailors)	110,702
ASSET (scientific)	not given	Bakers	26,000	Foundry workers	69,289
		CEU	25,000	AESD	66,217
		ASSET	21,000	NATSOPA (printers)	45,832
		FBU	20,500	Musicians	32,417
		CWU	20,000	ASSET	31,819
		TWU	16,000	Bakers	31,182
		ACTAT (broadcasting)	7,000	FBU	27,000
				CEU	20,936
				LTS (typographers)	20,000
				SCMA (drivers)	20,000
				ASW (scientific)	18,350
				TWU	17,103
				CWU	16,045
				ACTAT	12,271
TOTAL	1,226,050	TOTAL	1,970,000	TOTAL	3,050,431

Table 6.1. *Continued*

2. Other national affiliates

1955	1959–60	1964–5
NALSO	NALSO	Labour Peace Fellowship
Labour League of Youth	Labour Peace Fellowship	ILP
ILP	ILP	National Cypriot Committee
VFS	National Cypriot Committee	Connolly Association
Britain–Malaya Committee	Peace Pledge Union	Christian Socialist Movement
North African Liberation Committee (British Section)	Britain–Malaya Committee	Free Oman Committee
	IUSY Hostels	Iraqi Students' Society (UK)
		Venezuelan National Liberation Front (UK)
		British Guiana Freedom Association
		Indian Workers' Association of Great Britain

3. Regional affiliates

1955	1959–60	1964–5
London Co-operative Political Committee	NUM Derbyshire Area	NUM Derbyshire Area
	NUM Leicester Area	NUM Kent Area
	NUM Scottish Area	NUM Leicester Area
	NUM South Wales Area	NUM Midland Area
	London Co-operative Political Committee	NUM Scottish Area
		NUM South Wales Area
		London Co-operative Political Committee

TABLE 6.1. *Continued*

4. Local affiliates	1955	1959–60	1963	1964–5
CLPS and Borough Labour parties	158	122	133	90
Young Socialists branches	6	—[a]	70	18
Local Labour parties	78	73	42	31
Labour Women's sections	8	—	—	—
Co-operative organisations	108	86	52	37
Trades Councils	19	30	51	38
Trade union branches	70	204	177	110
Trade union district committees	—	37	36	26
Other local organisations[b]	26	53	37	24
Total local affiliates	473	605	596	374

5. Individual members and sponsors	1955	1959–60	1964–5
Individual members	838	634	374
Sponsoring MPs	72	119	107
Other sponsors[c]	—	35	55

Notes:

[a] The Labour Party did not have a youth wing in 1959–60, between the disbandment of the League of Youth in 1955 and the establishment of the Young Socialists in 1960.

[b] Including local colonial peoples' groups, ILP branches (1955 only) etc.

[c] Including a number of peers, trade union leaders, a smattering of bishops, and an assortment of liberal celebrities such as Benjamin Britten, Augustus John, and Dame Sybil Thorndyke.

Sources: MCF Annual Reports, 1955, 1959–60, 1963, 1964–5.

then, from 1955, in Grays Inn Road, its base for sixteen years. This was always overcrowded, particularly since at various times the space was shared with assorted nationalist groups in London, including the Uganda National Congress, the Zimbabwe African Peoples' Union, the Zambian United National Independence Party, the Free Oman Committee, and the British Guiana Freedom Association.[26]

Financial crisis was recurrent. The two early full-time officers, Douglas Rogers and Joseph Murumbi, had to subsist on a salary intended for one. Most office work was done on a voluntary basis.[27] The Movement was never able to afford more than three full-timers: being overwhelmingly dependent on affiliation fees which were not always reliably paid. There were some donations, including overseas ones; Nnamdi Azikiwe made at least one substantial gift and the Ghanaian CPP several.[28]

Thus the day-to-day running of the Movement was the responsibility of a rather small group of people. The most prominent public face of the organisation was of course Brockway—the press often referred to the Movement as being his, and certainly without his range of contacts, his prestige among Third World politicians, and his remarkable work rate the British anticolonial lobby would not have existed in anything like the same form. Behind the scenes, though, an almost equally central role was taken by successive General Secretaries. The first was Douglas Rogers, a long-standing colleague of Brockway's in the ILP, COPAI, and other organisations. He was soon joined by Joseph Murumbi, who had been Acting General Secretary of KAU in the early stages of the Kenyan Emergency. He had left Kenya intending to undertake a tour of India, Egypt, Britain, and America to publicise the Kenyan nationalist cause. But 'by the time I arrived in England I knew that if I came back [to Kenya] I

[26] See MCF committee minutes, circulars, reports, etc., 1954–6 *passim* (MCF and Benn papers) for early moves. The CWU offices were made available by Dick Beech, editor of the union's journal and member of the first MCF Central Council. Additional domestic information from interviews with Lord Brockway, Tony Benn, Barbara Haq, and Kay Beauchamp.
[27] 'Report from Head Office' (17 Dec. 1954) (Benn papers); Joe Murumbi, unpublished draft autobiography and interview transcripts, 159–60 (hereafter Murumbi).
[28] Azikiwe to Brockway (19 July 1963) (MCF papers). Executive Committee minutes (16 Apr. 1959, 15 Oct. 1959) and Executive Report (18 Mar. 1961) record donations of £400, £100, and £100 respectively from the CPP. Stephen Howe, 'Anti-Colonialism in British Politics: The Left and the End of Empire, 1939–1964 (Oxford University D.Phil. thesis, 1984), 288–9, gives more detail on the MCF's finances.

would be locked up'.[29] He therefore stayed, began working with
Brockway and Rogers whom he already knew through COPAI, and
became Joint Secretary of the MCF soon after its foundation.[30] He
was viewed with great suspicion by many in Britain. While to the *New
Statesman* he was 'one of the most moderate and thoughtful of the
African leaders', others accused him as a Mau Mau instigator; as, by
innuendo, did *The Times*.[31] His movements were watched by Special
Branch officers;[32] and some Labour politicians apparently refused to
share public platforms with him.[33]

Rogers and Murumbi thus shared the post of General Secretary
until the former went to Ghana in early 1956 and the latter resigned
because he believed the MCF's stance on Suez to be insufficiently
radical. Murumbi worked for a time with the Moroccan Embassy in
London and later returned to Kenyan politics, rising to become the
country's Vice-President.[34] Replacing him at the MCF was Helen
Bastable, who had already worked full-time for the Movement on a
voluntary basis since 1955. She in her turn resigned in order to join
her family in Australia.[35] Replacing Rogers from 1956 was Patricia
Rushton, who in 1959 was succeeded by John Eber. Eber, whose
background in Malayan politics has been discussed on pp. 215–19
above, and who became an even more controversial figure than
Murumbi, was eventually replaced as General Secretary in 1965 by
Barbara Haq, an Englishwoman formerly resident in Pakistan and
married to a Pakistani Marxist politician. She had been working on
the MCF's Trade Union Committee and South-East Asia Committee
for some years and as a full-time MCF officer from late 1961.[36]

---

[29] Murumbi, 136.

[30] Ibid. 136–8, 150–2, 156–7.

[31] 'London Diary' (Kingsley Martin), *NS&N* (12 Sept. 1953) (see also Brockway's
letter in the same issue); *The Times* (23 May and 26 Sept. 1953).

[32] Murumbi, 139–40, 145–6.

[33] Interviews with Stan Newens and Tony Benn. Murumbi's own statements at the
time all indicated a thoroughgoing constitutionalism. For his views of the Emergency
see his memoirs *passim* and the Introduction which he co-wrote with Bildad Kaggia,
Fred Kubai, and Achieng Oneko (leading figures of KAU's more socially radical
wing), in Donald N. Barnett and Karari Njama, *Mau Mau from Within* (MacGibbon &
Kee, 1966).

[34] For Murumbi's resignation see Central Council minutes (2 May 1957) (Benn
papers).

[35] For Bastable's resignation see Executive Committee minutes (16 June 1958)
(Benn papers).

[36] Interview with Barbara Haq, Executive Committee minutes (18 Dec. 1961)
(MCF papers).

Successive Secretaries—perhaps especially Murumbi, Eber, and Haq—took a major part in policy-making for the MCF. Eber visited almost every African country during his period in the office, attempting to cement co-operation between nationalist movements and seeking an advisory role for several of them, as with his drafting of proposals for economic development in the Gambia and for Obote's Ugandan Peoples' Congress.[37] Barbara Haq was later to play an important part in bringing together the two sides in the negotiations which ended the Sudanese civil war.[38]

One particularly important group from overseas involved with the MCF, however, was that of Southern African *émigrés*. These included Leon and Rolene Szur and Mary Klopper, all active in anticolonial circles since the period of the COPAI; Aberdeen MP Bob Hughes, who had been brought up in South Africa; authors Ronald Segal (editor of the banned oppositional journal *Africa South*), Ruth First (active in the ANC until her murder in Mozambique in 1982) and Masizi Kunene (London representative of the ANC, poet and translator of Zulu traditional verse); nationalist lawyer and later ANC leader Oliver Tambo; and trade unionists E. S. (Solly) Sachs and Simon Ber Zukas. Other prominent figures among the non-British activists in the MCF included at various times George Padmore, Arthur Scerri (subsequently a Maltese Cabinet Minister), Albert Rene (later President of the Seychelles), and Abdulrahman Babu (Zanzibari revolutionary and Tanzanian Minister).

IV. THE MCF AND THE LEFT IN PARLIAMENT

A major part of the MCF's work, both in Parliament and in the country, was carried on by sympathetic MPs. By October 1955 seventy-two were sponsors of the Movement; and this number continued to grow during the 1950s, reaching 119 in 1960 and falling only slightly thereafter even when, as we have seen, wider support for the MCF

[37] MCF Executive Report (22 July–14 Sept. 1961); Eber's Diary of his 1962 African trip; report of conversation with UPC leaders (11 Oct. 1961) (MCF). Bob Edwards was also involved in the Gambian talks, and recalled that at the head of the Gambians' list of economic needs was a Coca Cola factory!

[38] Interviews with Barbara Haq and M. Omer Beshir (who was then chief negotiator on the Sudanese Government side).

had flagged considerably. There were very wide divergences in the level of MCF activity among these Members. Some seem to have given little more than their names and occasional cheques: these inactive supporters included some of the more prominent, like Harold Wilson and Richard Crossman. Others came to make the colonies a major parliamentary specialisation. These, a fluctuating core of between twenty and forty MPs—a considerable expansion from the four or five who worked closely with Brockway in 1950—would come regularly for MCF-organised meetings at Westminster, might chair or participate in specialist committees of the Movement or in Area Councils in their constituencies, and helped direct a constant flow of parliamentary Questions and other forms of pressure on the Colonial Office.[39]

In assessing the activities of these parliamentarians, I shall not attempt here a general survey of post-war Parliaments' treatment of imperial questions—a task which has been fulfilled in some detail by David Goldsworthy[40]—but shall confine discussion to the part played by the anticolonialist left. It may first be noted that specialisation in colonial affairs was very far from being advantageous to the MPs concerned, whether in terms of their advancement within their party or in electoral popularity. Creech Jones's treatment by the electors in 1950 as well as by Attlee in the preceding years provided some indication of this; and when domestic race relations became an electoral issue in the 1960s (as colonial problems had not, on the whole, been in the 1950s) those who had devoted much of their time and energy to campaigning for racial equality both in the colonies and within Britain often seemed to suffer for it. There is no doubt that throughout the post-war period voting behaviour was primarily determined by considerations of domestic policy; and the opponents of left-wing politicians associated with anticolonial campaigns sometimes sought to play on this contrast between the preoccupations of such MPs and those of their electors. Thus at the time of the MCF's

[39] The following picture of MPs' activities is built up from MCF, Labour Party and FCB documents, Hansard, and interviews with Lord Brockway, Lord Hatch, Tony Benn, Bob Edwards, Bob Hughes, Barbara Haq, and Stan Newens.

[40] *Colonial Issues*, 64–110; 'Parliamentary Questions on Colonial Affairs: A Retrospective Analysis', *PA* 23/2 (1970); 'The Debate on a Parliamentary Committee for Colonial Affairs', *PA* 19/2 (1966). I am grateful to Dr Goldsworthy for help on this issue in personal communications. I have also relied, for background information, on D. N. Chester with Nona Bowring, *Questions in Parliament* (Oxford: Clarendon Press 1962).

foundation Benn's Conservative opponent in Bristol South-East sneered in a local magazine that:

Perhaps the people of Redfield like being told that Westminster has more important things to look after than their affairs. Personally, I doubt it . . . It was a pity from his point of view that Mr. Benn should have chosen Colonial affairs as his topic in an attempt to distract your attention from matters which more nearly concern your everyday lives.[41]

Later Brockway came under attack by his opponents in Slough for supposedly devoting all his time to colonial issues—a charge which he greeted with considerable indignation.[42] His narrow defeat against the national swing in 1964 was generally attributed to a combination of the effects of criticism of this kind, a more straightforward racist reaction against his campaigns on issues of racial justice, and some replication of the same attitudes within the local Labour Party itself. And when Patrick Gordon Walker was defeated in the explicitly racist Smethwick campaign, the man judged dispensable by Labour leaders in clearing a new seat for him was another veteran anticolonialist, Reg Sorensen.[43]

MCF MPs were, naturally, heavily concentrated on the left of the PLP; and many of them were associated with the various more-or-less organised groupings of the Labour left: Victory for Socialism, the Socialist Fellowship, Keep Left, and the Bevan group. Of the fifty-seven MPs who, defying a three-line Whip, voted against the Defence Estimates on 5 March 1952 (a revolt providing probably the clearest single index of Bevanite sympathies at the time), forty-four became MCF sponsors. All the key figures of the Keep Left and Bevan groups, excepting only the anomalous figure of Woodrow Wyatt in the former, were associated with the MCF: Crossman, Foot, Mikardo, Geoffrey Bing, Harold Davies, Hale, Mallalieu, Swingler, Jennie Lee, Julius and Sydney Silverman, Barbara Castle, Driberg, John Rankin, A. J. Irvine, Acland, and Bevan himself. Even this was a very diverse group: as several recent studies have emphasised, and as Crossman's *Backbench Diaries* vividly indicate, the left in Parliament was loosely knit indeed and the label 'Bevanite' little more than a convenient badge for a heterogenous group of occasional or persistent

[41] Robin Cooke in the *Redfield Review* (Apr. 1954) (copy in Benn papers).
[42] Interview with Lord Brockway.
[43] See Paul Foot, *Immigration and Race in British Politics* (Harmondsworth, Penguin, 1965).

dissenters.[44] Far from all the MCF MPs, however, fell into even this loose category: they included (admittedly usually as peripheral associates) people well to the right of the Labour Party on most issues like Dennis Howell and Geoffrey de Freitas.

Neither the MCF-sponsoring MPs nor the smaller inner group of active anticolonialists, then, was exclusively Bevanite. But nor were they a cross-section of the PLP. From 1955 to 1964, between 30 and 40 per cent of all Labour MPs were MCF sponsors at any one time; these included most of those clearly on the left, but very few of the right-wing trade union loyalists. MCF MPs shared, and in the case of the anticolonial activists probably accentuated, the social characteristics which tended to distinguish left from right within the PLP and which had led to the Bevanites being branded as a group of middle-class intellectuals (with all the pejorative connotations which that term carried in some Labour circles). A considerably higher proportion of the MCF MPs than of the PLP as a whole were graduates; many had been journalists, lawyers, or lecturers, relatively few were trade union sponsored; they were on average younger than the PLP as a whole.[45] There were exceptions, but the former trade union officials active in the MCF, such as Bob Edwards, George Craddock, Ernest Fernyhough, Walter Padley, and Walter Monslow, tended to be very atypical union MPs: autodidacts, individualists, and often ex-members of the ILP.

More generally, the ILP connection remained strong: almost every former ILP member in the House was a keen anticolonialist, including Brockway, Edwards, Padley, Jennie Lee, Rankin, James Carmichael, Emrys Hughes, and John Paton. Those Members predisposed towards concern for a wide range of humanitarian causes were likely to add colonial freedom to their lists: pacifists like Hughes or Frank Allaun, general-purpose idealists like Peter Freeman. In the 1955 Parliament,

[44] See Crossman, *Backbench Diaries*; Jenkins, *Bevanism*; Schneer, *Labour's Conscience*; Michael Foot, *Aneurin Bevan* ii. *1945–1960* (Davis-Poynter, 1973); Philip Williams, *Hugh Gaitskell* (Cape, 1979), 295–653; Anthony Howard, *Crossman* (Cape, 1990), chs. 10 and 11; Ian Mikardo, *Back-Bencher* (Weidenfeld & Nicolson, 1988); John Campbell, *Nye Bevan and the Mirage of British Socialism* (Weidenfeld & Nicolson, 1987), part 6; Francis Wheen, *Tom Driberg* (Chatto & Windus, 1990).

[45] S. E. Finer, H. B. Berrington, and D. J. Bartholemew, *Backbench Opinion in the House of Commons* (Oxford: Pergamon, 1961), shows that a similar profile applied to those signing Early Day Motions on anticolonial themes—but this is a very poor method of discovering MPs' opinions. Certainly those who signed MCF-drafted motions were not necessarily MCF activists, or even clear sympathisers. Some MPs will sign almost anything, some almost nothing, and some are renowned for their ability to cajole the most unlikely people into endorsing their pet resolutions.

nine Labour MPs declared themselves as absolute pacifists; they did not, by this time, include Brockway, but all were very involved in anticolonial campaigning and eight were active MCF members.[46]

Among these, some twenty especially active campaigners stood out. As well as those already mentioned, Brockway, Benn, Acland, Edwards, Driberg, Hale, and Sorensen, the most important included Stanley Awbery, Geoffrey Bing (later Attorney-General in Nkrumah's Ghana), Barbara Castle (President of the AAM, 1960–4), Anthony Greenwood (MCF Treasurer in the early 1960s and Colonial Secretary under Wilson), Judith Hart (MCF Vice-Chair and subsequently Minister for Overseas Development), Ian Mikardo, Maurice Orbach (Chair of the MCF's London Area Council), Leslie Plummer, John Rankin, John Stonehouse, Stephen Swingler, and Konni Zilliacus.

These MPs participated in a significant change in parliamentary attention to the colonies from the early 1950s. It would clearly be mistaken to assume that this change was simply or wholly a product of greater left-wing vigour on the issue. Yet there was undoubtedly a transformation in the level and nature of the left's responses to colonial developments; one which preceded that by other currents of parliamentary opinion. It may be that this would have taken place even had Brockway never re-entered Parliament or the MCF never been formed; and it is perhaps fruitless to speculate just how far and how fast change would have come under these circumstances. In order to appreciate the changes which did take place, and to evaluate the MCF's place in them, we may begin by glancing at the House of Commons's handling of colonial subjects before 1954.

Individuals on the left had for many years been complaining about Parliament's lack of concern for the problems of Britain's colonial subjects. In 1900 Edward Carpenter had spoken of:

> An empty House to hear the burden of the sorrows of India,
> And Irish questions treated with disdain.[47]

And in 1914 Brailsford had attacked the inadequacy of parliamentary scrutiny of the colonies.[48] The ILP had especially stressed this theme;

---

[46] *PN* (3 June 1955). They were George Craddock, Ernest Fernyhough, Leslie Hale, Emrys Hughes, Sir Fred Messer, John Rankin, Reg Sorensen, George Thomas, and Victor Yates. Only Sorensen was not an MCF activist, presumably because of his strong prior Fabian links.

[47] 'Empire', in Edward Carpenter, *Towards Democracy* (George Allen, 1913 edn.), 466.

[48] H. N. Brailsford, *The War of Steel and Gold* (Bell, 1914), 136–43.

in 1927 Graham Pole charged that Indian debates attracted at most '20 out of 415 Conservative Members ... mostly yawning or half-asleep'.[49] A few months later Ellen Wilkinson castigated the apathy towards Empire of the 'well-fed, rather stupid Tory back-benchers'.[50] The partisan aspect of these attacks was somewhat ill-placed: there is no evidence that Labour Members were any more conscientious in their attendance at colonial debates than their opponents. The FCB echoed and generalised the criticism in 1942: 'The House of Commons has in the past shown little general interest in colonial policy.'[51]

By the mid-1950s, at least some aspects of this situation had been transformed. John Hatch pointed to the 'passion' raised by Kenya and Guiana, Cyprus, Malta, Central Africa, Singapore, and other issues during the decade.[52] Yet as Goldsworthy notes, this may mean no more than that MPs, always prone to react to spectacular crises in the colonies whilst exhibiting apathy towards wider colonial issues, now had an unprecedented range of disorders to which to react.[53] Yet it does appear, despite this salutary caveat, that more had altered than the tempo of crises on the periphery. Parliamentary perceptions too had changed. MPs' responses to crisis were on the whole better informed, more vigorous, more rapid, embraced more Members, and aroused stronger partisan emotions than had been the case a decade before. Parliamentary scrutiny was also less than ever confined to reactions to crisis: by 1957, Benn was able to argue that in the colonial sphere 'the opportunities for raising matters in the House are very limited and Members feel frustrated in their attempts to bring out important matters'. He went on to call for more scope for back-benchers' participation, in an advisory capacity, at early stages in the Colonial Office decision-making process: MPs of all parties should be represented at constitutional conferences, should sit on Colonial Office bodies, and there should be a Parliamentary Committee on Colonial Affairs. He could make such suggestions knowing that he was speaking for a large number of back-benchers.[54] A decade earlier, the frustration would have been confined to a small group of

---

[49] *NL* (19 Aug. 1927).

[50] Ibid. (25 Nov. 1927).

[51] Fabian Colonial Bureau, *Downing Street and the Colonies* (FCB 1942), 80.

[52] 'The Opposition's Part in Colonial Policy' *Listener* (25 Apr. 1963), 702.

[53] *Colonial Issues*, 74.

[54] Benn, 'Colonial Affairs in the Commons': memorandum presented to Labour Party NEC–PLP Joint Committee (11 Feb. 1957) (Benn papers; copy and related documents also in Labour Party papers).

specialists, and Members simply could not have been found for the suggested functions.

It is evident that much of this alteration in atmosphere was attributable to the new and more active part played by left-wing Labour MPs. There had always been a minority who conceived of their role as being, in part, that of Members for India or for the colonies, and who argued that, since colonial peoples had no direct representation in Parliament, it was the duty of those sympathetic to their aspirations to fill the gap. As the political demands of the colonies were raised with ever greater urgency, so the number of those on the British left, prepared to be, as they saw it, the articulators of those demands at Westminster, grew larger.

From his re-entry into the House Brockway had assumed the role of a one-man alternative colonial service, backed by the COPAI and by the small back-bench group he gathered around him. By the end of 1953, it had already been noted that the front bench was growing uneasy at this clique's activities:

The Party's handling of Colonial matters has, it is said, been getting out of hand: the 'safe' men are now closing in, and Mr. Brockway's little outing may be ending. I wonder. The Constituencies back Mr. Brockway.[55]

Indeed, far from being constrained by the safe men, back-bench Labour activity continued to grow. And whereas in the late 1940s and early 1950s this involvement came primarily from the FCB, now the number of left-wingers with an apparently informed interest in the colonies was rapidly increasing. The figures for Questions to the Colonial Office rose by 72.6 per cent between 1950 and 1957, while the proportion of these asked by Labour Members also shot up. Of 905 Questions in 1949, 467 were asked by Labour MPs, 310 by Conservatives, and 128 by others (many of these being from the Labour Independents who had had the Whip withdrawn and from the two Communists). By 1958, of a total 1,258 Questions, 991 were the responsibility of Labour MPs, with only 262 Conservatives and 5 others.[56]

Three further enquiries present themselves. How large a part in these changes is attributable to the activities of the Labour left and

---

[55] Flavius, 'London Diary', *NS&N* (12 Dec. 1953).
[56] Calculated from figures in Goldsworthy, *Colonial Issues*, 79–84. Of course, Opposition MPs are always more likely to be active questioners; but on the other hand there were half as many Labour MPs again in 1949 as in 1958.

the MPs associated with the MCF? How far did the nature and tenor of parliamentary activity become influenced by these MPs? And what evidence is there for connections between pressure group activity outside Parliament and the treatment of colonial affairs at Westminster?

To answer the first question, we may examine which Labour MPs were asking Questions on colonial subjects during the 1950s, and what strands of opinion within the party they represented. Three years have been selected for this purpose: 1951, which marked the end of Labour's period in office and the beginning of rapid growth in left-wing activity on these issues; 1954 when the MCF was founded; and 1957, the high-water mark of MPs' interrogations of the Colonial Office. The figures in Table 6.2 relate to all Labour Questions clearly concerned with colonial subjects, not only those directed to the Colonial Secretary: thus Questions to the Secretary of State for War on Kenyan counter-insurgency, for instance, are included. Supplementary questions are included as separate entries, but Points of Order and other non-substantive interventions are excluded. The numbers asked by MPs closely associated with the FCB, and for 1954 and 1957 the MCF, are also shown in Table 6.3. These were, as noted above, not wholly mutually exclusive categories, nor in themselves necessarily indicative of a left–right division; but by the 1950s the FCB MPs were generally on the centre and right of the party, MCF ones on the left. Changes in their relative levels of activity may thus be taken not only as indications of the effectiveness of the FCB and MCF themselves, but as reflecting shifts in the political balance of parliamentary involvement in colonial affairs. This picture of a gradual shift to the left is reinforced in Table 6.4 which shows which individual MPs were dominating Labour's colonial activity.

So just as the overall level of parliamentary activity on colonial issues, and the proportion of that activity attributable to Labour Members, were growing, so also was the proportion of the Labour involvement for which the party's left wing was responsible. Table 6.3 shows that by 1957 more than two-thirds of all Labour colonial Questions were being asked by MCF sponsors; and since almost 80 per cent of all colonial Questions were now coming from Labour Members, it would seem that just over half of all colonial questions were the responsibility of MCF MPs. Not all of these, as we have seen, were necessarily left-wingers; and some had previously been active in the FCB as well. But Table 6.4 indicates the extent to which

TABLE 6.2. *Colonial questions asked by Labour MPs, 1951, 1954, and 1957*

Year and % change	Oral	Written	Total
1951	441	226	667
1954	954	554	1,508
1957	939	804	1,743
1954 % change on 1951	+116.3	+145.1	+126.1
1957 % change on 1954	−1.6	+45.1	+15.6
1957 % change on 1951	+112.9	+255.8	+161.3

TABLE 6.3. *Colonial questions asked by MPs associated with the FCB and MCF, 1951, 1954, and 1957*

	Oral	Written	Total
Questions asked by active FCB members			
1951	317	180	497
1954	325	248	573
1957	259	198	447
FCB Questions as % of Labour to total			
1951	71.9	79.6	74.5
1954	34.0	44.8	38.0
1957	27.6	24.6	25.6
Questions asked by MCF sponsors			
1954	508	254	762
1957	602	563	1,165
MCF Questions as % of Labour total			
1954	53.2	45.8	50.5
1957	64.1	70.0	66.8

the MCF MPs who came increasingly to dominate colonial Questions (17 of the 28 top scorers in 1957) were people who stood clearly on the left on a whole range of issues. Most of them were also unilateral nuclear disarmers and many had been involved with one or more organised left-wing grouping within the party: as had Acland, Allaun,

TABLE 6.4. *Labour MPs raising twenty or more questions on colonial subjects per year, 1951, 1954, and 1957*

Name of Labour MP	Number of questions (and affiliation)		
	1951	1954	1957
Acland, Sir Richard	36 (ab)	30 (cd)	
Allaun, F.			43 (c)
Awbery, S. S.	69 (b)	90 (bc)	47 (c)
Benn, A. Wedgwood		30 (cd)	57 (cd)
Brockway, A. F.	34	150 (cd)	234 (cd)
Callaghan, L. J.			59 (ab)
Castle, Barbara			52 (cd)
Cooper, G.	21 (b)		
Craddock, G.		37 (cd)	
Driberg, T.	25 (ab)	20 (bc)	
Dugdale, J.		44 (ab)	23 (ab)
Griffiths, J.		73 (ab)	24 (ab)
Hale, C. L.		33 (cd)	
Hughes, H.		26 (c)	21 (c)
Hynd, H.	25 (b)		
Hynd, J.	39 (ab)	26 (ab)	
Irving, S.			27 (c)
Jeger, Lena			41 (c)
Johnson, J.	66 (ab)	160 (ab)	148 (ab)
Jones, A. Creech			23 (ab)
Jones, D. T.		45 (b)	32 (ab)
Lee, Jennie		20 (cd)	27 (c)
MacPherson, M.			28
Marquand, H.			21 (b)
Noel-Baker, F.			73 (c)
Parker, J.	29 (ab)		
Plummer, Sir Leslie		25 (cd)	60 (cd)
Rankin, J.	43 (ab)	45 (abc)	52 (bcd)
Reid, T.	33	34	
Robinson, K.			49 (c)
Royle, C.			23 (c)
Sorenson, R.	104 (ab)	72 (ab)	48 (ab)
Stonehouse, J.			86 (cd)
Swingler, S.		30 (cd)	62 (cd)
Warbey, W.			25 (cd)
White, Eirene		63 (b)	32 (b)
Wyatt, W.	20 (b)		

Key:
a = member of FCB Advisory Committee in relevant year.
b = indicated by FCB papers to have been active in FCB in relevant year.
c = MCF sponsor in relevant year.
d = indicated by MCF papers to have been active in MCF in relevant year.

Brockway, Craddock, Driberg, Hale, Hector Hughes, Jennie Lee, Plummer, Rankin, Swingler, and Warbey.

Another striking feature of Table 6.4 is the poor performance of Labour's colonial front bench. Both Griffiths in 1954 and Callaghan in 1957 were far outstripped in levels of activity on their official subjects by many back-benchers. When one looks at the internal dynamics of Colonial Office Question Times, this impression is confirmed. Griffiths, Callaghan, and, during his brief period as Labour's colonial spokesperson, Bevan rarely initiated a line of attack on the Treasury benches. Rather they tended to enter the field only after a back-bencher such as Brockway or Sorensen had opened a breach; pursuing the issue with what often seems a lack of commitment and an imperfect command of the brief. Even more rarely do Questions originating from the Labour front bench display evidence of the detailed knowledge of specific colonial problems which both FCB and MCF activists could bring to bear. This suggests that the party's International and Commonwealth departments were, on the whole, less widely informed on colonial developments than were the two main pressure groups; although the weakness of the party's colonial research and information-gathering machinery was gradually remedied by Hatch. Between them, FCB and MCF virtually monopolised Labour's colonial expertise in Parliament: MPs closely associated with one or the other accounted, in 1954 and 1957, for 88.5 per cent and 92.4 per cent of all Labour colonial Questions. Of the most active individuals, only the very right-wing Tom Reid and Malcolm MacPherson were not linked to either group.

The military metaphors deployed above are more appropriate to the 1950s than they would have been for Parliament's handling of the Empire in almost any previous period. Perhaps not since the Governor Eyre controversy had events in the colonies—other than the defeat of British armies—aroused such emotion as they did in these years, and, as with Governor Eyre, it was allegations of brutality and oppression by colonial authorities and British troops which produced most bitterness. The issue which became the main focus of this feeling was the Kenyan Emergency; though similar allegations and similar anger arose over Cyprus and to a lesser extent Malaya. This revealed an almost unbridgeable gulf of perception between MCF anticolonialists and Ministers. The view of much of the left was passionately expressed by Harold Davies on 23 June 1954. The day was something of a watershed in colonial debate: for the first time, the entire Question period was taken up with colonial affairs, and also for the first time these Questions were almost monopolised by the Labour left. Davies's intervention highlighted the new, more confrontational style:

Does not the right hon. Gentleman think it is time we dropped the phraseology 'bandits and gangs' when what we are actually concerned with is the desire of these people for freedom and dignity? Is it not time we had a debate in this house on the entire African situation?[57]

Kenya aroused a feeling of profound indignation, spreading eventually well beyond the ranks of the far left, that the British Army was employing what Campbell-Bannerman had called in an earlier colonial conflict 'methods of barbarism'. During the same fraught Question Time as Davies's challenge, the following exchange took place:

RICHARD STOKES. . . . I ask the Minister how many of these people have been executed merely for having a single round of ammunition on their person? . . .

MR. LYTTELTON. The right hon. Gentleman should put a Question on the Paper about these matters. About 39 executions have taken place for possession of ammunition.

AN HON. MEMBER. Absolutely disgraceful.

MR. BOWLES. This is civilisation.

MR. LYTTELTON. Civilisation is broken down by the terrorists and not by ourselves . . . [58]

Under such circumstances any conception of bipartisanship in colonial policy—a doctrine, or rather an aspiration, in any case increasingly threadbare—could have but little chance of survival. If Lyttelton's final months at the Colonial Office were marked by a steadily rising temperature and ever more vigorous attacks from the left, Lennox-Boyd's first Question Time indicated that such attacks had become the norm—left-wing Labour MPs dominated the session from the start.[59]

So from about 1954 there was a rapid increase in Labour left-wing parliamentary activity on the colonies, and both the individuals and the attitudes involved coincided closely with the MCF's membership and views. How far, though, was the Movement itself orchestrating

---

[57] *HC. Deb.* (23 June 1954), cols. 413–14.
[58] Ibid., cols. 402–3. Stokes and Bowles were Labour MPs for Ipswich and Nuneaton respectively, and Bowles an MCF sponsor.
[59] Ibid. (20 Oct. 1954), cols. 1175–213.

this change? It would seem that it was doing so, to a considerable extent. After the MCF's foundation several MPs who had not previously taken part in questioning the Colonial Office began doing so: left-wingers like Michael Foot, Archie Manuel, Ian Mikardo, Walter Monslow, George Thomas, and Victor Yates; others who had previously featured only very infrequently, like George Craddock, Anthony Greenwood, Kenneth Robinson, and George Thomson also started to make regular appearances. Many of these new participants were displaying a previously unsuspected grasp of colonial detail; and there was evidence of concerted tactics. For some time previously, batches of consecutively numbered Questions from FCB MPs had appeared together on the Order Paper. From June 1954 similar groupings began to appear from MCF Members.[60] 'About sixty' of the Questions on Lennox-Boyd's first day in the hot seat were claimed to originate from the MCF.[61]

Effective interrogation required prior information on the subject concerned; and this often came to the MCF by somewhat covert means, as Murumbi recalled with reference to Kenya:

Well, we got information, you see I had letters from detainees. They used to come in a circuitous route, never come directly to me, they used to come to a certain address, and they'd be forwarded to me. Mbiyu Koinange used to get some information, individual students used to get some information. And my main source was of course Pinto [Pio Pinto Gamo, one of KAU's few Asian supporters]. But after Pinto's arrest of course that source stopped. We were getting a trickle of information.[62]

Probably the MCF never became, in strictly organisational terms, as efficient a Question-drafting machine as the FCB had been in its heyday; though the total numbers of MCF-inspired questions were considerably larger than those from the FCB.[63] The Fabians had set their sights specifically on an information-gathering role and on using

[60] For instance, ibid. (23 June 1954), *Written Answers*, cols. 23–7; (28 July 1954), *Written Answers*, cols. 46–60.

[61] Central Council minutes (27 Nov. 1954) (Benn papers).

[62] Murumbi, 163.

[63] Brockway claimed, clearly with some exaggeration, that MCF MPs had asked over 1,000 colonial Questions in the Movement's first eight months, 'Report from Head Office' (17 Dec. 1954). It was later suggested, probably more accurately, that in its first two years the Movement had raised over 1,900 issues with the Colonial Office, either in the House or by writing to Ministers; see Thomas Fox-Pitt, *Handbook for Federal Politicians* (MCF pamphlet, 1956), back cover. The very patchy survival of the Movement's early records makes computation impossible.

their expertise to spread awareness of colonial problems through Parliament and through official channels. The FCB's most active members developed their own regional specialisations and concentrated on raising issues, often of a very detailed nature, within these special fields, focusing especially on economic matters. The MCF, a bigger, more diffuse, more publicity-orientated body, adopted a very different style. MPs such as Brockway, Hale, and Castle concentrated on political rights rather than economic and social policies. MCF Questions were more likely to be aimed at challenging the Government than at elucidating information from it. On the whole MCF MPs concentrated less on building areas of specialisation, and more on posing a wide-ranging critique of colonial policy than did those of the FCB.

The sources of information on which the MCF drew were more likely to be radical nationalists and colonial trade unions, whereas the FCB's network drew much from liberal-minded colonial administrators. The most important difference lay, however, in the fact that the FCB sought to use Parliament to influence officials and Ministers whereas the MCF saw action in the House at least partly as a means towards mobilising opinion outside. The FCB had never aimed to be a public campaigning organisation, which was a major part of the MCF's *raison d'être*. The FCB also felt that it must be careful to 'lend no colour to the stock allegation that African opposition is "stirred up" by European extremists in London'.[64] The MCF never felt bound by these constraints. Its style, like that of the old ILP and the Labour left generally, was far more evangelical and less cautious than that of the Fabians. Charges from the right of extremism were inevitable and could be borne. They might even be welcomed if they overreached themselves and revealed the apparent intransigence of those who levelled them. Thus in early 1955, the Conservative Commonwealth Council accused the MCF of seeking to 'assault and sap the most civilising temporal influence in the modern world—British Colonial Rule' as a cover for 'furthering the Soviet international object of damaging the free European countries through their heavy colonial commitments'.[65] The MCF response was a gleeful decision to duplicate and circulate copies of the attack in Britain and abroad 'as an indication of the attitude of the Tory party'.[66] The MCF

---

[64] Rita Hinden to Fenner Brockway (23 May 1952), FCB 7/1/163.

[65] Conservative Commonwealth Council, *Colonial Rule: Enemies and Obligations* (Conservative Political Centre pamphlet, 1955), 1, 24.

[66] MCF Central Council minutes (6 Apr. 1955) (Benn papers).

calculated, no doubt correctly, that an attack on it which proceeded from the premiss that colonial rule was an unmixed good would do more damage to the assailants than to their target.

V. THE AREA COUNCILS—AND THE COMMUNIST PARTY

The MCF's hopes of arousing a mass anticolonial campaign rested in large part on its ability to extend its activities outside London—something previous groups with similar aims had almost wholly failed to do. The intention was that this should be accomplished by local organisations—Area Councils—throughout the country. During the first year ten of these were established, and in succeeding years at least another dozen. However, as Councils in some areas lapsed into inactivity after a time, it is doubtful whether more than twelve to fifteen were functioning at any one moment.[67] An initial plan to establish a further tier of local Councils seems to have been stillborn.[68] The Councils were intended to organise publicity and protests which would reach people not easily influenced from London, using the local press as much as possible, and to establish a nation-wide network of contacts with sympathisers, including both local Labour movement organisations and colonial immigrants and students.[69]

The levels of support and activity generated by Area Councils varied widely—as did their political complexion. By far the most effective was, not surprisingly, the London organisation. Indeed after the mid-1960s it appears that the London Area Council was actually retaining a higher degree of vitality than the national parent body.[70] Others with a high degree of activity included those of Birmingham and Merseyside. Here, perhaps largely because of the energy and dedication of those Councils' secretaries, an unusually large number of affiliates had been gained, a considerable individual membership kept busy with such measures as organising letters of protest to

[67] *A Policy for Colonial Freedom* (MCF namphlet, 1955), 21; MCF Annual Reports and correspondence with Area Council secretaries, *passim* (MCF papers).
[68] *Policy for Colonial Freedom*, 24.
[69] Ibid. 21; Minutes of Area Council secretaries' conference held at WASU (23–4 Sept. 1961); Annual Reports and correspondence (MCF papers).
[70] Minutes of discussion on future of MCF (n.d. but *c.*1968) (MCF papers); interviews with Barbara Haq, Kay Beauchamp, Stan Newens, and Lord Brockway.

Ministers and colonial Governors, and much local publicity gained for MCF views.[71]

Not all were so successful. Mary Klopper of Aberdeen Area Council had an intriguing explanation for the relative lack of support for the MCF in north-east Scotland: 'The Scots have no conscience about the colonies—they think the English are solely to blame.'[72] The peak period of Area Council activity was the late 1950s, and by the early 1960s there was a widespread feeling that it was falling away.[73] The Birmingham Council reported in 1964 that whilst institutional support, especially from trade unions, held steady, individual effort and public response were diminishing.[74] Even more disturbing were the explanations offered by some for this decline. The disillusioned Leeds Council secretary blamed a combination of local economic depression and the rise of working-class racism.[75]

By 1964–5 MCF organisation outside London was clearly in a state of advanced decay. The core of volunteers in the localities upon whom the Area Councils depended became ever harder to find. Whereas in the early and mid-1950s it would appear that interest in colonial and particularly African problems was growing amongst the politically aware, if not necessarily in the general public, during the early 1960s such concern was clearly diminishing. By 1963 John Eber was lamenting the 'futility' of trying to hold Day Schools to educate local Labour activists on the colonies.[76]

This decline of individual activism increased the likelihood of internal dissension, as relatively small groups were able to attain more influence. In particular dissension was likely to grow, as it had done in most left-wing pressure groups at some point, between mainstream Labour supporters and adherents of more militant ideologies. Such dissensions were not a major feature of the MCF's early years. The tasks facing the Movement seemed so urgent that members were far more concerned with getting things done than with one another's precise ideological affiliations. Brockway's political style, an emotional

[71] Area Councils' correspondence and 1961 secretaries' conference.

[72] Mary Klopper to Lian Eber, John Eber's wife, then Area Organiser (20 Nov. 1962) (MCF).

[73] Annual Reports and correspondence, *passim*; interviews with Barbara Haq and Lord Brockway.

[74] Report of Birmingham Area Council AGM (1964) (MCF).

[75] Mrs N. Segal, Leeds Area secretary, to John Eber (n.d. but c.Nov. 1963) (MCF papers).

[76] John Eber to H. Hardcastle of Bristol Area Council (6 May 1963) (MCF papers).

rather than a theoretical socialism, was opposed to any tendency to draw up internal lines of controversy within the left. MCF conferences seem invariably to have featured large numbers of unanimously approved resolutions and relatively few contentious votes; after the 1960 conference the Birmingham delegation were moved to complain that this meant wasting a great deal of time on motions 'which everyone connected with the MCF would be bound to accept'.[77] MCF meetings in the late 1950s and early 1960s were on occasion marked by disturbances; but these resulted not from internal left-wing dispute but from attacks by the League of Empire Loyalists.

Yet an organisation concerning itself with such a range of emotionally charged issues and including people with such a range of political perspectives as did the MCF could not hope to escape serious divisions within its ranks. From the late 1950s such divisions emerged in various ways. There were naturally arguments over the politics of particular colonial territories; probably the sharpest coming over the Malayan issue. There was dispute between those who saw the role of the MCF as being to exert pressure specifically over British colonial policy, and those who envisaged it as a vehicle for a more general and more militant campaign on the whole range of issues concerned with the Third World.[78] Thirdly, there was controversy over participation by members and supporters of the Communist Party.

It would be wrong to assume that CPGB attitudes to colonialism inevitably brought Communists into conflict with other sections of the left. The CPGB espoused the same broad aims, at least in the short term, as did most anticolonialists: the demand for political independence and future economic co-operation for development; the need for left-wingers in Britain and colonial nationalist movements to work closely together; sharp criticism of Conservative colonial policy. Where there were active Communist Parties in colonial territories, as in Malaya, the CPGB naturally supported these whereas the Labour left, on the whole, did not. Even there, non-Communist

[77] Birmingham Area Council report on 1960 MCF AGM (n.d. but late 1960) (MCF papers).

[78] See MCF Special Executive meeting minutes (22 Oct. 1959), where Eber (taking the latter view) clashed with Brockway (taking the former) on this issue. The same contention revived at Executive meetings of 27 Oct. 1960 and 15 Dec. 1960. In late 1959 MCF participated in joint discussions with other left-wing groups (VFS, UDC, Tribune, *New Left Review*, and the New Left Clubs) with the aim of evolving joint policies; see Executive minutes (17 Dec. 1959).

radicals such as Douglas Rogers might take a relaxed view: 'There is nothing sinister or surprising about there being Communists in the colonial Empire. The mystery is that there are not more of them.'[79] And in the majority of cases where there was no such party, the CP championed the cause of 'bourgeois' nationalist movements, in accordance with the theory that these represented a 'progressive national bourgeoisie' which, if not socialist, was at least anti-imperialist and concerned with national independence, state sponsored economic development, and social reform.

Many other groups on the British left—not only Trotskyists, but those brought up in the ILP tradition and, later, supporters of Maoist ideas—expressed more radical views on colonial issues than did the CPGB. In a period when the Cold War, the rigid Stalinism of the CPGB leaders, and the vehement anti-Communism of Labour and TUC leaderships combined to imbue relations between CPGB and Labour with a profound antagonism, there was something nearer to a commonality of views on the colonies than in most other spheres. The sharpest point of dissension was over international trade unionism. Labour and the TUC naturally used their influence to press colonial unions to join the ICFTU; the CPGB urged association with the WFTU. More generally and in the longer term, the CPGB argued that the newly independent states should form close economic and other ties with the Soviet bloc, whilst the Labour right believed they should associate with the West, and the Labour and independent lefts wanted some kind of non-aligned position. As the Communists, too, had come after 1953 to regard non-aligned status as a large step in the right direction for post-colonial states, this also did not provide a major barrier to co-operation.

Thus individual Communists participated in MCF activities from the beginning—in contrast to Brockway's previous organisations from which they had been wholly absent. The most prominent of these re-called, albeit with a touch of retrospective air-brushing, that they and the Labour left 'despite our many political differences, worked together amicably in trying to build a strong anti-imperialist movement'.[80] Brockway, for his part, stressed that despite his opposition to the general policies of the Communist Party he 'paid tribute' to the efforts of individual Communists in the anticolonial movement.[81] On

---

[79] Douglas Rogers, 'A Test of Sincerity', *Suara Merdeka* (Aug. 1955).
[80] Idris Cox, personal communication.
[81] Interview with Lord Brockway.

the other hand, any form of association with the CPGB would carry danger for the MCF; not least that of proscription by the Labour Party. Prior to the Movement's inaugural conference, the CPGB had offered its co-operation, but Douglas Rogers 'had replied on behalf of the sponsors of the Conference Arrangement Committee to the effect that in their view association with the Communist Party would be prejudicial to the work of the Movement'.[82] Later, a number of local Communist branches sought to affiliate to MCF Area Councils; but the Movement ruled that whilst individuals might join and trade unions be permitted to appoint representatives to MCF bodies whatever their political allegiance, affiliations by organisations which the Labour Party proscribed were not allowed.[83]

The majority of MCF supporters were left-wing Labour or were concerned with colonial issues on libertarian grounds. They might well be suspicious of the CPGB as an organisation, and they might well not trust the Communists on many domestic issues, but there was an emotional predilection towards left unity from below; and colonial affairs were seen in many quarters as a sphere in which the real divisions lay between left and right—including left-wing and right-wing Labour—rather than between Labour activists and other groups on the left. The attitude was summarised by one Area Council Secretary who wrote that the local communist leader was participating in MCF activities and that 'on the question of AFRICAN freedom there is no doubt about his sincerity'.[84] Similarly, when Jack Woddis, CPGB International Secretary and the Party's main African expert at the time, became the first Communist (or at least the first open one!) to join the MCF Central Council in 1961, there is no indication of particular friction between him and other Council members. Indeed Woddis collaborated very closely with Leon Szur, though their political views diverged sharply.[85]

There were, though, instances of more serious difficulty concerning the affairs of one or two Area Councils. The situation in Bristol, in

---

[82] Central Council minutes (27 Nov. 1954) (Benn papers).

[83] See Bert Pearce, Chairman of Cardiff Communist Party, to Helen Bastable (5 Oct. 1960); Bastable to Pearce (10 Oct. 1960); John Eber to P. McAuley Wirral Area Council (19 Apr. 1963 and 8 Dec. 1964) (MCF papers).

[84] P. McAuley to Lian Eber (24 Apr. 1964) (MCF papers).

[85] Interview with Lord Brockway. Szur, though not a member of any of the Trotskyist sects, was sympathetic to Trotsky's views. He and Woddis co-wrote the MCF's pamphlet on neo-colonialism.

particular, seems very much to have worried Eber.[86] The main and increasing base of CP strength in the MCF, however, lay in the London Area Council. This had, especially after the late 1950s, a high proportion of CPGB members and sympathisers involved, and this led to friction with the national organisation. The London Council was chaired successively by two Labour MPs, Maurice Orbach and William Warbey, who, whilst clearly not 'fellow travellers' in the 1930s sense, were both bitter critics of Labour foreign policy along lines which indicated a certain sympathy with Communist views and the Soviet stance.[87] It may be assumed that they were less averse to working with Communists on the Area Council than most Labour figures would have been. A number of prominent London Communists were active in the Council from early on, including Kay Beauchamp, Idris Cox, Billy Strachan, and Jack Woddis, but where policies which they proposed were not supported by the Labour majority they seem to have had little impact. Thus when Strachan, early in 1955, sought to commit the London MCF to a demand for the immediate independence of the West Indian colonies this was opposed on grounds of practicality and defeated.[88] As late as 1960 there seem to have been few if any CPGB members on the London Executive.[89]

Successive secretaries of the Council, none the less, were evidently open to suspicion of being close supporters of the Communist Party. Ian Page, the longest-serving London secretary, who also held various other prominent posts in the Movement, was a member of the Labour Party but clearly held views which were at least close to those of the CP. Like Eber, he had been involved in the fraught area of Malayan left-wing politics (his wife, Gladys Lim, was the sister of Lim Hong Bee), had attended international Communist-sponsored conferences, and wrote on occasion for the CPGB-dominated *Labour*

[86] John Eber to Henry Hardcastle, Bristol Area Council (16 Jan. 1963); Daphne Morgan, Bristol, to Eber (19 Jan. 1963); Eber to Hardcastle (16 Apr. 1963) (MCF papers). It is clear from this and related correspondence that the secretary of the Bristol Council (who should remain anonymous here) was persistently falsifying information on MCF activities and disrupting the Movement's work; though in ways that suggest personal rather than party political motives. The fact that Eber, in this case and elsewhere, attributed such problems to Communist activity and worried about CP influence is interesting in view of the controversy surrounding Eber himself.

[87] Warbey had difficulties with both the PLP and his own constituency on this score: see Robert Jackson, *Rebels and Whips* (Macmillan, 1968), 67–8, 268.

[88] Report of London Area Council conference (30 Jan. 1955) (MCF London Area papers).

[89] London Area Conference Report (1960) (MCF London Area papers).

Monthly. Such connections are the stuff of smear campaigns—and indeed Page, together with many others involved in the MCF and Anti-Apartheid, were thus smeared in an extraordinary Monday Club exposé of the 'puppeteers' supposedly manipulating African discontent from London.[90] Yet in this case there was some substance to the allegations: Page was apparently prepared not only to work closely with CPGB members but to encourage and facilitate contacts between African trade unions and the Soviet bloc.[91] This may indicate merely a desire to encourage a non-aligned position among colonial movements in face of overwhelming British and US influence on them; but a different and less straightforward explanation is more plausible.

Page's successor as London secretary, Solly Sachs, was likewise sympathetic to the Communist line, even though he had in fact been expelled from the South African Communist Party over thirty years earlier, and had been appointed to the London area post after the MCF Executive had persuaded the London Council out of their original intention to appoint Sam Kahn, a CPGB member and, like Sachs, formerly prominent in the SACP. Eber had suggested that such an appointment:

was a matter of concern, in view of the approach of a Labour Government, and of the already substantial number of British CP members on the London EC ... CP influence on the London EC was prejudicing the confidence and support of Labour Party and other people towards the MCF.[92]

It is the nature of such fears which gives significance to the internal arguments of the MCF over Communist involvement—attention to

[90] Harold Soref and John Greig, *The Puppeteers* (Tandem Books, 1965). This remarkable work is premissed on the belief that anticolonialism could never have found its way into any African mind unless it had first been planted there by scheming British Marxists.

[91] Page's articles are in *LM* (June and Dec. 1958, Aug. 1961, and June 1963). His report on the 1961 Casablanca AATUF conference (MCF papers) shows him inclined to evaluate the progressiveness of African trade unionists in terms of their hostility towards the Western powers and support for the USSR. For his establishing contacts between African and Soviet bloc unions, see e.g. Page to A. W. Wagoina of the Uganda Federation of Labour (20 June and 7 July 1961) (MCF papers). It may be added that two prominent CPGB members, on separate occasions, suggested to the present author their suspicion that Page was an agent for an (unspecified) security service.

[92] Executive minutes (15 July 1964) (MCF papers). On Sachs's political background, see Jack Simons and Ray Simons, *Class and Colour in South Africa, 1850–1950* (2nd edn., International Defence and Aid Fund, 1983), and Christopher J. Sansom, 'The British Labour Movement and Southern Africa, 1918–55' (Birmingham University Ph.D. thesis, 1982).

which might otherwise seem trivial or ungenerous given the relative absence of substantive policy differences between the CPGB and other sections of the left over political decolonisation. For in so far as the influence of the Movement was dependent on its ability to infuse its distinctive anticolonial stance into official Labour policy it had to walk the line between pressurising and wholly antagonising the Labour leadership—and allegations of pro-Communism were a sure way of destroying the relationship. The fortunes of the MCF were closely bound up with those of the left in the Labour Party in pressing for a more radical colonial policy. The next chapter turns to these fortunes, the conflicts between the MCF and the party, and the simultaneous changes in attitudes to the colonies within the Communist Party and other left-wing groups.

7

Campaigns and Schisms, 1954–1964

Between 1954 and the election of a Labour Government in 1964 political decolonisation proceeded with accelerating rapidity in Britain's remaining colonies, particularly during the 'winds of change' era of Macmillan and MacLeod. Immediately preceding this shift to what Churchill had stigmatised as the policy of 'scuttle', however, there was the last-ditch attempt militarily to reassert Britain's imperial role in the Suez adventure. Reactions on the anticolonialist left to these events were dominated by the Movement for Colonial Freedom, which saw its policies in large part adopted by the Labour Party during these years; but which also found itself embroiled in major controversy with the party, centring on attitudes to Malaya. There were also clashes with the British Labour movement over the future of colonial trade unionism. Meanwhile the CPGB, shaken by the revelations of Krushchev's 'secret speech' and the invasion of Hungary, was undergoing a contentious reappraisal of its own attitudes to the colonial world. And there emerged, partly from the crisis of British Communism, a New Left with distinctive views on these issues. This chapter traces these developments, concluding with the anticolonialists' reactions to the new Wilson Government in 1964.

I. THE MCF, THE LABOUR PARTY, AND DECOLONISATION

In 1961 the Labour Party agent for Leith wrote to Helen Bastable of the MCF that he had tried to enlist the support of the MCF Edinburgh Area Council for a Labour electoral campaign and that:

I was surprised to be told that the MCF was non-political—or at any rate non-party . . . If MCF are not prepared to recognise that the Labour Party is their best bet—and to help it, they are not really doing all they can to help themselves. At the last General Election it was obvious to every African how much a Labour victory would mean to them.[1]

Bastable's reply was that the MCF was indeed 'non-party' in the sense of not being affiliated to Labour, but that:

Our work has been accepted officially by the LP's Commonwealth Committee as complementary to that of the LP in the colonial sphere . . . We believe that an organisation which concentrates its whole attention on the colonial question publicising a wide range of people both within and outside the LP is necessary, and is indeed a way of bringing men of goodwill into the LP and into electoral support for it.[2]

The reply was a more accurate picture of the Movement's relationship to Labour and its colonial policies than was the suggestion that the MCF was non-political; but it was not the whole truth. The relationship was rather more complex, and more conflictual, than the bland reference to complementary activities would indicate.

The MCF's officers had opened sharp criticism of official Labour policy little more than a year after the Movement's foundation. In *Tribune*'s special issue for the 1955 Labour Conference, Douglas Rogers launched a stinging attack on party attitudes:

Last year the Labour Party conference was practically delirious with self-congratulation because for the first time it devoted a whole session to colonial affairs. It should have felt shame at the years of silence.

Last year Labour adopted a programme that set forth a comprehensive plan for moving the colonies to self-government. Comprehensive—but woolly! Where is the evidence that Labour really means to fight for colonial freedom? Where is the evidence of any serious challenge to the Tories on their colonial policy during the last twelve months?

Nowhere is there any sense of urgency. Labour must act quickly and resolutely or its tidy plans of constitutional advance will be swept away in a whirlpool of violence.[3]

Rogers's article drew an angry reply from new Labour Commonwealth Officer John Hatch, who pointed to the progress which had been made in Labour Party policy, the increased activity of Labour MPs on colonial issues (apparently forgetting that much of this activity came from the very MCF MPs who were increasingly critical of

---

[1] A. Biggar to Helen Bastable (18 Oct. 1961) (MCF papers).
[2] Bastable to Biggar (20 Oct. 1961) (MCF papers).
[3] Douglas Rogers, 'Challenge the Tories' Colonial Madness: Let's Have some Action!' *Tribune* (14 Oct. 1955).

the lead their front bench was giving), and suggesting that 'unlike Douglas Rogers, parties [i.e. CLPs] have noticed what has been done and are appreciative of it'.[4]

Before this disagreement was to issue forth in a full-scale row, however, the Suez crisis had intervened. The British left's reactions to this clearly displayed the way in which the MCF and other anticolonial critics effectively operated as the advance guard of Labour Party policy: issues and stances which they adopted would sooner or later be picked up by the party itself.

The cynical might regard the Suez affair as a godsend for anticolonialists. The MCF since its foundation, and left-wing individuals for decades before that, had been depicting Conservative Governments as being fixated on anachronistic and aggressive notions of imperial might and military adventure. Eden's actions over Suez seemed to confirm the left's worst suspicions; and because they had entertained such beliefs long before Gaitskell and the Labour front bench could bring themselves to do so, they had prepared. Discussions of the Labour response to the crisis have not noted the role of the MCF in laying the foundations and providing much of the driving force for the Labour campaign.[5] In a broad sense, it might be said that the Movement's activities over the previous two years had done much to create the atmosphere in which the left's anti-imperialism could focus around Suez. More specifically it was the MCF, and the Suez Emergency Committee which it launched in the summer of 1956, which provided the main focus for opposition to Eden's policy in the country.

In the weeks preceding the invasion, the Labour Party was deeply and publicly split on the issue. In the first week of August, the MCF organised a declaration by twenty-three Labour MPs that they 'are not prepared to support this or any British Government in the use of force not sanctioned by the Security Council', and mounted the first protest meetings against the Government's stance, with Brockway,

---

[4] John Hatch, letter, *Tribune* (21 Oct. 1955).

[5] See Leon Epstein, *British Politics in the Suez Crisis* (Urbana, Ill.: University of Illinois Press, 1964); Hugh Thomas, *The Suez Affair* (Weidenfeld & Nicolson, 1967); Keith Kyle, *Suez* (Weidenfeld & Nicolson, 1991); Wm. Roger Louis and Roger Owen (eds.), *Suez 1956: The Crisis and its Consequences* (Oxford: Oxford University Press, 1989), and for Labour reactions, Philip Williams, *Hugh Gaitskell* (Cape, 1979), 418–43, and Michael Foot, *Aneurin Bevan*, ii. *1945–1960* (Granada, 1975), 514–46 (both of which somewhat gloss over the inconsistencies and hesitations of their heroes' positions).

Castle, Soper, A. J. P. Taylor, and Kingsley Martin among the speakers. They peaked with a London rally on 16 September where Brockway, Benn, and Hale addressed a reported 7,000-strong crowd.[6] Meanwhile William Warbey castigated Gaitskell for being 'anxious to present a complete show of national unity and to damp down inconvenient criticism even from moderate and "respectable" quarters of the party'.[7] Even Bevan was seen by much of the left as unreliable on this question: 'As a disciple of Mr. Bevan, I was most disappointed to see "Our Nye" climbing onto the Eden–Gaitskell bandwaggon of hate against Nasser', wrote one irate correspondent to *Tribune*.[8]

The PLP meeting of 31 October showed how deep were the divisions among Labour MPs. Some, like Fred Lee, called for a general strike against the Government's policy; others like Stanley Evans asserted that opposing the Government would destroy parliamentary democracy and that the UN was not worth supporting anyway.[9] The call for a general strike met with but little favour: one Labour politician, then a youthful Trotskyist, recalls arriving at the 6 November Trafalgar Square demonstration with thousands of duplicated leaflets advocating such a course. He met with a group of dockers who took one look at the leaflets, laughed at them, and scattered the lot to the winds.[10]

By 25 October the Emergency Committee, operating from the MCF offices and using the Movement's staff, had held over 240 protest meetings throughout the country[11]—and in the weeks that followed many hundreds more were convened, some by the MCF and the Committee, some by local Labour parties, some more or less spontaneous.[12] The left proved to be wrong in their prediction as to how Gaitskell would react to the outbreak of hostilities. After what seemed to his critics like a long initial period of hesitation, his prescription to Labour MPs by 31 October was exactly what the MCF and the Emergency Committee had been advocating:

[6] *PN* (21 Sept. 1956).

[7] Text of MPs' letter and notes of meetings in MCF London Area files; Warbey's article in *Tribune* (10 Aug. 1956). (The reference to moderate and respectable quarters is, one presumes, not to himself.)

[8] Letter in *Tribune* (17 Aug. 1956).

[9] Tony Benn's 'Suez Diary' (typescript in Benn papers), entry for 31 Oct. 1956.

[10] Interview with Stan Newens—who now regards this ridicule as entirely appropriate.

[11] MCF Executive minutes (18 Sept. 1956); North Africa Committee minutes (25 Oct. 1956) (Benn papers).

[12] See *PN*, *NS&N*, and *Tribune* (Sept.–Nov. 1956), *passim*, for notices of many such meetings.

we should carry the fight to the country with an immediate national campaign in complete and utter opposition to this war. He warned us that we would be vilified and attacked as traitors but that we were bound in a solemn duty to do this until we had brought about an end to this war.[13]

The agitation against the Suez adventure was to be remembered within Labour's ranks as a period when the party had briefly united behind a leader who 'spoke for England' against aggression. So, eventually and in a limited sense, it was. Yet the initial drive to organise an anti-Suez campaign in the country had come from the anticolonialist left rather than the leadership.[14] During the invasion opposition on the grounds initially argued by the MCF—essentially based on adherence to the terms of the UN Charter—was not only picked up by the Labour leaders but was shared in more covert form by many Conservatives.[15] But that response was belated, coming into focus only after the invasion itself had taken place, and concealed deep divisions. Some in Labour's ranks refused to condemn the invasion; some argued against it essentially on pragmatic grounds of the damage caused to Britain's standing as a world power; some (including of course most of the left) regarded adherence to international law and principles as the real issue. Such divisions, largely covert during the Suez affair's impassioned crescendo, were to re-emerge in more open and dramatic form in the left's fragmented and confused reactions to an extraordinary epilogue to Empire, a distorted echo of Suez—the Falklands war of 1982.[16]

Whatever the ambivalences within the PLP, there was little doubt about the vehemence of opposition to the invasion among Labour constituency activists. Here the anticolonialism of the left seemed unquestioningly accepted: if the Kenyan Emergency had been a slow-burning fire warming support for the sentiments expressed by groups like the MCF, Suez was a flash of intense heat. Yet though Suez clearly strengthened anti-imperialism within the Labour move-

[13] Benn, 'Suez Diary' entry for 31 Oct. 1956.

[14] The major demonstration in Trafalgar Square on 6 Nov. had originally been called by the MCF, but was handed over to the Labour Party when the latter stirred on the issue (interviews with Tony Benn, Lord Brockway, and Kay Beauchamp; Fenner Brockway, *Towards Tomorrow* (Hart Davis, MacGibbon, 1977), 211).

[15] See Benn's 'Suez Diary' and Richard Crossman, *The Backbench Diaries of Richard Crossman* (Hamilton and Cape, 1981), 532–44, for some of the backstage manœuvring over Conservative rebellions and projected ministerial resignations in the crisis.

[16] On which see Clive Christie, 'The British Left and the Falklands War', *PQ* 55 (1984).

ment and contributed to the speed of later decolonisation, the emotional reaction in the country at large tended to move in the opposite direction. Opinion polls indicated that public sentiment, showing a large majority opposed to the use of force before and at the start of the invasion, rallied to support the Government's actions as fighting began, and even more in retrospect. Positive desire to retain imperial power may have eroded substantially by the 1950s; but in crisis public reactions would still rally to the defence of a British world role.

Two years after this moment of relative unity, there was a serious argument between the MCF and official Labour views over Malaya. This was almost the only important case in which the stance adopted by the Movement was not only more radical than, but was diametrically opposed to, that of the party. There had been sharp differences of emphasis, at least, since 1954. Whilst the official Labour line was critical of some of the means adopted to combat the guerrillas, it adhered like the Government to the belief that the fighting was primarily the responsibility of the Communists, defended the use of British troops to crush them, and supported the South-East Asia Treaty Organisation. The MCF, on the other hand, called for a negotiated end to the conflict, considered the Government's offer of an amnesty to the guerrillas to be unsatisfactory if not fraudulent, demanded wholly elected legislatures in the Malayan territories and commitment to a firm date for independence, and denounced the 'application of SEATO on an unwilling people'.[17]

By the late 1950s the gulf between the positions of party and Movement had opened far further than this—whereas in many other fields of colonial policy the party's views had moved a fair way towards those of the MCF. The latter opposed plans for a Malaysian federation, continued to call for a negotiated settlement with the MCP guerrillas, and had become fiercely critical not only of the continued British presence but also of many of the leading local nationalist politicians. Initially the MCF had sought co-operation with all the leading nationalist parties in the region despite their deep

---

[17] MCF, 'Questions for your Candidate' (prepared for 1955 General Election, May 1955, mimeo), 1, 6–7; *A Policy for Colonial Freedom* (MCF pamphlet, 1955), 10–11. In Aug. 1954 Brockway had launched a campaign for amnesties—to involve convicted prisoners as well as detainees and active guerrillas—in Malaya and Kenya: *PN* (6 Aug. 1954); and in late 1955 the MCF's London Area Council held a Trafalgar Square rally calling for a negotiated Malayan peace: *PN* (8 Nov. 1955.)

differences;[18] and Brockway, while expressing concern about the disunity of the Malayan and Singapore socialists and about their unwillingness to negotiate with, or grant civil liberties to, the Communists, had characteristically anticipated that all such problems 'could be adjusted in a self-governing Malaya'.[19]

By 1956, the MCF protested to Lennox-Boyd about continued denials of civil rights in Singapore; and in 1958 similar protests were directed at Commonwealth Relations Secretary Lord Home and at the Premiers of the now internally self-governing Malaya and Singapore. It was this latter complaint, signed by thirty-three MFC-supporting MPs and two peers, which precipitated the stormy passage with the Labour leaders. The MCF letter argued that:

The conflict is internal, and, in our view, if the Malayan Government is not prepared to negotiate the termination of hostilities, it should not now depend upon forces from this country. Indeed, this seems to us incompatible with the independence of Malaya.[20]

The attack was thus directed equally at the British Government and at the local rulers, then in the process of transition to full independence—but, in the MCF's eyes, still tied in both military and economic terms to British imperialism. The Movement's actions upset the Labour leadership and its colonial experts for three reasons. First, they were concerned lest the party should be associated with the views expressed which might, especially abroad, be taken for Labour policies. As James Griffiths said in dissociating himself, Callaghan, and the front bench from the statement: 'when a letter signed by so many Labour MPs is published... many people will think it is an official pronouncement by the Party.'[21]

Second, the MCF accusations were directed at ruling parties

[18] MCF South-East Asia Committee minutes (3 Nov. 1954) (Benn papers).

[19] Fenner Brockway, article in *Tribune* (6 Jan. 1956).

[20] Letter signed by Brockway and 34 others, to Lord Home, Tunku Abdul Rahman, and Lee Kuan Yew (copies in MCF, Benn, and LP papers). The following account is based on MCF, FCB, and Labour Party records, various contemporary periodicals, and interviews. As noted above the person at the centre of the controversy, John Eber, did not wish to be interviewed. Partly for this reason, aspects of the dispute remain unclear. It may also be noted here that Goldsworthy (*Colonial Issues in British Politics, 1945–1961* (Oxford: Oxford University Press, 1971), 328) refers to an earlier dispute between Labour Party and MCF over a speech by Ghanaian politician Joe Appiah. I have found no reference to such a dispute in any contemporary document, and assume that the memory of Lord Brockway (Goldsworthy's source for this supposed incident) was here at fault.

[21] Statement issued 3 Apr. 1958 (copies in Benn and LP papers).

in Malaya and Singapore with which Labour maintained friendly relations. Lee Kuan Yew's People's Action Party (PAP) in Singapore, in particular, was looked upon with favour by Labour's colonial spokespeople; and seen by both the Labour Party and FCB as a democratic socialist organisation deserving strong support.[22] Even the ILP apparently believed that 'Lee Kuan Yew is by personal conviction Left-wing, almost a Marxist'.[23] Attacks on the Singapore Government were not popular with British Labour.

Third, it was suspected that the reason why the MCF adopted this position on Malaya was that its policies had been influenced by a group of Malayan Communists or pro-Communists. Mohamed Sopiee of the Malayan High Commission in London charged that 'meetings sponsored by the Movement for Colonial Freedom ... have afforded a platform for people who are known to be representatives and sympathisers of the Malayan Communist terrorists ... this letter ... has been inspired by the same agents of the Malayan Communist terrorists'.[24] The FCB similarly accused the MCF of:

actively seeking advice from a small group of Malayans in London who ... have for years been the helpers and trail-blazers of the Malayan Communist party ... There is a struggle on in Singapore between democratic socialism on one hand and communism on the other. It is time that socialist members of the Movement for Colonial Freedom realised this.[25]

Brockway, responding to this attack, was at pains both to rebut the charge of Communist infiltration and to stress the ethical case for the MCF's intervention:

These communications were authorised by the Executive of the Movement for Colonial Freedom, which is composed entirely of members of the Labour Party, and were written by myself ... you do not name the alleged supporters of the Communist Party on our South East Asia Committee, but it would appear that among others you refer to Mr. John Eber. Mr. Eber has made a detailed personal statement to our Executive, and we have come unanimously to the conclusion that the allegations against him are untrue ... It was argued that the victims of the deportations, detentions and bans were Communists, but it is precisely because the MCF believes in basic human rights that in

---

[22] See *Venture* editorial (July 1958) and Callaghan's report of his Asian trip (Spring 1959), LP/CSC/58/44. Hatch and Callaghan had had to convince a sceptical Gaitskell that the PAP itself was not an MCP front (interview with Lord Hatch).

[23] Editorial note, *SL* (11 Aug. 1962).

[24] Sopiee to signatories of MCF letter (n.d. but early Apr. 1958) (Benn papers).

[25] *Venture* editorial (July 1958).

contrast to the methods of totalitarian dictatorships we oppose the setting aside of civil liberties in order to crush political opponents.[26]

Brockway was correct in believing that Eber, who was shortly thereafter to become the MCF's General Secretary, was the prime target of the accusation. This had become clear in *Venture*'s reply to Eber's own letter of protest, in which he denied that he was or had ever been a 'fellow traveller'.[27] Both the FCB and the Labour Commonwealth Officer had collected evidence, though much of it from strongly partisan sources, on the political activities of Eber and his associates in Britain.[28] Brockway was sufficiently perturbed to contact Malcolm MacDonald, who had been Governor-General in Malaya at the outbreak of the Emergency, about the allegations. MacDonald's reply was noncommittal.[29]

Judgement on such matters is inevitably highly subjective. It is clear that Eber had worked closely with MCP members in the MDU and later in Britain; and that some of those associated with the Britain–Malaya Committee and the MCF's South-East Asia Committee were sympathetic to Communist views. It is less clear, however, that there was justice in the vague charges of Eber being a 'trail-blazer' or 'agent' for the MCP in Britain in the sense that, for instance, Lim Hong Bee evidently was. Indeed as we have seen, Eber in his capacity as MCF General Secretary was to display distinct hostility to CPGB activity in the MCF. His views were undoubtedly very left wing; but whatever they may have been in the 1940s they were considerably different from—indeed in many respects more radical than—those of the CPGB by the end of the 1950s.[30]

The NEC Commonwealth Subcommittee was told by the party leaders to pursue the matter further. It had several meetings with Brockway and other MCF representatives before and after the 1958 Party Conference, and was persuaded to take no disciplinary action.

---

[26] Letter in *Venture* (Oct. 1958).

[27] Eber's letter and appended editorial comment, ibid.

[28] See *Hang Tuah* (Bulletin of Political Group of the Malay Society of Great Britain), 3 (Jan.–Feb. 1958); *Suara Merdeka* (organ of the Malayan Forum) (Oct. 1956); 'Note on the Malayan Merdeka Forum' (2 Aug. 1956); Hilda Selwyn-Clarke to John Hatch (10 Oct. 1958); Commonwealth Department memorandum on MCF to NEC (July 1958), Com. 1957–8/14; Goh Keng Swee to T. F. Betts (28 July 1958); and related material; all in LPCD.

[29] Malcolm MacDonald to Fenner Brockway (29 Sept. 1958) (MCF papers).

[30] Had he become in some sense a Maoist? That is the most plausible label for his later stance; though direct evidence is lacking.

As *The Times* pointed out, it was evident that the MCF 'are not in unbearably hot water... but Mr. Fenner Brockway is likely to be requested to treat Social Democratic leaders in the Commonwealth with more discretion and fellow feeling'.[31] Brockway wrote in very conciliatory tones to Morgan Phillips, saying that the MCF 'realise that the greatest hope of Britain contributing towards the freedom of the colonial peoples lies in the return of a Labour Government which will implement the policies adopted by the Party'. The Movement would henceforth concentrate its efforts on winning support for those policies. He pointed out that the only issues on which MCF and party had clashed were those of Malaya and Singapore, and 'over the rest of the vast field of colonial affairs the difficulty has not arisen'.[32] The MCF agreed in future to consult the party before making any statement on Malaya.

Yet Eber and others continued to argue for a more militant position on South-East Asia within the MCF, and opposition to plans for Federation was maintained. Eber retained his dislike both for the British presence and the feudal position of the indigenous rulers:

The British 'presence' in Malaya has been so continuous and so strong that Malayan politics is like a mythical world, borne aloft on the back of an elephant—but what if the elephant stumbles? British imperialism in Malaya and Malayan reaction have made themselves so interdependent that if one falls, both fall. But the elephant is tired and old...[33]

The MCF campaign against the idea of the Malaysian federation won little support in Britain, or even within the Labour movement. Although there can be little doubt that the Movement was correct in arguing that the federation proposals met with widespread opposition (but probably not the majority opposition they claimed), and that the referendum in Singapore on the issue was accompanied by malpractice, the MCF Annual Report of 1964 lamented that such arguments had made no impression.[34]

The long-running differences over Malaya were the exception

---

[31] *The Times* (22 Sept. 1958). As this report noted, the clash on Malaya coincided with a major victory for the MCF's views in another sphere, when the NEC made its first commitment to back legislation against racial discrimination.

[32] Fenner Brockway to Morgan Phillips (27 Oct. 1958) (copies in MCF and LP).

[33] John Eber in *Colonial Freedom News* (July 1960).

[34] MCF, Annual Report (1964), 8; see also MCF leaflet, *No to Malaysia* (n.d. but early 1963); London Area memorandum, 'Crisis in Brunei' (17 Dec. 1962); Executive Reports and South-East Asia Committee minutes (1961–4), *passim.*

rather than the rule in relations between the MCF and Labour. Whilst there remained an inevitable margin of difference in attitudes between a left-wing pressure group and a party leadership dominated by the 'revisionist' right wing, Labour Party policy moved in the direction pointed out by the anticolonial left on issue after issue. On opposition to the Central African Federation, on target dates for independence in East Africa, on the need to negotiate with the nationalists—including Kenyatta—in Kenya, on federation and the transfer of power in the West Indies, on recognition of the PPP's right to form a government if it won an election in Guiana, on proposals for Third World economic aid, on a Race Relations Act in Britain, on international action against South Africa, on one person one vote in the plural societies of the Empire, the party's position of the early 1960s was essentially what the MCF's had been in the mid-1950s. Apart from Malaya, and apart of course from the general decline in its own level of activity after the 1950s, the Movement faced two major disappointments.

The first was perhaps wholly predictable. In 1955 the MCF had attempted once more to activate Brockway's old dream of an effective international anticolonialist body bringing together on a permanent basis like-minded movements in Europe, Asia, and Africa. A World Conference for Colonial Liberation was planned for the end of the year in Margate. It was backed by a wide variety of international organisations, fourteen colonial political parties (including the CPP of Ghana, the Uganda National Congress, the Guiana CPP, the Northern Rhodesian ANC, and the Singapore PPP), and assorted European parties—though these last were mostly small bodies of the ILP type. The conference went ahead, but rather few even of the groups who sponsored it sent delegates, and most major nationalist parties went wholly unrepresented.[35] The intended permanent organisation never materialised, except on paper. The grandiose-sounding World Council for Colonial Liberation and International Council for Economic and Social Co-operation established at Margate appear

---

[35] See Press Release announcing conference (n.d. but *c.* Sept. 1955), Provisional Programme (n.d. but *c.* Oct. 1955), FCB 20/2/138 and 139; MCF Central Committee minutes (1955), *passim*, and conference report in *PN* (25 Nov. 1955). For a sample of dissatisfied delegates' comments, see *Bulletin* of the Malay Society of Great Britain (15 Dec. 1955) (LP/Malaya box). Among the few Third World movements which were represented were the Syrian and Jordanian Ba'ath: not democratic socialists by anyone's definition. In interview, Lord Brockway admitted that the conference was a complete disappointment.

never to have functioned at all. Meanwhile the COPAI, which retained a nominal existence after the foundation of the MCF and which the Margate meeting was intended to revitalise, continued to atrophy. The London organisation, run by Douglas Rogers, was nominal, its functions having been taken over by MCF; the Paris body was vestigial. Thus once more and for the last time, as with the League Against Imperialism in the late 1920s and the COPAI in the late 1940s, the aspiration for a world-wide, unified anticolonial organisation faded into nothing. Henceforth such international co-operation as there was to be in this sphere lay between and was organised by the Third World movements and governments themselves, with British anticolonialists reduced essentially to an observer's role.

The other major disappointment for the MCF was over Cyprus. The failure of its hopes here was fivefold. Its efforts to build contacts with groups representing both Greek and Turkish Cypriots came to nothing. It had many members from Britain's Greek Cypriot community, and links with their radical organisations like the National Cypriot Committee. But not only did it not gain support from Turkish Cypriots; it had to face fears that they would seek violently to disrupt its meetings on Cyprus.[36] This failure led to a second: the MCF, like the British left as a whole, was deeply divided over its attitudes to Enosis (union with Greece). British anticolonialists were never happy with the principle, but most aligned themselves with what appeared to be majority Greek Cypriot demands; and in many eyes adherence to the aim of a firm and imminent target date for British withdrawal in practice implied acceptance of union with Greece.[37] Brockway, in his usual starry-eyed fashion, expressed the belief that if Cyprus were given full independence it would surely not choose to become 'merely a province of Greece'; so that Turkish fears would be allayed and peace cemented.[38] Few even among his close colleagues, however, could share this quite unrealistic view.

Coupled with this was the fact, particularly uncomfortable for a

[36] See the exchange of letters on this in advance of a proposed MCF rally on Cyprus in May 1958; Wedgwood Benn to Barbara Castle (14 Apr. 1958); Sir Vincent Tewson to Benn (17 Apr. 1958); Benn to Tom Driberg (29 Apr. 1958); Fenner Brockway to Benn (8 May 1958) (Benn papers).

[37] See e.g. *The Times* (1 Dec. 1957); and material in Driberg papers on his Cyprus visits (Driberg C3).

[38] Fenner Brockway, *PN* (14 Feb. 1958).

group like the MCF, that in Cyprus the most militant nationalists, in the sense of those campaigning most vigorously (indeed violently) for British withdrawal, the followers of Grivas and Makarios, were also bitterly hostile to the left. Thus the belief, plausible if often facile in most colonial situations, that supporting radical nationalism also meant supporting socialists was quite untenable in the Cypriot case. Brockway continued to clutch at straws: perhaps at least Makarios's followers could be persuaded to adopt non-violent means. Thus he pressed Makarios, in discussion, to take the initiative in proposing negotiation with the British, and to end the armed struggle. The Cypriot leader responded uncompromisingly: he would call for talks only if Britain first lifted Emergency rule; and said that while he 'desired violence to end . . . how could he repudiate men whose actions arose from a love of their country and its liberties?'.[39] Later Brockway, undaunted, appealed publicly to the Archbishop to 'Use Gandhi's Techniques'.[40] The appeals won no response.

The third problem flowed in part from this, and lay in the failure of the British left either successfully to press for a negotiated end to the fighting or to exercise effective pressure to curb excesses by British troops. Whereas in the Kenyan case the Labour Party as a whole eventually came round to the view that the security forces were guilty of significant abuses, over Cyprus the left's complaints on this score were utterly repudiated by Gaitskell.[41] Finally, the failure to influence the Labour front bench extended to general policy towards Cypriot independence. Whereas in almost every other instance Labour moved gradually towards advocating target dates for decolonisation, in this one it actually shifted the other way, in accepting the Foot proposals of June 1958.[42] It might be argued, as it is by David Goldsworthy, that in thus changing its policy Labour actually helped facilitate the eventual settlement, and that this change in the long run accelerated decolonisation.[43] At the time, however, this argument found very few takers on the left; and the subsequent fate

[39] Fenner Brockway, 'My Talk with Makarios', ibid. (3 May 1957).

[40] Fenner Brockway, ibid. (4 July 1958).

[41] See his statement, *HC Deb.* (12 Nov. 1958), col. 390.

[42] Some of the Labour left's arguments against the change of position are rehearsed in Benn's speech to the PLP meeting on Cyprus of 26 June 1958 (speech notes in Benn papers).

[43] *Colonial Issues*, 352–7. The argument, in essence, is that adoption of a bipartisan policy both removed the Greek Cypriots' capacity to play off the British parties against one another and pushed them towards a more conciliatory position.

of the island may lead one to doubt the wisdom of the resulting bipartisan British policy.

II. THE TRADE UNIONS

One of the most far-reaching transformations in British political activity on colonial issues between the 1930s and the 1950s lay in the trade union sphere. Whereas there had been very little interest in things imperial from British unions for most of the inter-war period, the TUC and some individual unions had begun to play a more active role from the late 1930s. Only in the late 1950s, however, did positive involvement in this field—as opposed to negative criticism of prevailing attitudes within the official trade union structures—become a major preoccupation of the anticolonial lobby. Once again it was the MCF which made the main effort here; and since the pattern of development of colonial unionism was one of the most controversial aspects of decolonisation, and the TUC took a very dim view of outside bodies involving themselves in what it regarded as its proper sphere, the Movement found itself engaged in further clashes with authority.

In retrospect, many of those involved with the MCF were to see its most important achievement as having been in developing widespread trade union support and involving many unions for the first time in sustained critical attention to colonial developments.[44] The degree of organisational support which the Movement gained in the unions was striking. How far, and in what ways, such affiliations were reflected in active involvement, and what the effects of this were, are more complex matters. Generalisations about British trade unionism must always be handled with caution: the variations in structure, tradition, and outlook between unions were and are very wide. Thus it is obviously generally true to say that the more left-wing unions were more likely to affiliate to the MCF, and more likely to play an active part once affiliated. Yet it is often difficult to ascribe a clear left or right position to a given union: political balances vary both over time and between different levels of a union's structure. These might have unpredictable effects on a union's relationship with the MCF. Thus the ETU maintained its affiliation during and after its traumatic shift

---

[44] A claim made in interview especially by Bob Edwards and Barbara Haq.

from Communist to right-wing leadership; the AEU, with a strong Communist element but a right-wing majority and leaders, at one point disaffiliated but later rejoined.[45]

In its dealings with the union movement the MCF emphasised, naturally enough, those aspects of colonial struggles which had particular relevance to trade unionism. It pointed out that unions in the colonies were often at the forefront of nationalist efforts. It stressed the particular difficulties facing unions in many colonial territories—dissolution by the authorities, restrictions on activities, the internment or banishing of leaders, forcible suppression of strikes, refusal to allow trade unionists to engage in legitimate political activity, and of course the very low wages and poor conditions of most colonial workers. It suggested the parallels between these conditions and those faced by the British Labour movement in its earliest years and further suggested that 'the struggle of British Trade Unions is still, despite the many advances already won, directly linked with the Trade Union struggle in colonial and neo-colonial countries'.[46] Thus the appeal to self-interest characteristic of earlier attempts to arouse solidarity was on occasion revived, albeit in almost meaninglessly vague terms. The involvement of British unions in colonial affairs, it was claimed, could have three types of effect: to aid and encourage the colonial workers themselves; to spread knowledge and awareness of colonial workers' problems among their British counterparts; and to bring additional pressure to bear on the authorities over their treatment of colonial unions: 'the support of British Trade Unions in these cases undoubtedly has a profound influence on the Colonial Office and other authorities concerned.'[47]

How effective, then, was the MCF's Trade Union Committee in fulfilling these three aims? For the first, it seems to have been able to intervene with some success in a large number of individual cases; helping colonial, and especially African unions in dispute with

---

[45] In interview, Ernie Roberts, former Assistant General Secretary of the AEU and for many years leader of its left-wing faction, pointed out that the union's right-wing leaders, William Carron and John Boyd, held rather more radical views on colonial affairs and race relations than they did on most subjects. There were, none the less, clashes with the AEU over Roberts's involvement with the MCF: see C. W. Hallett to Ian Page (13 Nov. and 11 Dec. 1959); Page to Hallett (14 Nov. and 15 Dec. 1959) (MCF papers).

[46] John Eber to G. H. Lowthian, General Secretary of AUBTW (May 1962—no day given) (MCF papers).

[47] Ibid.

employers or with the authorities. In its early months, the Movement organised places and funding for African unionists to take NCLC courses (in implicit rivalry with the TUC's funding of places for colonial unionists at Ruskin College), and the sending of literature to colonial unions.[48] Later, aid took two main forms: offering advice and assistance directly, and initiating and co-ordinating financial and other help from individual British unions to their colonial counterparts. A few examples may suffice to indicate the way in which this was done. During the early 1960s the MCF was acting as a clearing house and organiser of appeals for help from unions in Aden, Basutoland, Kenya, Nigeria, Northern Rhodesia, South Africa, Swaziland, and Tanganyika, among others.[49] Requests poured into the MCF office: for money to buy a typewriter from Sierra Leone (for which £50 was sent); for the Nigerian mineworkers' strike fund (£300 was raised); for aid in publicising the detentions of Aden TUC leaders (on which questions were raised in Parliament and letters of protest sent); for help in a strike of Tanganyikan railwaymen (for which £500 was raised from the NUR alone, with donations and messages of support from many other unions); and a host of others. In sum, it would appear that during this period the range of contacts established, and the level of aid transmitted, between the MCF and colonial trade unions was more extensive than the comparable activities of any other British organisation, probably including the TUC itself.[50] Even very small sums of money sent from Britain might be of enormous importance under the conditions of penury, skeletal organisation, and often semi-legality characteristic of infant African trade unionism. Funds sufficient to buy a typewriter, a duplicator, or a motor car could make all the difference to the effective functioning of a union.

The response of the TUC to a request that they should aid the

[48] See for instance MCF Practical Aid Subcommittee minutes (21 Oct. 1954) (Benn papers).

[49] See, *inter alia*, correspondence in the files for these territories, and for the London Area Council and Trade Union Committee, and Executive Reports (1960–3) (MCF papers).

[50] See H. N. Georgestone, Sierra Leone Council of Labour, to Ian Page (21 Nov. 1960); Page to Georgestone (23 Dec. 1960); S. U. Bassey, General Secretary, Nigeria TUC, to Ian Page (15 Feb. 1961); telegrams from Aden TUC to Bob Edwards during Dec. 1963 (kindly loaned to me, with related material, by Mr Edwards); correspondence between Eber, Page, R. A. Jackson of the CWU, S. Nguka and C. S. Kasanga Tumbo of the Tanganyika African Railway Union, and various British union secretaries and branch officials (Mar. to May 1960) (MCF papers).

Tanganyikan railway strikers was indicative of the reasons why, despite the fact that the TUC was supposedly committed to supporting trade unionism in the British colonial territories, the MCF felt that it had a vital independent role to play. The TUC stated that it would continue to deal with East African affairs through its usual channels, and that 'a member of staff of the Commonwealth Section is in Nairobi giving advice and assistance to the railway workers there'.[51] As R. A. Jackson of the MCF's Trade Union Committee commented with some heat and much justice: 'The fatuousness of this is apparent.'[52] A TUC officer hundreds of miles away working with an entirely different union in a different territory could be of no imaginable help to the Tanganyikan railwaymen.

The TUC's approach to colonial affairs in this period was at best conventional, bureaucratic, slow moving, and unimaginative. To some trade unionists involved with the MCF it seemed to be, from their point of view, considerably worse even than that. The TUC's International Department, they alleged, would do nothing to upset the Colonial and Foreign Offices, and in effect took its instructions from them.[53] Such accusations are echoed by at least one academic observer:

For over twenty-five years the TUC and individual unions have not only been consulted on labour relations policy, they have in effect (through the system of Labour officers and participation on the Colonial Labour Advisory Board) been part of the colonial administration.[54]

These suspicions on the British left were shared in at least equal measure by many colonial trade unionists, who came to regard the TUC and the ICFTU, especially in Africa, as tools of the 'neo-colonial' policies of Britain and the USA. The leaders of the militant Pan-African trade union federation, the AATUF, expressed this view with particular ferocity.[55]

[51] Quoted in letter from R. A. Jackson to Ian Page (5 Apr. 1960) (MCF papers).
[52] Ibid.
[53] Interviews with Bob Edwards and Ernie Roberts; and numerous subsequent informal conversations with officials of SACTU, AATUF, etc. Much circumstantial evidence has been adduced in support of this view; and it was suggested, quite plausibly, that the position of co-operation and/or subservience originated under Bevin. See also Peter Weiler, *British Labour and the Cold War* (Stanford, Calif.: Stanford University Press, 1988), chs. 3 and 6.
[54] D. I. Davies, 'The Politics of the TUC's Colonial Policy', *PQ* 35/1 (1964), 23.
[55] 'Background and Prospects of the AATUF' (Accra: AATUF, n.d. but early 1961; mimeo in MCF papers).

All these were attitudes with which many in the MCF would have agreed: especially, but by no means only, those of them sympathetic to Communism. Such suspicions about the TUC's and ICFTU's roles in Africa were given further strength at the time of the AATUF's founding conference, when copies of what purported to be a secret British Cabinet document detailing full-blown conspiracies were distributed. The document suggested that the TUC and the British Government were working closely together to corrupt and subvert African union leaders, in competition with the USA which was attempting the same means for its own ends (and had succeeded with Kenyan leader Tom Mboya); and that a major aim of these dubious practices was to undermine African trade union autonomy.[56]

Whether this supposed Cabinet paper is genuine is not known—it must seriously be doubted. Its distribution and reception are of importance none the less, for it and subsequent leaked (or forged) international trade union documents brandished by both sides both indicated and intensified the profound hostility with which the various protagonists—ICFTU, WFTU, and AATUF—regarded one another. That atmosphere compounded already existing tensions within the British Labour movement about attitudes to colonial unionism.

The MCF was sympathetic to the strongly political orientation of much colonial trade unionism; and some supporters were keen also on the Communist leanings discerned in various colonial unions. The TUC decidedly disliked both. Thus in British Guiana where there were two rival union structures, the Man Power Citizens' Association and the Guiana Industrial Workers' Union, the TUC regarded the latter as unacceptably closely linked to Jagan and the PPP and fostered the former, which the left saw as little more than a company union.[57] In South Africa the MCF supported and established very close links with SACTU, which the TUC again treated with some suspicion as espousing radical nationalism and having Communists among its leaders. The MCF's officers believed SACTU to be the only representative non-racial body of South African workers, but because of the TUC's attitude was unsure whether it should address its

[56] Mimeoed document marked 'Secret. Annexe to Cabinet Paper on Policy in Africa. Draft 21/12/59' (copy in MCF papers, presumably that obtained by Page in Casablanca and referred to in his report). For a brief outline of the background to this affair, see Immanuel Wallerstein, *Africa: The Politics of Unity* (New York: Random House, 1967), 176–211.

[57] MCF Caribbean Committee report to Central Council (27 Feb. 1955) (Benn papers).

appeals to British unions in terms of support for SACTU in particular or South African workers in general.[58] The Movement did have some success, however, in influencing TUC policy towards South Africa: the support which the TUC gave to the movement for boycott of South African goods resulted from MCF lobbying.[59] After the MCF had founded the AAM much of its trade union work was handed over to the latter, which also drew very substantial trade union support.

The TUC's International Department obviously felt that it should have a monopoly on trade union activity in the colonial field. It resented MCF interference and sharply criticised the Movement for involving itself in this way. The General Council complained in 1957 that such activity 'by a body which is not staffed or equipped to deal with trade union matters' was thoroughly unhelpful, and British unions should not support it: 'The General Council does not approve of the intervention of the Movement for Colonial Freedom in the trade union field.'[60]

A sharper clash came over the question of relations with the AATUF. It was inevitable that a body such as this—highly politicised, Pan-Africanist, aggressively suspicious of neo-colonialism and of the ICFTU—would meet with the hostility of the TUC. The MCF, on the other hand, was in regular contact with the AATUF, organised meetings for its leader, John Tettegah, in Britain, and received the heartfelt thanks of the Federation for its support.[61] The Movement organised British trade union responses to the AATUF's founding conference: sending representatives, arranging articles in praise of the Federation in British socialist journals, and collecting messages of support from British unions.[62] This duly brought trouble from the TUC again—and indeed the MCF was sailing very close to the wind in this, identifying itself with an organisation which was deeply antagonistic to the TUC and ICFTU, and which drew much of its

---

[58] Leon Szur to Barbara Haq (17 Dec. 1963) (MCF papers). Ironically, British trade union support for SACTU later became almost general, just as SACTU itself was reduced to being an almost wholly exile organisation.

[59] See *TUC Annual Report* (1960), 42–3; MCF Executive Report (18 Aug. to 1 Oct. 1960) (MCF papers).

[60] *TUC Annual Report* 1957, 224–5.

[61] Charles Heymann, AATUF, to Ian Page (5 Dec. 1961) (MCF papers).

[62] MCF Executive minutes (28 Apr. 1960); John Tettegah to Ian Page (29 July 1961); Page to Mahjoub ben Seddik, AATUF (30 July 1961); Page's report on Casablanca conference (MCF papers).

international backing from Communist organisations. TUC General Secretary Sir Vincent Tewson expressed strong displeasure to the MCF's representative, ASSET General Secretary Harry Knight.[63] Under sharp attack, the MCF agreed, as it had done when threatened by the Labour Party, to a compromise: in future, all non-political trade union matters would be sent to the TUC for action.[64]

As to the MCF's level of success in arousing awareness and activity about colonial problems among British trade unionists, generalisations are again difficult. There was certainly an impact on those unions and union members who were already politicised or disposed towards an interest in international issues, but little evident success in involving the apathetic or parochial majority. Thus whilst it did rather more than merely preach to the converted, its activities did little to challenge the lack of interest in foreign, and especially Third World affairs in most parts of the British trade union movement. Interest, and at least verbal and financial expressions of solidarity, might briefly be awakened, only to fade again. In particular, the aim of bringing home to the trade union movement arguments about links between colonial underdevelopment, Commonwealth immigration, and British race relations was not fulfilled. Probably the most intensive efforts of the MCF to reach out to rank and file trade unionists came on this issue: in 1962, for instance, 100,000 MCF leaflets were distributed in workplaces aimed at rebutting the notion that colonial immigrants were a threat to jobs.[65]

The MCF and its offshoots played a pioneering role in arousing opposition to racial discrimination with the Labour movement—but the dramatic evidence which the later 1960s were to bring of the salience of popular racism is itself a testimony to the failure of these efforts. The Movement and its Area Councils gained the support of hundreds of trade union branches and district committees; but such support would involve primarily trade unionists who were already active on other political issues and in the Labour or Communist Parties, and might mean no more than the nominal consent of less active members. *Solidarity*, the MCF journal for trade unionists, apparently had a circulation of about 3,000: certainly a respectable figure, but tiny as a proportion of the membershp even of the affiliated

---

[63] MCF Executive minutes (26 May 1960 and 28 July 1960) (MCF papers).
[64] Ibid. The promise was regularly, and perhaps understandably, broken.
[65] Trade Union Committee minutes (28 July 1960) (MCF papers).

unions.[66] Special conferences for trade unionists also sometimes drew large numbers of participants, especially in areas with strong traditions of union radicalism.[67] The efforts of the MCF to get British unions to invite colonial trade unionists to address their annual conferences, and to carry articles on colonial subjects in their journals, were fairly successful; but again the audience at union conferences is by definition, and the readership of union journals tends to be, composed of activists. The general conclusion with regard to MCF influence on trade union members, as with Labour Party members, must then be that it achieved a considerable amount in terms of awakening consciousness of colonial problems among the existing circles of the politically active; but, unlike, for instance, CND, it did little to mobilise the previously uninvolved.

III. THE COMMUNIST PARTY—
AND THE NEW LEFT

In 1954 the CPGB held a second major conference of Communist Parties from 'countries within the sphere of British Imperialism'. This brought together representatives from a slightly wider range of colonial and Commonwealth territories than had its predecessor in 1947, including Australia, Canada, Cyprus, Iraq, Ireland, and the Sudan; with observers from Trinidad, Egypt, and Jamaica and reports from Malaya, the West Indies, India, Ceylon, Nigeria, Mauritius, and British Guiana given by British-resident nationals of those countries.[68]

Palme Dutt's long statement introducing the conference, The Way Forward, was largely devoted to analysing the changes in imperialism which he believed to have taken place since 1947, and the consequent altered views of the Communist movement. He identified six major developments in the situation of the colonial world:

1. The victory of the Chinese revolution;
2. The independence of India—and here he adopted the new Soviet

---

[66] Interview with Barbara Haq.

[67] For instance in South Wales, where about 450 miners attended a meeting on Kenya in early 1960; see MCF Executive Report (6 Jan. to 9 Mar. 1960) (MCF papers).

[68] *Allies for Freedom* (CPGB pamphlet, 1954). It is noteworthy that this conference was held within a fortnight of the MCF's founding conference; but neither gathering seems to have made any reference to the other.

attitude of praising Nehru's non-aligned stance and efforts 'in the cause of peace' whilst contrastingly, not to say contradictorily, lambasting the internal policies of the 'bankrupt Congress regime, representing the rule of big capitalists and landlords';[69]

3. The advance of colonial liberation movements elsewhere;
4. The 'offensive of US Imperialism', penetrating both Britain itself and the colonies;
5. The resulting crisis of British imperialism, manifested in 'intensified colonial exploitation' and 'catastrophic decline in the standard of living of the colonial peoples';[70]
6. The headlong drive towards a new world war induced by the aggressive advance of American, and the defensive desperation of British, imperialism, as a result of which: 'The colonial peoples are dragged against their will in the wake of the war camp.'[71]

Palme Dutt therefore urged—not, one suspects, to the great surprise of his audience—that the fight for peace was the most urgent priority for the colonial as for other peoples. Those who believed that this was a secondary consideration for the colonised, or even that the Cold War made decolonisation easier to attain, were seeking 'to separate the colonial peoples from the camp of democracy and peace, and thereby to weaken their struggle by isolating them from their strongest allies'.[72] Turning to the struggle for national liberation itself, he announced that the CPGB's previous distinctions between those countries where independence was on the immediate agenda and those where a longer struggle for democratic rights was in prospect (distinctions which had met with sharp criticism within the left) no longer applied. 'The struggle for national liberation is breaking out in every territory of the British Empire, without distinction of so-called backwardness of development.'[73] Meanwhile the US threat to both Britain and the colonies meant that a common fight of 'all the peoples of the British Empire, including the British people' against American imperialism must be mounted.[74]

Events since 1947 had also, Palme Dutt suggested, brought 'a deepening of the understanding of the meaning of national

[69] R. Palme Dutt, ibid. 8.
[70] Ibid. 14.
[71] Ibid. 15. Palme Dutt was never averse to mixing his metaphors.
[72] Ibid. 20.
[73] Ibid. 23.
[74] Ibid.

independence'. Whereas previously the CPGB had drawn a clear distinction between real and false independence, depending on the relationship between former colonial master and new state, now the real test was the post-colonial state's attitude to 'the whole camp of imperialism'—in other words, above all to the USA.[75] This would itself be an expression of the stance of those who held state power in the ex-colony: whether it was the 'upper sections of the bourgeoisie ... allied to imperialism' or 'the working class, in alliance with the peasantry and with all sections, including the national bourgeoisie, prepared to resist imperialism'.[76] This latter alliance found its model in the idea of the People's Democracy—a notion initially applied to the countries of Eastern Europe but now shown by the Chinese experience to be fully applicable to colonial and semi-colonial countries.[77] For the African and other colonies to emulate this model, the working class must come to the fore, as Palme Dutt asserted was already happening, for instance, in Kenya, and active Communist Parties formed in these countries.[78]

The position enunciated here on patterns of development for anticolonial movements is clearly a transitional one. There is a limited recognition of the progressive potential of the national bourgeoisie in the colonial revolution, and in particular of the fact that the foreign policy of states under progressive bourgeois leadership might be worthy of critical support—though only Nehru's India is singled out in this respect. On the other hand, the insistence that the upper strata of the colonial bourgeoisie are irredeemably tied to imperialism, that the working class must take the lead in attaining genuine independence, and that to this end independent Communist Parties must be founded, remains strong and strident, thus keeping the analysis tied to the orthodoxy of the Stalin era.

After 1956 this position underwent considerable alteration, as the CPGB—once more in large part following in the footsteps of the Soviet Union's policy—took an ever more charitable view of bourgeois nationalist leaderships, offering its verbal support to nationalist leaders from Jagan through Nehru, Nkrumah, and Nyerere to such unlikely figures as Hastings Banda as supposed embodiments of the

[75] Ibid. 25
[76] Ibid. 25–6.
[77] Ibid. 26–7.
[78] Ibid. 27–8.

progressive national bourgeoisie.[79] Thus in 1951 the CPGB was urging Jamaican Marxists to push at all times to bring forward militant working-class demands within the nationalist movement, to reject the fraudulent notion of non-alignment proposed by the PNP leaders, and to draw workers and unemployed leaders into organised Marxist groups.[80] In 1954, for Nigeria, a dual strategy was proposed: recognition of the NCNC and, to a lesser extent, the Action Group as the major anti-imperialist organisations whilst trying to win them over to a more progressive policy; and simultaneous attempts to bring together the scattered Nigerian Marxist circles into a Communist Party.[81] By 1960 interest centred almost wholly on the possibilities for evolution towards socialist ideas *within* the main colonial nation-alist movements; no emphasis was laid on the practicability or desirability of forming independent Marxist parties. Indeed the Marxist United Working People's Party of Nigeria, whose foundation was precisely what the CPGB had been calling for in 1954, was now condemned as 'sectarian and dogmatic' and criticised for its 'complete isolation from the national movement'.[82]

Among the African leaders, by the early 1960s, Nkrumah in particular was regarded with high hopes. 'Dr Nkrumah's definition of socialism is nearer to the Marxist standpoint than that of any non-Communist leader in Africa', suggested the CPGB in 1963.[83] Whilst the party was not of course quite unaware of the variations in local circumstances between, for instance, Jamaica, Nigeria, and Ghana or the way those circumstances changed over the decade, it is clear that these different evaluations owed far more to a shifting theoretical orientation than to analysis of individual colonial situations. Indeed,

[79] Thus whilst John Hatch, in July 1959, recognised that Banda 'has deteriorated ... not only being looked on as a Messiah but acting like one. He obviously considers himself to be a complete dictator' (Report of Central Africa trip (July 1959), LP/CSC/58/53/0), Idris Cox of the CPGB wrote of the 'love and affection' felt for Banda 'by all Africans ... [he] stands out like a giant among pygmies' (*WN* (1 Aug. 1959), 371). Cox, of course, had the advantage of having never visited Nyasaland.

[80] CPGB letter to Richard Hart (Nov. 1951) (dated in Hart's hand: Hart papers 4/8). Mr Hart was unable to recall the author—but it is evident from style, content, and context that this was an official statement of the CP's views on Jamaica rather than an individual communication. The drafter of the letter is most likely to have been Michael Carritt.

[81] 'What Next in Nigeria', part 2, *WN* (14 Aug. 1954), 649–52.

[82] CPGB memorandum, 'African National Movements and Leaders' (anon., but clearly by Jack Woddis, late 1960; Marx Memorial Library files).

[83] 'African Socialism and Marxism', document prepared by the CPGB Africa Committee (13 Dec. 1963) (anon., but probably drafted by Idris Cox; MML files).

as Alec Gordon suggests, the very formulation of the theory of the national bourgeoisie and the canonical status it assumed led to a rather desperate search for candidates for the label in any and every colonial country:

For example, the 1959 Marxist Seminar brought together the representatives of twelve communist parties from all three continents of the Third World. *All* of them claimed to identify a vigorous national bourgeoisie in their respective countries, and if any of them, or of the others present, thought there was one country in the three continents without a national bourgeoisie, no mention was made of it.[84]

During the late 1950s official Communist theory developed, in conjunction with this concept of the national bourgeoisie, the notion that, in countries where such a class, together with other progressive forces, was in power, a non-capitalist path to development might be pursued. This was characterised by a non-aligned and anti-imperialist stance in international affairs, a policy of self-reliant economic development drawing aid from both capitalist and socialist countries, largely under state control and accompanied by agrarian reform, and the eventual building of an industrial sector.[85] While not itself socialist, such a path—on which, for instance, Nkrumah's Ghana was held to be heading—laid the foundations for socialism. CPGB writers adopted and expounded this idea in a number of works relating to Africa, though they cannot be claimed to have made any very original contribution to it.[86] They were especially concerned to point out that, whilst the idea of the non-capitalist road implied that

---

[84] Alec Gordon, 'The Theory of the "Progressive" National Bourgeoisie', *Journal of Contemporary Asia*, 3/2 (1973), 199. The fullest contemporary CPGB expression of views on this issue is Idris Cox's contribution to the seminar, in Leipzig, to which Gordon refers: *World Marxist Review* (Aug. 1959). On the background to these ideas, see Hélène Carrère d'Encausse and Stuart R. Schram, *Marxism and Asia* (Allen Lane, 1969), and Stephen Clarkson, *The Soviet Theory of Development: India and the Third World in Marxist–Leninist Scholarship* (Macmillan, 1978), esp. chs. 7–11.

[85] The standard Soviet expressions of this theory are I. Andreyev, *The Non-Capitalist Way: Soviet Experience and the Liberated Countries* (Moscow: Progress Publishers, 1977); R. A. Ulyanovsky, *Socialism and the Newly Independent Nations* (Moscow: Progress Publishers, 1974); and K. N. Brutents, *National Liberation Movements Today* (Moscow: Progress Publishers, 1977). On its emergence, see Carrère d'Encausse and Schram, *Marxism and Asia*, 74–9, 287–91, 306–16; also Joe Slovo, 'A Critical Appraisal of the Non-Capitalist Path and the National-Democratic State in Africa', *Marxism Today* (June 1974); Fred Halliday and Maxine Molyneux, *The Ethiopian Revolution* (New Left Books, 1981), ch. 7.

[86] See Jack Woddis, *Africa: The Way Ahead* (Lawrence & Wishart, 1963); Idris Cox, *Socialist Ideas in Africa* (Lawrence & Wishart, 1966).

different countries could pursue different means in moving towards socialism, the essential model of an achieved socialist society remained the USSR. Thus the notion of a specific 'African Socialism' as expounded by Senghor or Nyerere and defended by Hatch or Brockway was wholly rejected.

This new theoretical stance, and the consequently far more favourable attitude expressed by the CPGB towards the major existing nationalist movements, were relatively uncontroversial within the party. Criticism emerged only in the early 1960s, when a small number of CPGB members adopted the Maoist viewpoint in the wake of the Sino-Soviet schism. These, like the Chinese themselves, regarded the Soviet-line Communists' approval of bourgeois colonial nationalism as one of the most significant among their many revisionist heresies.[87] At the time, these were very marginal criticisms, at least within Britain; very few British Communists became converts to Maoism, though some small organisations of the anticolonialist fringe did adopt a pro-Chinese view largely because China emerged during the 1960s as apparently a more militant anticolonial power than the USSR. Most active of these was the British Guiana Freedom Association, led by Guianese accountant Johnny James, which was associated with the MCF. (James, an MCF Executive member in the mid-1960s, later played a key role among the militants who tore apart the Campaign Against Racial Discrimination in 1967).[88] More important was that the CPGB's more ecumenical attitude to colonial nationalism facilitated its co-operation on these issues with other groups on the left: within front organisations like the Kenya Committee and the Association for African Freedom—the latter a tiny London group producing the monthly *Africa Bulletin* in 1954–7[89]— and increasingly within the MCF. By the early 1960s CPGB anticolonial activity was largely channelled into the latter organisation.

If this transformation of attitudes to non-Communist nationalism and to the prospect for non-capitalist development aroused little dissent in the CPGB, the same could not be said of all colonial

---

[87] See letter by Michael McCreery (later founder of the first British Maoist group) in *WN* (18 Nov. 1961), 568–9, attacking an article by Kay Beauchamp which praised Nkrumah.

[88] See B. W. Heinemann, Jun., *The Politics of the Powerless* (Oxford University Press/Institute of Race Relations, 1972), ch. 5.

[89] On ceasing operations in Apr. 1957, *Africa Bulletin*, run by M. Bassett, urged its supporters to work instead in the MCF.

issues. During the later 1950s two questions were heatedly debated within the party: the familiar controversy over the consequences of imperialism for British workers, and the problem of post-independence relationships between Britain and her ex-colonies. On the first, there were renewed complaints that the party was failing to present the anticolonial struggle as what its own theory said it should be: an integral part of the struggle of the British working class. Idris Cox hammered away at this issue time after time;[90] and Frank Oruwari, a Nigerian CPGB member, turned it into a general critique of the party's priorities:

This lukewarm attitude to the colonial question does disservice to the British Labour movement and to the colonial peoples, some of whom do not refrain from accusing the Party of parading ringing words which has [*sic*] become the stock-in-trade of the world progressive movement... The campaign against colonial wars and repressions is one of those issues which are most likely to draw very wide and divergent sections of the public into mass action. Many Liberal and Labour people who normally read sinister motives into every action taken by Communists will not hesitate to endorse and support a campaign in aid of the freedom of some remote outpost of empire.[91]

The CP, Oruwari charged, had failed to seize such opportunities; and had neither mobilised British workers nor made sufficient effort to recruit and arouse colonial people in Britain.

Calling for more effort to arouse British workers against colonialism was simple enough, but the issue of those workers' economic gain or loss from the system they were being called upon to destroy remained as vexed as it had been in the 1920s. In March 1957 the Birmingham Town Branch of the party used the letters column of *World News* (the nearest thing to an open forum of debate within the CPGB, and rather more open in the aftermath of Hungary and the Secret Speech than before) to argue that *all* the people of Britain were beneficiaries of the proceeds from colonial exploitation:

This is ignored in the present draft [of the party programme] which promises everything to everyone, without facing the real difficulties which exist now and could increase with the recognition of the sovereignty of the colonial countries.[92]

---

[90] See his articles in *WN* (31 Jan. 1959 and 25 Mar. 1961); and his booklet, *Empire Today* (Lawrence & Wishart, 1960).
[91] From CPGB 24th Congress Report, *WN* (28 Apr. 1956), 270–1.
[92] Letter in *WN* (23 Mar. 1957).

The official party view was presented a few months later, but was remarkable for its vagueness. There were, it was suggested, no real benefits to the British people from colonialism since trade between free peoples would bring greater rewards and 'There is no guarantee that even a tiny share of the big profits from the colonies means higher wages in Britain.'[93] This was a curious formulation—'no guarantee'—apparently deliberately evading the question whether in fact any section of the British work-force *did* receive such a share; and thus remaining agnostic on whether the classical Leninist theory of the labour aristocracy remained valid.

Implicitly, however, it would seem that Lenin was being thrown overboard. That at least was how Peter Seltman, another who was later to become a Maoist, read the article. In a lengthy reply he stormed that the party line 'stands in diametrical opposition to the conclusions arrived at by Lenin'. Yet Seltman's argument was not merely a pious rehash of Vladimir Ilyich; indeed it in effect anticipates the unequal exchange theory of Arghiri Emmanuel. Because of unequal technological development, there was far higher productivity of labour in the metropolitan countries, thus enabling the bourgeoisie to concede higher wages there whilst extracting super-profits primarily in the colonies. Therefore the section of the working class in Britain profiting from imperialism had 'become the dominant force', so that the whole of the British proletariat gained from Empire. The new (and he believed final) crisis of imperialism, however, opened the prospect that this situation and the consequent reactionary tendency of British workers would be reversed. But unless the CPGB clarified its thinking on these issues it would be unable to offer a lead out of the crisis.[94]

Kay Beauchamp responded to this argument on behalf of the CPGB leadership. Seltman's presentation of Lenin, she suggested, was 'one-sided'. Lenin had seen the 'bribe' of a minority of workers as coexisting with 'oppression and insecurity for the mass of the workers in imperialist countries, as well as for the colonial peoples'. Far from it being the case, as Seltman had argued, that the tendencies described in the theory of the labour aristocracy had grown stronger since the 1930s: 'In fact, in Lenin's view, the classic period of the

---

[93] 'Must We Have Colonies?', in *WN* Special Issue, 'Together Against Imperialism' (29 June 1957). Not signed, but presumably by Idris Cox.
[94] P. E. Seltman, 'Colonial Exploitation and the British Workers', *WN* (31 Aug. 1957), 558–9.

complete domination of opportunism was in Britain in the last half of the nineteenth century' (a somewhat eccentric reading of Lenin!). Beauchamp concluded that:

imperialism has never been in the interests of the *majority* of British workers, even in the narrow economic sense . . . the real choice before the British people is not capitalism with colonies or capitalism without colonies, but imperialism or socialism.[95]

An extensive correspondence followed. One reader quite reasonably complained that debate was being conducted by 'quotation from the past rather than realistic analysis'; and went on to assert that both sides in the debate had underestimated the effects of class struggle within Britain. The only sense in which British workers had gained from colonialism was that the latter had provided an alternative to fascism for the British ruling class, thereby postponing the final struggle for power.[96] Ian Watson from Glasgow felt that whilst in the past colonialism had weakened the British class struggle (whether through economic bribes or some other means he did not say) now the rising of the colonial peoples was altering that: true Marxist leadership would soon sweep away both capitalism and colonialism.[97]

Seltman hit back in January 1958, correctly pointing out that Beauchamp had omitted to address his central point, which was on the difference between British and colonial living standards and the causes of this difference. She had failed to understand the distinction between *relative* impoverishment and an *absolute* rise in living standards in Britain. The important thing now was to recognise that this imperialist era was coming to an end; the Labour Party's views (which he characterised as 'We are doing well out of the Empire') were becoming increasingly out of touch. The CP must fill the gap, and thus far had wholly failed to do so. Unless it presented revolutionary theory to the masses it would 'degenerate into a Social Democratic Party of the worst type'.[98]

The following month Idris Cox had what the CPGB leadership evidently intended to be the last word. Seltman, he said, had distorted Lenin—and he went on himself wildly to distort Seltman's argument.

[95] Kay Beauchamp, 'Has the Empire Improved Our Living Standards?', ibid. (9 Nov. 1957), 708–9. Emphasis in original.
[96] Letter from 'P. S. (Kent)', ibid. (23 Nov. 1957), 748.
[97] Letter from Ian Watson, ibid.
[98] Letter from Peter Seltman, ibid. (4 Jan. 1958), 5–6.

He attacked him for saying that colonial exploitation was the sole determinant of British living standards (which Seltman had not done), whereas Britain's general international situation was the determining factor. In the present position, Cox argued, it was not economically possible for British imperialism to corrupt any substantial section of the working class, though 'it must be recognised that the impact of imperialist ideology (fortified by its alliance with US imperialism) is still strong'.[99] This last was again an odd suggestion, since the CPGB had been claiming for more than a decade that American imperialism was undermining and taking over the British Empire. How, therefore, it might be held to fortify British imperialist ideology—unless the meaning being attached to the term 'imperialism' had shifted in mid-sentence—is hard to see.

Also during 1956–8, the Communist Party engaged in an even more intense—if often equally abstract—internal debate over the notion, presented in party programmes since the mid-1940s, of post-independence fraternal association between Britain and the ex-colonies. In December 1956 Idris Cox pointed out (as Richard Hart had noticed almost ten years before) that the party programme muddled the Empire, the Commonwealth, and the colonies—Communists were guilty, he said, of 'a slavish adherence to existing *forms* of the Empire political structure which serves only to hide the real *content* of imperialist exploitation'. A related but more serious defect lay in attachment to the idea of fraternal association:

whatever phrase we use to present a future 'association' of the 'existing countries of the empire' cannot fail to give the impression that we seek to create a new kind of empire on the ruins of the breakdown of the existing system.[100]

A response to this call for change in CPGB policy came from Jean Feldman:

a socialist Britain cannot give independence unconditionally and in all circumstances. We could not give a colonial people 'freedom' to be snapped up by another imperialist power and used as a puppet in the struggle against us. And this could easily happen in a colony which has learnt to hate us as enemies. It is essential to link self-determination with the obligation to join us in an anti-imperialist alliance.[101]

---

[99] Idris Cox, 'What Determines British Living Standards', ibid. (22 Feb. 1958), 126–7.
[100] Letter from Idris Cox, ibid. (1 Dec. 1956), 770–1.
[101] Letter, ibid. (2 Feb. 1957), 77.

This attitude, there seems little doubt, merely spelt out with brutal frankness what lay implicit in the party's programme. A new Empire was indeed to be built on the ruins of the old, under the title of an anti-imperialist alliance, membership of which would be obligatory. Once again the contrast between the early Bolsheviks' proclamation of the right to secede and the later practical denial of that right cannot have been far from many minds. The counter-attack was not slow in coming: Margot Parish, a CPGB member who had been active in the Kenya Committee and other anticolonialist organisations charged that Feldman's contention, 'supported by a large body of opinion inside our Party... is in fact imperialism in reverse'. Communists, she declared, must support the right to self-determination without qualifications. 'Any other standpoint exposes us as complete and utter hypocrites.'[102]

The clash was carried to the 25th (Special) Party Congress of the CPGB. This was the most explosive gathering in British Communist history, with the dissidents who wanted a more critical attitude to the USSR and a more democratic internal regime in the party fighting a losing battle against the hardliners. Most of those critics thereafter left the party in disgust. The Congress's most famous debate, that on Inner Party Democracy, has been much discussed.[103] Almost forgotten is that the party leaders did suffer one defeat at that Congress: over the formula of fraternal association for ex-colonies. More remarkably still, Rajani Palme Dutt, guardian of party orthodoxy for more than thirty years, led the dissident faction on the issue. A move to replace the phrase 'fraternal association' with the far less specific 'fraternal relations' (which did not carry the same overtones of formal and possible enforceable links) had been rejected by the party's International Committee, by fifteen votes to three. Yet, Palme Dutt argued on behalf of the minority, the overwhelming majority of CPGB members from colonial countries supported the minority formula; and none of the other Communist Parties in the Empire had ever accepted the fraternal association idea. Many colonial peoples,

---

[102] Letter, ibid. (9 Mar. 1957), 156.

[103] See the accounts of the 1956 battles by John Saville, Malcolm MacEwen, and Margot Heinemann in *The Socialist Register 1976* and David Widgery (ed.), *The Left in Britain, 1956–1968* (Harmondsworth: Penguin, 1976), 43–91. The bitterness is well captured by John McLoughlin's interruption of Moscow loyalist Andrew Rothstein's speech. The latter had been warning that criticism of the USSR would be used by 'the enemy'. At which McLoughlin, a working-class dissident, roared 'You are the enemy, you lying old swine!' (ibid. 59).

he pointed out, were suspicious of all British political parties: 'If we announce that we intend to transform the Empire into some new organisation called a fraternal association we are giving needless grounds for such suspicions.' There was, he warned, a danger of the CPGB succumbing to 'great-power chauvinism'.[104]

Émile Burns, like Palme Dutt a veteran of over thirty years' campaigning on colonial issues, replied on behalf of the Executive majority. He protested that the association envisaged would be, and had always been intended to be, purely voluntary. He pointed out that many ex-colonial countries had chosen to remain in the Commonwealth for good economic and political reasons: how much stronger would those reasons be when Britain became socialist! To fail to maintain association between Britain and the colonies 'would be to repudiate Britain's responsibility for the past and for the future ... I hope that you will reject the purely negative approach of the minority'.[105]

This was an extraordinary speech, directly echoing many of the classic arguments deployed against the anticolonial left by their opponents—that theirs was 'purely negative' opposition to Empire; that to seek decolonisation without preconditions or continued links was to evade Britain's historic responsibility; that the Commonwealth (which the CP had always derided as a neo-colonialist arrangement) was a valuable fraternal association. To hear these arguments from a Communist towards the end of decolonisation is remarkable. It is hardly surprising that this appeal failed to convince the delegates, and that one of the very few defeats for the leadership in the CPGB's history took place. Henceforth the party advocated only fraternal relations between the former countries of the Empire.

The anti-Stalinist dissidents who had resigned or been expelled from the CPGB in the battles of 1956–7 took various political directions thereafter. Some abandoned politics altogether; some fulfilled the expectations of the party loyalists by moving far to the right; some entered the Labour Party. A fairly large group, however, including some of the CPGB's erstwhile leading intellectuals, sought in a number of ways to carry on what they saw as the positive aspects of the British Communist tradition within new political forms. These groups, most influential among whom were those clustered around an

---

[104] Report of 25th Congress Discussion, *WN* (18 May 1957), 315.
[105] Ibid. 316–17.

independent socialist journal, *The New Reasoner*, edited by John Saville and Edward Thompson, became the nucleus of the so-called New Left. They soon attracted to their ranks a new generation of recruits from among those radicalised by CND, together with some of the less orthodox of the Trotskyists. The New Left was extremely varied in formation and ideology, and soon clear generational divisions were to appear within it. An important common theme at the start, none the less, was the notion of socialist humanism, most eloquently expressed by Edward Thompson; and implying a strong ethical condemnation equally of capitalism, of Stalinism, and of colonialism.

The *New Reasoner* devoted much of its editorial space to colonial and Third World subjects: and it expressed in unusually pure form (if one unusually infused with historical self-consciousness) the mixture of socialist arguments and Radical-Liberal humanitarian appeals characteristic of British anticolonialism. What Thompson and Saville made of the tradition is best conveyed by quoting *in extenso* from their commentary on the Cyprus conflict. They began by invoking the memory of the Governor Eyre controversy, and the role played by the intellectual leaders of British liberalism, exemplified by John Stuart Mill, in exposing the atrocity. They went on:

All this is grimly relevant to our situation today. The record of Britain's colonial administration in the post-war years in Palestine, Kenya and Cyprus—to mention only the countries where the worst of our misdeeds have been committed—cries out for the courage and the passionate sense of justice displayed by Mill ... Socialists do not need reminding of the duties of international solidarity, and of the absolute political and ethical prohibition, which their principles dictate, against participating in any degree whatsoever, direct or indirect, in the repression of a movement for national self-determination. But, in appealing to the Parliamentary Labour Party, and to the kept Labour press, it is no longer fruitful to appeal to any socialist principle. We must therefore ask them: do you in *any* sense respect the liberal and radical traditions symbolised by Mill?[106]

The New Left which took shape in the 1950s, then, largely from the wreckage of hopes in British Communism, espoused an anticolonialism which was recognisably in direct line of descent from the arguments of the early British socialist sects and their Radical-Liberal contemporaries. The principles of the right to national self-determination,

---

[106] John Saville and Edward Thompson, 'John Stuart Mill and EOKA', *The New Reasoner*, 7 (Winter 1958–9), 5–11. Emphasis in original.

opposition to aggression, racial equality, and a generalised internationalism survived where the economic arguments against colonialism splintered or faded. The attempt to prove that Britain or the British working class suffered economically from Empire was never able to command widespread conviction or attain complete coherence. What continued to resonate was the deeply held view that colonialism was an evil for British society, as well as for the colonised, because it was morally corrupting, inimical to the better self of British, or English, national identity.[107]

IV. NEO-COLONIALISM

Extensive formal colonial empires were, in most eyes, clearly doomed by the mid-1950s and virtually dead by the mid-1960s. The original and primary task of anticolonialist movements was in sight of completion. What had replaced, or would replace colonialism? British radicals came up with three main kinds of answer: sometimes combined or overlapping.

First was the view that transition to independence for the former colonies was a genuine revolution: political, social, and indeed moral. There might be continued attempts by declining colonial powers, and more certainly and dangerously by white settler communities, to retain one or other form of control. There were also persisting problems of economic underdevelopment, largely if not entirely caused by colonial exploitation, which it was the duty of the former imperial powers to remedy. But overall a new world order was in the making, marked by a repudiation of oppressive and exploitative relations between peoples, and the main question for Britain was whether her rulers would have the political vision to participate in it. To do so would require a major programme of overseas aid; sometimes argued for as part of a radically new direction in Britain's overseas economic relations as a whole, orientated towards links with the post-colonial states. It also necessitated intense efforts to overcome the racial antagonisms which were seen as legacies of colonialism: above all in southern Africa and in Britain itself. The

[107] The historical work of Saville and Thompson, with that of many other radical and ex-Communist British historians, derived much of its passion as well as its choice of subject-matter from the desire to salvage and revive this idea of an alternative national tradition.

campaign against colonialism, then, was replaced by two parallel crusades: against hunger and poverty, and against racism. This was the attitude taken by many liberals and most of the Labour left, and perhaps especially by the nexus of pacifists, ex-members of the ILP, and New Leftists for whom Brockway was becoming a kind of father figure.

The second response held that political independence was at root a fraud; or at least that Britain was trying her utmost to make it so. The change from Empire to Commonwealth was a purely semantic one.[108] Britain was seeking, with at least partial success, to maintain her imperial role by transferring authority to approved if not manufactured successors, retaining exploitative economic arrangements, and tying new states to the former colonial metropole through manipulative political, diplomatic, cultural, and military structures.

A third argued that the decline of the old colonial powers was genuine, but marked not so much the rise of Asia and Africa as that of the USSR and more particularly the USA. Thus a new imperialism threatened to perpetuate or supplant the old. One version of this belief saw Soviet Communism as the primary threat to the post-colonial world: a perception which itself had both social-democratic and far left anti-Stalinist variants. Another, associated with the remaining proponents of the Third Force idea, claimed that both superpowers were equally dangerous, and equally culpable. The emergent Third World states, and the non-aligned movement in which several of them took the lead, offered the best if not the only hope of carving out a path wholly independent of both. Indeed Third Force ideas were given a new lease of life from the 1955 Bandung conference, the 1962 Accra anti-nuclear summit, and similar events sponsored by various newly independent governments.[109]

The most influential version of this thesis, however, saw the United States as the main if not sole culprit in pursuing a new imperialism. This claim was of course an increasingly central one for Communists, including the CPGB, from the late 1940s onwards:

---

[108] A charge made at greatest length in R. Palme Dutt, *The Crisis of Britain and the British Empire* (Lawrence & Wishart, 1953). John Strachey launched an interesting counter-attack in support of the reality of decolonisation and the progressiveness of the Commonwealth in *The End of Empire* (Gollancz, 1959), 195–200, 249–50.

[109] For a vividly hostile historical sketch of these tendencies on the British left, seen as manifestations of imperialist pacifism, see James Hinton, *Protests and Visions: Peace Politics in 20th Century Britain* (Hutchinson, 1989), esp. 177–8, 180–1, 185.

though it was shared by many non-Communists and even some Conservatives. As we have seen, it was utilised by CP theorists like Palme Dutt in conjunction with the assertion that a declining and now subservient British imperialism was seeking to maintain its hold by new means. Thus anticolonialism was combined with British nationalism in the notion of a dual national liberation struggle of both British and colonial peoples against both British and American imperialism. Palme Dutt argued that:

The expansionist aims of American imperialism in relation to the British Empire are unconcealed. These aims grow daily more aggressive and emphatic...the most modern Conservative 'patriots' of imperialism (or, rather, of super-imperialism) [want] to hand over the British Empire on a plate to the American masters.[110]

So much of the anticolonialist left, especially but not only Marxists, came to believe some variant, or more often mixture, of the second and third arguments about decolonisation. They held that Britain and other colonial powers were seeking to exert control or influence by new, less direct means; and that simultaneously the USA was building a new informal empire. The term which came into widespread use in the early 1960s to describe these phenomena was of course 'neo-colonialism'. The origins of the word are uncertain. Its ubiquity in Third World political discourse probably owed more to Kwame Nkrumah than anyone else; but neither he nor the ghost-writers he increasingly used after 1957 invented it. Palme Dutt himself was, as Basil Davidson noted, often credited with the coinage; but he denied it, telling Davidson that 'I would never have personally invented such a barbarous term...since I preferred the simple English, "the New Colonialism"'.[111] Equally, the word was never clearly defined: evidently it, almost as much as 'imperialism' itself, functioned as a word of rhetoric and suspicion more than of analysis.

The third All-African Peoples' Conference in Cairo in 1961 had listed eight forms of neo-colonialism: a charge-sheet approvingly cited by the MCF's Jack Woddis and Leon Szur:

1. Puppet governments in independent new states;
2. Grouping states into federations linked to the imperialist powers;

---

[110] Palme Dutt, *Crisis of Britain and the British Empire*, 486–8.
[111] R. Palme Dutt letter to Basil Davidson of 18 Jan. 1974, quoted in Davidson, *Let Freedom Come: Africa in Modern History* (Boston, Mass.: Atlantic-Little Brown, 1978), 412.

3. Balkanisation and deliberate fragmentation of new states;
4. Continuation of economic dependence;
5. Integration into imperialist-dominated economic blocs, perpetuating underdevelopment;
6. Economic penetration through capital investment and loans;
7. Direct monetary control;
8. Retention of military bases by former colonial powers.[112]

It was a somewhat haphazard list: points 4, 5, and 6, for instance, seem to be the same phenomenon differently described. In contrast to such eclectic uses of the term by African nationalists, it entered British political debate almost exclusively from the pens of Marxists, and was used to describe primarily *economic* processes. As Woddis and Szur said in the MCF's pamphlet on the subject: 'The real purpose of neo-colonialism is to ensure the continued exploitation of economic resources, and wherever possible to extend economic influence and domination.'[113] Within the MCF, enthusiasm for polemicising on the issue clearly came from the organisation's Marxist and Communist element, from Woddis, Szur, John Eber, and Ian Page, rather than from Brockway or other Labour people.

Thus Woddis, in his and Szur's pamphlet and more explicitly in drafting MCF 'Speakers' Notes on Neo-Colonialism', presented an orthodox Communist view of colonialism and decolonisation radically different in language from the moral appeals of almost all earlier MCF propaganda. Colonialism was distinguished above all by deliberate underdevelopment: monocultural agrarian economies directed to exports in favour of the colony-owning power, total dependence on imports for even the most elementary manufactured goods, lack of 'basic facilities and social welfare'.[114] Neo-colonialism aimed to perpetuate this; and had been resorted to because the rise of the USSR, even more than that of colonial nationalism, had 'weakened world imperialism'. Where they could, colonial powers sought to retain direct control. Where they could not, it resorted to a battery of political, military, cultural, diplomatic, and above all economic means to retain 'essentially the same' relationships as hitherto.[115]

[112] Resolution from 1961 All-African Peoples' Congress, Cairo, cited in MCF, *What is Neo-Colonialism?* (MCF pamphlet, 1961), 11–12.

[113] Ibid. 4.

[114] Jack Woddis, 'Speakers' Notes on Neo-Colonialism', sent to John Eber (20 Feb. 1963) (MCF papers).

[115] Ibid. 10.

The European Community too was seen as a 'collective form of neo-colonialism' in that it enabled joint exploitation of African territories by a group of European powers; and of course the World Bank and IMF were neo-colonial institutions *par excellence.*[116] The way out of this trap for ex-colonies lay in industrialisation, economic planning, the development of a dominant state sector in the economy, land reform, government control of foreign trade, and investment leading to the eventual nationalisation of imperialist monopolies. Most extensively discussed by Woddis was, perhaps predictably, the benefits of 'socialist aid' from the USSR and other Communist states. This was argued to be in every way different from the West's manipulative aid projects, selfless and non-exploitative. This was partly so on the rather peculiar grounds that: 'Not a penny of socialist money is invested in a developing country, and therefore not a penny profit is taken out.'[117] And finally, Woddis urged once more that neo-colonialism, like colonialism, was damaging to Britain too:

Since the big British monopoly firms still exploiting the newly independent states are the same firms, the same interests, often the same people exploiting the British working class and holding back social progress in Britain, we have a common interest in helping the newly independent people to win their complete liberation by winning economic independence and cutting themselves free from military entanglements.[118]

Such attempts to link the future of the former colonies intimately with that of Britain were, however, never widely espoused beyond the narrow circles of the left's colonial specialists. And the orthodox Communist version of these arguments was, of course, substantially discredited by its entirely uncritical attitude to Soviet aims, to the USSR's attempts to manipulate colonial nationalist movements and newly independent states, and to the Soviet dictatorship itself. In relation to the economics of decolonisation as in response to late colonial wars, a fresher and more imaginative reaction came from New Left writers.

Perhaps the most powerful left-wing riposte to both Communist apologetics and traditional anticolonialism came from Peter Worsley in *Out of Apathy*, the influential collection of New Left essays edited by Edward Thompson in 1960. Suez, so Worsley argued, had shown how little room for manœuvre old-style colonialism now had. Its decline had been evident ever since Indian independence became

[116] Ibid. 12–13.   [117] Ibid. 15.   [118] Ibid. 16.

inevitable, even though it had appeared to gain a new lease of life in the 1950s wars of decolonisation. That appearance was misleading, since 'at any moment, the interests of *colon* and settler, planter and mine company, might conflict with the overall diplomatic and economic strategy of the "Free World" in its contest with Communism'.[119] And when they did, the latter would inevitably prevail—however desperately the French in Algeria, especially, might fight against history's verdict. Britain had been apparently wiser than France; but her 'surrender' to junior partnership with the USA, passing up the post-war opportunity to forge a non-aligned path, had led her too into deadly dangerous waters. The 'traditional Left' had almost entirely missed the significance of this: 'preoccupied primarily with resistance to these gross and brutal forms of imperialism [like apartheid and the Kenyan Emergency] . . . the Left's reaction has itself become traditionalised, and the newer forms of imperialism have gone unchallenged because they are so often unrecognised.'[120]

The picture Worsley then went on to draw of the 'new imperialism' was not in essence so very different from the emerging critique of neo-colonialism presented elsewhere on the left. But he did at least emphasise that the damaging effects of the Cold War on the underdeveloped world did not stem only from one side; that even a Britain subordinate to the USA still played a semi-autonomous role in many of her traditional spheres of influence; and that within this not only the traditional imperial interests but also, and increasingly, new social and economic forces in Britain were deeply involved in global networks of exploitation. Whatever its inadequacies, here was sketched a picture of dying colonialism and new world alignments which, unlike most other British left-wing thinking about decoloni-sation, looked forward to the politics of the 1960s and beyond.

V. 1964—FROM NEW DAWN
TO NEW DISAPPOINTMENT

Bidding farewell to Labour's Commonwealth Department in his last report, John Hatch said that his decision to leave had been made easy by the fact that 'the broad lines of the Party's Commonwealth and

[119] Peter Worsley, 'Imperial Retreat', in E. P. Thompson (ed.), *Out of Apathy* (Stevens & Sons for New Left Books, 1960), 106.
[120] Ibid. 111–12.

colonial policy are now firmly laid down and well established'. The British Labour movement, he believed, had now awoken to its responsibilities to the colonial peoples. Close personal ties had been built up between Labour and socialist and nationalist movements throughout the Commonwealth; and he believed that Labour's pressure was now having a considerable effect on the Conservative Government's colonial policy. So important did he feel this to be that he actually informed Iain Macleod that it was the latter's enlightened policies which enabled him, Hatch, to leave his Labour Party post with a feeling that the job was largely done.[121]

The view that Macleod and Macmillan had in effect done what Labour would have wanted to do in granting political independence to most of the remaining colonies did not of course extend to all parts of the Labour Party, nor to every area of colonial policy. It certainly did not spread into a generalised feeling of goodwill towards Conservative colonial Ministers. Indeed many on the left regarded Macleod's successor, Duncan Sandys, as the most difficult, obdurate, and arrogant Minister they had ever had to deal with at the Colonial Office.[122] It did mean, though, that by the time the Wilson Government assumed office in 1964 most of the bitterly contested issues of the 1950s had been disposed of in one way or another. And for the colonial questions which still remained unresolved—most crucially the fate of Southern Rhodesia—anticolonialists felt they had every reason to expect that the new Government would be on their side.

Wilson's Government seemed committed not only to rapid decolonisation and dismantling white settler power in most of the remaining imperial possessions, but to many other policies long advocated by anticolonialists. It was pledged to introduce major initiatives in overseas aid and to work for the eradication of world poverty: something on which the new Prime Minister had himself written with passion during the 1950s.[123] It had declared its intention of taking legislative action against racial discrimination in Britain: something long campaigned for by Brockway and the Movement for Colonial Freedom. The MCF, in particular, felt that it could virtually

---

[121] Hatch's last report to CSC (June 1961), LP/CSC/60/13. Conversation with Macleod reported in interview with author by Lord Hatch.

[122] A view expressed in interview by Tony Benn, Lord Brockway, and Bob Edwards.

[123] Harold Wilson, *The War on World Poverty: An Appeal to the Conscience of Mankind* (Gollancz, 1953).

count on this Government as its own; just as had the FCB that of 1945. There were seven MCF sponsors in the Cabinet, including Wilson himself. The new Ministers for the Colonies and for Overseas Development, Anthony Greenwood and Barbara Castle, had been actively involved in MCF campaigns for years.

These hopes of the anticolonial left for the Wilson Government were, of course, to be bitterly disappointed. Its policies—or perhaps rather its lack of them—over Rhodesia; its stance on the Nigerian Civil War, on immigration, in support of the USA over Vietnam, and on many other aspects of relations between Britain and the under-developed world were to be the subject of denunciation and recrimination from the left throughout Wilson's terms of office.

Perhaps more bitter were the frustrated or betrayed hopes for post-colonial development in the new states themselves. Those who had believed that the ending of formal colonial rule would virtually in and of itself unblock paths to economic growth, no less than those who had expected it to resolve ethnic, religious, and ideological tensions within colonial territories, and those who expected it to usher in socialist transformation in both colonies and metropole—and we have seen all these beliefs held on the left in the post-war years—found themselves disappointed. Nationalist leaders whom the British left had championed, even identified themselves with, fell victim to military coups or factional strife. Some saw their newly created countries collapse before their eyes. Some saw power snatched from their hands. Perhaps saddest of all for their British supporters, some moved towards dictatorship in order to retain power. Fenner Brockway recalled a miserable last meeting with an old friend:

I saw Nkrumah again only a few weeks before his overthrow . . . I asked for a few words with him alone and pleaded once more for the release of untried political prisoners, some of whom I was convinced were innocent of inciting violence. It might be so, answered the President, but when a conspiracy was planned it was better that a few innocent victims should suffer than that the conspiracy should succeed. I told him that his actions were making our support in England for African freedom more difficult. 'Perhaps you, too, Fenner, are a necessary victim' Kwame said.[124]

[124] Brockway, *Towards Tomorrow*, 206.

8

Conclusions

The story of British anticolonialism is one of success in failure, and of failure in success. The post-war British left did not attain more than a fraction of the diverse objectives which it had set for itself. Socialism, whatever that was, had not come to Britain. Nor had nuclear disarmament, industrial democracy, extended social ownership, economic equality, a fundamental and irreversible shift in the balance of wealth and power. Decolonisation was the great exception. Here, and almost here alone, the left saw its hopes realised and its predictions brought to pass. We have traced the fortunes of a series of radical groups, usually small in size and often apparently marginal to the political process, proclaiming militant opposition to British colonialism. It was an opposition which, though drawing many of its arguments from Marxism, rested primarily on ethical claims derived from an older political language of democratic radicalism. Within this language of anticolonialism, we have seen two claims emerge as paramount. One was that the Empire was in some sense damaging to the British people. Here the dominant strand of socialist discourse moved from an initial polarity between Little Englandism (the workers' movement has no interest, in any sense of that term, in the Empire) and Constructive Imperialism (the workers' movement can build a better Empire, create a more viable role for Britain as a world power). It moved through a range of attempts, none of them fully convincing, to argue an economic relationship between imperialism and the fate of the British working class; but returned always, and ever more influentially at least within the left, to the assertion that imperialism was a form of moral contagion thwarting hopes for democratic or socialist change in Britain.

The other claim was that of the absolute right to national self-determination; and this became ever more compelling as colonial nationalist movements arose to make that demand their own. With them arose the new hope that the states emerging from decolonisation, able to avoid both the mistakes of previous attempts at social trans-

formation and the embrace of the superpowers, could provide models
for the world to follow. Such hopes, expressed at various times since
the 1930s by Pan-Africanists, ILP anticolonialists, Keep Left, and
Third Force proponents, attained their most heightened form in the
1960s with the New Left. The most extreme manifestations of this
outlook—what came pejoratively to be called Third Worldism, the
pinning of wild hopes and investment of enormous emotional capital
in every emergent African, Asian, or Latin American revolutionary
movement—were found among those caught in the long hangover of
May 1968. Some took refuge in celebration of Third World revolution
as an escape from their failure to have any political influence in
their own countries. Some came to dream, or more than dream,
of importing Third World revolution into the advanced capitalist
countries; or, as with some British socialists' attachment to the IRA,
to embrace terrorist movements in a foul parody of earlier relationships between metropolitan anticolonialists and colonial nationalists.
Such excesses in the aftermath of the 'colonial revolution' testify
in their own way to decolonisation's importance for the left. A
transformation which they had argued for and predicted, movements
which they had fostered in their infancy, had come into their own.
In the 1930s the demand for complete and general colonial independence was the exclusive preserve of tiny minorities in British politics.
Within a generation the demand had been fulfilled.

Yet few of the further consequences expected to flow from
decolonisation had in fact followed. 'Imperialism', Lenin had proclaimed, 'is the eve of the socialist revolution.' Imperialism had meant
many different things to different people in the decades after Lenin's
death. But in so far as it was identified primarily with the colonial
empires (and we have followed the ways in which this did become the
dominant understanding, even among those whose ideological bent
supposedly committed them to other meanings) then it had largely
come to an end—but such revolutions as there had been in the
interim had not come in the former imperial metropoles. As late
as 1957 a British Communist writer had said that the choice lay
not between capitalism with colonies and capitalism without colonies,
but between imperialism and socialism. Capitalism had ducked the
terms of that choice and shown itself quite able to carry on without
colonies.

Much of the British left's thinking about the economic consequences of decolonisation was thus shown to have been the purest

messianism.[1] Given a general lack of rigorous, realistic forward projection, assessments of the likely pattern of future post-colonial development—and thus a major part of the basis on which attitudes to colonial nationalism were formulated—rested almost by default on evaluations of the past colonial record. Fabians tended to believe that whatever had been the motivation for acquiring colonies in the first place, the colonial relationship had brought benefits to the colonised which could not have been won in any other way. They believed it possible and necessary, therefore, for the final stages of colonialism to be administered so as to provide a viable basis for post-colonial progress; and came to see the consequence of this view as being that the duty of metropolitan socialists was to install the necessary machinery, even if this meant resisting the claims of impatient local élites and prolonging colonial rule.

Those who believed that colonial rule inevitably implied, and was motivated by, economic exploitation naturally concluded that European rule was itself the major obstacle to any form of social and economic development. Progress could come only under indigenous leadership; and the duty of metropolitan socialists was therefore to encourage the rapid assumption to power of that leadership, after which new forms of co-operation between equals could be evolved.

Inevitably then proponents of the former view found themselves cast in the role of apologists for the colonial past, believers in the latter as apologists for the excesses of successor regimes. Avowed anticolonialists became retrospective captives to an ideology of trusteeship which they had never accepted; adherents to the ethic of self-determination came to wear some of the oldest and most threadbare clothes of a Leninism to which very few of them were

---

[1] Anticolonial activists were by no means necessarily more ignorant of colonial realities than were their opponents. Some had extensive firsthand experience, others developed a wide range of colonial contacts. But conversely, there was an obvious general shortage of real expertise, which helped facilitate the pervasive gullibility about nationalist claims. Almost as often as political passion for colonial issues grew from prior personal involvement or expertise, the reverse happened; British political activists developed a firsthand engagement because they had initially become interested in colonial problems for other, and often fairly abstract, reasons. For some, the two never really came together, perhaps especially amongst Communists; thus the CPGB's Idris Cox and Jack Woddis, for instance, were Party 'colonial experts' long before they had travelled in Britain's tropical colonies to any considerable extent (or, in Cox's case, at all). Involvement might result from what was little more than a chain of accidents, as in Basil Davidson's case or the intriguing career of Geoffrey Bing—on which see his memoirs, *Reap the Whirlwind* (MacGibbon & Kee, 1968).

conscious adherents. In retrospect, most left-wing socialists in the former colony-owning powers came to see what they or their counterparts before the mid-1960s had lauded as a colonial revolution as having been, in reality, merely a transition to neo-colonialism. The radical pessimism of Richard Crossman, Rita Hinden, or John Strachey—all of whom had argued that the prospects for any sort of democracy, let alone a democratic socialism, in post-colonial states were bleak in the extreme[2]—now seemed rather more in tune with reality than the enthusiasm of other socialist prognoses. Neither the Fabian Colonial Bureau's original belief in the potential for constructive continuity between enlightened late colonialism and its successors, nor the Movement for Colonial Freedom's faith in the innate socialist virtue of nationalist leaders, had worn very well.

Most British socialists have argued since the 1960s that the real problems of the Third World and of Britain's relations with it began to be confronted only after political independence. Many of the anticolonialists have asserted at length that they knew, even during the heat of the battles over decolonisation, that this would always be so. One does not doubt the sincerity of the claim, and occasionally the record bears them out. It is clear, though, that most did not see the issue at all in these terms at the time. Whilst most talked then of a colonial revolution, and many have argued since that what emerged was an essential continuity, a neo-colonial world system, during the period of decolonisation itself they operated in practice on the assumption that what was at stake was a far simpler process: a mere transfer of power.

This narrowing of focus, ironically, imparted a surprising degree of flexibility to anticolonialists' responses to the nationalist movements. Believing as they generally did that the transfer of political power was the precondition for all other prospects of positive change, they were able to embrace almost any significant nationalist movement and view it as a progressive force. The closeness of the concentration on self-determination, coupled with the looseness of the categories through which hopes of longer-term developments were apprehended,

---

[2] R. H. S. Crossman, 'Towards a Philosophy of Socialism', in *New Fabian Essays* (Turnstile Press, 1953), 16–25; Rita Hinden, 'New Nations', 'The Odds Against Democracy', and 'Understanding Africa', *Socialist Commentary* (Aug. 1959, Feb. 1961, and Oct. 1961); John Strachey, *The End of Empire* (Gollancz, 1959), 208–10. Strachey, it is true, took a rather sanguine view of the matter; arguing that new states were unlikely to sustain Western-style democracy but that this was less important than that they should have strong, stable government.

facilitated a freedom from prescriptive attitudes towards nationalism which neither Fabian nor classical Marxist approaches could approximate. Precisely because the left's ideals on the pattern of development in ex-colonial territories seemed further removed from immediate possibilities of realisation than those of Labour's right wing or moderate Conservatives, these ideals imposed few direct constraints on the left's short-term perspectives. They therefore brought a lighter burden of preconceptions and policy preferences to their dealings with the nationalists than did others. The very cloudiness of their conception of the future of socialism in underdeveloped countries enabled them to conflate nationalism and socialism, and to be more open to co-operation with nationalists than were those with strong prescriptive predispositions towards a particular pattern of economic and social development. The relative lack of paternalism on the left owed as much to this as to abstract good intentions. Their very idealism enabled them to respond pragmatically; whilst more practical reformers hardened to dogma.

This freedom of action—irresponsibility, in the view of their critics—was also valuable in bringing pressure to bear on authority in Britain, whether within the Labour movement or on government. Yet it remains extraordinarily difficult to assess how significant, in some overall balance, that pressure may have been. The limitations on a global evaluation have been rehearsed at length in Chapter 1. They may be recapitulated briefly by saying that we still do not have access to important parts of the official record; that many aspects of metropolitan politics in decolonisation remain virtually unstudied (like its economic consequences, the nature of media coverage, and the role of public opinion); that the historiographical debate has barely begun, with little sophisticated theoretical or comparative work yet attempted; and that there are great intrinsic difficulties in evaluating patterns of cause and effect in complex, multidimensional historical processes. David Goldsworthy comments in relation to United Nations, American, Soviet, and Indian attacks on British colonialism after 1945 that:

To what extent international criticism actually did impel change (or at least acceleration) in the last phase of British colonial policy is not, in general, an answerable question. International and domestic forces impinged on colonial policy as a complex; hence attempts to isolate and measure the effect of any one force will seldom be very rewarding.[3]

---

[3] 'Britain and the International Critics of British Colonialism, 1951–56', *JCCP* 29/1 (1991).

This evidently applies with equal force for domestic anticolonialism: indeed with greater force, since internal pressure groups are less readily isolatable as a discrete influence than are foreign governments.

Having said this, the possible influence of radical anticolonialists can be subdivided into three categories: their impact, direct or indirect, on British policy-making; their influence on colonial nationalist movements; and whatever they may have contributed to the altered global climate after 1945. The last can rapidly be disposed of. Undoubtedly the dramatic transformation of the international political scene after 1945—above all the greatly increased weight of the USA and USSR in world affairs—created an atmosphere increasingly inhospitable to Britain's imperial role in political, economic, and indeed cultural terms. Equally obviously, the domestic critics of colonialism within Britain had little direct role in this. Although the MCF and other anticolonial lobbies sought intermittently to gain a voice at the United Nations and elsewhere (lobbying at the UN through Roger Baldwin of the International League for the Rights of Man), there is no evidence at all that this carried any weight. As we have seen, even the most concerted attempts at international co-operation, those seeking to bring together British and French anticolonialists as at Puteaux in 1948, had few lasting results. Although there were continuing efforts at governmental Franco-British colonial co-operation, especially in West Africa,[4] British and French anticolonialisms were almost always *parallel* rather than connecting movements.

Only with political movements in the colonies themselves, then, was there significant, intimate, and prolonged co-operation. How important an influence on their thinking and action was the British left? Answers vary, naturally, quite enormously with time and place. They also vary with different types of colonial political actors: British-educated nationalist leaders were of course far more keenly aware of the benefits—and limitations—of working closely with sympathisers in Britain than were peasant rebels. And it seems reasonable to suggest that the general political philosophies, notions of party organisation, and post-colonial development strategies would be more heavily shaped by British socialist influences than would the particular tactics of the nationalist struggle. Indeed a loud and ostentatious refusal to have one's tactics shaped by any metropolitan influence, even a socialist one, was an increasingly necessary badge of

[4] A story now told in John Kent, *The Internationalisation of Colonialism: Britain, France, and Black Africa, 1939–1956* (Oxford: Oxford University Press, 1992).

political legitimacy for post-war nationalist movements. Specific instances have been discussed at various points throughout this book: ranging from the very heavy ideological influence of British Labour on Anglophone Caribbean nationalism or the Maltese Labour Party, through the exaggerated hopes many Kenyan activists placed in their British sympathisers, to the virtual absence of such influences in Burma.

Even less possible to evaluate with any precision is the longer-term ideological inheritance. It is a commonplace (but surely an untestable one) that the influence of British Labour philosophy, as opposed to that of French or Portuguese Communists, helped shape the distinctive post-independence political culture of many former British colonies: Nehru's, Nyerere's, or Kaunda's 'humanistic' socialism, the social democracy of many Caribbean islands, of Malta and Gibraltar, as well as of Australia and New Zealand. It has frequently been noted that a strikingly high proportion of the post-colonial states that have retained pluralist democratic systems are former British colonies. Myron Weiner suggests that 'every country with a population of at least 1 million (and almost all the smaller countries as well) that has emerged from colonial rule since World War II and has had a continuous democratic experience is a former British colony'.[5]

The significance of the claim has been queried; partly because considerably more former British colonies did *not* retain democracy, especially in Africa. And explanations for it have been disputed. Weiner, followed by Samuel Huntington and Larry Diamond, attribute it to the transfer of institutions; with Britain, unlike other decolonisers, usually ensuring a transitional period in which legal, administrative, and electoral structures were established and into which local élites were socialised.[6] Recently others have questioned the emphasis on élites and suggested instead that the granting of relative freedom to organise and propagandise for political parties and trade unions had greater weight.[7] Evidently, none of these

---

[5] 'Empirical Democratic Theory', in Myron Weiner and Ergun Ozbudun (eds.), *Competitive Elections in Developing Countries* (Washington, DC: American Enterprise Institute, 1987), 20.

[6] Samuel Huntington, 'Will More Countries Become Democratic?', *Political Science Quarterly*, 99/2 (1984); Larry Diamond, 'Introduction', in id., Juan J. Linz, and Seymour M. Lipset (eds.), *Democracy in Developing Countries: Asia* (Boulder, Colo.: Lynne Rienner,1989).

[7] Dietrich Rueschemeyer, Evelyne Huber Stephens, and John D. Stephens, *Capitalist Development and Democracy* (Cambridge: Polity,1992), esp. 225–9, 236–44, 249–68.

conditions applies to all British decolonisations. A further hypothesis may tentatively be suggested: that those former British colonies where democracy has survived have tended to be ones where contacts and ideological influences between nationalists and British democratic socialists had been relatively close and long lasting. Evidently enough, this can have been at most a minor variable; and numerous exceptions immediately suggest themselves. But even if the positive influence of British anticolonialists in helping make some post-colonial polities relatively free, stable, and just was an extremely subsidiary one, this was surely an enduringly worthwhile role to have played.

Apart from ideological influence, there is the dimension of direct aid to be considered. Again this varied very considerably. It rarely, if ever, took militant forms. There were no British parallels for the French Communists' short-lived direct action campaign against the Rif war; or for the French socialist network around Francis Jeanson which aided the FLN by smuggling arms and money.[8] Although there is fragmentary, largely anecdotal evidence of the CPGB acting as a conduit for funds from the Soviet Union for various colonial parties and trade unions, the scale and significance of this will be impossible to assess so long as the relevant records remain closed. And it does not appear to have operated in situations of colonial war: CPGB solidarity with the Malayan or Mau Mau guerrillas seems to have been almost exclusively verbal.

Yet even if British socialist help for colonial nationalists never took such dramatic forms as a minority of French leftists essayed, one also does not find British equivalents for Albert Memmi's or Frantz Fanon's bitter dismissals of metropolitan radicals as total irrelevancies to the process of decolonisation.[9] It is very unlikely that in any particular instance aid, advice, or influence from the British left to colonial nationalists decisively shaped their success or failure. It may have strengthened, or at least provided additional self-confidence for, particular individuals and parties against their rivals—acting to some degree as a counterweight to the colonial authorities' favouring of others. Unofficial British contacts may thus have aided Nkrumah against the UGCC, Maltese Labour against the Nationalist Party,

[8] On the campaign against the Rif war, see David H. Slavin, 'The French Left and the Rif War, 1925–4', *JCH* 26 (1991); on Jeanson's activities, Alistair Horne, *A Savage War of Peace* (Macmillan, 1977), 237–8, 415–17.

[9] See Albert Memmi, *The Colonizer and the Colonized* (Boston, Mass.: Beacon, 1967; orig. pub. in French 1957), 27–44; Frantz Fanon, *Towards the African Revolution* (Harmondsworth: Penguin, 1970; orig. pub. in French 1964), 86–101.

Jamaica's PNP against Bustamante: though all in ways that cannot be quantified.

To turn now to the left's role in the domestic politics of decolonisation, this too must be subdivided into direct and indirect influences. Direct influences—that is, pressure from anticolonial lobbies exercised directly upon Ministers and civil servants and leading to concrete, demonstrable results in terms of changed policies or decisions—would be easiest to establish. *If*, that is, they could be shown to have operated at all. But, as has been emphasised, in any major decision in decolonisation such pressure was only a part (undoubtedly always a subsidiary one) of the influence brought to bear on the Government.

In the case of the far-left groups who were so active in anticolonialist politics throughout our period, like Communists and Trotskyists, the presence even of a very subsidiary direct impact of this kind must be doubted. Ministers and civil servants were only with extreme rarity willing to receive representations from known Communists or other members of the far left; unless they were wearing another hat, like that of trade union leader, which entitled them at least to a courteous hearing. Even distinguished academics with significant colonial expertise were routinely excluded from official advisory roles, as were Basil Davidson and Thomas Hodgkin, if they were thought to have Marxist sympathies. So moderate a social democratic figure as W. M. Macmillan was largely marginalised: his advisory involvement in the Seretse Khama case came only over the protests of officials who thought his views insufficiently safe.[10] And other impeccably orthodox and undoubtedly expert social democrats, Arthur Lewis and Thomas Balogh, were—before the latter's uneasy induction into Harold Wilson's inner circle—employed not by the British Government, but by those of states like Ghana and Malta to battle against British officialdom.

It is in relation to more minor decisions, especially concerning civil liberties and the behaviour of the legal and security services in the colonies, that one might expect to find evidence of direct pressure from anticolonialist MPs and others bringing direct results. A prima-facie case for such influence has, I think, been shown in several instances above. To go further than this would involve extensive investigation of a very wide range of official papers which—even if

[10] See Michael Crowder, 'Professor Macmillan goes on Safari', in Hugh Macmillan and Shula Marks, *Africa and Empire* (Temple Smith, 1989).

many of the relevant files were open, which they are not—would be beyond the scope of this study.[11]

The left's indirect influence on policy is a richer as well as a more complex theme. It must in its turn be subdivided, between the anticolonialists' parliamentary role, their influence on political parties, their ideas' presence in trade unions and other social organisations, pressure through the mass media, and effect on public opinion.

Anticolonialist influences in the trade unions have already been discussed at length. On the media it is not possible to say anything much. For the period of decolonisation, there is as yet no serious study of press and broadcasting coverage of colonial issues; either in general or, with the partial exception of the Suez crisis, for specific areas and incidents. Even for the inter-war years our knowledge is severely limited.[12] We have noted the strong support given to anticolonial campaigning by certain journals of the left, notably the *New Statesman, Tribune*, the *Daily Worker*, and *Peace News*. Nearer the mainstream, the *Manchester Guardian, Daily Herald*, and *Observer* also consistently advocated rapid decolonisation and were sharply critical of British policy. The last especially, under David Astor, adopted African freedom as something of a crusade in the 1950s and 1960s. Beyond this, there is little evidence of strong anticolonialist influences on Fleet Street. But the converse is also true: that after 1945 there was—with the partial exceptions of the *Telegraph* and *Express*—little positive editorial enthusiasm for the imperial mission in the British Press.

Chapter 6 traced in some detail the parliamentary activities of the left. It indicated that from the mid-1950s radical anticolonialist MPs, mostly associated with the MCF, came virtually to dominate Commons discussion of colonial affairs—being responsible, for instance, for over half of all Questions to Ministers on colonial subjects. This happened in a context of considerably increased parliamentary time devoted to the Empire,[13] and a sharp rise in the

[11] A preliminary trawl of Colonial Office papers in this sphere yielded almost nothing; unsurprisingly, hardly any relevant documents have been released under the thirty-year rule.

[12] John M. MacKenzie, *Propaganda and Empire* (Manchester: Manchester University Press, 1984), and id. (ed.), *Imperialism and Popular Culture* (Manchester: Manchester University Press, 1986), both discuss cinema, children's periodicals, and, to some degree, broadcasting, but not the news media; and almost wholly confine themselves to the production rather than the reception or possible impact of such discourses.

[13] See David Goldsworthy, *Colonial Issues in British Politics, 1945–1961* (Oxford: Oxford University Press, 1971), ch. 3.

number of MPs apparently taking a close interest in these issues. In the 1920s and 1930s colonial specialists, whether anticolonialist or Empire loyalist, had been very few in number and overwhelmingly concentrated on India. In the 1950s a considerably larger group with more diverse interests, especially African, and with a higher proportion very sharply critical of British policy, was active.

Yet increased activity by no means necessarily implies augmented influence. It is arguable that Parliament played a larger part in shaping policy in the colonial sphere than it did in most other policy areas: not despite, but precisely *because* of the indirectness of its role. Constitutional theory gave Westminster considerable power in relation to Britain's overseas dependencies; especially Crown Colonies. In practice this was severely limited by the extent to which colonial decisions were made and policies formulated by the men on the spot and Colonial Office staff; in ways not directly accountable to or subject to full scrutiny by Parliament or, of course, the local populations. Yet this in its turn encouraged at Westminster the ideas of vicarious representation and proxy accountability. Notions of special responsibility were strongly pushed by some individual MPs, especially active anticolonialists; at times, and apparently increasingly, they were shared by the House as a whole. When Parliament, moved by such considerations, sought to exercise these functions, its potential weight in shaping official decision-making was all the greater because of the weakness and distance of other influences: the absence, indirectness, or extreme selectivity of electoral and economic determinations for colonial policy in the last years of Empire.

But this begs the basic question of whether Parliament, during the years of decolonisation, functioned effectively in shaping policy in any sphere. The controversy on this point was almost as vigorous, and as difficult to resolve, in the 1950s as it has been in more recent times.[14] Certainly it is hard to find cases where major colonial policy decisions were clearly and directly shaped by parliamentary activity. This is partly because of the extent to which such decisions were made in

[14] It is impossible even to begin to summarise the literature here. For orthodox views of parliamentary sovereignty in the post-war era, see for instance Herbert Morrison, *Government and Parliament* (Oxford: Oxford University Press, 1954), esp. chs. 6–8, or Ronald Butt, *The Power of Parliament* (Constable, 1967). For arguments far more sceptical about Parliament's real power, see Bernard Crick, *The Reform of Parliament* (Weidenfeld & Nicolson, 1964), and more recently, Ian Harden and Norman Lewis, *The Noble Lie: The British Constitution and the Rule of Law* (Hutchinson, 1986), esp. chs. 4 and 5.

secretive and unaccountable ways. It is partly because of the degree of—albeit conditional—bipartisanship which marked colonial affairs for much of the era of decolonisation. But above all, it is a consequence of the fact that parliamentary activity never operated in isolation, but as part of a complex of pressures on policy which are extremely difficult to disentangle or their relative weights apportion.

Individual back-benchers and interested groups of MPs could bring some influence to bear.[15] We have already seen that in the colonial sphere this may have had unusual weight comparative to the role of the official Opposition. None the less even on colonial matters the British political process was heavily shaped by the party system. For pressure groups and campaigners, winning a major party's support for a particular policy or attitude remained crucial. It has been shown how relatively unsuccessful—indeed relatively inactive— Labour's anticolonial left was in this regard before 1939 and again under the Attlee Governments. After 1951 the story became radically different, with the policy of groups like the MCF increasingly becoming, on most remaining colonial questions, that of the party. And whereas a decade earlier Labour had been fairly sharply divided on colonial questions with the radical anticolonialists a distinct minority, it was after about 1955 relatively cohesive. The retrospective judgement of James Callaghan, Labour's Colonial spokesman in 1957–61, was apt if bland: 'At a time when Labour was deeply divided by the bitter Bevanite controversy, these were matters on which we could agree . . . a field in which there was broad unity.'[16]

But of course the Conservatives were in power during these years of the anticolonialists' greatest organisational coherence, parliamentary activism, and capacity for public campaigning. Thus any major influence on officialdom the latter might have would obviously in large part be dependent on how far the Opposition could shape policy. The strongest argument that it was able substantially to do so was made by John Hatch near the end of our period. He suggested that because of Labour's special relationship with colonial nationalist

---

[15] Again there is a very substantial literature on back-benchers' roles and influence. For summaries see P. G. Richards, *The Backbenchers* (Faber & Faber, 1974), and D. N. Chester with Nona Bowring, *Questions in Parliament* (Oxford: Clarendon Press, 1962). For a range of individual Members' views, John Biffen, *Inside the House of Commons* (Grafton, 1989); Alf Dubs, *Lobbying: An Insider's Guide to the Parliamentary Process* (Pluto, 1988); John Grant, *Member of Parliament* (Michael Joseph, 1974); and Austin Mitchell, *Westminster Man* (Methuen, 1982).

[16] *Time and Change* (Collins, 1987; Fontana edn. 1988), 119.

leaders, its views were 'a weightier consideration when colonial policy is being discussed than in any other branch of government business'. Labour was able to 'represent colonial grievances, advise colonial leaders on attitudes towards government decisions, and sometimes mediate between these representatives and British ministers'.[17] The argument is compelling; though it may well be, as Goldsworthy shows, that it is somewhat overstated and that such influence depended in addition on Labour's being 'a reasonably credible alternative government'.[18]

Much the same case can be made, *mutatis mutandis*, for radical anticolonialists operating independently of the official party structures, or partly so. Although the mediating role might be less often open to them, the representational and advisory ones were—as has been shown above—often more actively undertaken by left-wing groups than by the Labour front bench. And in cases where official Labour was unwilling to represent or mediate for nationalist movements, because of their perceived extremism, pro-Communism, or recourse to violence then the left (occasionally even the Communists) were the only available channels. This occurred in different ways in Kenya, Malaya, Guiana, Cyprus, Aden, and Sierra Leone, amongst other controversial passages in decolonisation. It is noteworthy, however, that in almost all these instances the colonial groups whom the radical left or sections of it backed, but official Labour did not, failed to obtain their objectives.

In particular, as we have seen, armed revolt in the colonies was always sharply divisive within the British left, and the mostly Communist minority prepared to support or endorse guerrilla war against British rule found itself extremely isolated. Labour Party Conferences just seven times, between 1945 and 1964, debated resolutions referring to any of Britain's wars of decolonisation. It never had a debate specifically and solely on any of them. One, in 1956, called for racial justice and an end to collective punishments in Kenya. This was carried. There were three calls for the withdrawal of British armed forces from colonies, one in 1952 and two in 1954: two referring specifically to Malaya, one also to Kenya. These were all easily defeated. The major MCF-inspired resolution, also in 1954, referred to the need to liberalise colonial policy to avoid frustration

---

[17] John Hatch, 'The Opposition's Part in Colonial Policy', *Listener* (25 Apr. 1963). See also Goldsworthy's careful evaluation of Hatch's claims in *Colonial Issues*, 341–5.
[18] Ibid. 344.

being 'exploited by Communist and terrorist elements'. It was remitted. One in 1958 'deplored' the violence in Cyprus, blamed the Conservative Government, and supported self-government there. It was withdrawn. And one in 1953 said that 'the repression of Mau Mau is necessary, but the economic and social causes of this reversion to barbarism demand radical treatment' and that in Malaya 'it is necessary to combat Communist terrorism'. This, unsurprisingly, was carried. Even in advocating an alternative policy to that of the Government, the Labour mainstream shared its political language.[19]

As to anticolonialism in public opinion, a wide variety of suggestions has been made as to its general profile: all of them necessarily highly speculative. John Strachey, as was noted at the start of this work, believed that strong anticolonial sentiment in the Labour movement and 'the most politically conscious' of the working class was decisive in enabling a relatively smooth and rapid decolonisation.[20] Here if nowhere else, Strachey's views were those of most of the left and of most anticolonialists. But clearly they were overstated: active involvement in anticolonial campaigning was always a minority pursuit even amongst the highly politicised. As Kingsley Amis—then a socialist of sorts—sceptically noted in relation to the Cyprus conflict:

Here at any rate is something which potentially unites the romantic with the practical man. But what gets done about it? Compare what gets done about it with what would have got done about it in the Thirties. In my innocence I asked one of my Labour party sociological friends why there weren't protest meetings all over the place, why people weren't organising something. 'We run meetings all right,' he said, 'but nobody turns up. Have you ever tried protesting to an empty hall?'[21]

And even so dispirited a view of the popular resonance of anticolonialism made one evidently erroneous assumption, and one unconsciously revealing one. The error was to assume that protest would necessarily have been more widespread in an earlier period. It was not: compare his friend's reported remark with Edward Thompson's exactly parallel complaint that in the 1930s the mere mention of India would empty the smallest hall. The inadvertently telling point is Amis's unargued assumption that colonial questions

[19] F. W. S. Craig (ed.), *Conservative & Labour Party Conference Decisions, 1945–1981* (Parliamentary Research Services, 1982), 123–5, 257, 263.
[20] Strachey, *End of Empire*, 215.
[21] *Socialism and the Intellectuals* (Fabian Tract 304, 1957).

were the natural concern only of the intelligentsia and the middle class. But so it was. Decolonisation was most of the time a remarkably marginal issue in British politics. Not one general election after 1918 featured the Empire as a major campaign issue, or one which appears significantly to have influenced voting behaviour. Much of the time, as has been shown, the major disagreements ran within rather than between the parties. But no party split on colonial questions either; despite Tory Suez Group and 'kith and kin' rebellions, and a few rather minor Labour back-bench revolts.

It is generally agreed, then, that we are dealing here with the role of élites and of the highly politically conscious, rather than mass views. Most accounts stress less the positive rise of anticolonial sentiment than the erosion of élite enthusiasm. Robert Holland suggests that the advance of a new middle class supplanted imperialism's former political constituency. The new class was interested in consumerism or welfarism rather than overseas commitments, within an insular and later a European rather than an imperial framework. Governments were constrained to follow these preferences.[22] More conservative commentators like Correlli Barnett and A. P. Thornton claim that the rise of democracy and of a politics dominated by the urban bourgeoisie rather than aristocracies inevitably doomed imperialism: replacing a spirit both adventurous and autocratic with a moralistic and egalitarian one.[23] The family resemblance between this and the Anderson–Nairn thesis is evident; though the ethos which Barnett and Thornton view as positive but defunct is regarded by Anderson and Nairn as deplorable but still living.

Ronald Robinson and John Darwin propose more subtle arguments. Robinson's famous notion of imperialism's moral disarmament suggests that colonisers saw ethical justifications as being 'as vital to them as surplus capital or high velocity guns'.[24] Such justifications, centred on the 'device' of trusteeship, seemed for decades almost infinitely adjustable. They

served to justify empire at its most vulnerable point. If the hurly-burly of politics in England [*sic*] had been allowed to play on the paradox of a parliamentary democracy holding an empire in subjection, the will to rule might have frayed and snapped at the centre. The device of trusteeship put

[22] R. F. Holland, *European Decolonization, 1918–1981* (Macmillan, 1985), 208–10.

[23] Correlli Barnett, *The Collapse of British Power* (Methuen, 1972); A. P. Thornton, *The Imperial Idea and its Enemies* (Macmillan, 1959).

[24] 'The Moral Disarmament of African Empire, 1919–1947', *JICH* 7/1 (1979), 86.

off this confrontation of principles indefinitely . . . [and] served to convert the anti-imperialists of one generation into the imperialists of the next.[25]

But in the event this process could *not* be perpetuated indefinitely. Incorporating notions of racial equality, self-determination, and economic progress, drawn from and intended to disarm metropolitan radicals, proved incompatible with the 'ancient racial prejudices' of the colonialists. They 'found themselves unable to live up to their pretensions' and so were forced to 'hand over their tasks to nationalists and achieve the purposes of trusteeship by other means'.[26]

Darwin usefully emphasises the 'highly differentiated and unpredictable' nature of public attitudes; and has the advantage, writing after the Falklands war and the apparent resurgence of English/British nationalism during the 1980s, of being able to see earlier assumptions about the deimperialising of popular sentiment as exaggerated.[27] Enthusiasts for the Raj in India, believers in the Commonwealth ideal, adherents to the kith and kin lobby in Africa, and supporters of Britain's global strategic role were defending very different kinds of Empire and might have little in common. It may well be that *all* of these lost their ideological appeal after 1945: though evidently if the first vanished rather quickly, the last has persisted into the 1990s. Policy-makers sought to avert two very different kinds of domestic criticism. On the one hand, they wanted to avoid being seen to capitulate to external pressure, whether from violent nationalist movements or from foreign powers. Hence the need to assert the *appearance* of continuity and authority. This meant that threats from guerrillas, or from a Nasser or, much later, a Galtieri, centrally involved fears of the domestic repercussions of losing prestige. Positions might then be held which on more rational—especially economic—calculation would have been abandoned.[28]

On the other hand, there was a domestic battle for the moral high ground, and here Darwin's argument connects with Robinson's:

If evidence appeared that colonial control depended too heavily upon coercion, policy brutality or too rough a justice, then the humanitarian

[25] 'The Moral Disarmament of African Empire, 1919–1947', *JICH* 7/1 (1979), 88.
[26] Ibid. 100, 101.
[27] John Darwin, *The End of the British Empire* (Oxford: Blackwell, 1991), 17. See also id., 'The Fear of Falling', *Transactions of the Royal Historical Society*, 5th ser. 36 (1986).
[28] David Goldsworthy, 'Keeping Change Within Bounds', *JICH* 18/1 (1990), and 'Britain and the International Critics of British Colonialism', *JCCP* 29/1 (1991), suggests a similar view.

instincts on which the champions of empire had played so artfully for so long ... might be roused successfully against the continuation of empire, in its classical form. If the politics of colonial rule could be ... presented starkly as a *moral* problem in which champions of freedom struggled against the tyranny of a police state, then all or most of the advantage which conservative defenders of empire at home normally enjoyed against their political opponents would begin to dribble away.[29]

That moral claim was of course the central theme of radical anticolonialist argument throughout. Had it gained overwhelming force by the 1950s? Yes and no. The actively mobilising capacity of their case was, as has been shown, always limited. But it was an ever-present threat. To governments eager to pre-empt possible crisis and confrontation, at home as in the colonies themselves, there could never be any guarantee that the *relative* lack of popular protest over Malaya, Kenya, or Cyprus would continue to be replicated. Suez was the great warning signal, even if Labour's opposition to the war did not command majority support. And meanwhile, more gradually but more pervasively, the whole language of colonial debate had been transformed.

If domestic race relations were still, though decreasingly, presented as a colonial question, then colonial issues were increasingly articulated in the language of race. This was the worst possible ground on which defenders of Britain's colonial role could fight, if they wished—as they desperately did—to maintain an image of moral ascendency both at home and in the international arena. However bigoted the real, underlying racial views of Conservative politicians, or of majority public opinion, may have been (and few political questions have been more bitterly, and perhaps undecidably, contested than this), there could after 1945 be no public, explicit defence of Empire in terms of racial hierarchy. Any politician or party which wished to retain legitimacy had to employ the discourse of universal political rights; whether they did so opportunistically or, as Macleod seemed to do in defending his colonial policy, with real conviction: 'I believe quite simply in the brotherhood of man—men of all races, of all colours, of all creeds. I think it is this that must be at the centre of our thinking.'[30]

Of course this delegitimising of the language of racial superiority

---

[29] Darwin, *End of the British Empire*, 20. Emphasis in original.
[30] Conservative Party Annual Conference Report (1961), 25.

was only in small degree attributable to the activities of British anticolonialists. The historical debate continues over where the main responsibility lies: the shock of the Nazi Holocaust, the propaganda needs of the Cold War, the self-assertion of colonised peoples, or some general, global advance of liberal universalism. But while colonialism could no longer effectively be defended in the language of race, there were also no longer convincing alternative languages available.

By the 1950s if not earlier, such real faith as there had ever been in an imperial mission had been almost wholly lost. Most of the traditional positive arguments in favour of British colonial rule had come to seem absurd or anachronistic to any audience outside the far right wing of the Conservative Party. In the absence of such arguments the perpetuation of colonial structures—which were so often in direct contravention of the practice and the proclaimed ethos of the domestic British political system—depended in large part on inertia.

In any argument over political change, the burden of proof is in practice laid on the advocates of change. Where they cannot adduce compelling arguments in support of their desired project, inertia will prevail. The anticolonialist ethic both stated a strong moral case for change, and absolved its proponents of the responsibility for making a more detailed practical case. If unconditional British recognition of colonial self-determination was, as they asserted, morally imperative and practically self-sufficient—since only the new indigenous leaders could set the agenda for the future—the burden of proof was thrust back on to the defenders of colonial rule.

They could not sustain it. They could not appeal to public opinion, since this was overwhelmingly apathetic; and the more informed it was the more critical it was likely to be.[31] They could not, at least after about 1948, appeal to their own plans for more gradual and constructive change, since these lay in tatters: torn by the nationalists, squeezed by the Treasury, suffocated by piles of unsold groundnuts. The British mode of rule in Africa had once aptly been described as 'apathy tempered by riots'. In so far as the colonial system was, after 1945, no longer able to reform itself in ways that would satisfy its growing numbers of internal and external critics, its perpetuation was dependent on that lethargy of colonial rule being matched by a

---

[31] See G. K. Evens, *Public Opinion on Colonial Affairs* (HMSO NS 119, June 1948).

lethargy in British political control over it. The activities of British anticolonialists played a major part in ensuring that the lethargy could not be reproduced, nor the riots ignored, in Britain. Colonial rulers, by definition, are not accountable to their subjects. In practice, the British political system had made them accountable to it only in the most intermittent and inadequate fashion. The anticolonialism of the left established an accountability by proxy. Therein lies its major contribution to bringing about decolonisation.

Bibliography

Unpublished sources

Africa Bureau papers: Rhodes House, Oxford.

Anthony Wedgwood Benn papers: in possession of Tony and Caroline Benn, London.

Thomas Driberg (Lord Bradwell) papers: Christ Church library, Oxford.

Fabian Colonial Bureau papers: Rhodes House, Oxford.

C. W. W. Greenidge papers: Rhodes House, Oxford.

Richard Hart papers: microfilm copies at Institute of Commonwealth Studies, London.

Thomas Hodgkin papers: in possession of Dorothy Hodgkin, Ilmington, Warwickshire.

Arthur Creech Jones papers: Rhodes House, Oxford.

Labour Party papers: Labour Party library, Walworth Road, London.

Marx Memorial Library: miscellaneous papers of Communist Party of Great Britain and associated organisations, Marx House, London.

Movement for Colonial Freedom papers: consulted at offices of Liberation (formerly the Movement for Colonial Freedom), now at School of Oriental and African Studies, London.

Joseph Murumbi: interview transcripts and draft autobiography, in Mr Murumbi's possession, Kenya: copies made available through the kindness of Ms Ann Thurston.

Revolutionary Communist Party: papers of the RCP and associated organisations, Nuffield College, Oxford.

Interviews

Miss Kay Beauchamp; Rt. Hon. Tony Benn, MP; Lord Brockway; Bob Edwards; Mrs Barbara Haq; Richard Hart; Lord Hatch of Lusby; Dr Julius

Lewin; Stan Newens, MEP; Ernie Roberts; John Stonehouse.

Numerous other participants in, and commentators on, anticolonial movements kindly provided information in informal discussions and written communications.

Journals

Only contemporary political periodicals consulted are listed here; articles in scholarly journals are separately cited.

Africa and the Colonial World (associated with MCF)
Africa Bulletin (Association for African Freedom)
Africa Newsletter (CPGB Africa Committee)
Anti-Imperialist Review (League Against Imperialism)
Britain–Malaya (Britain–Malaya Committee)
Colonial Freedom News (MCF—initially entitled *Prod*)
Communist Review (CPGB)
Daily Herald
Daily Worker
Inside the Empire (CPGB)
International Press Correspondence (Comintern)
Labour Monthly (associated with CPGB)
Labour Research (associated with CPGB)
Left (associated with ILP)
Malayan Monitor (associated with CPGB and MCP)
Militant (associated with RCP)
New Leader (ILP—after 1948 *Socialist Leader*)
Newsletter of the League of Coloured Peoples
New Reasoner
New Statesman (and Nation)
Pan-Africa
Peace News
Socialist Appeal (associated first with Workers' International League, later with RCP)
Socialist Outlook (The Club)
Socialist Review (State Capitalism Group)
The Times
Tribune
Venture (FCB)
West Indies Newsletter (CPGB West Indies Committee)
World Marxist Review (Cominform)
World News and Views (CPGB)

Books

Place of publication is London unless otherwise stated.

AARONOVITCH, S., and AARONOVITCH, K., *Crisis in Kenya* (Lawrence & Wishart, 1947).

ABRAHAMS, PETER, *A Wreath for Udomo* (Faber & Faber, 1956).

ACLAND, RICHARD, *Unser Kampf* (Harmondsworth: Penguin, 1940).

ADDISON, PAUL, *The Road to 1945* (Cape, 1975).

AGERON, CHARLES ROBERT, *L'Anticolonialisme en France de 1871 à 1914* (Paris: Presses Universitaires de France, 1973).

AHMED, MESBAHUDDIN, *The British Labour Party and the Indian Independence Movement, 1917–1939* (Oriental University Press, 1987).

AJAYI, J. F. A. DE, and CROWDER, MICHAEL (eds.), *History of West Africa*, ii (Longmans, 1974).

ALBERTINI, RUDOLPH VON, *Decolonization* (New York: Doubleday, 1971).

AMIN, SAMIR, *Delinking: Towards a Polycentric World* (Zed Books, 1990).

—— *Maldevelopment: Anatomy of a Global Failure* (Zed Books, 1990).

ANDERSON, PERRY, and BLACKBURN, ROBIN (eds.), *Towards Socialism* (Fontana, 1965).

ANDREYEV, I., *The Non-Capitalist Way: Soviet Experience and the Liberated Countries* (Moscow: Progress Publishers, 1977).

ANSPRENGER, FRANZ, *The Dissolution of the Colonial Empires* (Routledge, 1989).

ANSTEY, ROGER, *The Atlantic Slave Trade and British Abolition, 1760–1810* (Macmillan, 1975).

ARRIGHI, GIOVANNI, *The Geometry of Imperialism: The limits of Hobson's Paradigm* (New Left Books, 1978).

ATTFIELD, JOHN, and WILLIAMS, STEPHEN (eds.), *1939: The Communist Party and the War* (Lawrence & Wishart, 1984).

ATTLEE, CLEMENT, *The Labour Party in Perspective* (Gollancz, 1937).

—— *Empire into Commonwealth* (Oxford: Oxford University Press, 1961).

BARNES, LEONARD, *Caliban in Africa* (Gollancz, 1930).

—— *The New Boer War* (L. & V. Woolf, 1932).

—— *The Duty of Empire* (Gollancz, 1935).

—— *Empire or Democracy?* (Gollancz, 1939).

—— *Soviet Light on the Colonies* (Harmondsworth: Penguin, 1944).

BARNETT, CORELLI, *The Collapse of British Power* (Methuen, 1972).

BARNETT, DONALD N., and NJAMA, KARARI, *Mau Mau from Within* (MacGibbon & Kee, 1966).

BAUMGART, W., *Imperialism: The Idea and Reality of British and French Colonial Expansion, 1880–1914* (Oxford: Oxford University Press, 1982).

BEININ, JOEL, *Was the Red Flag Flying There?* (I. & B. Tauris, 1990).

BELL, GEOFFREY, *Troublesome Business: The Labour Party and the Irish Question* (Pluto, 1982).

BELLAMY, JOYCE, and Saville, John (eds.), *Dictionary of Labour Biography*, vii (Macmillan, 1984).

BENENSON, PETER (ed.), *Gangrene* (John Calder, 1959).

BENSON, MARY, *Tshekedi Khama* (Faber & Faber, 1960).

BERMAN, BRUCE, *Control and Crisis in Colonial Kenya: The Dialectic of Domination* (James Currey, 1990).

BERRINGTON, H., *Backbench Opinion in the House of Commons, 1945–55* (Oxford: Pergamon, 1973).

BIFFEN, JOHN, *Inside the House of Commons* (Grafton, 1989).

BING, GEOFFREY, *Reap the Whirlwind* (MacGibbon & Kee, 1968).

BLACKBURN, ROBIN, *The Overthrow of Colonial Slavery* (Verso, 1988).

—— (ed.), *Ideology in Social Science* (Fontana, 1972).

BLAXLAND, GREGORY, *J. H. Thomas: A Life for Unity* (Frederick Muller, 1964).

BLUNDELL, Sir MICHAEL, *So Rough a Wind* (Weidenfeld & Nicolson, 1964).

BONWICK, COLIN, *English Radicals and the American Revolution* (Chapel Hill, NC: University of North Carolina Press, 1977).

BORNSTEIN, SAM, and RICHARDSON, AL, *Against the Stream: A History of the Trotskyist Movement in Britain, 1924–38* (Socialist Platform, 1986).

—— and —— *War and the International: A History of the Trotskyist Movement in Britain, 1938–1949* (Socialist Platform, 1986).

BRAILSFORD, H. N., *The War of Steel and Gold: A Study of the Armed Peace* (Bell, 1914).

—— *The Levellers and the English Revolution*, ed. Christopher Hill (2nd edn., Nottingham: Spokesman, 1976).

BRANSON, NOREEN, *History of the CPGB, 1927–1941* (Lawrence & Wishart, 1985).

BRAUDEL, FERNAND, *Écrits sur l'histoire* (Paris: Flammarion, 1969).

—— *Civilisation & Capitalism 15th–18th Century*, iii. *The Perspective of the World* (Collins, 1984).

BRERETON, BRIDGET, *A History of Modern Trinidad, 1783–1962* (Heinemann, 1981).

BRETT, E. A., *Colonialism and Underdevelopment in East Africa* (Heinemann, 1973).

BREWER, ANTHONY, *Marxist Theories of Imperialism: A Critical Survey* (Routledge & Kegan Paul, 1980).

BROCKWAY, FENNER, *Inside the Left* (Allen & Unwin, 1942).

—— *African Journey* (Gollancz, 1955).

—— *Outside the Right* (Allen & Unwin, 1963).

—— *African Socialism* (Bodley Head, 1963).

—— *The Colonial Revolution* (Hart Davis, MacGibbon, 1973).

—— *Towards Tomorrow* (Hart Davis, MacGibbon, 1977).

BROWN, GORDON, *Maxton* (Edinburgh: Mainstream, 1986).

BRUTENTS, K. N., *National Liberation Movements Today* (Moscow: Progress Publishers, 1977).

BUDEIRI, M., *The Palestine Communist Party, 1918–1948: Arab and Jew in the Struggle for Internationalism* (Ithaca Press, 1979).

BUHLE, PAUL, *C. L. R. James: The Artist as Revolutionary* (Verso, 1988).

—— (ed.), *C. L. R. James: His Life and Work* (Allison & Busby, 1986).

BULLOCK, ALAN, *Ernest Bevin, Foreign Secretary* (Heinemann, 1983).

BUTT, RONALD, *The Power of Parliament* (Constable, 1967).

CABRAL, A., *Unity and Struggle* (Heinemann, 1980).

CALDER, ANGUS, *The People's War* (Cape, 1969).

CALLAGHAN, [L.] James, *Time and Change* (Collins, 1987).

CALLAGHAN, JOHN, *British Trotskyism: Theory and Practice* (Oxford: Blackwell, 1984).

CAMPBELL, JOHN, *Nye Bevan and the Mirage of British Socialism* (Weidenfeld & Nicolson, 1987).

CARPENTER, EDWARD, *Towards Democracy* (George Allen, 1913; orig. pub. 1883).

CARRÈRE D'ENCAUSSE, HÉLÈNE, and SCHRAM, STUART R., *Marxism and Asia* (Allen Lane, 1969).

CARRITT, M., *A Mole in the Crown* (Hove: the author, 1985).

CEADEL, MARTIN, *Pacifism in Britain, 1914–1945: The Defining of a Faith* (Oxford: Oxford University Press, 1980).

Centre for Contemporary Cultural Studies, *The Empire Strikes Back: Race and Racism in 'Seventies Britain* (CCCS/Hutchinson, 1982).

CESAIRE, AIME, *Discours sur le colonialisme* (Paris: Presence Africaine, 1955).

CHANDOS, OLIVER LYTTELTON, Viscount, *The Memoirs of Lord Chandos* (Bodley Head, 1962).

CHEAH BOON KHENG, *The Masked Comrades: A Study of the Communist United Front in Malaya, 1945–48* (Singapore: Times Books International, 1979).

CHESTER, D. N., with BOWRING, NONA, *Questions in Parliament* (Oxford: Clarendon Press, 1962).

CLARKE, PETER, *Liberals and Social Democrats* (Cambridge: Cambridge University Press, 1978).

CLARKSON, STEPHEN, *The Soviet Theory of Development: India and the Third World in Marxist–Leninist Scholarship* (Macmillan, 1978).

COHEN, PHILIP, and BAINS, HARWANT S. (eds.), *Multi-Racist Britain* (Macmillan, 1988).

COHEN, ROBIN, *Labour and Politics in Nigeria, 1945–71* (Heinemann, 1974).

COLLINS, CANON L. JOHN, *Faith Under Fire* (Leslie Frewin, 1966).

COLLOTTI PISCHEL, E., and ROBERTAZZI, C., *L'Internationale communiste et les problèmes coloniaux* (Paris: Mouton, 1968).

James Connolly: Selected writings, ed. Peter Berresford Ellis (Harmondsworth: Penguin, 1973).

CONSTANTINE, STEPHEN, *The Making of British Colonial Development Policy, 1914–1940* (Frank Cass, 1984).

CORFIELD, F. D., *Historical Survey of the Origins and Growth of Mau Mau,* Cmd. 1030 (HMSO, 1960).

CORISH, PATRICK J. (ed.), *Radicals, Rebels and Establishments,* Historical Studies, xv (Belfast: Appletree Press, 1985).

COX, IDRIS, *Socialist Ideas in Africa* (Lawrence & Wishart, 1966).

CRAIG, F. W. S. (ed.), *Conservative & Labour Party Conference Decisions, 1945–1981* (Parliamentary Research Services, 1982).

CRAIG, SUSAN (ed.), *Contemporary Caribbean: A Sociological Reader,* 2 vols. (Port of Spain, Trinidad: the author, 1982).

CRICK, BERNARD, *The Reform of Parliament* (Weidenfeld & Nicolson, 1964).

—— *George Orwell: A Life* (Secker & Warburg, 1980).

CRICK, MICHAEL, *Militant* (Faber & Faber, 1984; 2nd edn., *The March of Militant,* Faber & Faber, 1986).

CROSSMAN, R. H. S. (ed.), *New Fabian Essays* (Turnstile Press, 1953).

—— *The Backbench Diaries of Richard Crossman,* ed. Janet Morgan (Hamilton & Cape, 1981).

DALTON, HUGH, *Call Back Yesterday* (Frederick Muller, 1953).

DARWIN, JOHN, *Britain and Decolonisation: The Retreat from Empire in the Postwar World* (Macmillan, 1988).

—— *The End of the British Empire: The Historical Debate* (Oxford: Blackwell, 1991).

DAVIDSON, BASIL, *Report on Southern Africa* (Jonathan Cape, 1952).

—— *Which Way Africa?* (Harmondsworth: Penguin, 1964).

—— *Let Freedom Come: Africa in Modern History* (Boston, Mass.: Atlantic-Little Brown, 1978).

—— *Crossroads in Africa* (Nottingham: Spokesman, 1980).

DEUTSCHER, ISAAC, *The Prophet Outcast: Trotsky 1929–1940* (Oxford: Oxford University Press, 1963).

DEWAR, HUGO, *Communist Politics in Britain* (Pluto, 1976).

DIAMOND, LARRY, LINZ, JUAN, J., and LIPSET, SEYMOUR M. (eds.), *Democracy in Developing Countries: Asia* (Boulder, Colo.: Lynne Rienner, 1989).

DOWSE, R. E., *Left in the Centre* (Longmans, 1966).

DRESCHER, SEYMOUR, *Capitalism and Antislavery* (Macmillan, 1986).

DRIBERG, TOM, *Ruling Passions* (Cape, 1977).

DRUCKER, H. M., *Doctrine and Ethos in the Labour Party* (Allen & Unwin, 1979).

DRUHE, DAVID N., *Soviet Russia and Indian Communism* (New York: Bookman Associates, 1959).

DRYSDALE, JOHN, *Singapore: Struggle for Success* (Singapore: Times Books International/Allen & Unwin, 1984).

DUBS, ALF, *Lobbying: An Insider's Guide to the Parliamentary Process* (Pluto, 1988).

DUFF, P., *Left, Left, Left: A Personal Account of Six Protest Campaigns, 1945–1965* (Allison & Busby, 1971).

DURBIN, ELIZABATH, *New Jerusalems: The Labour Party and the Economics of Democratic Socialism* (Routledge & Kegan Paul, 1985).

DUTFIELD, MICHAEL, *A Marriage of Inconvenience* (Unwin Hyman, 1990).

DUTT, R. PALME, *Modern India* (Martin Lawrence, 1927).

—— *India Today* (Gollancz, 1940).

—— *Britain's Crisis of Empire* (Lawrence & Wishart, 1949).

—— *The Crisis of Britain and the British Empire* (Lawrence & Wishart, 1953).

EMMANUEL, ARGHIRI, *Unequal Exchange: A Study of the Imperialism of Trade* (New York: Monthly Review, 1972).

EPSTEIN, LEON, *British Politics in the Suez Crisis* (Urbana, Ill.: University of Illinois Press, 1964).

Fabian Colonial Bureau, *Downing Street and the Colonies* (FCB 1942).

Fabian Society, *Where Stands Democracy? A Collection of Essays by Members of the Fabian Society* (Macmillan, 1940).

FANON, FRANTZ, *Towards the African Revolution* (Harmondsworth: Penguin, 1970; orig. pub. in French 1964).

FEUER, LEWIS, *Imperialism and the Anti-Imperialist Mind* (Buffalo: Prometheus Books, 1986).

FIELDHOUSE, D. K., *Economics and Empire, 1830–1914* (Weidenfeld & Nicolson, 1973).

—— *Unilever Overseas* (Croom Helm, 1976).

—— (ed.), *The Theory of Capitalist Imperialism* (Longmans, 1967).

FINER, S. E., BERRINGTON, H. B., and BARTHOLEMEW, D. J., *Backbench Opinion in the House of Commons* (Oxford: Pergamon, 1961).

FISCHER, GEORGES, *Le Parti Travailliste et la décolonisation de l'Inde* (Paris: Maspero, 1966).

FOOT, MICHAEL, *Aneurin Bevan*, i. *1897–1945* (MacGibbon & Kee, 1962). ii. *1945–1960* (Davis-Poynter, 1973); paperback edn. (Granada, 1975).

FOOT, PAUL, *Immigration and Race in British Politics* (Harmondsworth: Penguin, 1965).

FOOTE, GEOFFREY, *The Labour Party's Political Thought* (Croom Helm, 1985).

FRANSMAN, M. (ed.), *Industry and Accumulation in Africa* (Heinemann, 1982).

FRYER, PETER, *Staying Power: The History of Black People in Britain* (Pluto, 1984).

FYFE, CHRISTOPHER (ed.), *African Studies Since, 1945: A Tribute to Basil Davidson* (Longman, 1976).

GALLAGHER, JOHN, *The Decline, Revival and Fall of the British Empire*, ed. Anil Seal (Cambridge: Cambridge University Press, 1982).

—— JOHNSON, GORDON, and SEAL, ANIL (eds.), *Locality, Province and Nation: Essays on Indian Politics, 1870–1940* (Cambridge: Cambridge University Press, 1973).

GEISS, IMMANUEL, *The Pan-African Movement* (New York: Africana Publishing Co., 1974).

GEORGE, T. J. S., *Krishna Menon* (New York: Taplinger, 1965).

GIFFORD, PROSSER, and LOUIS, WM. ROGER, *The Transfer of Power in Africa: Decolonization 1940–1960* (New Haven, Conn.: Yale University Press, 1982).

—— and —— *Decolonization and African Independence: The Transfers of Power 1960–1980* (New Haven, Conn.: Yale University Press, 1988).

GOLDSWORTHY, DAVID, *Colonial Issues in British Politics, 1945–1961: From 'Colonial Development' to 'Wind of Change'* (Oxford: Oxford University Press, 1971).

GOPAL, SARVEPALLI, *Jawaharlal Nehru*, i. *1889–1947* (Cape, 1975).

GORDON, M. R., *Conflict and Consensus in Labour's Foreign Policy 1914–1965* (Stanford, Calif.: Stanford University Press, 1969).

GORNY, JOSEPH, *The British Labour Movement and Zionism, 1917–1948* (Frank Cass, 1983).

GRANT, JOHN, *Member of Parliament* (Michael Joseph, 1974).

GREGORY, ROBERT, *Sidney Webb and East Africa: Labour's Experiment with the Doctrine of Native Paramountcy* (Berkeley, Calif.: University of California Press, 1962).

GRIFFITHS, RICHARD, *Fellow Travellers of the Right: British Enthusiasts for Nazi Germany, 1933–39* (Constable, 1980).

GRIMAL, HENRI, *Decolonization* (Routledge & Kegan Paul, 1978).

GUHA, RANAJIT, *A Rule of Property for Bengal* (2nd edn., New Delhi: Orient Longman, 1982).

—— (ed.), *Subaltern Studies VI* (Delhi: Oxford University Press, 1989).

GUPTA, PARTHA SARATHI, *Imperialism and the British Labour Movement, 1914–1964* (Macmillan, 1975).

HADEN-GUEST, LESLIE, *Labour and the Empire* (Labour Publishing Co., 1926).

HAITHCOX, J. P., *Communism and Nationalism in India* (Princeton, NJ: Princeton University Press, 1971).

HALL, S., CRITCHER, C., JEFFERSON, T., CLARKE, J., and ROBERTS, B., *Policing the Crisis: Mugging, the State and Law and Order* (Macmillan, 1978).

HALLIDAY, FRED, and MOLYNEAUX, MAXINE, *The Ethiopian Revolution* (New Left Books, 1981).

HAQQI, S. A. H., *The Colonial Policy of the Labour Government, 1945–51* (Aligarh: Aligarh University Press, 1960).

HARDEN, IAN, and LEWIS, NORMAN, *The Noble Lie: The British Constitution and the Rule of Law* (Hutchinson, 1986).

HARDING, NEIL, *Lenin's Political Thought*, ii. *Theory and Practice in the Socialist Revolution* (Macmillan, 1981).

HARNETTY, PETER, *Imperialism and Free Trade* (Manchester: Manchester University Press, 1972).

HARRIS, KENNETH, *Attlee* (Weidenfeld & Nicolson, 1982).

HARROD, JEFFREY, *Trade Union Foreign Policy: A Study of British and American Trade Union Activities in Jamaica* (Macmillan, 1972).

HART, RICHARD, *Rise and Organise: The Birth of the Workers and National Movements in Jamaica (1936–1939)* (Karia Press, 1989).

HATCH, JOHN, *Two African Statesmen: Kaunda of Zambia and Nyerere of Tanzania* (Secker & Warburg, 1976).

HATHAWAY, ROBERT M., *Ambiguous Partnership: Britain and America, 1944–1947* (New York: Columbia University Press, 1981).

HEFFER, ERIC, *Never a Yes Man: The Life and Politics of an Adopted Liverpudlian* (Verso, 1991).

HEINEMANN, B. W., JUN., *The Politics of the Powerless: A Study of the Campaign Against Racial Discrimination* (Oxford University Press/Institute of Race Relations, 1972).

HETHERINGTON, P., *British Paternalism and Africa, 1920–1940* (Frank Cass, 1978).

HINDEN, RITA, *Empire and After* (Essential Books, 1949).

—— (ed.), *Fabian Colonial Essays* (Allen & Unwin, 1945).

HINTON, JAMES, *Protests and Visions: Peace Politics in 20th Century Britain* (Hutchinson, 1989).

—— and HYMAN, RICHARD, *Trade Unions and Revolution: The Industrial Politics of the Early British Communist Party* (Pluto, 1975).

HOBSBAWM, E. J., *Revolutionaries* (Weidenfeld & Nicolson, 1973).

HOBSON, J. A., *The Psychology of Jingoism* (Grant Richardson, 1901).

—— *Imperialism: A Study* (James Nisbet & Co., 1902).

HODGKIN, THOMAS, *Nationalism in Colonial Africa* (Frederick Muller, 1956).

HOLLAND, R. F., *European Decolonisation, 1918–1981* (Macmillan, 1985).

HOLMES, COLIN (ed.), *Immigrants and Minorities in British Society* (Allen & Unwin, 1978).

HOOKER, J. R., *Black Revolutionary: George Padmore's Path from Communism to Pan-Africanism* (New York: Praeger, 1967).

HORNE, ALISTAIR, *A Savage War of Peace* (Macmillan, 1977).

HOWARD, ANTHONY, *Crossman: The Pursuit of Power* (Cape, 1990).

HOWELL, DAVID, *A Lost Left* (Manchester: Manchester University Press, 1986).

HOWE, STEPHEN, *Decolonisations: Postcoloniality, Culture, and the Politics of Identity* (Verso, forthcoming 1993).

HUGHES, EMRYS, *Keir Hardie* (Allen & Unwin, 1956).

HUTCHINSON, FRANCIS, *The Illusion of Permanence* (Princeton, NJ: Princeton University Press, 1967).

HYAM, RONALD, *The Failure of South African Expansion, 1908–1948* (Macmillan, 1972).

—— (ed.), *British Documents on the End of Empire: Series A*, ii. *The Labour*

Government and the End of Empire, 1945–1951, 4 vols, (HMSO for the Institute of Commonwealth Studies, 1992).

HYNDMAN, H. M., *England for All: A Textbook of Democracy*, ed. C. Tsuzuki (Brighton: Harvester, 1973; orig. pub. 1881).

—— *The Awakening of Asia* (Cassell, 1919).

India League, *Condition of India: Being the Report of the Delegation sent to India by the India League, in 1932* (Essential News Ltd., 1933).

JACKSON, ROBERT, *Rebels and Whips: An Analysis of Dissension, Discipline and Cohesion in British Political Parties* (Macmillan, 1968).

JACKSON, T. A., *Solo Trumpet* (Lawrence & Wishart, 1953).

JAGAN, CHEDDI, *Forbidden Freedom* (Lawrence & Wishart, 1954).

—— *The West on Trial* (Michael Joseph, 1966).

JAMES, C. L. R., *The Black Jacobins: Toussaint l'Ouverture and the San Domingo Revolution* (Allison & Busby, 1980; orig. pub. 1938).

—— *Notes on Dialectics* (Allison & Busby, 1980; orig. pub. 1948).

—— *Nkrumah and the Ghana Revolution* (Allison & Busby, 1977; orig. pub. 1962).

—— *The Future in the Present* (Allison & Busby, 1977).

—— *Spheres of Existence* (Allison & Busby, 1980).

—— *At the Rendezvous of Victory* (Allison & Busby, 1984).

JENKINS, MARK, *Bevanism: Labour's High Tide* (Nottingham: Spokesman, 1979).

JONES, ARTHUR CREECH (ed.), *New Fabian Colonial Essays* (Hogarth, 1959).

JONES, GARETH STEDMAN, *Languages of Class* (Cambridge: Cambridge University Press, 1983).

JONES, JACK, *My Lively Life* (John Long, 1928).

JOYCE, PATRICK, *Visions of the People* (Cambridge: Cambridge University Press, 1991).

KADALIE, CLEMENTS, *My Life and the ICU*, ed. Stanley Trapido (Frank Cass, 1970).

KAHLER, MILES, *Decolonization in Britain and France* (Princeton, NJ: Princeton University Press, 1984).

KAYE, Sir CECIL, *Communism in India* (Delhi: Government Publishers, 1926).

KEATLEY, PATRICK, *The Politics of Partnership* (Harmondsworth: Penguin, 1963).

KEMP, TOM, *Theories of Imperialism* (Dennis Dobson, 1967).

KENDALL, WALTER, *The Revolutionary Movement in Britain, 1900–1921* (Weidenfeld & Nicolson, 1969).

KENNEDY, PAUL, *Strategy and Diplomacy, 1870–1945* (Allen & Unwin, 1983).

KENT, JOHN, *The Internationalisation of Colonialism: Britain, France, and Black Africa, 1939–1956* (Oxford: Oxford University Press, 1992).

KILLICK, TONY, *Development Economics in Action: A Study of Economic Policies in Ghana* (Heinemann, 1978).

KILLINGRAY, DAVID, and RATHBONE, RICHARD (eds.), *Africa and the Second World War* (Macmillan, 1986).

KING, F., and MATTHEWS, G. (eds.), *About Turn: The British Communist Party and the Second World War: The Verbatim Record of the Central Committee Meetings of 25 September and 2–3 October, 1939* (Lawrence & Wishart, 1990).

KIRKMAN, W. P., *Unscrambling an Empire: A Critique of British Colonial Policy, 1956–1966* (Chatto & Windus, 1966).

KISCH, RICHARD, *The Days of the Good Soldiers: Communists in the Armed Forces WWII* (Journeyman Press, 1985).

KLUGMANN, JAMES, *History of the Communist Party of Great Britain*, 2 vols. (Lawrence & Wishart, 1968, 1969).

KNEI-PAZ, BARUCH, *The Social and Political Thought of Leon Trotsky* (Oxford: Oxford University Press, 1978).

KNOWLES, WILLIAM H., *Trade Union Development and Industrial Relations in the British West Indies* (Berkeley, Calif.: University of California Press, 1959).

KNOX, WILLIAM, *James Maxton* (Manchester: Manchester University Press, 1987).

KOEBNER, RICHARD, and SCHMIDT, H. DAN, *Imperialism: The Story and Significance of a Political Word, 1840–1960* (Cambridge: Cambridge University Press, 1964).

KOLKO, GABRIEL, *The Politics of War* (Weidenfeld & Nicolson, 1969).

KOSS, STEPHEN (ed.), *The Pro-Boers* (Chicago: Chicago University Press, 1973).

KYLE, KEITH, *Suez* (Weidenfeld & Nicolson, 1991).

LAGUERRE, JOHN GAFFAR, *The Social and Political Thought of the Colonial Intelligentsia* (Mona, Jamaica: Institute of Social and Economic Research, 1982).

LANGLEY, J. AYODELE, *Pan-Africanism and Nationalism in West Africa, 1900–1945* (Oxford: Oxford University Press, 1973).

LANSBURY, G., *Labour's Way with the Commonwealth* (Methuen, 1935).

LASKI, HAROLD (ed.), *Programme for Victory: A Collection of Essays Prepared for the Fabian Society* (Routledge, 1941).

LEE, FRANCIS, *Fabianism and Colonialism: The Life and Political Thought of Lord Sydney Olivier* (Defiant Books, 1988).

LEE, J. M., *Colonial Development and Good Government: A Study of the Ideas Expressed by the British Official Classes in Planning Decolonisation, 1939–1964* (Oxford: Clarendon Press, 1967).

—— and PETTER, MARTIN, *The Colonial Office, War and Development Policy* (Maurice Temple Smith for Institute of Development Studies, 1982).

LENIN, V. I., *Imperialism, the Highest Stage of Capitalism* (Peking: Foreign Languages Press, 1975; orig. pub. 1916).

—— *Left-Wing Communism: An Infantile Disorder* (Peking: Foreign Languages Press, 1975; orig. pub. 1920).

LEWIS, GORDON K., *The Growth of the Modern West Indies* (New York: Monthly Review, 1968).

—— *Slavery, Imperialism and Freedom: Studies in English Radical Thought* (New York: Monthly Review, 1978).

LEWIS, RUPERT, *Marcus Garvey: Anti-Colonial Champion* (Karia Press, 1987).

LEYS, NORMAN, *A Last Chance in Kenya* (Hogarth, 1931).

—— *The Colour Bar in East Africa* (Hogarth, 1941).

LIAUZU, CLAUDE, *Aux origines des tiers-mondismes: colonisés et anti-colonialistes en France* (1919–1939) (Paris: L'Harmattan, 1982).

LICHTHEIM, GEORGE, *Marxism in Modern France* (New York: Columbia University Press, 1966).

—— *A Short History of Socialism* (Fontana, 1975).

LOUIS, WM. ROGER, *Imperialism at Bay: The United States and the Decolonization of the British Empire, 1941–1945* (Oxford: Oxford University Press, 1978).

—— *The British Empire in the Middle East, 1945–1951* (Oxford: Oxford University Press, 1984).

—— and OWEN, ROGER (eds.), *Suez 1956: The Crisis and its Consequences* (Oxford: Oxford University Press, 1989).

LUXEMBURG, ROSA, and BUKHARIN, NIKOLAI, *Imperialism and the Accumulation of Capital*, ed. Ken Tarbuck (Allen Lane, 1972).

MACDONALD, J. RAMSAY, *Labour and the Empire* (George Allen, 1907).

MACFARLANE, L. G., *The British Communist Party: Its Origins and Development until 1929* (MacGibbon & Kee, 1966).

MACINTYRE, STUART, *A Proletarian Science: Marxism in Britain 1918–1933* (Cambridge: Cambridge University Press, 1980).

—— *Little Moscows: Communism and Working-Class Militancy in Inter-War Britain* (Croom Helm, 1980).

MACKENZIE, JOHN M., *Propaganda and Empire* (Manchester: Manchester University Press, 1984).

—— (ed.), *Imperialism and Popular Culture* (Manchester: Manchester University Press, 1986).

MACKENZIE, NORMAN, and MACKENZIE, JEANNE, *The First Fabians* (Weidenfeld & Nicolson, 1977).

MCKIBBIN, ROSS, *The Evolution of the Labour Party, 1910–1924* (Oxford: Oxford University Press, 1974).

MACLANE, CHARLES B., *Soviet Strategies in Southeast Asia* (Princeton, NJ: Princeton University Press, 1966).

MCLENNAN, GREGOR, *Marxism and the Methodologies of History* (Verso, 1981).

MACMILLAN, HUGH, and MARKS, SHULA (eds.), *Africa and Empire: W. M. Macmillan, Historian and Social Critic* (Temple Smith for Institute of Commonwealth Studies, 1989).

MACMILLAN, MONA, *Champion of Africa: W. M. Macmillan, The Second Phase* (Long Wittenham: the author, 1985).

MACMILLAN, W. M., *Warning from the West Indies* (Faber & Faber, 1936; 2nd edn., Harmondsworth: Penguin, 1938).

—— *Africa Emergent* (Faber & Faber, 1938; 2nd edn., Harmondsworth: Penguin, 1949).

—— *The Road to Self-Rule: A Study in Colonial Evolution* (Faber & Faber, 1959).

MCNAIR, JOHN, *James Maxton: The Beloved Rebel* (Allen & Unwin, 1953).

MAKONNEN, T. R., *Pan-Africanism from Within* (Nairobi: Oxford University Press, 1973).

MALLIA-MILANES, VICTOR (ed.), *The British Colonial Experience, 1800–1964: The Impact on Maltese Society* (Malta: Mireva Publications, 1988).

MANDEL, ERNEST, *Trotsky: A Study in the Dynamic of His Thought* (New Left Books, 1979).

MANGAN, J. A. (ed.), *Making Imperial Mentalities* (Manchester: Manchester University Press, 1990).

MARSEILLE, JACQUES, *Empire colonial et capitalisme français* (Paris: Albin Michel, 1984).

MARTIN, TONY, *Race First* (Westport, Conn.: Greenwood Press, 1976).

—— *The Pan-African Connection* (Dover, Mass.: The Majority Press, 1983).

MARX, KARL, *The Revolutions of 1848*, ed. David Fernbach (Harmondsworth: Penguin, 1973).

—— and ENGELS, FRIEDRICH, *On Colonialism* (Moscow: Progress Publishers, 1959).

—— and —— *Collected Works* (Lawrence & Wishart, 1975–).

MASANI, M. R., *The Communist Party of India* (Derek Verschoyle, 1954).

MEANS, GORDON K., *Malaysian Politics* (Hutchinson, 1965).

MEMMI, ALBERT, *The Colonizer and the Colonized* (Boston, Mass.: Beacon, 1967; orig. pub. in French 1957).

MERLE, MARCEL (ed.), *L'Anticolonialisme Européen de Las Casas à Karl Marx* (Paris: Armend Colin, 1969).

MIDDLEMASS, R. K., *The Clydesiders* (Hutchinson, 1965).

MIKARDO, IAN, *Back-Bencher* (Weidenfeld & Nicolson, 1988).

MILBURN, JOSEPHIRE, *British Business and Ghanaian Independence* (Hanover, NH: New England University Press, 1977).

MILIBAND, R., and SAVILLE, J. (eds.), *The Socialist Register* (Merlin, annually, 1962–).

MILL, J. S., *Utilitarianism, Liberty, and Representative Government* (Everyman edn., 1968).

MINKIN, LEWIS, *The Labour Party Conference* (Manchester: Manchester University Press, 2nd edn., 1980).

MITCHELL, AUSTIN, *Westminster Man* (Methuen, 1982).

MOMMSEN, WOLFGANG, and OSTERHAMMEL, JUERGEN (eds.), *Imperialism and After: Continuities and Discontinuities* (Allen & Unwin/German Historical Institute, 1986).

MONETA, JACOB (ed.), *La Politique du PCF dans la question coloniale, 1920–1963* (Paris: Maspero, 1971).

MOORE, R. J., *Escape from Empire: The Attlee Government and the Indian Problem* (Oxford: Oxford University Press, 1983).

MOREL, E. D., *Nigeria: Its Peoples and Its Problems* (Smith, Elder and Co., 1911).

MORGAN, AUSTEN, *James Connolly: A Political Biography* (Manchester: Manchester University Press, 1988).

MORGAN, D. J., *The Official History of Colonial Development*, 5 vols. (Macmillan, 1980).

MORGAN, KENNETH O., *Labour in Power, 1945–1951* (Oxford: Oxford University Press, 1984).

MORGAN, Kevin, *Against Fascism and War* (Manchester: Manchester University Press, 1989).

MORLEY, JOHN, *The Life of Richard Cobden* (Chapman & Hall, 1879).

MORRIS-JONES, W. H., and FISCHER, GEORGES (eds.), *Decolonisation and After* (Frank Cass, 1980).

MORRISON, HERBERT, *Government and Parliament* (Oxford: Oxford University Press, 1954).

MORRISON, SYBIL, *I Renounce War* (Sheppard Press, 1962).

MUNROE, TREVOR, *The Politics of Constitutional Decolonization: Jamaica, 1944–62* (Kingston, Jamaica: Institute of Social and Economic Research, 1972).

MURPHY, J. T., *New Horizons* (John Lane, 1941).

MURRAY-BROWN, JEREMY, *Kenyatta* (Fontana, 1974).

NAIRN, TOM, *The Break-Up of Britain: Crisis and Neo-Nationalism* (Verso, 2nd edn., 1981).

—— *The Enchanted Glass* (Century Hutchinson, 1988).

NANDA, B. R. (ed.), *Socialism in India* (Delhi: Vikas, 1971).

NEHRU, JAWAHARLAL, *The Discovery of India* (Meridian, 1946).

NEUMANN, FRANZ, *Behemoth: The Structure and Practice of National Socialism* (Gollancz, 1942).

NEWTON, K., *The Sociology of British Communism* (Allen Lane, 1969).

NGUGI WA THIONG'O, *A Grain of Wheat* (Heinemann, 1967).

NICHOLSON, MARJORIE, *The TUC Overseas: The Roots of Policy* (Allen & Unwin, 1986).

NKRUMAH, KWAME, *Ghana: The Autobiography of Kwame Nkrumah* (Edinburgh: Nelson, 1957).

NORTON, PHILIP, *Dissension in the House of Commons, 1945–74* (Macmillan, 1975).

OLUSANYA, G. O., *The West African Students' Union and the Politics of Decolonisation, 1925–1958* (Ibadan: Daystar Press, 1982).

ORWELL, GEORGE, *Collected Essays, Journalism and Letters*, 4 vols. (Harmondsworth: Penguin, 1976).

OVENDALE, RITCHIE (ed.), *The Foreign Policy of the British Labour Governments, 1945–51* (Leicester: Leicester University Press, 1984).

OVERSTREET, GENE, and WINDMILLER, MARSHALL, *Communism in India* (Berkeley, Calif.: University of California Press, 1959).

OXAAL, IVOR, *Black Intellectuals Come to Power: The Rise of Creole Nationalism in Trinidad and Tobago* (Cambridge, Mass.: Harvard University Press, 1968).

PADMORE, GEORGE, *Africa: Britain's Third Empire* (Dennis Dobson, 1949).

—— *The Gold Coast Revolution* (Dennis Dobson, 1953).

—— *Pan-Africanism or Communism?* (Dennis Dobson, 1956).

PEARCE, R. D., *The Turning Point in Africa: British Colonial Policy, 1938–48* (Frank Cass, 1982).

PELLING, HENRY, *The British Communist Party: A Historical Profile* (Adam & Charles Black, 1958).

—— *Popular Politics and Society in Late Victorian Britain* (Macmillan, 1968).

—— *The Labour Governments, 1945–51* (Macmillan, 1984).

PHILLIPS, ANNE, *The Enigma of Colonialism: British Policy in West Africa* (James Currey, 1989).

PIMLOTT, BEN, *Hugh Dalton* (Cape, 1985).

—— (ed.), *Fabian Essays in Socialist Thought* (Heinemann, 1984).

—— (ed.), *The Political Diary of Hugh Dalton, 1918–40, 1945–60* (Jonathan Cape, 1986).

POCOCK, J. G. A., *The Machiavellian Moment* (Princeton, NJ: Princeton University Press, 1975).

—— *Politics, Language and Time* (2nd edn., Chicago: Chicago University Press, 1989).

PORTER, BERNARD, *Critics of Empire* (Macmillan, 1968).

POST, KEN, *Arise Ye Starvelings: The Jamaican Labour Rebellion of 1938 and its Aftermath* (The Hague: Institute of Social Studies, 1978).

—— *Strike the Iron: A Colony at War, Jamaica, 1939–1945*, 2 vols. (Atlantic Highlands, NJ: Humanities Press, 1981).

PRICE, RICHARD, *An Imperial War and the British Working Class* (Routledge & Kegan Paul, 1972).

PRITT, D. N., *The Autobiography of D. N. Pritt*. iii. *The Defence Accuses* (Lawrence & Wishart, 1966).

PUGH, PATRICIA, *Educate, Agitate, Organise: 100 Years of Fabian Socialism* (Methuen, 1984).

RAMDIN, RON, *The Making of the Black Working Class in Britain* (Gower, 1987).

RANGER, T. O. (ed.), *Emerging Themes in African History* (Heinemann, 1968).

RATHBONE, RICHARD (ed.), *British Documents on the End of Empire: Series B*, i. *Ghana*, 2 vols. (HMSO for the Institute of Commonwealth Studies, 1992).

RAY, SIBNARAYAN (ed.), *Selected Works of M. N. Roy*, i. *1917–1922* (Delhi: Oxford University Press, 1987).

REE, JONATHAN, *Proletarian Philosophers* (Oxford: Oxford University Press, 1984).

REX, JOHN, and TOMLINSON, SALLY, *Colonial Immigrants in a British City* (Routledge & Kegan Paul, 1979).

REY, PIERRE-PHILIPE, *Colonialisme, neo-colonialisme et transition au capitalisme* (Paris: Maspero, 1971).

REYNOLDS, REGINALD, *My Life and Crimes* (Jarrolds, 1956).

RICH, PAUL, *Race and Empire in British Politics* (Cambridge: Cambridge University Press, 1986).

RICHARDS, P. G., *The Backbenchers* (Faber & Faber, 1974).

ROBERTS, B. C., *Labour in the Tropical Territories of the Commonwealth* (Bell, 1964).

ROBINSON, C., *Black Marxism: The Making of the Black Radical Tradition* (Zed, 1983).

ROBINSON, K., *The Dilemmas of Trusteeship* (Oxford: Oxford University Press, 1965).

ROBINSON, RONALD, and GALLAGHER, JOHN, with DENNY, ALICE, *Africa and the Victorians: The Official Mind of Imperialism* (Macmillan, 1961).

ROLPH, C. H., *Kingsley: The Life, Letters and Diaries of Kingsley Martin* (Gollancz, 1973).

ROTHSTEIN, THEODORE, *Egypt's Ruin* (Fifield, 1910).

—— (as John Bryan), *Essays in Socialism and War* (British Socialist Party, 1917).

—— *From Chartism to Labourism* (Martin Lawrence, 1929).

RUBINSTEIN, DAVID (ed.), *People for the People* (Ithaca, 1973).

RUESCHEMEYER, DIETRICH, HUBER STEPHENS, EVELYNE, and STEPHENS, JOHN D., *Capitalist Development and Democracy* (Cambridge: Polity, 1992).

SAID, EDWARD W., *The Question of Palestine* (Routledge & Kegan Paul, 1980).

SAKLATVALA, SEHRI, *The Fifth Commandment* (Salford: Miranda Press, 1991).

SAMUEL, RAPHAEL (ed.), *People's History and Socialist Theory* (Routledge & Kegan Paul, 1981).

—— (ed.), *Patriotism: The Making and Unmaking of British National Identity*, 3 vols. (Routledge & Kegan Paul, 1989).

SARTRE, J-P., *Critique of Dialectical Reason* (New Left Books, 1976).

SCHNEER, JONATHAN, *Labour's Conscience: The Labour Left, 1945–51* (Unwin Hyman, 1988).

SCOTT, MICHAEL, *A Time to Speak* (Faber & Faber, 1958).

SEAL, ANIL, *The Emergence of Indian Nationalism* (Cambridge: Cambridge University Press, 1968).

SEMMEL, BERNARD, *Imperialism and Social Reform: British Social-Imperial Thought, 1895–1914* (Allen & Unwin, 1960).

SEN, AMARTYA, *Poverty and Famines: An Essay on Entitlement and Deprivation* (Oxford: Oxford University Press, 1981).

SEYD, PATRICK, and WHITELEY, PAUL, *Labour's Grass Roots* (Oxford: Oxford University Press, 1992).

SHAW, GEORGE BERNARD (ed.), *Fabianism and the Empire: A Manifesto of the Fabian Society* (Fabian Society, 1900).

SHIPLEY, PETER, *Revolutionaries in Modern Britain* (Bodley Head, 1976).

SHORT, ANTHONY, *The Communist Insurrection in Malaya, 1948–1960* (Frederick Muller, 1975).

SIMONS, JACK, and SIMONS, RAY, *Class and Colour in South Africa, 1850–1950* (2nd edn., International Defence and Aid Fund, 1983).

SITHOLE, NDABANINGI, *African Nationalism* (2nd edn., Oxford: Oxford University Press, 1968).

SLATER, MONTAGU, *The Trial of Jomo Kenyatta* (Secker & Warburg, 1955).

SOREF, HAROLD, and GREIG, JOHN, *The Puppeteers: An Examination of those Organisations and Bodies concerned with the Elimination of the White Man in Africa* (Tandem Books, 1965).

SPRATT, PHILIP, *Blowing Up India: Reminiscences and Reflections of a Former Comintern Emissary* (Calcutta: Prachi Prakashan, 1955).

SQUIRES, MIKE, *Saklatvala: A Political Biography* (Lawrence & Wishart, 1990).

STOKES, ERIC, *The English Utilitarians and India* (Oxford: Oxford University Press, 1959).

STONEHOUSE, JOHN, *Prohibited Immigrant* (Bodley Head, 1960).

STRACHEY, JOHN, *The End of Empire* (Gollancz, 1959).

STRANGE, SUSAN, *Sterling and British Policy* (Oxford: Oxford University Press, 1971).

STUDDERT-KENNEDY, GERALD, *British Christians, Indian Nationalists, and the Raj* (Delhi: Oxford University Press, 1991).

STURGIS, JAMES L., *John Bright and the Empire* (Athlone Press, 1969).

TANDON, YASH (ed.), *Debate on Class, State and Imperialism* (Dar es Salaam: Tanzania Publishing House, 1982).

TAYLOR, A. J. P., *The Troublemakers: Dissent over Foreign Policy, 1792–1939* (Hamish Hamilton, 1957).

TEMU, A. and SWAI, B., *Historians and Africanist History: A Critique* (Zed Books, 1981).

THOMAS, HUGH, *The Suez Affair* (Weidenfeld & Nicolson, 1967).

THOMPSON, E. P., *William Morris: Romantic to Revolutionary* (2nd edn., Merlin, 1977).

—— *Writing by Candlelight* (Merlin, 1980).

—— *Customs in Common* (Merlin, 1991).

—— (ed.), *Out Of Apathy* (Stevens & Sons for New Left Books, 1960).

THOMPSON, LAURENCE, *Robert Blatchford: Portrait of an Englishman* (Gollancz, 1951).

THORNE, CHRISTOPHER, *Allies of a Kind: The United States, Britain and the War against Japan, 1941–1945* (Oxford: Oxford University Press, 1978).

THORNTON, A. P., *The Imperial Idea and its Enemies* (Macmillan, 1959).

THROUP, DAVID W., *Economic and Social Origins of Mau Mau* (James Currey, 1987).

TINKER, HUGH (ed.), *Burma: The Struggle for Independence*, i. *From Military Occupation to Civil Government*; ii. *From General Strike to Independence* (HMSO, 1983, 1984).

TSUZUKI, CHUSHICHI, *H. M. Hyndman and British Socialism* (Oxford: Oxford University Press, 1961).

ULYANOVSKY, R. A., *Socialism and the Newly Independent Nations* (Moscow: Progress Publishers, 1974).

—— *The Cominteon and the East*, 3 vols. (Moscow: Progress Publishers, 1978, 1979, 1981).

UPWARD, EDWARD, *The Rotten Elements* (Heinemann, 1969).

VANSINA, JAN, *Paths in the Rainforests: Towards a History of Political Tradition in Equatorial Africa* (James Currey, 1990).

VITAL, DAVID, *Zionism: The Formative Years* (Oxford: Oxford University Press, 1982).

WALEY, DANIEL, *British Public Opinion and the Abyssinian War* (Maurice Temple Smith, 1975).

WALKER, PATRICK GORDON, *The Commonwealth* (Secker & Warburg, 1962).

WALLERSTEIN, IMMANUEL, *Africa: The Politics of Unity* (New York: Random House, 1967).

—— *The Modern World System*, 3 vols. (New York: Academic Press, 1974, 1980, 1989).

—— *The Capitalist World Economy* (Cambridge: Cambridge University Press, 1979).

WARREN, BILL, *Imperialism, Pioneer of Capitalism* (New Left Books, 1980).

WASSERMAN, GARY, *Politics of Decolonization: Kenya Europeans and the Land Issue, 1960–1965* (Cambridge: Cambridge University Press, 1976).

WEDGWOOD, JOSIAH, *Essays and Adventures of a Labour MP* (Allen & Unwin, 1924).

WEILER, PETER, *British Labour and the Cold War* (Stanford, Calif.: Stanford University Press, 1988).

WEINER, MYRON, and OZBUDUN, ERGUN (eds.), *Competitive Elections in Developing Countries* (Washington, DC: American Enterprise Institute, 1987).

WHEEN, FRANCIS, *Tom Driberg: His Life and Indiscretions* (Chatto & Windus, 1990).

WHYTE, JOHN, *Interpreting Northern Ireland* (Oxford: Oxford University Press, 1990).

WIDGERY, DAVID (ed.), *The Left in Britain, 1956–1968* (Harmondsworth: Penguin, 1976).

WIENER, MARTIN J., *English Culture and the Decline of the Industrial Spirit, 1850–1980* (Cambridge: Cambridge University Press, 1981).

WILLIAMS, PHILIP, *Hugh Gaitskell* (Cape, 1979).

WILSON, HAROLD, *The War on World Poverty: An Appeal to the Conscience of Mankind* (Gollancz, 1953).

WINDMULLER, J. P., *The International Trade Union Movement* (Deventer: Kluwer, 1980).

WINTER, J. M. (ed.), *The Working Class in Modern British History* (Cambridge: Cambridge University Press, 1983).

WINTRINGHAM, TOM, *New Ways of War* (Harmondsworth: Penguin Special, Aug. 1940).

WODDIS, JACK, *Africa: The Way Ahead* (Lawrence & Wishart, 1963).

—— *Introduction to Neo-Colonialism* (Lawrence & Wishart, 1967).

WOLF, ERIC, *Europe and the People without History* (Berkeley, Calif.: University of California Press, 1982).

WOODHOUSE, MICHAEL, and PEARCE, BRIAN, *Essays on the History of Communism in Britain* (New Park, 1975).

WOOLF, LEONARD, *Downhill All the Way: An Autobiography of the Years 1919–1939* (Hogarth, 1967).

WORCESTER, KENT, *C. L. R. James: A Political Biography* (Lanham, Md.: North & South Press, 1988).

WORSLEY, PETER, *The Three Worlds* (Weidenfeld & Nicolson, 1984).

WRIGHT, FRANK, *Northern Ireland. A Comparative Analysis* (Dublin: Gill & Macmillan, 1988).

Pamphlets

The following list includes not only pamphlets cited in the footnotes, but also attempts to catalogue all radical, critical, and left-wing pamphlet material which I have been able to trace published in Britain on colonial subjects between 1918 and 1964. Undoubtedly this remains a far from complete list of such material. Place of publication is London unless otherwise stated. Pamphlets attributed to an organisation are those where no individual author is given, and are published by the organisation unless otherwise noted.

ALLEN, ELIZABETH A., *Citizen of the Colonies in Cyprus* (Committee for Cyprus Afairs, n.d. but *c*.1950).

AMIS, KINGSLEY, *Socialism and the Intellectuals* (Fabian Tract 304, 1957).

Anti-Slavery and Aborigines' Protection Society, *A Draft Colonial Mandate submitted to the Commission on Mandates* (1919).

Association for World Peace, *War on Want: A Plan for World Development* (1952; written by Sir Richard Acland, Leslie Hale, Mary Rosser, and Harold Wilson).

AUDIT, GEORGE, *Egypt and a Labour Government* (CPGB 1947).

BANDA, HASTINGS K., and NKUMBULA, HARRY, *Federation in Central Africa* ('On behalf of Nyasaland and Northern Rhodesian Africans in UK', May, 1949).

BARNES, LEONARD, *The Future of Colonies* (Hogarth 'Day to Day' series 32, 1936).

—— *Skeleton of Empire* ('Fact' series 3, June, 1937).

BIRCH, LIONEL, *The Demand for Colonies* (League of Nations Union, 1936).

BOLSOVER, PHILIP, *Kenya: What Are the Facts?* (CPGB, May 1953).

BOWEN, W., *Colonial Trade Unions* (FCB, Oct. 1954).

BRADLEY, BEN, *Colonies, Mandates and Peace* (CPGB 1936).

—— *India: What We Must Do* (CPGB 1942).

—— *India's Famine: The Facts* (CPGB, Nov. 1943).

—— *The Colonies and the Future* (CPGB Study Syllabus, 1944).

—— (introd.), *India's Problems* (CPGB 1942).

—— and HUTCHINSON, LESTER, *India and a New Dictatorship* (LAI British section, n.d. but 1934).

BRAILSFORD, H. N., *India in Chains* (Socialist League, n.d. but 1937?).

BRANSON, NOREEN (ed.), *British Soldier in India: The Letters of Clive Branson* (CPGB 1944).

BRIDGEMAN, REGINALD, *The Meerut Conspiracy Case* (LAI 1931).

British Guiana Freedom Association, *Independence for British Guiana Now* (1963).

British Youth Peace Assembly, *Life in the Empire No. 1: The Bengal Peasant* (n.d.).

BROCKWAY, FENNER, *India and its Government* (Labour Publishing Co., 1921).

—— *The Way Out* (ILP 'Socialist Britain' series 2, 1942).

—— *Why Mau Mau?* (COPAI 1953).

—— *British Protectorates: Key to South African Freedom* (UDC, July 1957).

—— *1960: Africa's Year of Destiny* (MCF 1960).

—— *What is the MCF?* (MCF, n.d. but *c.*1963).

—— *The White Dictators of Southern Rhodesia* (MCF, n.d. but *c.*1963).

BURNS, ELINOR, *British Imperialism in Malaya* (Labour Research Department, 1926).

—— *British Imperialism in China* (Labour Research Department, 1926).

—— *British Imperialism in East Africa* (Labour Research Department, 1926).

—— *British Imperialism in West Africa* (Labour Research Department, 1927).

BURNS, ÉMILE, *Imperialism: An Outline Course for Students' Classes and Study Circles* (Labour Research Department, 1927).

BUXTON, CHARLES RODEN, *The Black Man's Rights* (ILP, n.d. but 1925).

—— *The Future of Empire* (Friends' Peace Committee, n.d. but *c.*1936).

Caribbean Labour Congress (London Branch), *Federation and Self-Government Now or Colonialism and Slavery for Ever* (1951).

CARRITT, MICHAEL, *India* (CPGB 1941).

CHIUME, M. W. KANYAMA, *Nyasaland Speaks: An Appeal to the British People* (UDC/MCF 1959).

CLEGG, ARTHUR, *Hands Off Indonesia* (CPGB, Jan. 1946).

Committee for the Rights of Oman/MCF, *The Oman Question in the United Nations* (MCF, n.d. but *c.*1963).

Communist Party of Great Britain, *Introduction to Communist International Theses on the National and Colonial Question* (1921).

—— *Is India Different? The Class Struggle in India* (1927).

—— *The Revolutionary Movement in the Colonies* (VI Comintern Congress theses, Modern Books, 1929).

—— *Class Against Class: The General Election Programme of the CPGB* (1929).

—— *Palestine: Terror or Peace* (1938).

—— *War! Communist Policy* (Central Committee manifesto, 2 Sept. 1939).

—— *Peace or War?* (Central Committee manifesto, 7 Oct. 1939).

—— *The Empire and the War* (1940).

—— *The Colonies: The Way Forward* (memorandum by Executive Committee, Nov. 1944).

—— *R. Palme Dutt in India: Souvenir of His Travels* (London District Committee, n.d. but 1946).

—— *We Speak for Freedom: 1947 Conference of Empire Communist Parties Report* (1947).

—— *Stop the War in Malaya* (Sept. 1948).

—— *London Labour and Colonial Freedom* (London District Committee, Apr. 1954).

—— *Allies for Freedom: 1954 Conference of Empire Communist Parties Report* (1954).

—— *Africa in World History*, History Group 'Our History' series 14, Introd. Desmond Buckle (1959).

—— *Africa: 1960* (1960).

—— /Communist Party of India, *Imperialism and Labour: The Meaning of British Policy in India. An Appeal to the Workers of Great Britain by the CPI* (1925).

Congress of Peoples Against Imperialism, *Congress of the Peoples of Europe, Africa and Asia* (1948).

—— *Charter of the Congress of the Peoples Against Imperialism* (1948).

—— *The Colonial Peoples' Appeal to the United Nations* (1952).

Conservative Commonwealth Council, *Colonial Rule: Enemies and Obligations* (Conservative Political Centre, 1955).

COWLING, J. W., *Forced Labour in the Colonies* (*PN*, July 1943).

CRIPPS, Stafford, *Empire* (India League, 1938).

CRUZ, GERALD DE, *Facing Facts in Malaya* (UDC 1952).

CUNARD, NANCY, and PADMORE, GEORGE, *The White Man's Duty* (W. H. Allen, 1942; enlarged edn. Manchester: Panaf Service Ltd., July 1945).

Cyprus Affairs Committee, *Cyprus Presents its Case to the World* (n.d. but *c*.1950).

DANGE, S. A., *India and You* (Daily Worker League; n.d. but *c*.1945; introd. Clemens Dutt).

—— *In the Rear of the 14th Army: Why India is Not Mobilised* (the author, Dec. 1944).

DANQUAH, J. B., *Friendship and Empire: Impression of the Africa Conference* (FCB Colonial Controversy series 5, 1949).

DAVIDSON, BASIL, *Tomorrow's Africa? A Report on Some New Trends* (MCF/UDC 1962).

DAVIES, CLEMENT, *Famine in India: Our Duty* (India Relief Committee, n.d. but late 1943).

DJASSI, ABEL (pseud. of Amilcar Cabral), *The Facts About Portugal's African Colonies* (UDC 1960).

DUMPLETON, C. W., *Colonial Development Corporation* (Fabian Society Research series 186, 1957).

DUTT, Clemens, *'Conspiracy Against the King'* (National Meerut Prisoners' Defence Committee, June 1930).

DUTT, R. PALME, *Empire 'Socialism'* (CPGB 1925).

—— *Free the Colonies!* (National Minority Movement, n.d.).

—— *The Communist Party in the Fight Against Imperialism* (World News, 1952).

—— *Stand by Congo* (CPGB 1960).

EBER, JOHN, *Malaya's Freedom is Vital to Britain* (Britain–Malaya Committee, 1954).

EVENS, G. K., *Public Opinion on Colonial Affaire* (HMSO NS 119, June 1948).

Fabian Colonial Bureau, *Labour in the Colonies* (Fabian Research series 61, 1942).

—— *Kenya: White Man's Country?* (Fabian Research series 78, 1944).

—— *Hunger or Health in the Colonies* (Fabian Society Research series 80, 1944).

—— *Four Colonial Questions* (Fabian Research series 88, 1944).

—— *Colonies and International Conscience* (Fabian Research series 92, 1945).

—— *Kenya Controversy* (Colonial Controversy series 4, 1947).

—— *Advance to Democracy* (Colonial Controversy series 8, 1952).

—— *East African Future* (Colonial Controversy series 9, 1952).

—— *Opportunity in Kenya* (Fabian Research series 162, 1953).

FLETCHER, EILEEN, *Truth About Kenya* (MCF/PN 1955, foreword by Leslie Hale).

FOX-PITT, THOMAS, *Handbook for Federal Politicians* (MCF 1956).

GLADING, PERCY, *The Meerut Conspiracy Case* (CPGB, n.d. but 1933).

GRIFFITHS, JAMES, HINDEN, RITA, and CREECH JONES, ARTHUR, *The Way Forward* (FCB Colonial Controversy series 7, 1950).

HART, RICHARD, *Origins and Development of the Working Class in the English-Speaking Caribbean Area, 1897–1937* (Community Education Trust, n.d.).

HATCH, JOHN, *The Intelligent Socialist's Guide to Africa* (Tribune, 1952).

HEWITT, DOROTHY, *Truth About India* (India League, 1941).

HINDEN, RITA, *The Colonies—And Us* (Fabian Special pamphlet 4, n.d.).

—— *Socialists and the Empire: Five Years' Work of the Fabian Colonial Bureau* (Fabian Society, n.d. but *c*.1945).

—— *The Labour Party and the Colonies* (Labour Discussion series 8, 1946).

—— *Common Sense and Colonial Development* (Fabian Research series 131, 1949).

—— *No Cheer for Central Africa* (Fabian Research series 197, 1958).

HODGKIN, THOMAS, *The Colonial Empire: A Student's Guide* (Workers' Educational Association Study Outline 7, 1942).

—— *Freedom for the Gold Coast?* (UDC 1951).

HORRABIN, J. F., *The Break with Imperialism* (Socialist League, n.d. but *c*.1934).

—— *A Short History of the British Empire* (National Council of Labour Colleges, Tillicoutry, 1946).

HUGHES, EMRYS, *British Guiana: Iron Hand and Wooden Head: An Indictment of Mr. Oliver Lyttelton* (*PN* 1953).

Hull Youth Group, League of Nations Union, *Civilisation and Empire* (Hull: E. M. Frost, 1936, foreword by A. A. Milne).

HUTCHINSON, LESTER, *Meerut, 1929–1932* (Manchester: Meerut Defence Committee, 1932).

Independent Labour Party, *Socialism and the Empire* (Empire Policy Committee report, 1926).

—— *ILP Policy: The Basic Resolutions Adopted by the Annual Conference* (1936).

—— *Italy and Abyssinia: Should British Workers Take Sides?* (Controversy Special Supplement 1, 1936).

—— *Socialist Policy for 1938* (1938).

India League, *Britain's Prisoner* (1941).

—— *India! We Call on the People of Britain!* (July, 1942; speeches by Sorensen, Palme Dutt, and others).

—— *India and Victory: Our Immediate Task* (July, 1942; signed by P. G. Barstow, S. O. Davies, and Alexander Sloan).

—— *The Conflict in India* (Aug. 1942).

—— *The Prime Minister on India* (Sept. 1942; written by Krishna Menon).

—— *Independence* (Jan. 1943).

—— *The Indian Demand and British Policy: Gandhi–Viceroy Correspondence* (Feb. 1943).

—— *The White Paper Examined* (mimeo, Mar. 1943).

'Indian Communists in Great Britain', *An Open Letter to Fighters for Freedom* (Dilip Kumar Bose, n.d. but 1949).

International African Service Bureau, *The West Indies Today* (n.d. but *c.*1938).

JACKSON, T. A., *The British Empire* (CPGB 1922).

—— *What Is the British Empire to You?* (CPGB 1925).

JAGAN, CHEDDI, *What Happened in British Guiana?* (UDC 1954).

JEFFERY, NORA, *Hands Off the Middle East!* (CPGB, n.d. but 1958).

JOANNIDES, EVROS, *The Case for Cyprus* (Committee for Cyprus Affairs, 1937/8).

JOSHI, P. C., *The Indian Communist Party* (CPGB, Sept. 1942, foreword by Harry Pollitt).

JUPP, AUDREY, *Facing Facts in British Guiana* (UDC, n.d. but 1957).

KAUNDA, KENNETH, *Dominion Status for Central Africa?* (MCF/UDC 1958).

Keep Left (*New Statesman*, 1947; by 'A Group of Members of Parliament').

Keeping Left (*New Statesman*, 1950; by Richard Crossman, Ian Mikardo *et al.*).

Kenya Committee, *Kenya—Who Are the Terrorists?* (leaflet, n.d. but 1953/4).

—— *Kenya—We Must Make Peace* (leaflet, n.d. but 1953/4).

KLOPPER, MARY, *Algeria: The Full Story* (MCF, n.d.; foreword by Fenner Brockway).

KOINANGE, MBIYU, *Land Hunger in Kenya* (UDC 1952).

LABOUR PARTY, *The Empire in Africa: Labour's Policy* (1926).

—— *The Colonies* (1933).

—— *The Demand for Colonial Territories and Equality of Economic Opportunity* (1936).

—— *The Colonies: The Labour Party's Post-War Policy for the African and Pacific Colonies* (1943).

—— *Let Us Face the Future* (election manifesto, 1945).

—— *Speakers' Handbook, 1948–9* (1948).

—— *Statement on Policy on Colonial Affairs: From Colonies to Commonwealth* (1954).

—— *Facing Facts in the Colonies* (Policy Discussion pamphlet, 1955).

—— *Suez Crisis: Labour's Fight for Peace* (Sept. 1956).

—— *Labour's Colonial Policy (1) The Plural Society* (1956).

—— *Labour's Colonial Policy (2) Economic Aid* (1957).

—— *Labour's Colonial Policy (3) The Smaller Territories* (1957).

—— *Racial Discrimination* (1958).

Labour Party Research Department, 'Talking Points' series, *The Colonial Development Corporation* (Apr. 1951).

—— *Tory Colonial Policy* (Aug. 1952).

—— *Kenya* (Dec. 1952).

—— *Central African Federation* (Mar. 1953).

—— *British Guiana* (Nov. 1953).

—— *Colonial Policy* (Jan. 1954).

—— *Spotlight on the Colonies*, parts 1 and 2 (1955).

—— *Cyprus* (1956).

—— *The Plural Society* (1956).
—— *Gold Coast to Ghana* (1956).
——*Developments in Central Africa* (1956).
—— *Central Africa*, parts 1–3 (1959).
—— *Hola* (1959).
—— *Central African Federation* (1960).
Labour Research Department, *British Guiana* (1953).
League Against Imperialism, International Secretariat, *The Colonies and the Oppressed Nations in the Struggle for Freedom* (Berlin, 1931).
League Against Imperialism, British Section, *Report of National Conference, February 1931* (1931).
—— *The Mutiny in Meerut Jail* (1930).
—— *The Meerut Prisoners and the Charge Against Them* (Modern Books, n.d. but 1931).
——*Abyssinia* (n.d. but *c.*1935).
—— *The British Empire* (n.d. but *c.*1935).
—— *China's Appeal to British Workers* (n.d. but *c.*1936).
—— *China* (1936).
LEWIN, JULIUS, *Britain's Colour Bar in Africa* (UDC, n.d. but 1952).
LEWIS, W. ARTHUR, *Labour in the West Indies* (Fabian Research series 44, 1939; new edn. ed. Susan Craig, New Beacon, 1977).
MACINTYRE, STUART, *Imperialism and the British Labour Movement in the 1920s: An Examination of Marxist Theory* (CPGB History Group, 'Our History' series 64, 1975).
MCNAIR, JOHN, *Make Britain Socialist Now!* (ILP 'Socialist Britain' series 1, 1942).
—— *What the Independent Labour Party Stands for* (ILP 1945).
MATTERS, L. W., *India* (Hurricane Books, May 1942).
MBOYA, TOM, *The Kenya Question: An African Answer* (FCB 1956).
MEDORA, ALI and WODDIS, JACK, *Social Security in the Colonies* (WFTU 1953).
MENON, V. K. KRISHNA, *Why Must India Fight?* (India League, Jan. 1940).
—— *India, Britain and Freedom* (India League, n.d. but late 1941).
MOREL, E. D., *The African Problem and the Peace Settlement* (UDC 1917).
Movement for Colonial Freedom, *Facts About Kenya* (1954/5).
—— *Facts About Algeria* (1954/5).
—— *Facts About the Gold Coast* (1954/5).
—— *Facts About Morocco* (1954/5).
——*A Policy for Colonial Freedom* (1955).
——*Ashanti and the Future of the Gold Coast* (1955).
——*A Denial of Democracy: An Analysis of the Report of the British Guiana Constitutional Commission* (1955).
—— *Mau Mau and the White Settler in Kenya* (1955).
—— *Cyprus: The Solution* (with National Cypriot Committee, 1958).

—— *What is Neo-Colonialism?* (1961).

—— *Objects and Constitution* (1961).

—— *Colonialism and the Bomb* (1963).

—— *The Unholy Alliance: Salazar–Verwoerd–Welensky* (with Anti-Apartheid Movement and Council for Freedom in Portugal and the Colonies, n.d. but 1962; foreword by Basil Davidson, Introd. Conor Cruise O'Brien).

—— *No Colour Bar Against Commonwealth Immigrants* (n.d. but 1962).

—— *No to Malaysia* (n.d. but 1963/4).

——*A Labour Government, the Colonial Peoples and the New Nations* (n.d. but 1964).

MULIRA, E. M. K., *Troubled Uganda* (FCB Colonial Controversy series 6, 1950).

National Committee for the Defence of Children, *Children in the British Colonies* (n.d. but *c.*1952).

National Council for Civil Liberties, Overseas Subcommittee, *Civil Liberties in the Colonies* (Apr. 1954).

National Meerut Defence Committee, *The Meerut Trial: Facts of the Case* (1929).

National Minority Movement, *British Imperialism: An Outline of Workers' Conditions in the Colonies* (n.d. but *c.*1928).

National Peace Council, *Peace and the Colonial Problem* (1935/6).

—— *Our Trust in Central Africa* (with Central Africa Committee and Racial Unity, 1953).

NEHRU, JAWAHARLAL, *The Parting of Ways* (India League, Jan. 1940).

—— *The Cripps Mission* (India League, 1942).

—— *What India Wants* (India League, June 1942).

—— and AZAD, A. K., *India: What Next?* (India League, n.d. but *c.*1943).

NICHOLSON, MARJORIE, *Self-Government and the Communal Problem* (Fabian Research series 126, 1948).

—— *The Future of the British Colonial Empire* (London Institute for World Affairs, 1948).

NOEL, CONRAD, *The Meaning of Imperialism* (LAI British Section, 1929).

OKAFOR, AMANKE, *Nigeria: Why We Fight for Freedom* (the author, 1949; foreword by Paul Robeson).

OLORENSHAW, ARTHUR, *Our Forces in India* (CPGB, n.d. but *c.*1943).

One Way Only: A Socialist Analysis of the Present World Crisis (*Tribune*, 1951; foreword by Nye Bevan, Harold Wilson, and John Freeman).

Oxford University Socialist Club, *Seretse Khama: A Background Study of the Southern African Crisis* (with OU West African Students' Club and OU West Indian Club; publ. by A. Sackey, secretary of OU Seretse Khama Committee, Oxford, May 1950).

PADMORE, GEORGE (ed.), *History of the Pan-African Congress* (orig. pub. 1947; repr. Hammersmith Bookshop Ltd., 1963).

PAGE ARNOT, ROBIN, *How Britain Rules India* (CPGB 1929).

PALMER, H., *India* (Marx House syllabus, Lawrence & Wishart, n.d. but *c.*1943).

PAUL, WILLIAM, *Labour and the Empire* (Socialist Labour Party, n.d. but *c.*1917).

POLLITT, HARRY, *Malaya: Stop the War!* (CPGB, Jan. 1952).

—— *Indian Diary* (CPGB 1954).

PRITT, D. N., *India Our Ally?* (Frederick Muller, 1942).

RANGER, TERENCE, *Crisis in Southern Rhodesia* (FCB 1960).

RIDLEY, F. A., and EDWARDS, BOB, *The United Socialist States of Europe* (National Labour Press, 1944).

RIDLEY, GEORGE, *India* (Labour Party, n.d. but late 1942).

SAKLATVALA, SHAPURJI, *India in the Labour World* (Labour Publishing Co. for Workers' Welfare League of India, n.d.).

SCOTT, MICHAEL, *Shadow over Africa* (UDC, n.d. but 1950).

SELWYN-CLARKE, HILDA, *New Hope in Asia* (Co-operative Party, June 1952).

SILBERMAN, L., *Crisis in Africa* (FCB Colonial Controversy series 2, 1947).

SINGTON, DERRICK, *Malayan Perspective* (FCB Colonial Controversy series 10, 1953).

SIVANANDAN, A., *Race, Class and the State: The Black Experience in Britain* (Race and Class, 1976).

SORENSEN, REGINALD, *India and the Atlantic Charter* (India League, 1942).

—— *Famine, Politics—and Mr. Amery* (India League, Jan. 1944).

STONEHOUSE, JOHN, *Central Africa: After Monckton—What Next?* (UDC/MCF, n.d. but 1960; preface by Fenner Brockway).

TAYLOR, W. L., *The Trusts Versus the People* (National Labour Press, 1944).

United Nations Association, *Congo Challenge* (n.d. but 1960).

University Labour Federation, *India's Demand for Freedom* (Lawrence & Wishart, n.d. but *c.*1940).

VARGA, E., *The Imperialist Struggle for a New Redivision of the World* (Labour Monthly War series 1, n.d. but 1941).

VERULAM, FRANK, *Imperialism and the People* (Marx House syllabus, Lawrence & Wishart, n.d. but *c.*1943).

'Vigilantes', *Abyssinia* (*NS&N*, Sept. 1935).

WELLS, H. G., *Imperialism and the Open Conspiracy* (Criterion Miscellany series 3, Faber & Faber, 1929).

WODDIS, JACK, *Stop the War in Malaya* (CPGB, May 1950).

—— *The Mask is Off: An Examination of the Activities of Trade Union Advisers in the British Colonies* (Thames Publishers, June 1954).

Workers' Empire Exhibition Committee, *Come and See the Empire by the All Red Route* (National Labour Press, n.d. but 1938).

World Federation of Trade Unions, *Terror in Kenya* (repr. of articles in World Trade Union Movement fortnightly; Nov. 1952).

Articles

ABBOTT, G. C., 'A Re-examination of the 1929 Colonial Development Act', *EcHR* 24 (1971).

ALAVI, HAMZA, 'The State in Post-Colonial Societies: Pakistan and Bangladesh', *NLR* 74 (1972).

ANDERSON, PERRY, 'Components of the National Culture', *NLR* 50 (1968).

—— 'Figures of Descent', *NLR* 161 (1987).

CALLAGHAN, JOHN, 'The Heart of Darkness: Rajani Palme Dutt and the British Empire—A Profile', *Contemporary Record*, 5/2 (1991).

—— 'Jawaharlal Nehru and the Communist Party', *Journal of Communist Studies* 7/3 (1991).

COLLEY, L., 'Whose Nation? Class and National Consciousness in Britain, 1750–1830', *Past & Present*, 102 (1982).

COWEN, MICHAEL, 'Early Years of the Colonial Development Corporation: British State Enterprise Overseas during Late Colonialism', *African Affairs* (1984).

—— and SHENTON, ROBERT, 'The Origin and Course of Fabian Colonialism in Africa', *Journal of Historical Sociology*, 4/2 (1991).

CUNNINGHAM, HUGH, 'The Language of Patriotism, 1750–1914', *HWJ* 12 (1981).

DARWIN, J., 'The Fear of Falling: British Politics and Imperial Decline since 1900', *Transactions of the Royal Historical Society*, 5th ser. 36 (1986).

DAVIES, D. I., 'The Politics of the TUC's Colonial Policy', *PQ* 35/1 (1964).

DAVIES, I (D. I. Davies), 'The Labour Commonwealth', *NLR* 22 (1963).

DuBois, W. E. B., 'The African Roots of War', *Atlantic Monthly*, 115 (May, 1915).

DUFFIELD, IAN, 'History and the Historians', *History Today* (Sept. 1981).

ELEY, G., 'International Communism in the Heyday of Stalin', *NLR* 157 (1986).

EMMANUEL, A., 'White Settler Colonialism and the Myth of Investment Imperialism', *NLR* 73 (1972).

FERNBACH, DAVID, 'Tom Wintringham and Socialist Defence Strategy', *HWJ* 14 (1982).

FLINT, JOHN, 'Planned Decolonization and its Failure in British Africa', *African Affairs* 82/328 (1983).

FUREDI, F., 'Britain's Colonial Wars: Playing the Ethnic Card', *JCCP* 28/1 (1990).

GALLAGHER, JOHN, and ROBINSON, RONALD, 'The Imperialism of Free Trade', *EcHR* 6/1 (1953).

GOLDSWORTHY, DAVID, 'The Debate on a Parliamentary Committee for Colonial Affairs', *PA* 19/2 (1966).

—— 'Parliamentary Questions on Colonial Affairs: A Retrospective Analysis', *PA* 23/2 (1970).

—— 'Conservatives and Decolonization', *African Affairs* (1970).

—— 'Keeping Change Within Bounds: Aspects of Colonial Policy during the Churchill and Eden Governments, 1951–57', *JICH* 18/1 (1990).

—— 'Britain and the International Critics of British Colonialism, 1951–56', *JCCP* 29/1 (1991).

GORDON, ALEC 'The Theory of the "Progressive" National Bourgeoisie', *Journal of Contemporary Asia*, 3/2 (1973).

HATCH, J. 'The Opposition's Part in Colonial Policy', *Listener* (25 Apr. 1963).

HIGGINS, JIM, 'British Trotskyism, 1938–48', *International Socialism*, 13 (1963).

HINDS, ALLISTER E., 'Imperial Policy and Colonial Sterling Balances, 1943–56', *JICH* 19/1 (1991).

HINTON, JAMES, 'Coventry Communism: A Study of Factory Politics in the Second World War', *HWJ* 10 (1980).

HOPKINS, A. G., 'Imperial Business in Africa', parts 1 and 2, *JAH* 17 (1976).

HOWE, DARCUS, 'Bringing It All Back Home', *Race Today*, 6/3 (1974).

HUNTINGTON, SAMUEL, 'Will More Countries Become Democratic?', *Political Science Quarterly*, 99/2 (1984).

HYAM, RONALD, 'The Political Consequences of Seretse Khama: Britain, the Bamangwato and South Africa, 1948–1953', *Historical Journal*, 29 (1986).

—— 'Africa and the Labour Government, 1945–1951', *JICH* 16 (1988).

JOHNSON, HOWARD, 'The Political Uses of Commissions of Enquiry: (i) The Imperial-Colonial West Indian Context', *Social & Economic Studies*, 27/3 (1978).

JOSHI, P. C., 'R. P. Dutt and Indian Communism', *Indian Left Review* (July 1971).

JOSHI, SHIRLEY, and Carter, Bob, 'Labour's Role in the Creation of a Racist Britain', *Race and Class*, 25/3 (1984).

KIERNAN, V. G., 'India and the Labour Party', *NLR* 42 (1967).

—— 'The British Labour Movement and Imperialism', *SSLHB* 31 (1975).

MACDONAGH, O., 'The Anti-Imperialism of Free Trade', *EcHR* 2nd ser. 14/3 (1962).

MACDONALD, RODERICK, 'Dr. Harold Arundel Moody and the League of Coloured Peoples, 1931–1947: A Retrospective View', *Race*, 14/3 (1973).

MARSHALL, DAVID, 'Singapore's Struggle for Nationhood, 1945–1959', *Journal of South-East Asian Studies*, 1/2 (1970).

MOORHOUSE, H. F., 'The Marxist Theory of the Labour Aristocracy', *Social History*, 3/1 (1978).

NAIRN, TOM, 'Anatomy of the Labour Party', *NLR* 27 and 28 (1964).

—— 'The Left Against Europe?', *NLR* 75 (1972); pub. Harmondsworth: Penguin Books, 1973.

PANG CHENG LIAN, 'The People's Action Party, 1954–1963', *Journal of South-East Asian History*, 10/1 (1969).

PIAZZA, H. 'Jawaharlal Nehru und die Antiimperialistische Liga', *wiss. z. Karl Marx Univ. Leipzig*, 19/3 (1970).

—— 'Der Kampf der Komintern für ein antiimperialistische Weltfront', *Beitrage zur Geschichte der Arbeiterbewegung*, 2 (1969).

RAY, SIBNARAYAN, 'In Freedom's Quest: Life of M. N. Roy', *Radical Humanist*, (Aug. 1985 *et seq.*).

RICH, PAUL, 'A Question of Life and Death to England: Patriotism and the British Intellectuals, *c*.1886–1945', *New Community*, 15/4 (1989).

ROBINSON, R. E., 'The Moral Disarmament of African Empire, 1919–47', *JICH* 7/1 (1979).

SAMAROO, BRINSLEY, 'The Trinidad Workingmen's Association and the Origins of Popular Protest in a Crown Colony', *Social & Economic Studies*, 21/2 (1972).

SAMUEL, RAPHAEL, 'The Lost World of British Communism', *NLR* 154, 156, and 165 (1985–7).

SAVILLE, JOHN, 'The Communist Experience: A Personal Appraisal', *The Socialist Register, 1991* (1991).

—— and THOMPSON, EDWARD, 'John Stuart Mill and EOKA', *The New Reasoner*, 7 (Winter 1958–9).

SAYER, S., 'British Reaction to the Amritsar Massacre, 1919–1920', *Past & Present*, 131 (1991).

SIMPSON-HOLLEY, B., 'Members for Trinidad', *Journal of Caribbean History*, 6 (May, 1973).

SIVANANDAN, A., 'From Resistance to Rebellion', *Race & Class*, 23/2–3 (1982).

SKINNER, Q., 'Some Problems in the Analysis of Political Thought and Action', *Political Theory*, 2 (1974).

SLAVIN, DAVID H., 'The French Left and the Rif War, 1924–5: Racism and the Limits of Internationalism', *JCH* 26 (1991).

SLOVO, J., 'A Critical Appraisal of the Non-Capitalist Path and the National-Democratic State in Africa', *Marxism Today* (June, 1974).

SMITH, TONY, 'A Comparative Study of French and British Decolonisation', *Comparative Studies in Society & History*, 20/1 (1978).

SPITZER, LEO, and DENZER, LARAY, 'I. T. A. Wallace-Johnson and the West African Youth League', *Journal of African Historical Studies*, 6/3–4 (1973).

TAYLOR, MILES, 'Imperium et Libertas? Rethinking the Radical Critique of Imperialism during the Nineteenth Century', *JICH* 19/1 (1991).

THOMAS, T. 'The Workers' Theatre Movement', *HWJ* 4 (1977).

THOMPSON, E. P., 'The Peculiarities of the English', *Socialist Register* (1965).

—— 'Eighteenth-Century English Society: Class Struggle Without Class?', *Social History*, 3/3 (1980).

TINKER, HUGH, 'Burma's Struggle for Independence: The Transfer of Power Thesis Re-examined', *Modern Asian Studies*, 20 (1986).

TOMLINSON, B. R., 'The Contraction of England: National Decline and the Loss of Empire', *JICH* 11/1 (1982).

TURNBULL, C. M., 'British Planning for Post-War Malaya', *Journal of South-East Asian Studies*, 5/2 (1974).

WATERMAN, PETER, 'Communist Theory in the Nigerian Trade Union Movement', *Politics & Society*, 3/2 (1973).

YEO KIM WAH, 'A Study of Three Early Political Parties in Singapore, 1945–1955', *Journal of South-East Asian History*, 10/1 (1969).

Other printed sources

Hansard: Houses of Commons and of Lords debates, various dates.

Communist Party of Great Britain: Congress and Executive Reports, various dates.

Independent Labour Party: Conference Agendas, Reports, and NAC Reports, various dates.

Labour Party: Annual Conference Agendas and Reports, various dates.

Movement for Colonial Freedom: Annual Reports, various dates.

Trades Union Congress: Annual Reports, various dates.

Unpublished theses and papers

BOWDEN, JANE, 'Development and Control in British Colonial Policy, with Reference to Nigeria and the Gold Coast, 1935–1948' (Birmingham University Ph.D. thesis, 1980).

BRYAN, DAVID, 'The Development of Revisionist Thought among British Labour Intellectuals and Politicians, 1931–64' (Oxford University D.Phil. thesis, 1984).

BUSH, BARBARA, 'Britain and Black Africa in the Inter-War Years: Metropolitan Responses to the Growth of Race and Political Consciousness, with Specific Reference to West and South Africa.' (Sheffield University Ph.D. thesis, 1986).

DENZER, LaRAY E., 'I. T. A. Wallace-Johnson and the West African Youth League: A Case Study in West African Radicalism' (Birmingham University Ph.D. thesis, 1977).

GRUBER, H., 'The Comintern and the Negro Question', paper for International Labour History conference (Linz, 1984).

HOROWITZ, DAN, 'Attitudes of British Conservatives towards Decolonization in Africa during the Period of the Macmillan Government, 1957–63' (Oxford University D.Phil. thesis, 1967).

HOWE, STEPHEN, 'Anti-Colonialism in British Politics: The Left and the End of Empire, 1939–1964' (Oxford University D.Phil. thesis, 1984).

JONES, KATH, ' "A Quiet Fame": A Biography of Rita Hinden' (Ruskin College, Oxford, Dip. L. S. thesis, 1985).

KAARSHOLM, PREBEN, 'Imperialism and Romantic Anti-Capitalism' (Kultur og Samfund, Roskilde Universitetscenter, 1983).

MACDONALD, R. 'The Role of London's Black Press in the 1930s and 1940s', paper for History of Blacks in Britain conference (Institute of Education, London, 1981).

MACKENZIE, A. J. 'British Marxists and the Empire: Anti-Imperialist Theory and Practice, 1920–1945' (London University Ph.D. thesis, 1978).

NEMENZO, FRANSISCO, Jun., 'Revolution and Counter-Revolution. A Study of British Colonial Policy as a Factor in the Growth and Disintegration of National-Liberation Movements in Burma and Malaya' (Manchester University Ph.D. thesis, 1964).

PIAZZA, H., 'Koloniale Frage und Arbeitebewegung, 1917–1939', paper for International Labour History conference (Linz, 1984).

SANSOM, CHRISTOPHER J., 'The British Labour Movement and Southern Africa, 1918–55' (Birmingham University Ph.D. thesis, 1982).

SANDASHI, HARRIS B. K., 'The Politics of the Voice. An Examination and Comparison of British Pressure Groups (Capricorn Africa Society, the Africa Bureau, and the Movement for Colonial Freedom) which Sought to Influence Colonial Policies and Events. The Case of Central Africa, 1949–1962' (York University M. Phil. thesis, 1981).

TOMICKI, J., 'Sozialistische Arbeiter-Internationale und die Koloniale Frage', paper for International Labour History conference (Linz, 1984).

Index